FEDERAL RULES OF CIVIL PROCEDURE

with Selected Statutes and Cases — 2003

FEDERAL RULES OF CIVIL PROCEDURE

with Selected Statutes and Cases — 2003

Stephen C. Yeazell

David G. Price and
Dallas P. Price
Professor of Law
University of California
Los Angeles

ASPEN
PUBLISHERS

1185 Avenue of the Americas, New York, NY 10036
www.aspenpublishers.com

Permissions
Aspen Publishers
1185 Avenue of the Americas
New York, NY 10036

Printed in the United States of America

1 2 3 4 5 6 7 8 9 0

ISBN 0-7355-2817-9

ISSN 1074-4150

About Aspen Publishers

Aspen Publishers, headquartered in New York City, is a leading information provider for attorneys, business professionals, and law students. Written by preeminent authorities, our products consist of analytical and practical information covering both U.S. and international topics. We publish in the full range of formats, including updated manuals, books, periodicals, CDs, and online products.

Our proprietary content is complemented by 2,500 legal databases, containing over 11 million documents, available through our Loislaw division. Aspen Publishers also offers a wide range of topical legal and business databases linked to Loislaw's primary material. Our mission is to provide accurate, timely, and authoritative content in easily accessible formats, supported by unmatched customer care.

To order any Aspen Publishers title, go to *www.aspenpublishers.com* or call 1-800-638-8437.

To reinstate your manual update service, call 1-800-638-8437.

For more information on Loislaw products, go to *www.loislaw.com* or call 1-800-364-2512.

For Customer Care issues, e-mail *CustomerCare@aspenpublishers.com*; call 1-800-234-1660; or fax 1-800-901-9075.

Aspen Publishers
A Wolters Kluwer Company

CONTENTS

TABLE OF CASES

(References are to supplement page numbers.)
(Principal cases are in italics.)

PREFACE

The federal procedural system flows from four major sources of law: (1) the Constitution of the United States, (2) the Federal Rules (of Civil and Appellate Procedure), (3) the Judiciary Code (collected in Title 28 of the United States Code), and (4) cases applying and interpreting these three bodies of law. All of these sources are represented in this volume. This volume is intended to serve as a rules pamphlet for any civil procedure course. The statutes and rules reflect amendments through January 31, 2003. I am grateful to Christopher Baker for help in preparing this supplement.

Stephen C. Yeazell

April 2003

NOTE ON THE FEDERAL RULES OF CIVIL PROCEDURE

The Federal Rules of Civil Procedure govern the conduct of civil trials in federal courts. Their authority comes from Congress, but, unlike the Judiciary Code (Title 28 of the United States Code, found at page 273 of this supplement), the Rules are not a product of direct congressional legislation. Instead Congress has enacted 28 U.S.C. §2072 (the Rules Enabling Act), which authorizes the Supreme Court to promulgate rules of procedure.

Although the Rules Enabling Act gives the Supreme Court power to promulgate the Rules, the Justices do not in practice do the actual drafting. That process instead occurs in committees of the Judicial Conference, a supervisory and administrative arm of the federal courts. In 1988 a set of amendments to 28 U.S.C. §§2072-2074 formalized this committee process. Under these provisions the Judicial Conference appoints a standing committee on rules of practice, procedure, and evidence. This standing committee screens all recommendations for consistency. The Judicial Conference may also appoint committees with a more defined jurisdiction — for example, civil rules, rules of evidence, bankruptcy rules. Judges, practitioners, and scholars are appointed to these advisory committees. Each advisory committee considers proposals for amendments to the Rules, circulates drafts of proposed amendments to members of the bench and bar, revises in light of their comments, and then transmits the revised proposals to the Committee on Practice and Procedure, which reports to the Judicial Conference, which in turn recommends changes to the Supreme Court. In recent years the process surrounding Rule amendments has become more "transparent" — open to public and professional comment — and simultaneously slower and more contested.

The Court, if it concurs with the proposals, officially promulgates the revised Rules by May 1, to take effect on December 1 of the same year if Congress does not act in the meantime. The Court has rarely rejected outright a Rules amendment recommended by the Judicial Conference (although several justices have on occasion dissented from the promulgation of various sets of amendments).

Like the Supreme Court, Congress has usually acceded to the recommendations of the Judicial Conference. As with the Court, however, there have been exceptions. In the instance of the 1993 amendments, Congress came very close to exercising its power of disapproval in connection with the discovery rules; a bill that would have blocked the implementation of those proposals passed the

House of Representatives and died in the Senate only when that body adjourned without having acted on it.

The original Rules were promulgated in 1938. Since then there have been significant revisions in 1948, 1961, 1963, 1966, 1970, 1983, 1985, 1987, 1991, 1993, 1995, and 2000 (with technical amendments in 1971, 1975, 1996, 1997, 1999, 2001, and 2002). The most important changes in the past 30 years have been:

the 1966 amendments, which revised the rules for joinder of claims and parties;

the 1970 amendments, which revamped discovery procedures;

the 1983 amendments, which strengthened judicial control over the pretrial process and stiffened sanctions provisions;

the 1993 amendments, which changed the conception of service of process and discovery and revised the sanctions provisions of Rule 11.

the 2000 amendments, which further altered the rules for discovery and rewrote the Supplemental Admiralty Rules.

This supplement reprints portions of the advisory committee's notes for significant amendments after the Rule in question. Though they do not have the force of law, these notes often serve the same function for the Rules that legislative history does for statutes.

The Rules have been influential beyond the federal courts. A number of states (by one count about 35 of the 50 states) have chosen to adopt the Rules to govern their civil procedure, so that many lawyers who practice primarily in state courts will find their procedural systems similar or identical to Rules model.

FEDERAL RULES OF CIVIL PROCEDURE

with Selected Statutes and Cases — 2003

PART I

RULES AND STATUTES

FEDERAL RULES OF CIVIL PROCEDURE FOR THE UNITED STATES DISTRICT COURTS

As Amended Through December 1, 2001

TABLE OF RULES

III. Pleadings and Motions

IV. Parties

VI. Trials

Rule

VII. Judgment

Rule

VIII. Provisional and Final Remedies and Special Proceedings

IX. Special Proceedings

Rule

I. Scope of Rules — One Form of Action

Rule 1. Scope and Purpose of Rules

These rules govern the procedure in the United States district courts in all suits of a civil nature whether cognizable as cases at law or in equity or in admiralty, with the exceptions stated in Rule 81. They shall be construed and administered to secure the just, speedy, and inexpensive determination of every action.

As amended Dec. 29, 1948, eff. Oct. 20, 1949; Feb. 28, 1966, eff. July 1, 1966; Apr. 22, 1993, eff. Dec. 1, 1993.

Rule 2. One Form of Action

There shall be one form of action to be known as "civil action."

II. Commencement of Action; Service of Process, Pleadings, Motions, and Orders

Rule 3. Commencement of Action

A civil action is commenced by filing a complaint with the court.

Rule 4. Summons

(a) **Form.** The summons shall be signed by the clerk, bear the seal of the court, identify the court and the parties, be directed to the defendant, and state the name and address of the plaintiff's attorney or, if unrepresented, of the plaintiff. It shall also state the time within which the defendant must appear and defend, and notify the defendant that failure to do so will result in a judgment by default against the defendant for the relief demanded in the complaint. The court may allow a summons to be amended.

(b) **Issuance.** Upon or after filing the complaint, the plaintiff may present a summons to the clerk for signature and seal. If the summons is in proper form, the clerk shall sign, seal, and issue it to the plaintiff for service on the defendant. A summons, or a copy of the summons if addressed to multiple defendants, shall be issued for each defendant to be served.

(c) **Service with Complaint; by Whom Made.**

(1) A summons shall be served together with a copy of the complaint. The plaintiff is responsible for service of a summons and complaint within the time allowed under subdivision (m) and shall furnish the person effecting service with the necessary copies of the summons and complaint.

(2) Service may be effected by any person who is not a party and who is at least 18 years of age. At the request of the plaintiff, however, the court may direct

that service be effected by a United States marshal, deputy United States marshal, or other person or officer specially appointed by the court for that purpose. Such an appointment must be made when the plaintiff is authorized to proceed in forma pauperis pursuant to 28 U.S.C. §1915 or is authorized to proceed as a seaman under 28 U.S.C. §1916.

(d) Waiver of Service; Duty to Save Costs of Service; Request to Waive.

(1) A defendant who waives service of a summons does not thereby waive any objection to the venue or to the jurisdiction of the court over the person of the defendant.

(2) An individual, corporation, or association that is subject to service under subdivision (e), (f), or (h) and that receives notice of an action in the manner provided in this paragraph has a duty to avoid unnecessary costs of serving the summons. To avoid costs, the plaintiff may notify such a defendant of the commencement of the action and request that the defendant waive service of a summons. The notice and request

(A) shall be in writing and shall be addressed directly to the defendant, if an individual, or else to an officer or managing or general agent (or other agent authorized by appointment or law to receive service of process) of a defendant subject to service under subdivision (h);

(B) shall be dispatched through first-class mail or other reliable means;

(C) shall be accompanied by a copy of the complaint and shall identify the court in which it has been filed;

(D) shall inform the defendant, by means of a text prescribed in an official form promulgated pursuant to Rule 84, of the consequences of compliance and of a failure to comply with the request;

(E) shall set forth the date on which the request is sent;

(F) shall allow the defendant a reasonable time to return the waiver, which shall be at least 30 days from the date on which the request is sent, or 60 days from that date if the defendant is addressed outside any judicial district of the United States; and

(G) shall provide the defendant with an extra copy of the notice and request, as well as a prepaid means of compliance in writing.

If a defendant located within the United States fails to comply with a request for waiver made by a plaintiff located within the United States, the court shall impose the costs subsequently incurred in effecting service on the defendant unless good cause for the failure be shown.

(3) A defendant that, before being served with process, timely returns a waiver so requested is not required to serve an answer to the complaint until 60 days after the date on which the request for waiver of service was sent, or 90 days after that date if the defendant was addressed outside any judicial district of the United States.

(4) When the plaintiff files a waiver of service with the court, the action shall proceed, except as provided in paragraph (3), as if a summons and complaint

had been served at the time of filing the waiver, and no proof of service shall be required.

(5) The costs to be imposed on a defendant under paragraph (2) for failure to comply with a request to waive service of a summons shall include the costs subsequently incurred in effecting service under subdivision (e), (f), or (h), together with the costs, including a reasonable attorney's fee, of any motion required to collect the costs of service.

(e) **Service upon Individuals Within a Judicial District of the United States.** Unless otherwise provided by federal law, service upon an individual from whom a waiver has not been obtained and filed, other than an infant or an incompetent person, may be effected in any judicial district of the United States:

(1) pursuant to the law of the state in which the district court is located, or in which service is effected, for the service of a summons upon the defendant in an action brought in the courts of general jurisdiction of the State; or

(2) by delivering a copy of the summons and of the complaint to the individual personally or by leaving copies thereof at the individual's dwelling house or usual place of abode with some person of suitable age and discretion then residing therein or by delivering a copy of the summons and of the complaint to an agent authorized by appointment or by law to receive service of process.

(f) **Service upon Individuals in a Foreign Country.** Unless otherwise provided by federal law, service upon an individual from whom a waiver has not been obtained and filed, other than an infant or an incompetent person, may be effected in a place not within any judicial district of the United States:

(1) by any internationally agreed means reasonably calculated to give notice, such as those means authorized by the Hague Convention on the Service Abroad of Judicial and Extrajudicial Documents; or

(2) if there is no internationally agreed means of service or the applicable international agreement allows other means of service, provided that service is reasonably calculated to give notice:

(A) in the manner prescribed by the law of the foreign country for service in that country in an action in any of its courts of general jurisdiction; or

(B) as directed by the foreign authority in response to a letter rogatory or letter of request; or

(C) unless prohibited by the law of the foreign country, by

(i) delivery to the individual personally of a copy of the summons and the complaint; or

(ii) any form of mail requiring a signed receipt, to be addressed and dispatched by the clerk of the court to the party to be served; or

(3) by other means not prohibited by international agreement as may be directed by the court.

(g) Service upon Infants and Incompetent Persons. Service upon an infant or an incompetent person in a judicial district of the United States shall be effected in the manner prescribed by the law of the state in which the service is made for the service of summons or other like process upon any such defendant in an action brought in the courts of general jurisdiction of that state. Service upon an infant or an incompetent person in a place not within any judicial district of the United States shall be effected in the manner prescribed by paragraph (2)(A) or (2)(B) of subdivision (f) or by such means as the court may direct.

(h) Service upon Corporations and Associations. Unless otherwise provided by federal law, service upon a domestic or foreign corporation or upon a partnership or other unincorporated association that is subject to suit under a common name, and from which a waiver of service has not been obtained and filed, shall be effected:

(1) in a judicial district of the United States in the manner prescribed for individuals by subdivisions (e)(1), or by delivering a copy of the summons and of the complaint to an officer, a managing or general agent, or to any other agent authorized by appointment or by law to receive service of process and, if the agent is one authorized by statute to receive service and the statute so requires, by also mailing a copy to the defendant, or

(2) in a place not within any judicial district of the United States in any manner prescribed for individuals by subdivision (f) except personal delivery as provided in paragraph (2)(C)(i) thereof.

(i) Serving the United States, Its Agencies, Corporations, Officers, or Employees.

(1) Service upon the United States shall be effected

(A) by delivering a copy of the summons and of the complaint to the United States attorney for the district in which the action is brought or to an assistant United States attorney or clerical employee designated by the United States attorney in a writing filed with the clerk of the court or by sending a copy of the summons and of the complaint by registered or certified mail addressed to the civil process clerk at the office of the United States attorney and

(B) by also sending a copy of the summons and of the complaint by registered or certified mail to the Attorney General of the United States at Washington, District of Columbia, and

(C) in any action attacking the validity of an order of an officer or agency of the United States not made a party, by also sending a copy of the summons and of the complaint by registered or certified mail to the officer or agency.

(2)(A) Service on an agency or corporation of the United States, or an officer or employee of the United States sued only in an official capacity, is effected by serving the United States in the manner prescribed by Rule 4(i)(1) and by also sending a copy of the summons and complaint by registered or certified mail to the officer, employee, agency, or corporation.

(B) Service on an officer or employee of the United States sued in an individual capacity for acts or omissions occurring in connection with the performance of duties on behalf of the United States — whether or not the officer or employee is sued also in an official capacity — is effected by serving the United States in the manner prescribed by Rule 4(i)(1) and by serving the officer or employee in the manner prescribed by Rule 4(e), (f), or (g).

(3) The court shall allow a reasonable time to serve process under Rule 4(i) for the purpose of curing the failure to serve:

(A) all persons required to be served in an action governed by Rule 4(i)(2)(A), if the plaintiff has served either the United States attorney or the Attorney General of the United States, or

(B) the United States in an action governed by Rule 4(i)(2)(B), if the plaintiff has served an officer or employee of the United States sued in an individual capacity.

(j) Service upon Foreign, State, or Local Governments.

(1) Service upon a foreign state or a political subdivision, agency, or instrumentality thereof shall be effected pursuant to 28 U.S.C. §1608.

(2) Service upon a state, municipal corporation, or other governmental organization subject to suit shall be effected by delivering a copy of the summons and of the complaint to its chief executive officer or by serving the summons and complaint in the manner prescribed by the law of that state for the service of summons or other like process upon any such defendant.

(k) Territorial Limits of Effective Service.

(1) Service of a summons or filing a waiver of service is effective to establish jurisdiction over the person of a defendant

(A) who could be subjected to the jurisdiction of a court of general jurisdiction in the state in which the district court is located, or

(B) who is a party joined under Rule 14 or Rule 19 and is served at a place within a judicial district of the United States and not more than 100 miles from the place from which the summons issues, or

(C) who is subject to the federal interpleader jurisdiction under 28 U.S.C. §1335, or

(D) when authorized by a statute of the United States.

(2) If the exercise of jurisdiction is consistent with the Constitution and laws of the United States, serving a summons or filing a waiver of service is also effective, with respect to claims arising under federal law, to establish personal jurisdiction over the person of any defendant who is not subject to the jurisdiction of the courts of general jurisdiction of any state.

(l) Proof of Service. If service is not waived, the person effecting service shall make proof thereof to the court. If service is made by a person other than a United States marshal or deputy United States marshal, the person shall make affidavit thereof. Proof of service in a place not within any judicial district of the United States shall, if effected under paragraph (1) of subdivision (f), be made pursuant to the applicable treaty or convention, and shall, if effected under paragraph (2) or (3) thereof, include a receipt signed by the addressee or other evidence of delivery to the addressee satisfactory to the court. Failure to make proof of service does not affect the validity of the service. The court may allow proof of service to be amended.

(m) Time Limit for Service. If service of the summons and complaint is not made upon a defendant within 120 days after the filing of the complaint, the court, upon motion or on its own initiative after notice to the plaintiff, shall dismiss the action without prejudice as to that defendant or direct that service be effected within a specified time; provided that if the plaintiff shows good cause for the failure, the court shall extend the time for service for an appropriate period. This subdivision does not apply to service in a foreign country pursuant to subdivision (f) or (j)(1).

(n) Seizure of Property; Service of Summons Not Feasible.

(1) If a statute of the United States so provides, the court may assert jurisdiction over property. Notice to claimants of the property shall then be sent in the manner provided by the statute or by service of a summons under this rule.

(2) Upon a showing that personal jurisdiction over a defendant cannot, in the district where the action is brought, be obtained with reasonable efforts by service of summons in any manner authorized by this rule, the court may assert jurisdiction over any of the defendant's assets found within the district by seizing the assets under the circumstances and in the manner provided by the law of the state in which the district court is located.

As amended Jan. 21, 1963, eff. July 1, 1963; Feb. 28, 1966, eff. July 1, 1966; Apr. 29, 1980, eff. Aug. 1, 1980; Pub. L. 97-462, §2, Jan. 12, 1983, 96 Stat. 2527; Mar. 2, 1987, eff. Aug. 1, 1987; Apr. 22, 1993, eff. Dec. 1, 1993; Apr. 17, 2000, eff. Dec. 1, 2000.

Advisory Committee Notes, 1993 and 2000 Amendments

1993 amendments

Purposes of Revision. The general purpose of this revision is to facilitate the service of the summons and complaint. The revised rule explicitly authorizes a means for service of the summons and complaint on any defendant. While the methods of service so authorized always provide appropriate notice to persons against whom claims are made, effective service under this rule does not assure that personal jurisdiction has been established over the defendant served.

First, the revised rule authorizes the use of any means of service provided by the law not only of the forum state, but also of the state in which a defendant is served, unless the defendant is a minor or incompetent.

Second, the revised rule clarifies and enhances the cost-saving practice of securing the assent of the defendant to dispense with actual service of the summons and complaint. This practice was introduced to the rule in 1983 by an act of Congress authorizing "service-by-mail," a procedure that effects economic service with cooperation of the defendant. Defendants that magnify costs of service by requiring expensive service not necessary to achieve full notice of an action brought against them are required to bear the wasteful costs. This provision is made available in actions against defendants who cannot be served in the districts in which the actions are brought. . . .

. . . A new provision enables district courts to exercise jurisdiction, if permissible under the Constitution and not precluded by statute, when a federal claim is made against a defendant not subject to the jurisdiction of any single state. . . .

Subdivision (d). This text is new, but is substantially derived from the former subdivisions (c)(2)(C) and (D), added to the rule by Congress in 1983. The aims of the provision are to eliminate the costs of service of a summons on many parties and to foster cooperation among adversaries and counsel. The rule operates to impose upon the defendant those costs that could have been avoided if the defendant had cooperated reasonably in the manner prescribed. This device is useful in dealing with defendants who are furtive, who reside in places not easily reached by process servers, or who are outside the United States and can be served only at substantial and unnecessary expense. Illustratively, there is no useful purpose achieved by requiring a plaintiff to comply with all the formalities of service in a foreign country, including costs of translation, when suing a defendant manufacturer, fluent in English, whose products are widely distributed in the United States. See Bankston v. Toyota Motor Corp., 889 F.2d 172 (8th Cir. 1989). . . .

Paragraph (2) is new. It authorizes the exercise of territorial jurisdiction over the person of any defendant against whom is made a claim arising under any federal law if that person is subject to personal jurisdiction in no state. This addition is a companion to the amendments made in revised subdivisions (e) and (f).

This paragraph corrects a gap in the enforcement of federal law. Under the former rule, a problem was presented when the defendant was a non-resident of the United States having contacts with the United States sufficient to justify the application of United States law and to satisfy federal standards of forum selection, but having insufficient contact with any single state to support jurisdiction under state long-arm legislation or meet the requirements of the Fourteenth Amendment limitation on state court territorial jurisdiction. In such cases, the defendant was shielded from the enforcement of federal law by the fortuity of a favorable limitation on the power of state courts, which was incorporated into the federal practice by the former rule. In this respect, the revision responds to the suggestion of the Supreme Court made in Omni Capital Intl. v. Rudolf Wolff & Co., 484 U.S. 97, 111 (1987).

There remain constitutional limitations on the exercise of territorial jurisdiction by federal courts over persons outside the United States. These restrictions arise from the Fifth Amendment rather than from the Fourteenth Amendment, which limits state-court reach and which was incorporated into federal practice by the reference to state law in the text of the former subdivision (e) that is deleted by this revision. The Fifth Amendment requires that any defendant have affiliating contacts with the United States sufficient to justify the exercise of personal jurisdiction over that party. Cf. Wells Fargo & Co. v. Wells Fargo Express Co., 556 F.2d 406, 418 (9th Cir. 1977). There also may be a further Fifth Amendment constraint in that a plaintiff's forum selection might be so inconvenient to a defendant that it would be a denial of "fair play and substantial justice" required by the due process clause, even though the defendant had significant affiliating contacts with the United States. See DeJames v. Magnificent Carriers, 654 F.2d 280, 286 n.3 (3rd Cir.), cert. denied, 454 U.S. 1085 (1981). Compare World-Wide Volkswagen Corp. v. Woodson, 444 U.S. 286, 293-294 (1980); Insurance Corp. of Ireland v. Compagnie des Bauxites de Guinee, 456 U.S. 694, 702-703 (1982); Burger King Corp. v. Rudzewicz, 471 U.S. 462, 476-478 (1985); Asahi Metal Indus. v. Superior Court of Cal., Solano County, 480 U.S. 102, 108-113 (1987). See generally R. Lusardi, Nationwide Service of Process: Due Process Limitations on the Power of the Sovereign, 33 Vill. L. Rev. 1 (1988).

This provision does not affect the operation of federal venue legislation. See generally 28 U.S.C. §1391. Nor does it affect the operation of federal law providing for the change of venue. 28 U.S.C. §§1404, 1406. The availability of transfer for fairness and convenience under §1404 should preclude most conflicts between the full exercise of territorial jurisdiction permitted by this rule and the Fifth Amendment requirement of "fair play and substantial justice."

The district court should be especially scrupulous to protect aliens who reside in a foreign country from forum selections so onerous that injustice could result. "[G]reat care and reserve should be exercised when extending our notions of personal jurisdiction into the international field." Asahi Metal Indus. v. Superior Court of Cal., Solano County, 480 U.S. 102, 115 (1987), quoting United States v. First Natl. City Bank, 379 U.S. 378, 404 (1965) (Harlan, J., dissenting).

This narrow extension of the federal reach applies only if a claim is made against the defendant under federal law. It does not establish personal jurisdiction if the only claims are those arising under state law or the law of another country, even though there might be diversity or alienage subject matter jurisdiction as to such claims. If, however, personal jurisdiction is established under this paragraph with respect to a federal claim, then 28 U.S.C. §1367(a) provides supplemental jurisdiction over related claims against that defendant, subject to the court's discretion to decline exercise of that jurisdiction under 28 U.S.C. §1367(c).

2000 AMENDMENTS

Paragraph (2)(B) is added to Rule 4(i) to require service on the United States when a United States officer or employee is sued in an individual capacity for acts or omissions occurring in connection with duties performed on behalf of the United

States. Decided cases provide uncertain guidance on the question whether the United States must be served in such actions.

Rule 4.1. Service of Other Process

(a) Generally. Process other than a summons as provided in Rule 4 or subpoena as provided in Rule 45 shall be served by a United States marshal, a deputy United States marshal, or a person specially appointed for that purpose, who shall make proof of service as provided in Rule 4(l). The process may be served anywhere within the territorial limits of the state in which the district court is located, and, when authorized by a statute of the United States, beyond the territorial limits of that state.

(b) Enforcement of Orders: Commitment for Civil Contempt. An order of civil commitment of a person held to be in contempt of a decree or injunction issued to enforce the laws of the United States may be served and enforced in any district. Other orders in civil contempt proceedings shall be served in the state in which the court issuing the order to be enforced is located or elsewhere within the United States if not more than 100 miles from the place at which the order to be enforced was issued.

Rule 5. Serving and Filing Pleadings and Other Papers

(a) Service: When Required. Except as otherwise provided in these rules, every order required by its terms to be served, every pleading subsequent to the original complaint unless the court otherwise orders because of numerous defendants, every paper relating to discovery required to be served upon a party unless the court otherwise orders, every written motion other than one which may be heard ex parte, and every written notice, appearance, demand, offer of judgment, designation of record on appeal, and similar paper shall be served upon each of the parties. No service need be made on parties in default for failure to appear except that pleadings asserting new or additional claims for relief against them shall be served upon them in the manner provided for service of summons in Rule 4.

In an action begun by seizure of property, in which no person need be or is named as defendant, any service required to be made prior to the filing of an answer, claim, or appearance shall be made upon the person having custody or possession of the property at the time of its seizure.

(b) Making Service.

(1) Service under Rules 5(a) and 77(d) on a party represented by an attorney is made on the attorney unless the court orders service on the party.

(2) Service under Rule 5(a) is made by:

(A) Delivering a copy to the person served by:

(i) handing it to the person;

(ii) leaving it at the person's office with a clerk or other person in charge, or if no one is in charge leaving it in a conspicuous place in the office; or

(iii) if the person has no office or the office is closed, leaving it at the person's dwelling house or usual place of abode with someone of suitable age and discretion residing there.

(B) Mailing a copy to the last known address of the person served. Service by mail is complete on mailing.

(C) If the person served has no known address, leaving a copy with the clerk of the court.

(D) Delivering a copy by any other means, including electronic means, consented to in writing by the person served. Service by electronic means is complete on transmission; service by other consented means is complete when the person making service delivers the copy to the agency designated to make delivery. If authorized by local rule, a party may make service under this subparagraph (D) through the court's transmission facilities.

(3) Service by electronic means under Rule 5(b)(2)(D) is not effective if the party making service learns that the attempted service did not reach the person to be served.

(c) Same: Numerous Defendants. In any action in which there are unusually large numbers of defendants, the court, upon motion or of its own initiative, may order that service of the pleadings of the defendants and replies thereto need not be made as between the defendants and that any cross-claim, counterclaim, or matter constituting an avoidance or affirmative defense contained therein shall be deemed to be denied or avoided by all other parties and that the filing of any such pleading and service thereof upon the plaintiff constitutes due notice of it to the parties. A copy of every such order shall be served upon the parties in such manner and form as the court directs.

(d) Filing; Certificate of Service. All papers after the complaint required to be served upon a party, together with a certificate of service, must be filed with the court within a reasonable time after service, but disclosures under Rule 26(A)(1) or (2) and the following discovery requests and responses must not be filed until they are used in the proceeding or the court orders filing: (i) depositions, (ii) interrogatories, (iii) requests for documents or to permit entry upon land, and (iv) requests for admission.

(e) Filing with the Court Defined. The filing of papers with the court as required by these rules shall be made by filing them with the clerk of the court, except that the judge may permit the papers to be filed with the judge, in which event the judge shall note thereon the filing date and forthwith transmit them to the office of the clerk. A court may by local rule permit papers to be filed, signed, or verified by electronic means that are consistent with standards, if any, that the Judicial Conference of the United States establishes. A paper filed by electronic means in compliance with a local rule constitutes a written paper for the purpose of applying these rules. The clerk shall not refuse to accept for filing any paper presented for that purpose solely because it is not presented in proper form as required by these rules or any local rules or practices.

As amended Jan. 21, 1963, eff. July 1, 1963; Mar. 30, 1970, eff. July 1, 1970; Apr. 29, 1980, eff. Aug. 1, 1980; Mar. 2, 1987, eff. Aug. 1, 1987; Apr. 30, 1991, eff. Dec. 1, 1991; Apr. 22, 1993, eff. Dec. 1, 1993; Apr. 23, 1996, eff. Dec. 1, 1996; Apr. 17, 2000, eff. Dec. 1, 2000; Apr. 23, 2001, eff. Dec. 1, 2001.

Advisory Committee Notes, 2000 and 2001 Amendments

2000 Amendments

Rule 5(d) is amended to provide that disclosures under Rule 26(a)(1) and (2), and discovery requests and responses under Rules 30, 31, 33, 34, and 36 must not be filed until they are used in the action. "Discovery requests" includes deposition notices and "discovery responses" includes objections. The rule supersedes and invalidates local rules that forbid, permit, or require filing of these materials before they are used in the action. The former Rule 26(a)(4) requirement that disclosures under Rule 26(a)(1) and (2) be filed has been removed. Disclosures under Rule 26(a)(3), however, must be promptly filed as provided in Rule 26(a)(3). Filings in connection with Rule 35 examinations, which involve a motion proceeding when the parties do not agree, are unaffected by these amendments . . . .

The amended rule provides that discovery materials and disclosures under Rule 26(a)(1) and (a)(2) must not be filed until they are "used in the proceeding." This phrase is meant to refer to proceedings in court. This filing requirement is not triggered by "use" of discovery materials in other discovery activities, such as depositions. In connection with proceedings in court, however, the rule is to be interpreted broadly; any use of discovery materials in court in connection with a motion, a pretrial conference under Rule 16, or otherwise, should be interpreted as use in the proceeding.

2001 Amendments

Subparagraph (D) of Rule 5(b)(2) is new. It authorizes service by electronic means or any other means, but only if consent is obtained from the person served. The consent must be express, and cannot be implied from conduct. Early experience with electronic filing as authorized by Rule 5(d) is positive, supporting service by electronic means as well. Consent is required, however, because it is not yet possible to assume universal entry into the world of electronic communication . . . . The Rule 5(b)(2)(B) provision making mail service complete on mailing is extended in subparagraph (D) to make service by electronic means complete on transmission; transmission is effected when the sender does the last act that must be performed by the sender . . . .

Rule 6. Time

(a) Computation. In computing any period of time prescribed or allowed by these rules, by the local rules of any district court, by order of court, or by any applicable statute, the day of the act, event, or default from which the designated period of time begins to run shall not be included. The last day of the period so computed shall be included, unless it is a Saturday, a Sunday, or a legal holiday or, when the act to be done is the filing of a paper in court, a day on which weather or other conditions have made the office of the clerk of the district court inaccessible, in which event the period runs until the end of the next day which is not one of the aforementioned days. When the period of time prescribed or allowed is less than 11 days, intermediate Saturdays, Sundays, and legal holidays shall be excluded in the computation. As used in this rule and in Rule 77(c), "legal holiday" includes New Year's Day, Birthday of Martin Luther King, Jr., Washington's Birthday, Memorial Day, Independence Day, Labor Day, Columbus Day, Veterans Day, Thanksgiving Day, Christmas Day, and any other day appointed as a holiday by the President or the Congress of the United States, or by the state in which the district court is held.

(b) Enlargement. When by these rules or by a notice given thereunder or by order of court an act is required or allowed to be done at or within a specified time, the court for cause shown may at any time in its discretion (1) with or without motion or notice order the period enlarged if request therefor is made before the expiration of the period originally prescribed or as extended by a previous order, or (2) upon motion made after the expiration of the specified period permit the act to be done where the failure to act was the result of excusable neglect; but it may not extend the time for taking any action under Rules 50(b) and (c)(2), 52(b), 59(b), (d), and (e), and 60(b), except to the extent and under the conditions stated in them.

(c) Unaffected by Expiration of Term. Rescinded Feb. 28, 1966, eff. July 1, 1966.

(d) For Motions — Affidavits. A written motion, other than one which may be heard ex parte, and notice of the hearing thereof shall be served not later than 5 days before the time specified for the hearing, unless a different period is fixed by these rules or by order of the court. Such an order may for cause shown be made on ex parte application. When a motion is supported by affidavit, the affidavit shall be served with the motion; and, except as otherwise provided in Rule 59(c), opposing affidavits may be served not later than 1 day before the hearing, unless the court permits them to be served at some other time.

(e) **Additional Time After Service under Rule 5(b)(2)(B), (C), or (D).** Whenever a party has the right or is required to do some act or take some proceedings within a prescribed period after the service of a notice or other paper upon the party and the notice or paper is served upon the party under Rule 5(b)(2)(B), (C), or (D), 3 days shall be added to the prescribed period.

As amended Jan. 21, 1963, eff. July 1, 1963; Feb. 28, 1966, eff. July 1, 1966; Dec. 4, 1967, eff. July 1, 1968; Mar. 1, 1971, eff. July 1, 1971; Apr. 28, 1983, eff. Aug. 1, 1983; Apr. 29, 1985, eff. Aug. 1, 1985; Mar. 2, 1987, eff. Aug. 1, 1987; Apr. 29, 1999, eff. Dec. 1, 1999; Apr. 23, 2001, eff. Dec. 1, 2001.

III. Pleadings and Motions

Rule 7. Pleadings Allowed; Form of Motions

(a) **Pleadings.** There shall be a complaint and an answer; a reply to a counterclaim denominated as such; an answer to a cross-claim, if the answer contains a cross-claim; a third-party complaint, if a person who was not an original party is summoned under the provisions of Rule 14; and a third-party answer, if a third-party complaint is served. No other pleading shall be allowed, except that the court may order a reply to an answer or a third-party answer.

(b) **Motions and Other Papers.**

(1) An application to the court for an order shall be by motion which, unless made during a hearing or trial, shall be made in writing, shall state with particularity the grounds therefor, and shall set forth the relief or order sought. The requirement of writing is fulfilled if the motion is stated in a written notice of the hearing of the motion.

(2) The rules applicable to captions and other matters of form of pleadings apply to all motions and other papers provided for by these rules.

(3) All motions shall be signed in accordance with Rule 11.

(c) **Demurrers, Pleas, Etc., Abolished.** Demurrers, pleas, and exceptions for insufficiency of a pleading shall not be used.

As amended Jan. 21, 1963, eff. July 1, 1963; Apr. 28, 1983, eff. Aug. 1, 1983.

Advisory Committee Notes, 1983 Amendment

One of the reasons sanctions against improper motion practice have been employed infrequently is the lack of clarity of Rule 7. That rule has stated only generally that the pleading requirements relating to captions, signing, and other matters of form also apply to motions and other papers. The addition of Rule 7(b)(3) makes explicit the applicability of the signing requirement and the sanctions of Rule 11, which have been amplified.

Rule 7.1. Disclosure Statement

(a) Who Must File: Nongovernmental Corporate Party. A nongovernmental corporate party to an action or proceeding in a district court must file two copies of a statement that identifies any parent corporation and any publicly held corporation that owns 10% or more of its stock or states that there is no such corporation.

(b) Time for Filing; Supplemental Filing. A party must:

(1) file the Rule 7.1(a) statement with its first appearance, pleading, petition, motion, response, or other request addressed to the court, and

(2) promptly file a supplemental statement upon any change in the information that the statement requires.

As Added Apr. 29, 2002, eff. Dec. 1, 2002.

ADVISORY COMMITTEE NOTES, 2002 ADOPTION

Rule 7.1 is drawn from Rule 26.1 of the Federal Rules of Appellate Procedure, with changes to adapt to the circumstances of district courts that dictate different provisions for the time of filing, number of copies, and the like. The information required by Rule 7.1(a) reflects the "financial interest" standard of Canon 3C(1)(c) of the Code of Conduct for United States Judges. This information will support properly informed disqualification decisions in situations that call for automatic disqualification under Canon 3C(1)(c). It does not cover all of the circumstances that may call for disqualification under the financial interest standard, and does not deal at all with other circumstances that may call for disqualification. Although the disclosures required by Rule 7.1(a) may seem limited, they are calculated to reach a majority of the circumstances that are likely to call for disqualification on the basis of financial information that a judge may not know or recollect. Framing a rule that calls for more detailed disclosure will be difficult. . . .

Rule 8. General Rules of Pleading

(a) Claims for Relief. A pleading which sets forth a claim for relief, whether an original claim, counterclaim, cross-claim, or third-party claim, shall contain (1) a short and plain statement of the grounds upon which the court's jurisdiction depends, unless the court already has jurisdiction and the claim needs no new grounds of jurisdiction to support it, (2) a short and plain statement of the claim showing that the pleader is entitled to relief, and (3) a demand for judgment for the relief the pleader seeks. Relief in the alternative or of several different types may be demanded.

(b) Defenses; Form of Denials. A party shall state in short and plain terms the party's defenses to each claim asserted and shall admit or deny the averments upon which the adverse party relies. If a party is without knowledge or information sufficient to form a belief as to the truth of an averment, a party shall so state and this has the effect of a denial. Denials shall fairly meet the substance of the averments denied. When a pleader intends in good faith to deny only a part or a qualification of an averment, the pleader shall specify so much of it as is true and material and shall deny only the remainder. Unless the pleader intends in good faith to controvert all the averments of the preceding pleading, the pleader may make denials as specific denials of designated averments or paragraphs, or may generally deny all the averments except such designated averments or paragraphs as the pleader expressly admits; but, when the pleader does so intend to controvert all its averments, including averments of the grounds upon which the court's jurisdiction depends, the pleader may do so by general denial subject to the obligations set forth in Rule 11.

(c) Affirmative Defenses. In pleading to a preceding pleading, a party shall set forth affirmatively accord and satisfaction, arbitration and award, assumption of risk, contributory negligence, discharge in bankruptcy, duress, estoppel, failure of consideration, fraud, illegality, injury by fellow servant, laches, license, payment, release, res judicata, statute of frauds, statute of limitations, waiver, and any other matter constituting an avoidance or affirmative defense. When a party has mistakenly designated a defense as a counterclaim or a counterclaim as a defense, the court on terms, if justice so requires, shall treat the pleading as if there had been a proper designation.

(d) Effect of Failure to Deny. Averments in a pleading to which a responsive pleading is required, other than those as to the amount of damage, are admitted when not denied in the responsive pleading. Averments in a pleading to which no responsive pleading is required or permitted shall be taken as denied or avoided.

(e) Pleading to Be Concise and Direct; Consistency.

(1) Each averment of a pleading shall be simple, concise, and direct. No technical forms of pleadings or motions are required.

(2) A party may set forth two or more statements of a claim or defense alternately or hypothetically, either in one count or defense or in separate counts or defenses. When two or more statements are made in the alternative and one of them if made independently would be sufficient, the pleading is not made

insufficient by the insufficiency of one or more of the alternative statements. A party may also state as many separate claims or defenses as the party has regardless of consistency and whether based on legal, equitable, or maritime grounds. All statements shall be made subject to the obligations set forth in Rule 11.

(f) Construction of Pleadings. All pleadings shall be so construed as to do substantial justice.

As amended Feb. 28, 1966, eff. July 1, 1966; Mar. 2, 1987, eff. Aug. 1, 1987.

Rule 9. Pleading Special Matters

(a) Capacity. It is not necessary to aver the capacity of a party to sue or be sued or the authority of a party to sue or be sued in a representative capacity or the legal existence of an organized association of persons that is made a party, except to the extent required to show the jurisdiction of the court. When a party desires to raise an issue as to the legal existence of any party or the capacity of any party to sue or be sued or the authority of a party to sue or be sued in a representative capacity, the party desiring to raise the issue shall do so by specific negative averment, which shall include such supporting particulars as are peculiarly within the pleader's knowledge.

(b) Fraud, Mistake, Condition of the Mind. In all averments of fraud or mistake, the circumstances constituting fraud or mistake shall be stated with particularity. Malice, intent, knowledge, and other condition of mind of a person may be averred generally.

(c) Conditions Precedent. In pleading the performance or occurrence of conditions precedent, it is sufficient to aver generally that all conditions precedent have been performed or have occurred. A denial of performance or occurrence shall be made specifically and with particularity.

(d) Official Document or Act. In pleading an official document or official act it is sufficient to aver that the document was issued or the act done in compliance with law.

(e) Judgment. In pleading a judgment or decision of a domestic or foreign court, judicial or quasi-judicial tribunal, or of a board or officer, it is sufficient to aver the judgment or decision without setting forth matter showing jurisdiction to render it.

(f) Time and Place. For the purpose of testing the sufficiency of a pleading, averments of time and place are material and shall be considered like all other averments of material matter.

(g) Special Damage. When items of special damage are claimed, they shall be specifically stated.

(h) Admiralty and Maritime Claims. A pleading or count setting forth a claim for relief within the admiralty and maritime jurisdiction that is also within the jurisdiction of the district court on some other ground may contain a statement identifying the claim as an admiralty or maritime claim for the purposes of Rules 14(c), 38(e), 82, and the Supplemental Rules for Certain Admiralty and Maritime Claims. If the claim is cognizable only in admiralty, it is an admiralty or maritime claim for those purposes whether so identified or not. The amendment of a pleading to add or withdraw an identifying statement is governed by the principles of Rule 15. A case that includes an admiralty or maritime claim within this subdivision is an admiralty case within 28 U.S.C. §1292(a)(3).

As amended Feb. 28, 1966, eff. July 1, 1966; Dec. 4, 1967, eff. July 1, 1968; Mar. 30, 1970, eff. July 1, 1970; Mar. 2, 1987, eff. Aug. 1, 1987; Apr. 11, 1997, eff. Dec. 1, 1997.

Rule 10. Form of Pleadings

(a) Caption; Names of Parties. Every pleading shall contain a caption setting forth the name of the court, the title of the action, the file number, and a designation as in Rule 7(a). In the complaint the title of the action shall include the names of all the parties, but in other pleadings it is sufficient to state the name of the first party on each side with an appropriate indication of other parties.

(b) Paragraphs; Separate Statements. All averments of claim or defense shall be made in numbered paragraphs, the contents of each of which shall be limited as far as practicable to a statement of a single set of circumstances; and a paragraph may be referred to by number in all succeeding pleadings. Each claim founded upon a separate transaction or occurrence and each defense other than denials shall be stated in a separate count or defense whenever a separation facilitates the clear presentation of the matters set forth.

(c) Adoption by Reference; Exhibits. Statements in a pleading may be adopted by reference in a different part of the same pleading or in another pleading or in any motion. A copy of any written instrument which is an exhibit to a pleading is a part thereof for all purposes.

Rule 11. Signing of Pleadings, Motions, and Other Papers; Representations to Court; Sanctions

a) Signature. Every pleading, written motion, and other paper shall be y at least one attorney of record in the attorney's individual name, or, if the party is not represented by an attorney, shall be signed by the party. Each paper shall state the signer's address and telephone number, if any. Except when otherwise specifically provided by rule or statute, pleadings need not be verified or accompanied by affidavit. An unsigned paper shall be stricken unless omission of the signature is corrected promptly after being called to the attention of the attorney or party.

(b) Representations to Court. By presenting to the court (whether by signing, filing, submitting, or later advocating) a pleading, written motion, or other paper, an attorney or unrepresented party is certifying that to the best of the person's knowledge, information, and belief, formed after an inquiry reasonable under the circumstances, —

(1) it is not being presented for any improper purpose, such as to harass or to cause unnecessary delay or needless increase in the cost of litigation;

(2) the claims, defenses, and other legal contentions therein are warranted by existing law or by a nonfrivolous argument for the extension, modification, or reversal of existing law or the establishment of new law;

(3) the allegations and other factual contentions have evidentiary support or, if specifically so identified, are likely to have evidentiary support after a reasonable opportunity for further investigation or discovery; and

(4) the denials of factual contentions are warranted on the evidence or, if specifically so identified, are reasonably based on a lack of information or belief.

(c) Sanctions. If, after notice and a reasonable opportunity to respond, the court determines that subdivision (b) has been violated, the court may, subject to the conditions stated below, impose an appropriate sanction upon the attorneys, law firms, or parties that have violated subdivision (b) or are responsible for the violation.

(1) How Initiated.

(A) By Motion. A motion for sanctions under this rule shall be made separately from other motions or requests and shall describe the specific conduct alleged to violate subdivision (b). It shall be served as provided in Rule 5, but shall not be filed with or presented to the court unless, within 21 days after service of the motion (or such other period as the court may prescribe), the challenged paper, claim, defense, contention, allegation, or denial is not withdrawn or appropriately corrected. If warranted, the court may award to the party prevailing on the motion the reasonable expenses and attorney's fees incurred in presenting or opposing the motion. Absent exceptional circumstances, a law firm shall be held jointly responsible for violations committed by its partners, associates, and employees.

(B) On Court's Initiative. On its own initiative, the court may enter an order describing the specific conduct that appears to violate subdivision (b)

and directing an attorney, law firm, or party to show cause why it has not violated subdivision (b) with respect thereto.

*(2) **Nature of Sanction; Limitations.*** A sanction imposed for violation of this rule shall be limited to what is sufficient to deter repetition of such conduct or comparable conduct by others similarly situated. Subject to the limitations in subparagraphs (A) and (B), the sanction may consist of, or include, directives of a nonmonetary nature, an order to pay a penalty into court, or, if imposed on motion and warranted for effective deterrence, an order directing payment to the movant of some or all of the reasonable attorneys' fees and other expenses incurred as a direct result of the violation.

(A) Monetary sanctions may not be awarded against a represented party for a violation of subdivision (b)(2).

(B) Monetary sanctions may not be awarded on the court's initiative unless the court issues its order to show cause before a voluntary dismissal or settlement of the claims made by or against the party which is, or whose attorneys are, to be sanctioned.

*(3) **Order.*** When imposing sanctions, the court shall describe the conduct determined to constitute a violation of this rule and explain the basis for the sanction imposed.

(d) Inapplicability to Discovery. Subdivisions (a) through (c) of this rule do not apply to disclosures and discovery requests, responses, objections, and motions that are subject to the provisions of Rules 26 through 37.

As amended Apr. 28, 1983, eff. Aug. 1, 1983; Mar. 2, 1987, eff. Aug. 1, 1987; Apr. 22, 1993, eff. Dec. 1, 1993.

ADVISORY COMMITTEE NOTES, 1993 AMENDMENTS

Purpose of Revision . . .

The rule retains the principle that attorneys and pro se litigants have an obligation to the court to refrain from conduct that frustrates the aims of Rule 1. The revision broadens the scope of this obligation, but places greater constraints on the imposition of sanctions and should reduce the number of motions for sanctions presented to the court. New subdivision (d) removes from the ambit of this rule all discovery requests, responses, objections, and motions subject to the provisions of Rule 26 through 37.

Subdivision (a). Retained in this subdivision are the provisions requiring signatures on pleadings, written motions, and other papers. Unsigned papers are to be received by the Clerk, but then are to be stricken if the omission of the signature is not corrected promptly after being called to the attention of the attorney or pro se litigant. Correction can be made by signing the paper on file or by submitting a duplicate that contains the signature. A court may require by local rule that papers contain additional identifying information regarding the parties or attorneys, such as telephone numbers to facilitate facsimile transmissions, though, as for omission of a signature, the paper should not be rejected for failure to provide such information. . . .

Subdivisions (b) and (c). These subdivisions restate the provisions requiring attorneys and pro se litigants to conduct a reasonable inquiry into the law and facts before signing pleadings, written motions, and other documents, and prescribing sanctions for violation of these obligations. The revision in part expands the responsibilities of litigants to the court, while providing greater constraints and flexibility in dealing with infractions of the rule. The rule continues to require litigants to "stop-and-think" before initially making legal or factual contentions. It also, however, emphasizes the duty of candor by subjecting litigants to potential sanctions for insisting upon a position after it is no longer tenable and by generally providing protection against sanctions if they withdraw or correct contentions after a potential violation is called to their attention. . . .

The certification with respect to allegations and other factual contentions is revised in recognition that sometimes a litigant may have good reason to believe that a fact is true or false but may need discovery, formal or informal, from opposing parties or third persons to gather and confirm the evidentiary basis for the allegation. Tolerance of factual contentions in initial pleadings by plaintiffs or defendants when specifically identified as made on information and belief does not relieve litigants from the obligation to conduct an appropriate investigation into the facts that is reasonable under the circumstances; it is not a license to join parties, make claims, or present defenses without any factual basis or justification. Moreover, if evidentiary support is not obtained after a reasonable opportunity for further investigation or discovery, the party has a duty under the rule not to persist with that contention. Subdivision (b) does not require a formal amendment to pleadings for which evidentiary support is not obtained, but rather calls upon a litigant not thereafter to advocate such claims or defenses.

The certification is that there is (or likely will be) "evidentiary support" for the allegation, not that the party will prevail with respect to its contention regarding the fact. That summary judgment is rendered against a party does not necessarily mean, for purposes of this certification, that it had no evidentiary support for its position. On the other hand, if a party has evidence with respect to a contention that would suffice to defeat a motion for summary judgment based thereon, it would have sufficient "evidentiary support" for purposes of Rule 11. . . .

Arguments for extensions, modifications, or reversals of existing law or for creation of new law do not violate subdivision (b)(2) provided they are "nonfrivolous." This establishes an objective standard, intended to eliminate any "empty-head pure-heart" justification for patently frivolous arguments. However, the extent to which a litigant has researched the issues and found some support for its theories even in minority opinions, in law review articles, or through consultation with other attorneys should certainly be taken into account in determining whether paragraph (2) has been violated. Although arguments for a change of law are not required to be specifically so identified, a contention that is so identified should be viewed with greater tolerance under the rule.

The court has available a variety of possible sanctions to impose for violations, such as striking the offending paper; issuing an admonition, reprimand, or censure; requiring participation in seminars or other educational programs; ordering a fine payable to the court; referring the matter to disciplinary authorities (or, in the case of government attorneys, to the Attorney General, Inspector General, or agency head), etc. See Manual for Complex Litigation, Second, §42.3. The rule does not attempt to enumerate the factors a court should consider in deciding whether to impose a sanction or what sanctions would be appropriate in the circumstances; but, for emphasis, it does specifically note that a sanction may be nonmonetary as well as monetary. Whether the improper conduct was willful, or negligent; whether it was part of a pattern of activity, or an isolated event; whether it infected the entire pleading, or only one particular count or defense; whether the person has engaged in similar conduct in other litigation; whether it was intended to injure; what effect it had on the litigation process in time or expense; whether the responsible person is trained in the law; what amount, given the financial resources of the responsible person, is needed to deter that person from repetition in the same case; what amount is needed to deter similar activity by other litigants: All of these may in a particular case be proper considerations. The court has significant discretion in determining what sanctions, if any, should be imposed for a violation, subject to the principle that the sanctions should not be more severe than reasonably necessary to deter repetition of the conduct by the offending person or comparable conduct by similarly situated persons. . . .

The power of the court to act on its own initiative is retained, but with the condition that this be done through a show cause order. This procedure provides the person with notice and an opportunity to respond. The revision provides that a monetary sanction imposed after a court-initiated show cause order be limited to a penalty payable to the court and that it be imposed only if the show cause order is issued before any voluntary dismissal or an agreement of the parties to settle the claims made by or against the litigant. Parties settling a case should not be subsequently faced with an unexpected order from the court leading to monetary sanctions that might have affected their willingness to settle or voluntarily dismiss a case. Since show cause orders will ordinarily be issued only in situations that are akin to a contempt of court, the rule does not provide a "safe harbor" to a litigant for withdrawing a claim, defense, etc., after a show cause order has been issued on the court's own initiative. Such corrective action, however, should be taken into account in deciding what — if any — sanction to impose if, after consideration of the litigant's response, the court concludes that a violation has occurred.

Rule 12. Defenses and Objections — When and How Presented — by Pleading or Motion — Motion for Judgment on the Pleadings

(a) When Presented.

Unless a different time is prescribed in a statute of the United States, a [illegible] shall serve an answer

(A) within 20 days after being served with the summons and complaint, or

(B) if service of the summons has been timely waived on request under Rule 4(d), within 60 days after the date when the request for waiver was sent, or within 90 days after that date if the defendant was addressed outside any judicial district of the United States.

(2) A party served with a pleading stating a cross-claim against that party shall serve an answer thereto within 20 days after being served. The plaintiff shall serve a reply to a counterclaim in the answer within 20 days after service of the answer, or, if a reply is ordered by the court, within 20 days after service of the order, unless the order otherwise directs.

(3)(A) The United States, an agency of the United States, or an officer or employee of the United States sued in an official capacity, shall serve an answer to the complaint or cross-claim — or a reply to a counterclaim — within 60 days after the United States attorney is served with the pleading asserting the claim.

(B) An officer or employee of the United States sued in an individual capacity for acts or omissions occurring in connection with the performance of duties on behalf of the United States shall serve an answer to the complaint or cross-claim — or a reply to a counterclaim — within 60 days after service on the officer or employee, or service on the United States attorney, whichever is later.

(4) Unless a different time is fixed by court order, the service of a motion permitted under this rule alters these periods of time as follows:

(A) if the court denies the motion or postpones its disposition until the trial on the merits, the responsive pleading shall be served within 10 days after notice of the court's action; or

(B) if the court grants a motion for a more definite statement, the responsive pleading shall be served within 10 days after the service of the more definite statement.

(b) How Presented. Every defense, in law or fact, to a claim for relief in any pleading, whether a claim, counterclaim, cross-claim, or third-party claim, shall be asserted in the responsive pleading thereto if one is required, except that the following defenses may at the option of the pleader be made by motion: (1) lack of jurisdiction over the subject matter, (2) lack of jurisdiction over the person, (3) improper venue, (4) insufficiency of process, (5) insufficiency of service of process, (6) failure to state a claim upon which relief can be granted, (7) failure to join a party under Rule 19. A motion making any of these defenses shall be made before pleading if a further pleading is permitted. No defense or objection is waived by being joined with one or more other defenses or objections in a responsive pleading or motion. If a pleading sets forth a claim for relief to which the adverse party is not required to serve a responsive pleading, the adverse party may assert at the trial any defense in law or fact to that claim for relief. If, on a motion asserting the defense numbered (6) to dismiss for failure of the pleading to state a claim upon which relief can be granted, matters outside the pleading are presented to and not excluded by the court, the motion shall be treated as one for summary judgment and disposed of as provided in Rule 56, and all parties shall be given reasonable opportunity to present all material made pertinent to such a motion by Rule 56.

(c) **Motion for Judgment on the Pleadings.** After the pleadings are closed but within such time as not to delay the trial, any party may move for judgment on the pleadings. If, on a motion for judgment on the pleadings, matters outside the pleadings are presented to and not excluded by the court, the motion shall be treated as one for summary judgment and disposed of as provided in Rule 56, and all parties shall be given reasonable opportunity to present all material made pertinent to such a motion by Rule 56.

(d) **Preliminary Hearings.** The defenses specifically enumerated (1)-(7) in subdivision (b) of this rule, whether made in a pleading or by motion, and the motion for judgment mentioned in subdivision (c) of this rule shall be heard and determined before trial on application of any party, unless the court orders that the hearing and determination thereof be deferred until the trial.

(e) **Motion for More Definite Statement.** If a pleading to which a responsive pleading is permitted is so vague or ambiguous that a party cannot reasonably be required to frame a responsive pleading, the party may move for a more definite statement before interposing a responsive pleading. The motion shall point out the defects complained of and the details desired. If the motion is granted and the order of the court is not obeyed within 10 days after notice of the order or within such other time as the court may fix, the court may strike the pleading to which the motion was directed or make such order as it deems just.

(f) **Motion to Strike.** Upon motion made by a party before responding to a pleading or, if no responsive pleading is permitted by these rules, upon motion made by a party within 20 days after the service of the pleading upon the party or upon the court's own initiative at any time, the court may order stricken from any pleading any insufficient defense or any redundant, immaterial, impertinent, or scandalous matter.

(g) **Consolidation of Defenses in Motion.** A party who makes a motion under this rule may join with it any other motions herein provided for and then available to the party. If a party makes a motion under this rule but omits therefrom any defense or objection then available to the party which this rule permits to be raised by motion, the party shall not thereafter make a motion based on the defense or objection so omitted, except a motion as provided in subdivision (h)(2) hereof on any of the grounds there stated.

(h) Waiver or Preservation of Certain Defenses.

(1) A defense of lack of jurisdiction over the person, improper venue, insufficiency of process, or insufficiency of service of process is waived (A) if omitted from a motion in the circumstances described in subdivision (g), or (B) if it is neither made by motion under this rule nor included in a responsive pleading or an amendment thereof permitted by Rule 15(a) to be made as a matter of course.

(2) A defense of failure to state a claim upon which relief can be granted, a defense of failure to join a party indispensable under Rule 19, and an objection of failure to state a legal defense to a claim may be made in any pleading permitted or ordered under Rule 7(a), or by motion for judgment on the pleadings, or at the trial on the merits.

(3) Whenever it appears by suggestion of the parties or otherwise that the court lacks jurisdiction of the subject matter, the court shall dismiss the action.

As amended Dec. 27, 1946, eff. Mar. 19, 1948; Jan. 21, 1963, eff. July 1, 1963; Feb. 28, 1966, eff. July 1, 1966; Mar. 2, 1987, eff. Aug. 1, 1987; Apr. 22, 1993, eff. Dec. 1, 1993; Apr. 17, 2000, eff. Dec. 1, 2000.

Advisory Committee Notes, 1948 Amendments and 1966 Amendments

1948 Amendments

Subdivision (e). References in this subdivision to a bill of particulars have been deleted, and the motion provided for is confined to one for a more definite statement, to be obtained only in cases where the movant cannot reasonably be required to frame an answer or other responsive pleading to the pleading in question. With respect to preparations for trial, the party is properly relegated to the various methods of examination and discovery provided in the rules for that purpose. . . .

Rule 12(e) as originally drawn has been the subject of more judicial rulings than any other part of the rules, and has been much criticized by commentators, judges and members of the bar. See general discussion and cases cited in 1 Moore's Federal Practice, 1938, Cum. Supplement, §12.07, under "Page 657"; also, Holtzoff, New Federal Procedure and the Courts, 1940, 35-41. . . . The tendency of some courts freely to grant extended bills of particulars has served to neutralize any helpful benefits derived from Rule 8, and has overlooked the intended use of the rules on depositions and discovery. The words "or to prepare for trial" — eliminated by the proposed amendment — have sometimes been seized upon as grounds for compulsory statement in the opposing pleading of all the details which the movant would have to meet at the trial. On the other hand, many courts have in effect read these words out of the rule. . . .

1966 Amendments

Amended subdivision (h)(1)(A) eliminates [an] ambiguity and states that certain specified defenses which were available to a party when he made a preanswer motion, but which he omitted from the motion, are waived. The specified defenses are lack of jurisdiction over the person, improper venue, insufficiency of process, and insufficiency of service of process (see Rule 12(b)(2)-(5)). A party who by motion invites the court to pass upon a threshold defense should bring forward all the specified defenses he then has and thus allow the court to do a reasonably complete job. The waiver reinforces the policy of subdivision (g) forbidding successive motions.

By amended subdivision (h)(1)(B), the specified defenses, even if not waived by the operation of (A), are waived by the failure to raise them by a motion under Rule 12 or in the responsive pleading or any amendment thereof to which the party is entitled as a matter of course. The specified defenses are of such a character that they should not be delayed and brought up for the first time by means of an application to the court to amend the responsive pleading.

Since the language of the subdivisions is made clear, the party is put on fair notice of the effect of his actions and omissions and can guard himself against unintended waiver. It is to be noted that while the defenses specified in subdivision (h)(1) are subject to waiver as there provided, the more substantial defenses of failure to state a claim upon which relief can be granted, failure to join a party indispensable under Rule 19, and failure to state a legal defense to a claim (see Rule 12(b)(6), (7), (f)), as well as the defense of lack of jurisdiction over the subject matter (see Rule 12(b)(1)), are expressly preserved against waiver by amended subdivision (h)(2) and (3).

Rule 13. Counterclaim and Cross-Claim

(a) Compulsory Counterclaims. A pleading shall state as a counterclaim any claim which at the time of serving the pleading the pleader has against any opposing party, if it arises out of the transaction or occurrence that is the subject matter of the opposing party's claim and does not require for its adjudication the presence of third parties of whom the court cannot acquire jurisdiction. But the pleader need not state the claim if (1) at the time the action was commenced the claim was the subject of another pending action, or (2) the opposing party brought suit upon the claim by attachment or other process by which the court did not acquire jurisdiction to render a personal judgment on that claim, and the pleader is not stating any counterclaim under this Rule 13.

(b) Permissive Counterclaims. A pleading may state as a counterclaim any claim against an opposing party not arising out of the transaction or occurrence that is the subject matter of the opposing party's claim.

(c) Counterclaim Exceeding Opposing Claim. A counterclaim may or may not diminish or defeat the recovery sought by the opposing party. It may claim relief exceeding in amount or different in kind from that sought in the pleading of the opposing party.

(d) Counterclaim Against the United States. These rules shall not be construed to enlarge beyond the limits now fixed by law the right to assert counterclaims or to claim credits against the United States or an officer or agency thereof.

(e) Counterclaim Maturing or Acquired After Pleading. A claim which either matured or was acquired by the pleader after serving a pleading may, with the permission of the court, be presented as a counterclaim by supplemental pleading.

(f) Omitted Counterclaim. When a pleader fails to set up a counterclaim through oversight, inadvertence, or excusable neglect, or when justice requires, the pleader may by leave of court set up the counterclaim by amendment.

(g) Cross-Claim Against Co-Party. A pleading may state as a cross-claim any claim by one party against a co-party arising out of the transaction or occurrence that is the subject matter either of the original action or of a counterclaim therein or relating to any property that is the subject matter of the original action. Such cross-claim may include a claim that the party against whom it is asserted is or may be liable to the cross-claimant for all or part of a claim asserted in the action against the cross-claimant.

(h) Joinder of Additional Parties. Persons other than those made parties to the original action may be made parties to a counterclaim or cross-claim in accordance with the provisions of Rules 19 and 20.

(i) Separate Trials; Separate Judgments. If the court orders separate trials as provided in Rule 42(b), judgment on a counterclaim or cross-claim may be rendered in accordance with the terms of Rule 54(b) when the court has jurisdiction so to do, even if the claims of the opposing party have been dismissed or otherwise disposed of.

As amended Dec. 27, 1946, eff. Mar. 19, 1948; Jan. 21, 1963, eff. July 1, 1963; Feb. 28, 1966, eff. July 1, 1966; Mar. 2, 1987, eff. Aug. 1, 1987.

ADVISORY COMMITTEE COMMENTS, 1963 AMENDMENT

. . . When a defendant, if he desires to defend his interest in property, is obliged to come in and litigate in a court to whose jurisdiction he could not ordinarily be subjected, fairness suggests that he should not be required to assert counterclaims, but should rather be permitted to do so at his election. If, however, he does elect to assert a counterclaim, it seems fair to require him to assert any other which is compulsory within the meaning of Rule 13(a). Clause (2), added by amendment to Rule 13(a), carries out this idea. It will apply to various cases described in Rule 4(e), as amended, where service is effected through attachment or other process by which the court does not acquire jurisdiction to render a personal judgment against the defendant. Clause (2) will also apply to actions commenced in State courts jurisdictionally grounded on attachment or the like, and removed to the Federal courts.

Rule 14. Third-Party Practice

(a) **When Defendant May Bring in Third Party.** At any time after commencement of the action a defending party, as a third-party plaintiff, may cause a summons and complaint to be served upon a person not a party to the action who is or may be liable to the third-party plaintiff for all or part of the plaintiff's claim against the third-party plaintiff. The third-party plaintiff need not obtain leave to make the service if the third-party plaintiff files the third-party complaint not later than 10 days after serving the original answer. Otherwise the third-party plaintiff must obtain leave on motion upon notice to all parties to the action. The person served with the summons and third-party complaint, hereinafter called the third-party defendant, shall make any defenses to the third-party plaintiff's claim as provided in Rule 12 and any counterclaims against the third-party plaintiff and cross-claims against other third-party defendants as provided in Rule 13. The third-party defendant may assert against the plaintiff any defenses which the third-party plaintiff has to the plaintiff's claim. The third-party defendant may also assert any claim against the plaintiff arising out of the transaction or occurrence that is the subject matter of the plaintiff's claim against the third-party plaintiff. The plaintiff may assert any claim against the third-party defendant arising out of the transaction or occurrence that is the subject matter of the plaintiff's claim against the third-party plaintiff, and the third-party defendant thereupon shall assert any defenses as provided in Rule 12 and any counterclaims and cross-claims as provided in Rule 13. Any party may move to strike the third-party claim, or for its severance or separate trial. A third-party defendant may proceed under this rule against any person not a party to the action who is or may be liable to the third-party defendant for all or part of the claim made in the action against the third-party defendant. The third-party complaint, if within the admiralty and maritime jurisdiction, may be in rem against a vessel, cargo, or other property subject to admiralty or maritime process in rem, in which case references in this rule to the summons include the warrant of arrest, and references to the third-party plaintiff or defendant include, where appropriate, person who asserts a right under Supplemental Rule C(6)(b)(i) in the property arrested.

(b) **When Plaintiff May Bring in Third Party.** When a counterclaim is asserted against a plaintiff, the plaintiff may cause a third party to be brought in under circumstances which under this rule would entitle a defendant to do so.

(c) **Admiralty and Maritime Claims.** When a plaintiff asserts an admiralty or maritime claim within the meaning of Rule 9(h), the defendant or person who asserts a right under Supplemental Rule C(6)(b)(i), as a third-party plaintiff, may bring in a third-party defendant who may be wholly or partly liable, either to the plaintiff or to the third-party plaintiff, by way of remedy over, contribution, or otherwise on account of the same transaction, occurrence, or series of transactions or occurrences. In such a case the third-party plaintiff may also demand judgment against the third-party defendant in favor of the plaintiff, in which event the third-party defendant shall make any defenses to the claim of the plaintiff as well as to that of the third-party plaintiff in the manner provided in Rule 12 and the action shall proceed as if the plaintiff had commenced it against the third-party defendant as well as the third-party plaintiff.

As amended Dec. 27, 1946, eff. Mar. 19, 1948; Jan. 21, 1963, eff. July 1, 1963; Feb. 28, 1966, eff. July 1, 1966; Mar. 2, 1987, eff. Aug. 1, 1987; Apr. 17, 2000, eff. Dec. 1, 2000.

Rule 15. Amended and Supplemental Pleadings

(a) **Amendments.** A party may amend the party's pleading once as a matter of course at any time before a responsive pleading is served or, if the pleading is one to which no responsive pleading is permitted and the action has not been placed upon the trial calendar, the party may so amend it at any time within 20 days after it is served. Otherwise a party may amend the party's pleading only by leave of court or by written consent of the adverse party; and leave shall be freely given when justice so requires. A party shall plead in response to an amended pleading within the time remaining for response to the original pleading or within 10 days after service of the amended pleading, whichever period may be the longer, unless the court otherwise orders.

(b) **Amendments to Conform to the Evidence.** When issues not raised by the pleadings are tried by express or implied consent of the parties, they shall be treated in all respects as if they had been raised in the pleadings. Such amendment of the pleadings as may be necessary to cause them to conform to the evidence and to raise these issues may be made upon motion of any party at any time, even after judgment; but failure so to amend does not affect the result of the trial of these issues. If evidence is objected to at the trial on the ground that it is not within the issues made by the pleadings, the court may allow the pleadings to be amended and shall do so freely when the presentation of the merits of the action will be subserved thereby and the objecting party fails to satisfy the court that the admission of such evidence would prejudice the party in maintaining the party's action or defense upon the merits. The court may grant a continuance to enable the objecting party to meet such evidence.

(c) **Relation Back of Amendments.** An amendment of a pleading relates back to the date of the original pleading when

(1) relation back is permitted by the law that provides the statute of limitations applicable to the action, or

(2) the claim or defense asserted in the amended pleading arose out of the conduct, transaction, or occurrence set forth or attempted to be set forth in the original pleading, or

(3) the amendment changes the party or the naming of the party against whom a claim is asserted if the foregoing provision (2) is satisfied and, within the period provided by Rule 4(m) for service of the summons and complaint, the party to be brought in by amendment (A) has received such notice of the institution of the action that the party will not be prejudiced in maintaining a defense on the merits, and (B) knew or should have known that, but for a mistake concerning the identity of the proper party, the action would have been brought against the party.

The delivery or mailing of process to the United States Attorney, or United States Attorney's designee, or the Attorney General of the United States, or an agency or officer who would have been a proper defendant if named, satisfies the requirement of subparagraphs (A) and (B) of this paragraph (3) with respect to the United States or any agency or officer thereof to be brought into the action as a defendant.

(d) Supplemental Pleadings. Upon motion of a party the court may, upon reasonable notice and upon such terms as are just, permit the party to serve a supplemental pleading setting forth transactions or occurrences or events which have happened since the date of the pleading sought to be supplemented. Permission may be granted even though the original pleading is defective in its statement of a claim for relief or defense. If the court deems it advisable that the adverse party plead to the supplemental pleading, it shall so order, specifying the time therefor.

As amended Jan. 21, 1963, eff. July 1, 1963; Feb. 28, 1966, eff. July 1, 1966; Mar. 2, 1987, eff. Aug. 1, 1987; Apr. 30, 1991, eff. Dec. 1, 1991; Apr. 22, 1993, eff. Dec. 1, 1993.

Advisory Committee Notes, 1966 and 1991 Amendments

1966 Amendments

Subdivision (c). Prior to the 1966 amendments, Rule 15(c) contained only what is now its first sentence. The Advisory Committee commented upon the additions as follows:

Rule 15(c) is amplified to state more clearly when an amendment of a pleading changing the party against whom a claim is asserted (including an amendment to correct a misnomer or misdescription of a defendant) shall "relate back" to the date of the original pleading.

The problem has arisen most acutely in certain actions by private parties against officers or agencies of the United States. Thus an individual denied social security benefits by the Secretary of Health, Education, and Welfare may secure review of the decision by bringing a civil action against that officer within sixty days. 42 U.S.C. §405(g) (Supp. III, 1962). In several recent cases the claimants instituted timely action but mistakenly named as defendant the United States, the Department of HEW, the "Federal Security Administration" (a nonexistent agency), and a Secretary who had retired from the office nineteen days before. Discovering their mistakes, the claimants moved to amend their complaints to name the proper defendant; by this time the statutory sixty-day period had expired. The motions were denied on the ground that the amendment "would amount to the commencement of a new proceeding and would not relate back in time so as to avoid the statutory provision . . . that suit be brought within sixty days. . . ." Cohn v. Federal Security Adm., 199 F. Supp. 884, 885 (W.D.N.Y.1961). . . .

Analysis in terms of "new proceeding" is traceable to Davis v. L.L. Cohen & Co., 268 U.S. 638 (1925), and Mellon v. Arkansas Land & Lumber Co., 275 U.S. 460 (1928), but those cases antedate the adoption of the rules which import different criteria for determining when an amendment is to "relate back." As lower courts have continued to rely on the *Davis and Mellon* cases despite the contrary intent of the rules, clarification of Rule 15(c) is considered advisable.

Relation back is intimately connected with the policy of the statute of limitations. The policy of the statute limiting the time for suit against the Secretary of HEW would not have been offended by allowing relation back in the situations described above. For the government was put on notice of the claim within the stated period — in the particular instances, by means of the initial delivery of process to a responsible government official (see Rule 4(d)(4) and (5)). In these circumstances, characterization of the amendment as a new proceeding is not responsive to the reality, but is merely question-begging; and to deny relation back is to defeat unjustly the claimant's opportunity to prove his case. See the full discussion by Byse, Suing the "Wrong" Defendant in Judicial Review of Federal Administrative Action: Proposals for Reform, 77 Harv. L. Rev. 40 (1963); see also Ill. Civ. P. Act §46(4). . . . In actions between private parties, the problem of relation back of amendments changing defendants has generally been better handled by the courts, but incorrect criteria have sometimes been applied, leading sporadically to doubtful results. . . . Rule 15(c) has been amplified to provide a general solution. . . .

1991 Amendments

Paragraph (c)(1). This provision is new. It is intended to make it clear that the rule does not apply to preclude any relation back that may be permitted under the applicable limitations law. Generally, the applicable limitations law will be state law. If federal jurisdiction is based on the citizenship of the parties, the primary reference is the law of the state in which the district court sits. Walker v. Armco Steel Corp., 446 U.S. 740 (1980). If federal jurisdiction is based on a federal question, the reference may be to the law of the state governing relations between the parties. E.g., Board of Regents v. Tomanio, 446 U.S. 478 (1980). In some circumstances, the controlling limitations law may be federal law. E.g., West v. Conrail, Inc. 107 S. Ct. 1538 (1987). Cf. Burlington Northern R. Co. v. Woods, 480 U.S. 1 (1987); Stewart Organization v. Ricoh, 108 S. Ct. 2239 (1988). Whatever may be the controlling body of limitations law, if that law affords a more forgiving principle of relation back than the one provided in this rule, it should be available to save the claim. Accord, Marshall v. Mulrenin, 508 F.2d 39 (1st cir. 1974). If Schiavone v. Fortune, 106 S. Ct. 2379 (1986) implies the contrary, this paragraph is intended to make a material change in the rule.

Paragraph (c)(3). This paragraph has been revised to change the result in Schiavone v. Fortune, supra, with respect to the problem of a misnamed defendant. An intended defendant who is notified of an action within the period allowed by Rule 4(j) for service of a summons and complaint may not under the revised rule defeat the action on account of a defect in the pleading with respect to the defendant's name, provided that the requirements of clauses (A) and (B) have been met. If the notice requirement is met within the Rule 4(j) period, a complaint may be amended at any time to correct a formal defect such as a misnomer or misidentification. On the basis of the text of the former rule, the Court reached a result in Schiavone v. Fortune that was inconsistent with the liberal pleading practices secured by Rule 8. See Bauer, Schiavone: An Un-Fortune-ate Illustration of the Supreme Court's Role as Interpreter of the Federal Rules of Civil Procedure, 63 Notre Dame L. Rev. 720 (1988); Brussack, Outrageous Fortune: The Case for Amending Rule 15(c) Again, 61 S. Cal. L. Rev. 671 (1988); Lewis, The Excessive History of Federal Rule 15(c) and Its Lessons for Civil Rules Revision, 86 Mich. L. Rev. 1507 (1987).

In allowing a name-correcting amendment within the time allowed by Rule 4(m), this rule allows not only the 120 days specified in that rule, but also any additional time resulting from any extension ordered by the court pursuant to that rule, as may be granted, for example, if the defendant is a fugitive from service of the summons.

Rule 16. Pretrial Conferences; Scheduling; Management

(a) Pretrial Conferences; Objectives. In any action, the court may in its discretion direct the attorneys for the parties and any unrepresented parties to appear before it for a conference or conferences before trial for such purposes as

(1) expediting the disposition of the action;

(2) establishing early and continuing control so that the case will not be protracted because of lack of management;

(3) discouraging wasteful pretrial activities;

(4) improving the quality of the trial through more thorough preparation, and;

(5) facilitating the settlement of the case.

(b) Scheduling and Planning. Except in categories of actions exempted by district court rule as inappropriate, the district judge, or a magistrate judge when authorized by district court rule, shall, after receiving the report from the parties under Rule 26(f) or after consulting with the attorneys for the parties and any unrepresented parties by a scheduling conference, telephone, mail, or other suitable means, enter a scheduling order that limits the time

(1) to join other parties and to amend the pleadings;

(2) to file motions; and

(3) to complete discovery.

The scheduling order may also include

(4) modifications of the times for disclosures under Rules 26(a) and 26(e)(1) and of the extent of discovery to be permitted;

(5) the date or dates for conferences before trial, a final pretrial conference, and trial; and

(6) any other matters appropriate in the circumstances of the case.

The order shall issue as soon as practicable but in any event within 90 days after the appearance of a defendant and within 120 days after the complaint has been served on a defendant. A schedule shall not be modified except upon a showing of good cause and by leave of the district judge or, when authorized by local rule, by a magistrate judge.

(c) Subjects for Consideration at Pretrial Conferences. At any conference under this rule consideration may be given, and the court may take appropriate action, with respect to

(1) the formulation and simplification of the issues, including the elimination of frivolous claims or defenses;

(2) the necessity or desirability of amendments to the pleadings;

(3) the possibility of obtaining admissions of fact and of documents which will avoid unnecessary proof, stipulations regarding the authenticity of documents, and advance rulings from the court on the admissibility of evidence;

(4) the avoidance of unnecessary proof and of cumulative evidence, and limitations or restrictions on the use of testimony under Rule 702 of the Federal Rules of Evidence;

(5) the appropriateness and timing of summary adjudication under Rule 56;

(6) the control and scheduling of discovery, including orders affecting disclosures and discovery pursuant to Rule 26 and Rules 29 through 37;

(7) the identification of witnesses and documents, the need and schedule for filing and exchanging pretrial briefs, and the date or dates for further conferences and for trial;

(8) the advisability of referring matters to a magistrate judge or master;

(9) settlement and the use of special procedures to assist in resolving the dispute when authorized by statute or local rule;

(10) the form and substance of the pretrial order;

(11) the disposition of pending motions;

(12) the need for adopting special procedures for managing potentially difficult or protracted actions that may involve complex issues, multiple parties, difficult legal questions, or unusual proof problems;

(13) an order for a separate trial pursuant to Rule 42(b) with respect to a claim, counterclaim, cross-claim, or third-party claim, or with respect to any particular issue in the case;

(14) an order directing a party or parties to present evidence early in the trial with respect to a manageable issue that could, on the evidence, be the basis for a judgment as a matter of law under Rule 50(a) or a judgment on partial findings under Rule 52(c);

(15) an order establishing a reasonable limit on the time allowed for presenting evidence; and

(16) such other matters as may facilitate the just, speedy, and inexpensive disposition of the action.

At least one of the attorneys for each party participating in any conference before trial shall have authority to enter into stipulations and to make admissions regarding all matters that the participants may reasonably anticipate may be discussed. If appropriate, the court may require that a party or its representative be present or reasonably available by telephone in order to consider possible settlement of the dispute.

(d) **Final Pretrial Conference.** Any final pretrial conference shall be held as close to the time of trial as reasonable under the circumstances. The participants at any such conference shall formulate a plan for trial, including a program for facilitating the admission of evidence. The conference shall be attended by at least one of the attorneys who will conduct the trial for each of the parties and by any unrepresented parties.

(e) **Pretrial Orders.** After any conference held pursuant to this rule, an order shall be entered reciting the action taken. This order shall control the subsequent course of the action unless modified by a subsequent order. The order following a final pretrial conference shall be modified only to prevent manifest injustice.

(f) **Sanctions.** If a party or party's attorney fails to obey a scheduling or pretrial order, or if no appearance is made on behalf of a party at a scheduling or pretrial conference, or if a party or party's attorney is substantially unprepared to participate in the conference, or if a party or party's attorney fails to participate in good faith, the judge, upon motion or the judge's own initiative, may make such orders with regard thereto as are just, and among others any of the orders provided in Rule 37(b)(2)(B), (C), (D). In lieu of or in addition to any other sanction, the judge shall require the party or the attorney representing the party or both to pay the reasonable expenses incurred because of any noncompliance with this rule, including attorney's fees, unless the judge finds that the noncompliance was substantially justified or that other circumstances make an award of expenses unjust.

As amended Apr. 28, 1983, eff. Aug. 1, 1983; Mar. 2, 1987, eff. Aug. 1, 1987; Apr. 22, 1993, eff. Dec. 1, 1993.

Advisory Committee Notes, 1983 and 1993 Amendments

1983 Amendments

Introduction

Rule 16 has not been amended since the Federal Rules were promulgated in 1938. In many respects, the rule has been a success. For example, there is evidence that pretrial conferences may improve the quality of justice rendered in the federal courts by sharpening the preparation and presentation of cases, tending to eliminate trial surprise, and improving, as well as facilitating, the settlement process. See 6 Wright & Miller, Federal Practice and Procedure: Civil §1522 (1971). However, in other respects particularly with regard to case management, the rule has not always been as helpful as it might have been. Thus there has been a widespread feeling that amendment is necessary to encourage pretrial management that meets the needs of modern litigation. See Report of the National Commission for the Review of Antitrust Laws and Procedures (1979).

Major criticism of Rule 16 has centered on the fact that its application can result in over-regulation of some cases and under-regulation of others. In simple, run-of-the-mill cases, attorneys have found pretrial requirements burdensome. It is claimed that over-administration leads to a series of mini-trials that result in a waste of an attorney's time and needless expense to a client. Pollack, Pretrial Procedures More Effectively Handled, 65 F.R.D. 475 (1974). This is especially likely to be true when pretrial proceedings occur long before trial. At the other end of the spectrum, the discretionary character of Rule 16 and its orientation toward a single conference late in the pretrial process has led to under-administration of complex or protracted cases. Without judicial guidance beginning shortly after institution, these cases often become mired in discovery.

Four sources of criticism of pretrial have been identified. First, conferences often are seen as a mere exchange of legalistic contentions without any real analysis of the particular case. Second, the result frequently is nothing but a formal agreement on minutiae. Third, the conferences are seen as unnecessary and time-consuming in cases that will be settled before trial. Fourth, the meetings can be ceremonial and ritualistic, having little effect on the trial and being of minimal value, particularly when the attorneys attending the sessions are not the ones who will try the case or lack authority to enter into binding stipulations. See generally McCargo v. Hedrick, 545 F.2d 393 (4th Cir. 1976); Pollack, Pretrial Procedures More Effectively Handled, 65 F.R.D. 475 (1974); Rosenberg, The Pretrial Conference and Effective Justice 45 (1964).

There also have been difficulties with the pretrial orders that issue following Rule 16 conferences. When an order is entered far in advance of trial, some issues may not be properly formulated. Counsel naturally are cautious and often try to preserve as many options as possible. If the judge who tries the case did not conduct the conference, he could find it difficult to determine exactly what was agreed to at the conference. But any insistence on a detailed order may be too burdensome, depending on the nature or posture of the case.

Given the significant changes in federal civil litigation since 1938 that are not reflected in Rule 16, it has been extensively rewritten and expanded to meet the challenges of modern litigation. Empirical studies reveal that when a trial judge intervenes personally at an early stage to assume judicial control over a case and to schedule dates for completion by the parties of the principal pretrial steps, the case is disposed of by settlement or trial more efficiently and with less cost and delay than when the parties are left to their own devices. Flanders, Case Management and Court Management in United States District Courts 17, Federal Judicial Center (1977). Thus, the rule mandates a pretrial scheduling order. However, although scheduling and pretrial conferences are encouraged in appropriate cases, they are not mandated. . . .

1993 AMENDMENTS

Subdivision (c). The primary purposes of the changes in subdivision (c) are to call attention to the opportunities for structuring of trial under Rules 42, 50, and 52 and to eliminate questions that have occasionally been raised regarding the authority of the court to make appropriate orders designed either to facilitate settlement or to provide for an efficient and economical trial. The prefatory language of this subdivision is revised to clarify the court's power to enter appropriate orders at a conference notwithstanding the objection of a party. Of course settlement is dependent upon agreement by the parties and, indeed, a conference is most effective and productive when the parties participate in a spirit of cooperation and mindful of their responsibilities under Rule 1.

IV. Parties

Rule 17. Parties Plaintiff and Defendant; Capacity

(a) **Real Party in Interest.** Every action shall be prosecuted in the name of the real party in interest. An executor, administrator, guardian, bailee, trustee of an express trust, a party with whom or in whose name a contract has been made for the benefit of another, or a party authorized by statute may sue in that person's own name without joining the party for whose benefit the action is brought; and when a statute of the United States so provides, an action for the use or benefit of another shall be brought in the name of the United States. No action shall be dismissed on the ground that it is not prosecuted in the name of the real party in interest until a reasonable time has been allowed after objection for ratification of commencement of the action by, or joinder or substitution of, the real party in interest; and such ratification, joinder, or substitution shall have the same effect as if the action had been commenced in the name of the real party in interest.

(b) Capacity to Sue or Be Sued. The capacity of an individual, other than one acting in a representative capacity, to sue or be sued shall be determined by the law of the individual's domicile. The capacity of a corporation to sue or be sued shall be determined by the law under which it was organized. In all other cases capacity to sue or be sued shall be determined by the law of the state in which the district court is held, except (1) that a partnership or other unincorporated association, which has no such capacity by the law of such state, may sue or be sued in its common name for the purpose of enforcing for or against it a substantive right existing under the Constitution or laws of the United States, and (2) that the capacity of a receiver appointed by a court of the United States to sue or be sued in a court of the United States is governed by Title 28, U.S.C. §§754 and 959(a).

(c) Infants or Incompetent Persons. Whenever an infant or incompetent person has a representative, such as a general guardian, committee, conservator, or other like fiduciary, the representative may sue or defend on behalf of the infant or incompetent person. An infant or incompetent person who does not have a duly appointed representative may sue by a next friend or by a guardian ad litem. The court shall appoint a guardian ad litem for an infant or incompetent person not otherwise represented in an action or shall make such other order as it deems proper for the protection of the infant or incompetent person.

As amended Dec. 27, 1946, eff. Mar. 19, 1948; Dec. 29, 1948, eff. Oct. 20, 1949; Feb, 28, 1966, eff. July 1, 1966; Mar. 2, 1987, eff. Aug. 1, 1987; Apr. 25, 1988, eff. Aug. 1, 1988; Nov. 19, 1988, Pub. L. 100-690, Title VII, §7049, 102 Stat. 4401.

ADVISORY COMMITTEE NOTES, 1966 AMENDMENTS

[Amended Rule 17(a)] keeps pace with the law as it is actually developing. Modern decisions are inclined to be lenient when an honest mistake has been made in choosing the party in whose name the action is to be filed. . . . The provision should not be misunderstood or distorted. It is intended to prevent forfeiture when determination of the proper party to sue is difficult or when an understandable mistake has been made. It does not mean, for example, that, following an airplane crash in which all aboard were killed, an action may be filed in the name of John Doe (a fictitious person), as personal representative of Richard Roe (another fictitious person), in the hope that at a later time the attorney filing the action may substitute the real name of the real personal representative of a real victim, and have the benefit of suspension of the limitation period.

Rule 18. Joinder of Claims and Remedies

(a) Joinder of Claims. A party asserting a claim to relief as an original claim, counterclaim, cross-claim, or third-party claim, may join, either as independent or as alternate claims, as many claims, legal, equitable, or maritime, as the party has against an opposing party.

(b) Joinder of Remedies; Fraudulent Conveyances. Whenever a claim is one heretofore cognizable only after another claim has been prosecuted to a conclusion, the two claims may be joined in a single action; but the court shall grant relief in that action only in accordance with the relative substantive rights of the parties. In particular, a plaintiff may state a claim for money and a claim to have set aside a conveyance fraudulent as to that plaintiff, without first having obtained a judgment establishing the claim for money.

As amended Feb. 28, 1966, eff. July 1, 1966; Mar. 2, 1987, eff. Aug. 1, 1987.

Advisory Committee Notes, 1966 Amendments

The liberal policy regarding joinder of claims in the pleadings extends to cases with multiple parties. However, the language used in the second sentence of Rule 18(a) — "if the requirements of Rules 19 [necessary joinder of parties], 20 [permissive joinder of parties], and 22 [interpleader] are satisfied" — has led some courts to infer that the rules regulating joinder of parties are intended to carry back to Rule 18(a) and to impose some special limits on joinder of claims in multi-party cases. In particular, Rule 20(a) has been read as restricting the operation of Rule 18(a) in certain situations in which a number of parties have been permissively joined in an action. In Federal Housing Admr. v. Christianson, 26 F. Supp. 419 (D. Conn. 1939), the indorsee of two notes sued the three co-makers of one note, and sought to join in the action a count on a second note which had been made by two of the three defendants. There was no doubt about the propriety of the joinder of the three parties defendant, for a right to relief was being asserted against all three defendants which arose out of a single "transaction" (the first note) and a question of fact or law "common" to all three defendants would arise in the action. See the text of Rule 20(a). The court, however, refused to allow the joinder of the count on the second note, on the ground that this right to relief, assumed to arise from a distinct transaction, did not involve a question common to all the defendants but only two of them. . . .

If the court's view is followed, it becomes necessary to enter at the pleading stage into speculations about the exact relation between the claim sought to be joined against fewer than all the defendants properly joined in the action, and the claims asserted against all the defendants. . . . Thus if it could be found in the *Christianson* situation that the claim on the second note arose out of the same transaction as the claim on the first or out of a transaction forming part of a "series," and that any question of fact or law with respect to the second note also arose with regard to the first, it would be held that the claim on the second note could be joined in the complaint. . . . Such pleading niceties provide a basis for delaying and wasteful maneuver. It is more compatible with the design of the rules to allow the claim to be joined in the pleading, leaving the question of possible separate trial of that claim to be later decided. . . .

Rule 18(a) is now amended not only to overcome the *Christianson* decision and similar authority, but also to state clearly, as a comprehensive proposition, that a party asserting a claim (an original claim, counterclaim, cross-claim, or third-party claim) may join as many claims as he has against an opposing party. . . .

It is emphasized that amended Rule 18(a) deals only with pleading. As already indicated, a claim properly joined as a matter of pleading need not be proceeded with together with the other claims if fairness or convenience justifies separate treatment. . . .

Free joinder of claims and remedies is one of the basic purposes of unification of the admiralty and civil procedure. The amendment accordingly provides for the inclusion in the rule of maritime claims as well as those which are legal and equitable in character.

Rule 19. Joinder of Persons Needed for Just Adjudication

(a) Persons to Be Joined If Feasible. A person who is subject to service of process and whose joinder will not deprive the court of jurisdiction over the subject matter of the action shall be joined as a party in the action if (1) in the person's absence complete relief cannot be accorded among those already parties, or (2) the person claims an interest relating to the subject of the action and is so situated that the disposition of the action in the person's absence may (i) as a practical matter impair or impede the person's ability to protect that interest or (ii) leave any of the persons already parties subject to a substantial risk of incurring double, multiple, or otherwise inconsistent obligations by reason of the claimed interest. If the person has not been so joined, the court shall order that the person be made a party. If the person should join as a plaintiff but refuses to do so, the person may be made a defendant, or, in a proper case, an involuntary plaintiff. If the joined party objects to venue and joinder of that party would render the venue of the action improper, that party shall be dismissed from the action.

(b) Determination by Court Whenever Joinder Not Feasible. If a person as described in subdivision (a)(1)-(2) hereof cannot be made a party, the court shall determine whether in equity and good conscience the action should proceed among the parties before it, or should be dismissed, the absent person being thus regarded as indispensable. The factors to be considered by the court include: first, to what extent a judgment rendered in the person's absence might be prejudicial to the person or those already parties; second, the extent to which, by protective provisions in the judgment, by the shaping of relief, or other measures, the prejudice can be lessened or avoided; third, whether a judgment rendered in the person's absence will be adequate; fourth, whether the plaintiff will have an adequate remedy if the action is dismissed for nonjoinder.

(c) Pleading Reasons for Nonjoinder. A pleading asserting a claim for relief shall state the names, if known to the pleader, of any persons as described in subdivision (a)(1)-(2) hereof who are not joined, and the reasons why they are not joined.

(d) Exception of Class Actions. This rule is subject to the provisions of Rule 23.

As amended Feb. 28, 1966, eff. July 1, 1966; Mar. 2, 1987, eff. Aug. 1, 1987.

ADVISORY COMMITTEE NOTES, 1966 AMENDMENTS . . .

The Amended Rule

New subdivision (a) defines the persons whose joinder in the action is desirable. Clause (1) stresses the desirability of joining those persons in whose absence the court would be obliged to grant partial or "hollow" rather than complete relief to the parties before the court. The interests that are being furthered here are not only those of the parties, but also that of the public in avoiding repeated lawsuits on the same essential subject matter. Clause (2) (i) recognizes the importance of protecting the person whose joinder is in question against the practical prejudice to him which may arise through a disposition of the action in his absence. Clause (2) (ii) recognizes the need for considering whether a party may be left, after the adjudication, in a position where a person not joined can subject him to a double or otherwise inconsistent liability. See Reed, 55 Mich. L. Rev. at 330, 338; Note, 65 Harv. L. Rev. at 1052-57; Developments in the Law, 71 Harv. L. Rev. at 881-85.

The subdivision (a) definition of persons to be joined is not couched in terms of the abstract nature of their interests — "joint," "united," "separable," or the like. See N.Y. Temporary Comm. on Courts, First Preliminary Report, [Legis. Doc. 1957;] Developments in the Law, supra, at 880. It should be noted particularly, however, that the description is not at variance with the settled authorities holding that a tortfeasor with the usual "joint-and-several" liability is merely a permissive party to an action against another with like liability. See 3 Moore's Federal Practice, §2153 (2d ed. 1963); 2 Barron & Holtzoff, Federal Practice & Procedure §513.8 (Wright ed. 1961). Joinder of these tortfeasors continues to be regulated by Rule 20; compare Rule 14 on third-party practice.

If a person as described in subdivision (a)(1)-(2) is amenable to service of process and his joinder would not deprive the court of jurisdiction in the sense of competence over the action, he should be joined as a party; and if he has not been joined, the court should order him to be brought into the action. If a party joined has a valid objection to the venue and chooses to assert it, he will be dismissed from the action.

Subdivision (b). When a person as described in subdivision (a)(1)-(2) cannot be made a party, the court is to determine whether in equity and good conscience the action should proceed among the parties already before it, or should be dismissed. That this decision is to be made in the light of pragmatic considerations has often been acknowledged by the courts. See Roos v. Texas Co., 23 F.2d 171 (2d Cir. 1927), cert. denied, 277 U.S. 587 (1928); Nites-Bement-Pond Co. v. Iron Moulders' Union, 254 U.S. 77, 80 (1920). The subdivision sets out four relevant considerations drawn from the experience revealed in the decided cases. The factors are to a certain extent overlapping, and they are not intended to exclude other considerations which may be applicable in particular situations.

The *first factor* brings in a consideration of what a judgment in the action would mean to the absentee. Would the absentee be adversely affected in a practical sense, and if so, would the prejudice be immediate and serious, or remote and minor? The possible collateral consequences of the judgment upon the parties already joined are also to be appraised. Would any party be exposed to a fresh action by the absentee, and if so, how serious is the threat? See the elaborate discussion in Reed, supra; cf. A. L. Smith Iron Co. v. Dickson, 141 F.2d 3 (2d Cir. 1944); Caldwell Mfg. Co. v. Unique Balance Co., 18 F.R.D. 258 (S.D.N.Y. 1955).

The *second factor* calls attention to the measures by which prejudice may be averted or lessened. The "shaping of relief" is a familiar expedient to this end. See e.g., the award of money damages in lieu of specific relief where the latter might affect an absentee adversely. Ward v. Deavers, 203 F.2d 72 (D.C. Cir. 1953); Miller & Lux, Inc. v. Nickel, 141 F. Supp. 41 (N.D. Calif. 1956). On the use of "protective provisions," see Roos v. Texas Co., supra; Atwood v. Rhode Island Hosp. Trust Co., 275 Fed. 513, 519 (1st Cir. 1921), cert. denied, 257 U.S. 661 (1922); cf. Stumpf v. Fidelity Gas Co., 294 F.2d 886 (9th Cir. 1961); and the general statement in National Licorice Co. v. Labor Board, 309 U.S. 350, 363 (1940).

Sometimes the party is himself able to take measures to avoid prejudice. Thus a defendant faced with a prospect of a second suit by an absentee may be in a position to bring the latter into the action by defensive interpleader. See Hudson v. Newell, 172 F.2d 848, 852, mod., 176 F.2d 546 (5th Cir. 1949); Gauss v. Kirk, F.2d 83, 86 (D.C. Cir. 1952); Abel v. Brayton Flying Service, Inc., 248 F.2d 713, 716 (5th Cir. 1957) (suggestion of possibility of counterclaim under Rule 13(h)); cf. Parker Rust-Proof Co. v. Western Union Tel. Co., 105 F.2d 976 (2d Cir. 1939), cert. denied, 308 U.S. 597 (1939). So also the absentee may sometimes be able to avert prejudice to himself by voluntarily appearing in the action or intervening on an ancillary basis. See Developments in the Law, supra, 71 Harv. L. Rev. at 882; Annot., Intervention or Subsequent Joinder of Parties as Affecting Jurisdiction of Federal Court Based on Diversity of Citizenship, 134 A.L.R. 335 (1941); Johnson v. Middleton, 175 F.2d 535 (7th Cir. 1949); Kentucky Nat. Gas Corp. v. Duggins, 165 F.2d 1011 (6th Cir. 1948); McComb v. McCormack, 159 F.2d 219 (5th Cir. 1947). The court should consider whether this, in turn, would impose undue hardship on the absentee. (For the possibility of the court's informing an absentee of the pendency of the action, see comment under subdivision (c) below.)

The *third factor* — whether an "adequate" judgment can be rendered in the absence of a given person — calls attention to the extent of the relief that can be accorded among the parties joined. It mashes with the other factors, especially the "shaping of relief" mentioned under the second factor. Cf. Kroese v. General Steel Castings Corp., 179 F.2d 760 (3d Cir. 1949), cert. denied, 339 U.S. 983 (1950).

The *fourth factor,* looking to the practical effects of a dismissal, indicates that the court should consider whether there is any assurance that the plaintiff, if dismissed, could sue effectively in another forum where better joinder would be possible. See Fitzgerald v. Haynes, 241 F.2d 417, 420 (3d Cir. 1957); Fouke v. Schenewerk, 197 F.2d 234, 236 (5th Cir. 1952); cf. Warfield v. Marks, 190 F.2d 178 (5th Cir. 1951).

The subdivision uses the word "indispensable" only in a conclusory sense, that is, a person is "regarded as indispensable" when he cannot be made a party and, upon consideration of the factors above-mentioned, it is determined that in his absence it would be preferable to dismiss the action, rather than to retain it.

A person may be added as a party at any stage of the action on motion or on the court's initiative (see Rule 21); and a motion to dismiss, on the ground that a person has not been joined and justice requires that the action should not proceed in his absence, may be made as late as the trial on the merits (see Rule 12(h) (2), as amended; cf. Rule 12(b) (7), as amended). However, when the moving party is seeking dismissal in order to protect himself against a later suit by the absent person (subdivision (a) (2) (ii)), and is not seeking vicariously to protect the absent person against a prejudicial judgment (subdivision (a) (2) (i)), his undue delay in making the motion can properly be counted against him as a reason for denying the motion. A joinder question should be decided with reasonable promptness, but decision may properly be deferred if adequate information is not available at the time. Thus the relationship of an absent person to the action, and the practical effects of an adjudication upon him and others, may not be sufficiently revealed at the pleading stage; in such a case it would be appropriate to defer decision until the action was further advanced. Cf. Rule 12(d). . . .

Subdivision (c) parallels the predecessor subdivision (c) of Rule 19. In some situations it may be desirable to advise a person who has not been joined of the fact that the action is pending, and in particular cases the court in its discretion may itself convey this information by directing a letter or other informal notice to the absentee.

Rule 20. Permissive Joinder of Parties

(a) Permissive Joinder. All persons may join in one action as plaintiffs if they assert any right to relief jointly, severally, or in the alternative in respect of or arising out of the same transaction, occurrence, or series of transactions or occurrences and if any question of law or fact common to all these persons will arise in the action. All persons (and any vessel, cargo or other property subject to admiralty process in rem) may be joined in one action as defendants if there is asserted against them jointly, severally, or in the alternative, any right to relief in respect of or arising out of the same transaction, occurrence, or series of transactions or occurrences and if any question of law or fact common to all defendants will arise in the action. A plaintiff or defendant need not be interested in obtaining or defending against all the relief demanded. Judgment may be given for one or more of the plaintiffs according to their respective rights to relief, and against one or more defendants according to their respective liabilities.

(b) **Separate Trials.** The court may make such orders as will prevent a party from being embarrassed, delayed, or put to expense by the inclusion of a party against whom the party asserts no claim and who asserts no claim against the party, and may order separate trials or make other orders to prevent delay or prejudice.

As amended Feb. 28, 1966, eff. July 1, 1966; Mar. 2, 1987, eff. Aug. 1, 1987.

Rule 21. Misjoinder and Nonjoinder of Parties

Misjoinder of parties is not ground for dismissal of an action. Parties may be dropped or added by order of the court on motion of any party or of its own initiative at any stage of the action and on such terms as are just. Any claim against a party may be severed and proceeded with separately.

Rule 22. Interpleader

(1) Persons having claims against the plaintiff may be joined as defendants and required to interplead when their claims are such that the plaintiff is or may be exposed to double or multiple liability. It is not ground for objection to the joinder that the claims of the several claimants or the titles on which their claims depend do not have a common origin or are not identical but are adverse to and independent of one another, or that the plaintiff avers that the plaintiff is not liable in whole or in part to any or all of the claimants. A defendant exposed to similar liability may obtain such interpleader by way of cross-claim or counter-claim. The provisions of this rule supplement and do not in any way limit the joinder of parties permitted in Rule 20.

(2) The remedy herein provided is in addition to and in no way supersedes or limits the remedy provided by Title 28, U.S.C. §§1335, 1397, and 2361. Actions under those provisions shall be conducted in accordance with these rules.

As amended Dec. 29, 1948, eff. Oct. 20, 1949; Mar. 2, 1987, eff. Aug. 1, 1987.

Rule 23. Class Actions

(a) **Prerequisites to a Class Action.** One or more members of a class may sue or be sued as representative parties on behalf of all only if (1) the class is so numerous that joinder of all members is impracticable, (2) there are questions of law or fact common to the class, (3) the claims or defenses of the representative parties are typical of the claims or defenses of the class, and (4) the representative parties will fairly and adequately protect the interests of the class.

(b) Class Actions Maintainable. An action may be maintained as a class action if the prerequisites of subdivision (a) are satisfied, and in addition:

(1) the prosecution of separate actions by or against individual members of the class would create a risk of

(A) inconsistent or varying adjudications with respect to individual members of the class which would establish incompatible standards of conduct for the party opposing the class, or

(B) adjudications with respect to individual members of the class which would as a practical matter be dispositive of the interests of the other members not parties to the adjudications or substantially impair or impede their ability to protect their interest; or

(2) the party opposing the class has acted or refused to act on grounds generally applicable to the class, thereby making appropriate final injunctive relief or corresponding declaratory relief with respect to the class as a whole; or

(3) the court finds that the questions of law or fact common to the members of the class predominate over any questions affecting only individual members, and that a class action is superior to other available methods for the fair and efficient adjudication of the controversy. The matters pertinent to the findings include: (A) the interest of members of the class in individually controlling the prosecution or defense of separate actions; (B) the extent and nature of any litigation concerning the controversy already commenced by or against members of the class; (C) the desirability or undesirability of concentrating the litigation of the claims in the particular forum; (D) the difficulties likely to be encountered in the management of a class action.

(c) Determination by Order Whether Class Action to Be Maintained; Notice; Judgment; Actions Conducted Partially as Class Actions.

(1) As soon as practicable after the commencement of an action brought as a class action, the court shall determine by order whether it is to be so maintained. An order under this subdivision may be conditional, and may be altered or amended before the decision on the merits.

(2) In any class action maintained under subdivision (b)(3), the court shall direct to the members of the class the best notice practicable under the circumstances, including individual notice to all members who can be identified through reasonable effort. The notice shall advise each member that (A) the court will exclude the member from the class if the member so requests by a specified date; (B) the judgment, whether favorable or not, will include all members who do not request exclusion; and (C) any member who does not request exclusion may, if the member desires, enter an appearance through counsel.

(3) The judgment in an action maintained as a class action under subdivision (b) (1) or (b) (2), whether or not favorable to the class, shall include and describe those whom the court finds to be members of the class. The judgment in an action maintained as a class action under subdivision (b) (3), whether or not favorable to the class, shall include and specify or describe those to whom the notice provided in subdivision (c) (2) was directed, and who have not requested exclusion, and whom the court finds to be members of the class.

(4) When appropriate (A) an action may be brought or maintained as a class action with respect to particular issues, or (B) a class may be divided into subclasses and each subclass treated as a class, and the provisions of this rule shall then be construed and applied accordingly.

(d) Orders in Conduct of Actions. In the conduct of actions to which this rule applies, the court may make appropriate orders: (1) determining the course of proceedings or prescribing measures to prevent undue repetition or complication in the presentation of evidence or argument; (2) requiring, for the protection of the members of the class or otherwise for the fair conduct of the action, that notice be given in such manner as the court may direct to some or all of the members of any step in the action, or of the proposed extent of the judgment, or of the opportunity of members to signify whether they consider the representation fair and adequate, to intervene and present claims or defenses, or otherwise to come into the action; (3) imposing conditions on the representative parties or on intervenors; (4) requiring that the pleadings be amended to eliminate therefrom allegations as to representation of absent persons, and that the action proceed accordingly; (5) dealing with similar procedural matters. The orders may be combined with an order under Rule 16, and may be altered or amended as may be desirable from time to time.

(e) Dismissal or Compromise. A class action shall not be dismissed or compromised without the approval of the court, and notice of the proposed dismissal or compromise shall be given to all members of the class in such manner as the court directs.

(f) Appeals. A court of appeals may in its discretion permit an appeal from an order of a district court granting or denying class action certification under this rule if application is made to it within ten days after entry of the order. An appeal does not stay proceedings in the district court unless the district judge or the court of appeals so orders.

As amended Feb. 28, 1966, eff. July 1, 1966; Mar. 2, 1987, eff. Aug. 1, 1987; Apr. 24 1998, eff. Dec. 1, 1998.

Advisory Committee Notes, 1966 Amendments

The amended rule describes in more practical terms the occasions for maintaining class actions; provides that all class actions maintained to the end as such will result in judgments including those whom the court finds to be members of the class, whether or not the judgment is favorable to the class; and refers to the measures which can be taken to assure the fair conduct of these actions. . . .

Subdivision (b)(1). The difficulties which would be likely to arise if resort were had to separate actions by or against the individual members of the class here furnish the reasons for, and the principal key to, the propriety and value of utilizing the class-action device. The considerations stated under clauses (A) and (B) are comparable to certain of the elements which define the persons whose joinder in an action is desirable as stated in Rule 19(a), as amended. See amended Rule 19(a)(2) (i) and (ii), and the Advisory Committee's Note thereto; Hazard, Indispensable Party: The Historical Origin of a Procedural Phantom, 61 Colum. L. Rev. 1254, 1259-60 (1961); cf. 3 Moore, [Federal Practice,] ¶223.08, at 3435.

Clause (A): One person may have rights against, or be under duties toward, numerous persons constituting a class, and be so positioned that conflicting or varying adjudications in lawsuits with individual members of the class might establish incompatible standards to govern his conduct. The class action device can be used effectively to obviate the actual or virtual dilemma which would thus confront the party opposing the class. The matter has been stated thus: "The felt necessity for a class action is greatest when the courts are called upon to order or sanction the alteration of the status quo in circumstances such that a large number of persons are in a position to call on a single person to alter the status quo, or to complain if it is altered, and the possibility exists that [the] actor might be called upon to act in inconsistent ways." Louisell & Hazard, Pleading and Procedure: State and Federal 719 (1962); see Supreme Tribe of Ben-Hur v. Cauble, 255 U.S. 356, 366-67 (1921). To illustrate: Separate actions by individuals against a municipality to declare a bond issue invalid or condition or limit it, to prevent or limit the making of a particular appropriation or to compel or invalidate an assessment, might create a risk of inconsistent or varying determinations. In the same way, individual litigations of the rights and duties of riparian owners, or of landowners' rights and duties respecting a claimed nuisance, could create a possibility of incompatible adjudications. Actions by or against a class provide a ready and fair means of achieving unitary adjudication. See Maricopa County Mun. Water Con. Dist. v. Looney, 219 F.2d 529 (9th Cir. 1955); Rank v. Krug, 142 F. Supp. 1, 154-59 (S.D. Calif. 1956), on app., State of California v. Rank, 293 F.2d 340, 348 (9th Cir. 1961); Gart v. Cole, 263 F.2d 244 (2d Cir. 1959), cert. denied, 359 U.S. 978 (1959); cf. Martinez v. Maverick Cty. Water Con. & Imp. Dist., 219 F.2d 666 (5th Cir. 1955); 3 Moore, supra, ¶223.11[2], at 3458-59.

Clause (B): This clause takes in situations where the judgment in a nonclass action by or against an individual member of the class, while not technically concluding the other members, might do so as a practical matter. The vice of an individual action would lie in the fact that the other members of the class, thus practically concluded, would have had no representation in the lawsuit. In an action by policy holders against a fraternal benefit association attacking a financial reorganization of the society, it would hardly have been practical, if indeed it would have been possible, to confine the effects of a validation of the reorganization to the individual plaintiffs. Consequently a class action was called for with adequate representation of all members of the class. See Supreme Tribe of Ben-Hur v. Cauble, 255 U.S. 356 (1921); Waybright v. Columbian Mut. Life Ins. Co., 30 F. Supp. 885 (W.D. Tenn. 1939); cf. Smith v. Swormstedt, 16 How. (57 U.S.) 288 (1853). For much the same reason actions by shareholders to compel the declaration of a dividend, the proper recognition and handling of redemption or pre-emption rights, or the like (or actions by the corporation for corresponding declarations of rights), should ordinarily be conducted as class actions, although the matter has been much obscured by the insistence that each shareholder has an individual claim. See Knapp v. Bankers Securities Corp., 17 F.R.D. 245 (E.D. Pa. 1954), affd., 230 F.2d 717 (3d Cir. 1956); Giesecke v. Denver Tramway Corp., 81 F. Supp. 957 (D. Del. 1949); Zahn v. Transamerica Corp., 162 F.2d 36 (3d Cir. 1947); Speed v. Transamerica Corp., 100 F. Supp. 461 (D. Del. 1951); Sobel v. Whittier Corp., 95 F. Supp. 643 (E.D. Mich. 1951), app. dism., 195 F.2d 361 (6th Cir. 1952); Goldberg v. Whittier Corp., 111 F. Supp. 382 (E.D. Mich. 1953); Dann v. Studebaker-Packard Corp., 288 F.2d 201 (6th Cir. 1961); Edgerton v. Armour & Co., 94 F. Supp. 549 (S.D. Calif. 1950); Ames v. Mengel Co., 190 F.2d 344 (2d Cir. 1951). (These shareholders' actions are to be distinguished from derivative actions by shareholders dealt with in new Rule 23.1). The same reasoning applies from an action which charges a breach of trust by an indenture trustee or other fiduciary similarly affecting the members of a large class of security holders or other beneficiaries, and which requires an accounting or like measures to restore the subject of the trust. See Boesenberg v. Chicago T. & T. Co., 128 F.2d 245 (7th Cir. 1942); Citizens Banking Co. v. Monticello State Bank, 143 F.2d 261 (8th Cir. 1944); Redmond v. Commerce Trust Co., 144 F.2d 140 (8th Cir. 1944), cert. denied, 323 U.S. 776 (1944); cf. York v. Guaranty Trust Co., 143 F.2d 503 (2d Cir. 1944), rev'd on grounds not here relevant, 326 U.S. 99 (1945).

In various situations an adjudication as to one or more members of the class will necessarily or probably have an adverse practical effect on the interests of other members who should therefore be represented in the lawsuit. This is plainly the case when claims are made by numerous persons against a fund insufficient to satisfy all claims. A class action by or against representative members to settle the validity of the claims as a whole, or in groups, followed by separate proof of the amount of each valid claim and proportionate distribution of the fund, meets the problem. Cf. Dickinson v. Burnham, 197 F.2d 973 (2d Cir. 1952), cert. denied, 344 U.S. 875 (1952); 3 Moore, supra, at ¶223.09. The same reasoning applies to an action by a creditor to set aside a fraudulent conveyance by the debtor and to appropriate the property to his claim, when the debtor's assets are insufficient to pay all creditors' claims. See Heffernan v. Bennett & Armour, 110 Cal. App. 2d 564, 243 P.2d 846 (1952); cf. City & Council of San Francisco v. Market Street Ry., 95 Cal. App. 2d 648, 213 P.2d 780 (1950). Similar problems, however, can arise in the absence of a fund either present or potential. A negative or mandatory injunction secured by one of a numerous class may disable the opposing party from performing claimed duties toward the other members of the class or materially affect his ability to do so. An adjudication as to movie "clearances and runs" nominally affecting only one exhibitor would often have practical effects on all the exhibitors in the same territorial area. Cf. United States v. Paramount Pictures, Inc., 66 F. Supp. 323, 341-46 (S.D.N.Y.1946), 334 U.S. 131, 144-48 (1948). Assuming a sufficiently numerous class of exhibitors, a class action would be advisable. (Here representation of subclasses of exhibitors could become necessary; see subdivision (c) (3) (B).)

Subdivision (b)(2). This subdivision is intended to reach situations where a party has taken action or refused to take action with respect to a class, and final relief of an injunctive nature or of a corresponding declaratory nature, settling the legality of the behavior with respect to the class as a whole, is appropriate. Delcaratory relief "corresponds" to injunctive relief when as a practical matter it affords injunctive relief or serves as a basis for later injunctive relief. The subdivision does not extend to cases in which the appropriate final relief relates exclusively or predominantly to money damages. Action or inaction is directed to a class within the meaning of this subdivision even if it has taken effect or is threatened only as to one or a few members of the class, provided it is based on grounds which have general application to the class.

Illustrative are various actions in the civil-rights field where a party is charged with discriminating unlawfully against a class, usually one whose members are incapable of specific enumeration. See Potts v. Flax, 313 F.2d 284 (5th Cir. 1963); Bailey v. Patterson, 323 F.2d 201 (5th Cir. 1963), cert. denied, 377 U.S. 972 (1964); Brunson v. Board of Trustees of School District No.1, Clarendon Cty., S.C., 311 F.2d 107 (4th Cir. 1962), cert. denied, 373 U.S. 933 (1963); Green v. School Bd. of Roanoke, Va., 304 F.2d 118 (4th Cir. 1962); Orleans Parish School Bd. v. Bush, 242 F.2d 156 (5th Cir. 1957), cert. denied, 354 U.S. 921 (1957); Mannings v. Board of Public Inst. of Hillsborough County, Fla., 277 F.2d 370 (5th Cir. 1960); Northcross v. Board of Ed. of City of Memphis, 302 F.2d 818 (6th Cir. 1962), cert. denied, 370 U.S. 944 (1962); Frasier v. Board of Trustees of Univ. of N. C., 134 F. Supp. 589 (M.D.N.C. 1955, 3-judge court), affd., 350 U.S. 979 (1956). Subdivision (b) (2) is not limited to civil-rights cases. Thus an action looking to specific or declaratory relief could be brought by a numerous class of purchasers, say retailers of a given description, against a seller alleged to have undertaken to sell to that class at prices higher than those set for other purchasers, say retailers of another description, when the applicable law forbids such a pricing differential. So also a patentee of a machine, charged with selling or licensing the machine on condition that purchasers or licensees also purchase or obtain licenses to use an ancillary unpatented machine, could be sued on a class basis by a numerous group of purchasers or licensees, or by a numerous group of competing sellers or licensors of the unpatented machine, to test the legality of the "tying" condition.

Subdivision (b)(3). In the situations to which this subdivision relates, class-action treatment is not as clearly called for as in those described above, but it may nevertheless be convenient and desirable depending upon the particular facts. Subdivision (b)(3) encompasses those cases in which a class action would achieve economies of time, effort, and expense, and promote uniformity of decision as to persons similarly situated, without sacrificing procedural fairness or bringing about other undesirable results. Cf. Chafee, [Some Problems of Equity 201 (1950).]

The court is required to find, as a condition of holding that a class action may be maintained under this subdivision, that the questions common to the class predominate over the questions affecting individual members. It is only where this predominance exists that economies can be achieved by means of the class-action device. In this view, a fraud perpetrated on numerous persons by the use of similar misrepresentations may be an appealing situation for a class action, and it may remain so despite the need, if liability is found, for separate determination of the damages suffered by individuals within the class. On the other hand, although having some common core, a fraud case may be unsuited for treatment as a class action if there was material variation in the representations made or in the kinds of degrees of reliance by the persons to whom they were addressed. See Oppenheimer v. F. J. Young & Co., Inc., 144 F.2d 387 (2d Cir. 1944); Miller v. National City Bank of N.Y., 166 F.2d 723 (2d Cir. 1948); and for like problems in other contexts, see Hughes v. Encyclopaedia Britannica, 199 F.2d 295 (7th Cir. 1952); Sturgeon v. Great Lakes Steel Corp., 143 F.2d 819 (6th Cir. 1944). A "mass accident" resulting in injuries to numerous persons is ordinarily not appropriate for a class action because of the likelihood that significant questions, not only of damages but of liability and defenses to liability, would be present, affecting the individuals in different ways. In these circumstances an action conducted nominally as a class action would degenerate in practice into multiple lawsuits separately tried. See Pennsylvania R.R. v. United States, 111 F. Supp. 80 (D.N.J. 1953); cf. Weinstein, 9 Buffalo L. Rev. at 469. Private damage claims by numerous individuals arising out of concerted antitrust violations may or may not involve predominating common questions. See Union Carbide & Carbon Corp. v. Nisley, 300 F.2d 561 (10th Cir. 1961), pet. cert. dism., 371 U.S. 801 (1963); cf. Weeks v. Bareco Oil Co., 125 F.2d 84 (7th Cir. 1941); Kainz v. Anheuser-Busch, Inc., 194 F.2d 737 (7th Cir. 1952); Hess v. Anderson, Clayton & Co., 20 F.R.D. 466 (S.D. Calif. 1957).

That common questions predominate is not itself sufficient to justify a class action under subdivision (b)(3), for another method of handling the litigious situation may be available which has greater practical advantages. Thus one or more actions agreed to by the parties as test or model actions may be preferable to a class action; or it may prove feasible and preferable to consolidate actions. Cf. Weinstein, supra, 9 Buffalo L. Rev. at 438-54. Even when a number of separate actions are proceeding simultaneously, experience shows that the burdens on the parties and the courts can sometimes be reduced by arrangements for avoiding repetitious discovery or the like. Currently the Coordinating Committee on Multiple Litigation in the United States District Courts (a subcommittee of the Committee on Trial Practice and Technique of the Judicial Conference of the United States) is charged with developing methods for expediting such massive litigation. To reinforce the point that the court with the aid of the parties ought to assess the relative advantages of alternative procedures for handling the total controversy, subdivision (b)(3) requires, as a further condition of maintaining the class action, that the court shall find that that procedure is "superior" to the others in the particular circumstances.

Factors (A)-(D) are listed, non-exhaustively, as pertinent to the findings. The court is to consider the interests of individual members of the class in controlling their own litigations and carrying them on as they see fit. See Weeks v. Bareco Oil

Co., 125 F.2d 84, 88-90, 93-94 (7th Cir. 1941) (anti-trust action); see also Pentland v. Dravo Corp., 152 F.2d 851 (3d Cir. 1945), and Chafee, supra, at 273-75, regarding policy of Fair Labor Standards Act of 1938, §16(b), 29 U.S.C. §216(b), prior to amendment by Portal-to-Portal Act of 1947, §5(a). [The present provisions of 29 U.S.C. §216(b) are not intended to be affected by Rule 23, as amended.]

In this connection the court should inform itself of any litigation actually pending by or against the individuals. The interests of individuals in conducting separate lawsuits may be so strong as to call for denial of a class action. On the other hand, these interests may be theoretic rather than practical: the class may have a high degree of cohesion and prosecution of the action through representatives would be quite unobjectionable, or the amounts at stake for individuals may be so small that separate suits would be impracticable. The burden that separate suits would impose on the party opposing the class, or upon the court calendars, may also fairly be considered. (See the discussion, under subdivision (c)(2) below, of the right of members to be excluded from the class upon their request.)

Also pertinent is the question of the desirability of concentrating the trial of the claims in the particular forum by means of a class action, in contrast to allowing the claims to be litigated separately in forums to which they would ordinarily be brought. Finally, the court should consider the problems of management which are likely to arise in the conduct of a class action.

Subdivision (c)(1). In order to give clear definition to the action, this provision requires the court to determine, as early in the proceedings as may be practicable, whether an action brought as a class action is to be so maintained. The determination depends in each case on satisfaction of the terms of subdivision (a) and the relevant provisions of subdivision (b). . . .

Whether the court should require notice to be given to members of the class of its intention to make a determination, or of the order embodying it, is left to the court's discretion under subdivision (d) (2). . . .

Subdivision (c)(3). . . . Although thus declaring that the judgment in a class action includes the class, as defined, subdivision (c) (3) does not disturb the recognized principle that the court conducting the action cannot predetermine the *res judicata* effect of the judgment; this can be tested only in a subsequent action. See Restatement, Judgments §86, comment (h), §116 (1942). The court, however, in framing the judgment in any suit brought as a class action, must decide what its extent or coverage shall be, and if the matter is carefully considered, questions of *res judicata*are less likely to be raised at a later time and if raised will be more satisfactorily answered. See Chafee, supra, at 294; Weinstein, supra, 9 Buffalo L. Rev. at 460. . . .

Rule 23.1. Derivative Actions by Shareholders

In a derivative action brought by one or more shareholders or members to enforce a right of a corporation or of an unincorporated association, the corporation or association having failed to enforce a right which may properly be asserted by it, the complaint shall be verified and shall allege (1) that the plaintiff was a shareholder or member at the time of the transaction of which the plaintiff complains or that the plaintiff's share or membership thereafter devolved on the plaintiff by operation of law, and (2) that the action is not a collusive one to confer jurisdiction on a court of the United States which it would not otherwise have. The complaint shall also allege with particularity the efforts, if any, made by the plaintiff to obtain the action the plaintiff desires from the directors or comparable authority and, if necessary, from the shareholders or members, and the reasons for the plaintiff's failure to obtain the action or for not making the effort. The derivative action may not be maintained if it appears that the plaintiff does not fairly and adequately represent the interests of the shareholders or members similarly situated in enforcing the right of the corporation or association. The action shall not be dismissed or compromised without the approval of the court, and notice of the proposed dismissal or compromise shall be given to shareholders or members in such manner as the court directs.

Added Feb. 28, 1966, eff. July 1, 1966; amended Mar. 2, 1987, eff. Aug. 1, 1987.

Rule 23.2. Actions Relating to Unincorporated Associations

An action brought by or against the members of an unincorporated association as a class by naming certain members as representative parties may be maintained only if it appears that the representative parties will fairly and adequately protect the interests of the association and its members. In the conduct of the action the court may make appropriate orders corresponding with those described in Rule 23(d), and the procedure for dismissal or compromise of the action shall correspond with that provided in Rule 23(e).

Added Feb. 28, 1966, eff. July 1, 1966.

Advisory Committee Note on the Adoption of Rule 23.2

Although an action by or against representatives of the membership of an unincorporated association has often been viewed as a class action, the real or main purpose of this characterization has been to give "entity treatment" to the association when for formal reasons it cannot sue or be sued as a jural person under Rule 17(b). See Louisell & Hazard, Pleading and Procedure: State and Federal 718 (1962); 3 Moore's Federal Practice ¶223.08 (2d ed. 1963). . . . Rule 23.2 deals separately with these actions, referring where appropriate to Rule 23.

Rule 24. Intervention

(a) Intervention of Right. Upon timely application anyone shall be permitted to intervene in an action: (1) when a statute of the United States confers an unconditional right to intervene; or (2) when the applicant claims an interest relating to the property or transaction which is the subject of the action and the applicant is so situated that the disposition of the action may as a practical matter impair or impede the applicant's ability to protect that interest, unless the applicant's interest is adequately represented by existing parties.

(b) Permissive Intervention. Upon timely application anyone may be permitted to intervene in an action: (1) when a statute of the United States confers a conditional right to intervene; or (2) when an applicant's claim or defense and the main action have a question of law or fact in common. When a party to an action relies for ground of claim or defense upon any statute or executive order administered by a federal or state governmental officer and agency or upon any regulation, order, requirement or agreement issued or made pursuant to the statute or executive order, the officer or agency upon timely application may be permitted to intervene in the action. In exercising its discretion the court shall consider whether the intervention will unduly delay or prejudice the adjudication of the rights of the original parties

(c) Procedure. A person desiring to intervene shall serve a motion to intervene upon the parties as provided in Rule 5. The motion shall state the grounds therefor and shall be accompanied by a pleading setting forth the claim or defense for which intervention is sought. The same procedure shall be followed when a statute of the United States gives a right to intervene. When the constitutionality of an act of Congress affecting the public interest is drawn in question in any action to which the United States or an officer, agency, or employee thereof is not a party, the court shall notify the Attorney General of the United States as provided in Title 28, U.S.C.§2403. When the constitutionality of any statute of a State affecting the public interest is drawn in question in any action in which that State or any agency, officer, or employee thereof is not a party, the court shall notify the attorney general of the State as provided in Title 28, U.S.C. §2403. A party challenging the constitutionality of legislation should call the attention of the court to its consequential duty, but failure to do so is not a waiver of any constitutional right otherwise timely asserted.

As amended Dec. 27, 1946, eff. Mar. 19, 1948; Dec. 29, 1948, eff. Oct. 20, 1949; Jan. 21, 1963, eff. July 1, 1963; Feb. 28, 1966, eff. July 1, 1966; Mar. 2, 1987, eff. Aug. 1, 1987; Apr. 30, 1991, eff. Dec. 1, 1991.

ADVISORY COMMITTEE NOTES, 1966 AMENDMENTS

. . . If an absentee would be substantially affected in a practical sense by the determination made in an action, he should, as a general rule, be entitled to intervene, and his right to do so should not depend on whether there is a fund to be distributed or otherwise disposed of. Intervention of right is here seen to be a kind of counterpart to Rule 19(a)(2)(i) on joinder of persons needed for a just adjudication: where, upon motion of a party in an action, an absentee should be joined so that he may protect his interest which as a practical matter may be substantially impaired by the disposition of the action, he ought to have a right to intervene in the action on his own motion. See Louisell & Hazard, Pleading and Procedure: State and Federal 749-50 (1962). . . .

Original Rule 24(a)(2), however, made it a condition of intervention that "the applicant is or may be bound by a judgment in the action," and this created difficulties with intervention in class actions. If the "bound" language was read literally in the sense of *res judicata*, it could defeat intervention in some meritorious cases. A member of a class to whom a judgment in a class action extended by its terms (see Rule 23(c)(3), as amended) might be entitled to show in a later action, when the judgment in the class action was claimed to operate as *res judicata* against him, that the "representative" in the class action had not in fact adequately represented him. If he could make this showing, the class-action judgment might be held not to bind him. See Hansberry v. Lee, 311 U.S. 32 (1940). If a class member sought to intervene in the class action proper, while it was still pending, on grounds of inadequacy of representation, he could be met with the argument: if the representation was in fact inadequate, he would not be "bound" by the judgment when it was subsequently asserted against him as *res judicata*, hence he was not entitled to intervene; if the representation was in fact adequate, there was no occasion or ground for intervention. See Sam Fox Publishing Co. v. United States, 366 U.S. 683 (1961); cf. Sutphen Estates, Inc. v. United States, 342 U.S. 19 (1951). This reasoning might be linguistically justified by original Rule 24(a)(2); but it could lead to poor results. Compare the discussion in International M. & I. Corp. v. Von Clemm, 301 F.2d 857 (2d Cir. 1962); Atlantic Refining Co. v. Standard Oil Co., 304 F.2d 387 (D.C. Cir. 1962). A class member who claims that his "representative" does not adequately represent him, and is able to establish that proposition with sufficient probability, should not be put to the risk of having a judgment entered in the action which by its terms extends to him, and be obliged to test the validity of the judgment as applied to his interest by a later collateral attack. Rather he should, as a general rule, be entitled to intervene in the action.

The amendment provides that an applicant is entitled to intervene in an action when his position is comparable to that of a person under Rule 19(a)(2)(i), as amended, unless his interest is already adequately represented in the action by existing parties. The Rule 19(a)(2)(i) criterion imports practical considerations, and the deletion of the "bound" language similarly frees the rule from undue preoccupation with strict considerations of *res judicata*.

The representation whose adequacy comes into question under the amended rule is not confined to formal representation like that provided by a trustee for his beneficiary or a representative party in a class action for a member of the class. A party to an action may provide practical representation to the absentee seeking intervention although no such formal relationship exists between them, and the adequacy of this practical representation will then have to be weighed. See International M. & I. Corp. v. Von Clemm, and Atlantic Refining Co. v. Standard Oil Co., both supra; Wolpe v. Poretsky, 144 F.2d 505 (D.C. Cir 1944), cert. denied, 323 U.S. 777 (1944); cf. Ford Motor Co. v. Bisanz Bros., 249 F.2d 22 (8th Cir. 1957); and generally, Annot., 84 A.L.R.2d 1412 (1962).

An intervention of right under the amended rule may be subject to appropriate conditions or restrictions responsive among other things to the requirements of efficient conduct of the proceedings.

Rule 25. Substitution of Parties

(a) Death.

(1) If a party dies and the claim is not thereby extinguished, the court may order substitution of the proper parties. The motion for substitution may be made by any party or by the successors or representatives of the deceased party and, together with the notice of hearing, shall be served on the parties as provided in Rule 5 and upon persons not parties in the manner provided in Rule 4 for the service of a summons, and may be served in any judicial district. Unless the motion for substitution is made not later than 90 days after the death is suggested upon the record by service of a statement of the fact of the death as provided herein for the service of the motion, the action shall be dismissed as to the deceased party.

(2) In the event of the death of one or more of the plaintiffs or of one or more of the defendants in an action in which the right sought to be enforced survives only to the surviving plaintiffs or only against the surviving defendants, the action does not abate. The death shall be suggested upon the record and the action shall proceed in favor of or against the surviving parties.

(b) Incompetency. If a party becomes incompetent, the court upon motion served as provided in subdivision (a) of this rule may allow the action to be continued by or against the party's representative.

(c) Transfer of Interest. In case of any transfer of interest, the action may be continued by or against the original party, unless the court upon motion directs the person to whom the interest is transferred to be substituted in the action or joined with the original party. Service of the motion shall be made as provided in subdivision (a) of this rule.

(d) Public Officers; Death or Separation from Office.

(1) When a public officer is a party to an action in an official capacity and during its pendency dies, resigns, or otherwise ceases to hold office, the action does not abate and the officer's successor is automatically substituted as a party. Proceedings following the substitution shall be in the name of the substituted party, but any misnomer not affecting the substantial rights of the parties shall be disregarded. An order of substitution may be entered at any time, but the omission to enter such an order shall not affect the substitution.

(2) A public officer who sues or is sued in an official capacity may be

described as a party by the officer's official title rather than by name; but the court may require the officer's name to be added.

As amended Dec. 29, 1948, eff. Oct. 20, 1949; Apr. 17, 1961, eff. July 19, 1961; Jan. 21, 1963, eff. July 1, 1963; Mar. 2, 1987, eff. Aug. 1, 1987.

V. Depositions and Discovery

Rule 26. General Provisions Governing Discovery; Duty of Disclosure

(a) Required Disclosures; Methods to Discover Additional Matter.

(1) Initial Disclosures. Except in categories of proceedings specified in Rule 26(a)(1)(E), or to the extent otherwise stipulated or directed by order, a party must, without awaiting a discovery request, provide to other parties:

(A) the name and, if known, the address and telephone number of each individual likely to have discoverable information that the disclosing party may use to support its claims or defenses, unless solely for impeachment, identifying the subjects of the information;

(B) a copy of, or a description by category and location of, all documents, data compilations, and tangible things that are in the possession, custody, or control of the party and that the disclosing party may use to support its claims or defenses, unless solely for impeachment;

(C) a computation of any category of damages claimed by the disclosing party, making available for inspection and copying as under Rule 34 the documents or other evidentiary material, not privileged or protected from disclosure, on which such computation is based, including materials bearing on the nature and extent of injuries suffered; and

(D) for inspection and copying as under Rule 34 any insurance agreement under which any person carrying on an insurance business may be liable to satisfy part or all of a judgment which may be entered in the action or to indemnify or reimburse for payments made to satisfy the judgment.

(E) The following categories of proceedings are exempt from initial disclosure under Rule 26(a)(1):

(i) an action for review on an administrative record;

(ii) a petition for habeas corpus or other proceeding to challenge a criminal conviction or sentence;

(iii) an action brought without counsel by a person in custody of the United States, a state, or a state subdivision;

(iv) an action to enforce or quash an administrative summons or subpoena;

(v) an action by the United States to recover benefit payments;

(vi) an action by the United States to collect on a student loan guaranteed by the United States;

(vii) a proceeding ancillary to proceedings in other courts; and

(viii) an action to enforce an arbitration award.

These disclosures must be made at or within 14 days after the Rule 26(f) conference unless a different time is set by stipulation or court order, or unless a party objects during the conference that initial disclosures are not appropriate in the circumstances of the action and states the objection in the Rule 26(f) discovery plan. In ruling on the objection, the court must determine what disclosures — if any — are to be made, and set the time for disclosure.

Any party first served or otherwise joined after the Rule 26(f) conference must make these disclosures within 30 days after being served or joined unless a different time is set by stipulation or court order. A party must make its initial disclosures based on the information then reasonably available to it and is not excused from making its disclosures because it has not fully completed its investigation of the case or because it challenges the sufficiency of another party's disclosures or because another party has not made its disclosures.

(2) ***Disclosure of Expert Testimony.***

(A) In addition to the disclosures required by paragraph (1), a party shall disclose to other parties the identity of any person who may be used at trial to present evidence under Rules 702, 703, or 705* of the Federal Rules of Evidence.

(B) Except as otherwise stipulated or directed by the court, this disclosure shall, with respect to a witness who is retained or specially employed to provide expert testimony in the case or whose duties as an employee of the party regularly involve giving expert testimony, be accompanied by a written report prepared and signed by the witness. The report shall contain a complete statement of all opinions to be expressed and the basis and reasons therefor; the data or other information considered by the witness in forming the opinions; any exhibits to be used as a summary of or support for the opinions; the qualifications of the witness, including a list of all publications authored by the witness within the preceding ten years; the compensation to be paid for the study and testimony; and a listing of any other cases in which the witness has testified as an expert at trial or by deposition within the preceding four years.

(C) These disclosures shall be made at the times and in the sequence directed by the court. In the absence of other directions from the court or stipulation by the parties, the disclosures shall be made at least 90 days before the trial date or the date the case is to be ready for trial or, if the evidence is intended solely to contradict or rebut evidence on the same subject matter identified by another party under paragraph (2)(B), within 30 days after the

*[Federal Rules of Evidence 702-705 describe the ways in which parties may introduce experts' testimony at trial. — Ed.]

disclosure made by the other party. The parties shall supplement these disclosures when required under subdivision (e)(1).

*(3) **Pretrial Disclosures.*** In addition to the disclosures required by Rule 26(a)(1) and (2), a party must provide to other parties and promptly file with the court the following information regarding the evidence that it may present at trial other than solely for impeachment:

(A) the name and, if not previously provided, the address and telephone number of each witness, separately identifying those whom the party expects to present and those whom the party may call if the need arises;

(B) the designation of those witnesses whose testimony is expected to be presented by means of a deposition and, if not taken stenographically, a transcript of the pertinent portions of the deposition testimony; and

(C) an appropriate identification of each document or other exhibit, including summaries of other evidence, separately identifying those which the party expects to offer and those which the party may offer if the need arises.

Unless otherwise directed by the court, these disclosures must be made at least 30 days before trial. Within 14 days thereafter, unless a different time is specified by the court, a party may serve and promptly file a list disclosing (i) any objections to the use under Rule 32(a) of a deposition designated by another party under Rule 26(a)(3)(B) and (ii) any objection, together with the grounds therefor, that may be made to the admissibility of materials identified under Rule 26(a)(3)(C). Objections not so disclosed, other than objections under Rules 402 and 403* of the Federal Rules of Evidence, are waived unless excused by the court for good cause.

*(4) **Form of Disclosures.*** Unless the court orders otherwise, all disclosures under Rule 26(a)(1) through (3) must be made in writing, signed, and served.

*(5) **Methods to Discover Additional Matter.*** Parties may obtain discovery by one or more of the following methods: depositions upon oral examination or written questions; written interrogatories; production of documents or things or permission to enter upon land or other property under Rule 34 or 45(a)(1)(C), for inspection and other purposes; physical and mental examinations; and requests for admission.

(b) Discovery Scope and Limits. Unless otherwise limited by order of the court in accordance with these rules, the scope of discovery is as follows:

*(1) **In General.*** Parties may obtain discovery regarding any matter, not privileged, that is relevant to the claim or defense of any party, including the existence, description, nature, custody, condition, and location of any books,

*[Federal Rule of Evidence 402 provides that evidence is admissible only if relevant; F.R.E. 403 excludes even relevant evidence if it is likely to prejudice, confuse or mislead the jury, or if it is likely to lead to unwarranted delay. — Ed.]

documents, or other tangible things and the identity and location of persons having knowledge of any discoverable matter. For good cause, the court may order discovery of any matter relevant to the subject matter involved in the action. Relevant information need not be admissible at the trial if the discovery appears reasonably calculated to lead to the discovery of admissible evidence. All discovery is subject to the limitations imposed by Rule 26(b)(2)(i), (ii), and (iii).

*(2) **Limitations.*** By order, the court may alter the limits in these rules on the number of depositions and interrogatories, or the length of depositions under Rule 30. By order or local rule, the court may also limit the number of requests under Rule 36. The frequency or extent of use of the discovery methods otherwise permitted under these rules and by any local rule shall be limited by the court if it determines that: (i) the discovery sought is unreasonably cumulative or duplicative, or is obtainable from some other source that is more convenient, less burdensome, or less expensive; (ii) the party seeking discovery has had ample opportunity by discovery in the action to obtain the information sought; or (iii) the burden or expense of the proposed discovery outweighs its likely benefit, taking into account the needs of the case, the amount in controversy, the parties' resources, the importance of the issues at stake in the litigation, and the importance of the proposed discovery in resolving the issues. The court may act upon its own initiative after reasonable notice or pursuant to a motion under Rule 26(c).

*(3) **Trial Preparation: Materials.*** Subject to the provisions of subdivision (b)(4) of this rule, a party may obtain discovery of documents and tangible things otherwise discoverable under subdivision (b)(1) of this rule and prepared in anticipation of litigation or for trial by or for another party or by or for that other party's representative (including the other party's attorney, consultant, surety, indemnitor, insurer, or agent) only upon showing that the party seeking discovery has substantial need of the materials in the preparation of the party's case and that the party is unable without undue hardship to obtain the substantial equivalent of the materials by other means. In ordering discovery of such materials when the required showing has been made, the court shall protect against disclosure of the mental impressions, conclusions, opinions, or legal theories of an attorney or other representative of a party concerning the litigation.

A party may obtain without the required showing a statement concerning the action or its subject matter previously made by that party. Upon request, a person not a party may obtain without the required showing a statement concerning the action or its subject matter previously made by that person. If the request is refused, the person may move for a court order. The provisions of Rule 37(a)(4) apply to the award of expenses incurred in relation to the motion. For purposes of this paragraph, a statement previously made is (A) a written statement signed or otherwise adopted or approved by the person making it, or (B) a stenographic, mechanical, electrical, or other recording, or a transcription thereof, which is a substantially verbatim recital of an oral statement by the person making it and contemporaneously recorded.

(4) Trial Preparation: Experts.

(A) A party may depose any person who has been identified as an expert whose opinions may be presented at trial. If a report from the expert is required under subdivision (a)(2)(B), the deposition shall not be conducted until after the report is provided.

(B) A party may, through interrogatories or by deposition, discover facts known or opinions held by an expert who has been retained or specially employed by another party in anticipation of litigation or preparation for trial and who is not expected to be called as a witness at trial only as provided in Rule 35(b) or upon a showing of exceptional circumstances under which it is impracticable for the party seeking discovery to obtain facts or opinions on the same subject by other means.

(C) Unless manifest injustice would result, (i) the court shall require that the party seeking discovery pay the expert a reasonable fee for time spent in responding to discovery under this subdivision; and (ii) with respect to discovery obtained under subdivision (b)(4)(B) of this rule the court shall require the party seeking discovery to pay the other party a fair portion of the fees and expenses reasonably incurred by the latter party in obtaining facts and opinions from the expert.

(5) Claims of Privilege or Protection of Trial Preparation Materials. When a party withholds information otherwise discoverable under these rules by claiming that it is privileged or subject to protection as trial preparation material, the party shall make the claim expressly and shall describe the nature of the documents, communications, or things not produced or disclosed in a manner that, without revealing information itself privileged or protected, will enable other parties to assess the applicability of the privilege or protection.

(c) Protective Orders. Upon motion by a party or by the person from whom discovery is sought, accompanied by a certification that the movant has in good faith conferred or attempted to confer with other affected parties in an effort to resolve the dispute without court action, and for good cause shown, the court in which the action is pending or alternatively, on matters relating to a deposition, the court in the district where the deposition is to be taken may make any order which justice requires to protect a party or person from annoyance, embarrassment, oppression, or undue burden or expense, including one or more of the following:

(1) that the disclosure or discovery not be had;

(2) that the disclosure or discovery may be had only on specified terms and conditions, including a designation of the time or place;

(3) that the discovery may be had only by a method of discovery other than that selected by the party seeking discovery;

(4) that certain matters not be inquired into, or that the scope of the disclosure or discovery be limited to certain matters;

(5) that discovery be conducted with no one present except persons designated by the court;

(6) that a deposition, after being sealed, be opened only by order of the court;

(7) that a trade secret or other confidential research, development, or commercial information not be revealed or be revealed only in a designated way; and

(8) that the parties simultaneously file specified documents or information enclosed in sealed envelopes to be opened as directed by the court.

If the motion for a protective order is denied in whole or in part, the court may, on such terms and conditions as are just, order that any party or other person provide or permit discovery. The provisions of Rule 37(a)(4) apply to the award of expenses incurred in relation to the motion.

(d) Timing and Sequence of Discovery. Except in categories of proceedings exempted from initial disclosure under Rule 26(a)(1)(E), or when authorized under these rules or by order or agreement of the parties, a party may not seek discovery from any source before the parties have conferred as required by Rule 26(f). Unless the court upon motion, for the convenience of parties and witnesses and in the interests of justice, orders otherwise, methods of discovery may be used in any sequence, and the fact that a party is conducting discovery, whether by deposition or otherwise, does not operate to delay any other party's discovery.

(e) Supplementation of Disclosures and Responses. A party who has made a disclosure under subdivision (a) or responded to a request for discovery with a disclosure or response is under a duty to supplement or correct the disclosure or response to include information thereafter acquired if ordered by the court or in the following circumstances:

(1) A party is under a duty to supplement at appropriate intervals its disclosures under subdivision (a) if the party learns that in some material respect the information disclosed is incomplete or incorrect and if the additional or corrective information has not otherwise been made known to the other parties during the discovery process or in writing. With respect to testimony of an expert from whom a report is required under subdivision (a)(2)(B) the duty extends both to information contained in the report and to information provided through a deposition of the expert, and any additions or other changes to this information shall be disclosed by the time the party's disclosures under Rule 26(a)(3) are due.

(2) A party is under a duty seasonably to amend a prior response to an interrogatory, request for production, or request for admission if the party learns that the response is in some material respect incomplete or incorrect and if the

additional or corrective information has not otherwise been made known to the other parties during the discovery process or in writing.

(f) Conference of Parties; Planning for Discovery. Except in categories of proceedings exempted from initial disclosure under Rule 26(a)(1)(E) or when otherwise ordered, the parties must, as soon as practicable and in any event at least 21 days before a scheduling conference is held or a scheduling order is due under Rule 16(b), confer to consider the nature and basis of their claims and defenses and the possibilities for a prompt settlement or resolution of the case, to make or arrange for the disclosures required by Rule 26(a)(1), and to develop a proposed discovery plan that indicates the parties' views and proposals concerning:

(1) what changes should be made in the timing, form, or requirement for disclosures under Rule 26(a), including a statement as to when disclosures under Rule 26(a)(1) were made or will be made;

(2) the subjects on which discovery may be needed, when discovery should be completed, and whether discovery should be conducted in phases or be limited to or focused upon particular issues;

(3) what changes should be made in the limitations on discovery imposed under these rules or by local rule, and what other limitations should be imposed; and

(4) any other orders that should be entered by the court under Rule 26(c) or under Rule 16(b) and (c).

The attorneys of record and all unrepresented parties that have appeared in the case are jointly responsible for arranging the conference, for attempting in good faith to agree on the proposed discovery plan, and for submitting to the court within 14 days after the conference a written report outlining the plan. A court may order that the parties or attorneys attend the conference in person. If necessary to comply with its expedited schedule for Rule 16(b) conferences, a court may by local rule (i) require that the conference between the parties occur fewer than 21 days before the scheduling conference is held or a scheduling order is due under Rule 16(b), and (ii) require that the written report outlining the discovery plan be filed fewer than 14 days after the conference between the parties, or excuse the parties from submitting a written report and permit them to report orally on their discovery plan at the Rule 16(b) conference.

(g) Signing of Disclosures, Discovery Requests, Responses, and Objections.

(1) Every disclosure made pursuant to subdivision (a)(1) or subdivision (a)(3) shall be signed by at least one attorney of record in the attorney's individual name, whose address shall be stated. An unrepresented party shall sign the disclosure and state the party's address. The signature of the attorney or party constitutes a certification that to the best of the signer's knowledge, information, and belief, formed after a reasonable inquiry, the disclosure is complete and correct as of the time it is made.

(2) Every discovery request, response, or objection made by a party represented by an attorney shall be signed by at least one attorney of record in the attorney's individual name, whose address shall be stated. An unrepresented party shall sign the request, response, or objection and state the party's address. The signature of the attorney or party constitutes a certification that to the best of the signer's knowledge, information, and belief, formed after a reasonable inquiry, the request, response, or objection is:

(A) consistent with these rules and warranted by existing law or a good faith argument for the extension, modification, or reversal of existing law;

(B) not interposed for any improper purpose, such as to harass or to cause unnecessary delay or needless increase in the cost of litigation; and

(C) not unreasonable or unduly burdensome or expensive, given the needs of the case, the discovery already had in the case, the amount in controversy, and the importance of the issues at stake in the litigation.

If a request, response, or objection is not signed, it shall be stricken unless it is signed promptly after the omission is called to the attention of the party making the request, response, or objection, and a party shall not be obligated to take any action with respect to it until it is signed.

(3) If without substantial justification a certification is made in violation of the rule, the court, upon motion or upon its own initiative, shall impose upon the person who made the certification, the party on whose behalf the disclosure, request, response, or objection is made, or both, an appropriate sanction, which may include an order to pay the amount of the reasonable expenses incurred because of the violation, including a reasonable attorney's fee.

As amended Dec. 27, 1946, eff. Mar. 19, 1948; Jan. 21, 1963, eff. July 1, 1963; Feb. 28, 1966, eff. July 1, 1966; Mar. 30, 1970, eff. July 1, 1970; Apr. 29, 1980, eff. Aug. 1, 1980; Apr. 28, 1983, eff. Aug. 1, 1983; Mar. 2, 1987, eff. Aug. 1, 1987; Apr. 22, 1993, eff. Dec. 1, 1993; Apr. 17, 2000, eff. Dec. 1, 2000.

Advisory Committee Notes, 1970, 1983, 1993, and 2000 Amendments

1970 Amendments . . .

Subdivision (b) — Scope of Discovery. This subdivision is recast to cover the scope of discovery generally. It regulates the discovery obtainable through any of the discovery devices listed in Rule 26(a).

All provisions as to scope of discovery are subject to the initial qualification that the court may limit discovery in accordance with these rules. Rule 26(c) (transferred from 30(b)) confers broad powers on the courts to regulate or prevent discovery even though the materials sought are within the scope of 26(b), and these powers have always been freely exercised. For example, a party's income tax return is generally held not privileged, 2A Barron & Holtzoff, Federal Practice and Procedure, §651.2 (Wright ed. 1961), and yet courts have recognized that interests in privacy may call for a measure of extra protection. E.g., Wiesenberger v. W. E. Hutton &

Co., 35 F.R.D. 556 (S.D.N.Y. 1964). Similarly, the courts have in appropriate circumstances protected materials that are primarily of an impeaching character. These two types of materials merely illustrate the many situations, not capable of governance by precise rule, in which courts must exercise judgment. The new subsections in Rule 26(b) do not change existing law with respect to such situations. . . .

Subdivision (b)(3). The rules are amended by eliminating the general requirement of "good cause" from Rule 34 but retaining a requirement of a special showing for trial preparation materials in this subdivision. The required showing is expressed, not in terms of "good cause" whose generality has tended to encourage confusion and controversy, but in terms of the elements of the special showing to be made: substantial need of the materials in the preparation of the case and inability without undue hardship to obtain the substantial equivalent of the materials by other means.

These changes conform to the holdings of the cases, when viewed in light of their facts. Apart from trial preparation, the fact that the materials sought are documentary does not in and of itself require a special showing beyond relevance and absence of privilege. The protective provisions are of course available, and if the party from whom production is sought raises a special issue of privacy (as with respect to income tax returns or grand jury minutes) or points to evidence primarily impeaching, or can show serious burden or expense, the court will exercise its traditional power to decide whether to issue a protective order. On the other hand, the requirement of a special showing for discovery of trial preparation materials reflects the view that each side's informal evaluation of its case should be protected, that each side should be encouraged to prepare independently, and that one side should not automatically have the benefit of the detailed preparatory work of the other side. See Field and McKusick, Maine Civil Practice 264 (1959). . . .

Materials assembled in the ordinary course of business, or pursuant to public requirements unrelated to litigation, or for other nonlitigation purposes are not under the qualified immunity provided by this subdivision. Goosman v. A. Duie Pyle, Inc., 320 F.2d 45 (4th Cir. 1963); cf. United States v. New York Foreign Trade Zone Operators, Inc., 304 F.2d 792 (2d Cir. 1962). No change is made in the existing doctrine, noted in the *Hickman* case, that one party may discover relevant facts known or available to the other party, even though such facts are contained in a document which is not itself discoverable. . . .

Subdivision (b)(3) reflects the trend of the cases by requiring a special showing, not merely as to materials prepared by an attorney, but also as to materials prepared in anticipation of litigation or preparation for trial by or for a party or any representative acting on his behalf. The subdivision then goes on to protect against disclosure the mental impressions, conclusions, opinions, or legal theories concerning the litigation of an attorney or other representative of a party. The *Hickman* opinion drew special attention to the need for protecting an attorney against discovery of memoranda prepared from recollection of oral interviews. The courts have steadfastly safeguarded against disclosure of lawyers' mental impressions and legal theories, as well as mental impressions and subjective evaluations of investigators and claim-agents. In enforcing this provision of the subdivision, the courts will sometimes find it necessary to order disclosure of a document but with portions deleted.

Rules 33 and 36 have been revised in order to permit discovery calling for opinions, contentions, and admissions relating not only to fact but also to the application of law to fact. Under those rules, a party and his attorney or other representative may be required to disclose, to some extent, mental impressions, opinions, or conclusions. But documents or parts of documents containing these matters are protected against discovery by this subdivision. Even though a party may ultimately have to disclose in response to interrogatories or requests to admit, he is entitled to keep confidential documents containing such matters prepared for internal use.

Party's Right to Own Statement. — An exception to the requirement of this subdivision enables a party to secure production of his own statement without any special showing. . . .

Courts which treat a party's statement as though it were that of any witness overlook the fact that the party's statement is, without more, admissible in evidence. Ordinarily, a party gives a statement without insisting on a copy because he does not yet have a lawyer and does not understand the legal consequences of his actions. Thus, the statement is given at a time when he functions at a disadvantage. Discrepancies between his trial testimony and earlier statement may result from lapse of memory or ordinary inaccuracy; a written statement produced for the first time at trial may give such discrepancies a prominence which they do not deserve. In appropriate cases the court may order a party to be deposed before his statement is produced. . . .

Witness' Right to Own Statement. — A second exception to the requirement of this subdivision permits a non-party witness to obtain a copy of his own statement without any special showing. Many, though not all, of the considerations supporting a party's right to obtain his statement apply also to the non-party witness. Insurance companies are increasingly recognizing that a witness is entitled to a copy of his statement and are modifying their regular practice accordingly.

1983 AMENDMENTS

Excessive discovery and evasion or resistance to reasonable discovery requests pose significant problems. Recent studies have made some attempt to determine the sources and extent of the difficulties. See Brazil, Civil Discovery: Lawyers' Views of its Effectiveness, Principal Problems and Abuses, American Bar Foundation (1980); Connolly, Holleman & Kuhlman, Judicial Controls and the Civil Litigative Process: Discovery, Federal Judicial Center (1978); Ellington, A Study of Sanctions for Discovery Abuse, Department of Justice (1979); Schroeder & Frank, The Proposed Changes in the Discovery Rules, 1978 Ariz. St. L.J. 475.

The purpose of discovery is to provide a mechanism for making relevant information available to the litigants. "Mutual knowledge of all the relevant facts gathered by both parties is essential to proper litigation." Hickman v. Taylor, 329 U.S. 495, 507 (1947). Thus the spirit of the rules is violated when advocates attempt to use discovery tools as tactical weapons rather than to expose the facts and illuminate the issues by overuse of discovery or unnecessary use of defensive weapons or evasive responses. All of this results in excessively costly and time-consuming activities that are disproportionate to the nature of the case, the amount involved, or the issues or values at stake.

Given our adversary tradition and the current discovery rules, it is not surprising that there are many opportunities, if not incentives, for attorneys to engage in discovery that, although authorized by the broad, permissive terms of the rules nevertheless results in delay. See Brazil, The Adversary Character of Civil Discovery: A Critique and Proposals for Change, 31 Vand. L. Rev. 1259 (1978). As a result, it has been said that the rules have "not infrequently [been] exploited to the disadvantage of justice." Herbert v. Lando, 441 U.S. 153, 179 (1979) (Powell, J., concurring). These practices impose costs on an already overburdened system and impede the fundamental goal of the "just, speedy, and inexpensive determination of every action." Fed. R. Civ. P. 1. . . .

Subdivision (g) — Signing of Discovery Requests, Responses, and Objections. Rule 26(g) imposes an affirmative duty to engage in pretrial discovery in a responsible manner that is consistent with the spirit and purposes of Rules 26 through 37. In addition, Rule 26(g) is designed to curb discovery abuse by explicitly encouraging the imposition of sanctions. The subdivision provides a deterrent to both excessive discovery and evasion by imposing a certification requirement that obliges each attorney to stop and think about the legitimacy of a discovery request, a response thereto, or an objection. The term "response" includes answers to interrogatories and to requests to admit as well as responses to production requests.

If primary responsibility for conducting discovery is to continue to rest with the litigants, they must be obliged to act responsibly and avoid abuse. With this in mind, Rule 26(g), which parallels the amendments to Rule 11, requires an attorney or unrepresented party to sign each discovery request, response, or objection. Motions relating to discovery are governed by Rule 11. However, since a discovery request, response, or objection usually deals with more specific subject matter than motions or papers, the elements that must be certified in connection with the former are spelled out more completely. The signature is a certification of the elements set forth in Rule 26(g).

Although the certification duty requires the lawyer to pause and consider the reasonableness of his request, response, or objection, it is not meant to discourage or restrict necessary and legitimate discovery. The rule simply requires that the attorney make a reasonable inquiry into the factual basis of his response, request, or objection.

The duty to make a "reasonable inquiry" is satisfied if the investigation undertaken by the attorney and the conclusions drawn therefrom are reasonable under the circumstances. It is an objective standard similar to the one imposed by Rule 11. See the Advisory Committee Note to Rule 11. See also Kinee v. Abraham Lincoln Fed. Sav. & Loan Assn., 365 F. Supp. 975 (E.D. Pa. 1973). In making the inquiry, the attorney may rely on assertions by the client and on communications with other counsel in the case as long as that reliance is appropriate under the circumstances. Ultimately, what is reasonable is a matter for the court to decide on the totality of the circumstances. . . .

Because of the asserted reluctance to impose sanctions on attorneys who abuse the discovery rules, see Brazil, Civil Discovery: Lawyers' Views of its Effectiveness, Principal Problems and Abuses, American Bar Foundation (1980); Ellington, A Study of Sanctions for Discovery Abuse, Department of Justice (1979), Rule 26(g) makes explicit the authority judges now have to impose appropriate sanctions and requires them to use it. This authority derives from Rule 37, 28 U.S.C. §1927, and the court's inherent power. See Roadway Express, Inc. v. Piper, 447 U.S. 752 (1980); Martin v. Bell Helicopter Co., 85 F.R.D. 654, 661-662 (D. Col. 1980); Note, Sanctions Imposed by Courts on Attorneys Who Abuse the Judicial Process, 44 U. Chi. L. Rev. 619 (1977). The new rule mandates that sanctions be imposed on attorneys who fail to meet the standards established in the first portion of Rule 26(g). The nature of the sanction is a matter of judicial discretion to be exercised in light of the particular circumstances. The court may take into account any failure by the party seeking sanctions to invoke protection under Rule 26(c) at an early stage in the litigation.

The sanctioning process must comport with due process requirements. The kind of notice and hearing required will depend on the facts of the case and the severity of the sanction being considered. To prevent the proliferation of the sanction procedure and to avoid multiple hearings, discovery in any sanction proceeding normally should be permitted only when it is clearly required by the interests of justice. In most cases the court will be aware of the circumstances and only a brief hearing should be necessary.

1993 AMENDMENTS

Subdivision (a). Through the addition of paragraphs (1) — (4), this subdivision imposes on parties a duty to disclose, without awaiting formal discovery requests, certain basic information that is needed in most cases to prepare for trial or make an informed decision about settlement. The rule requires all parties (1) early in the case to exchange information regarding potential witnesses, documentary evidence, damages, and insurance, (2) at an appropriate time during the discovery period to identify expert witnesses and provide a detailed written statement of the testimony that may be offered at trial through specially retained experts, and (3) as the trial date approaches to identify the particular evidence that may be offered at trial. . . .

Unlike subparagraphs (C) and (D), subparagraph (B) does not require production of any documents. Of course, in cases involving few documents a disclosing party may prefer to provide copies of the documents rather than describe them, and the rule is written to afford this option to the disclosing party. If, as will be more typical, only the description is provided, the other parties are expected to obtain the documents desired by proceeding under Rule 34 or through informal requests. The disclosing party does not, by describing documents under subparagraph (B), waive its right to object to production on the basis of privilege or work product protection, or to assert that the documents are not sufficiently relevant to justify the burden or expense of production. . . .

2000 AMENDMENTS

Purposes of Amendments. The Rule 26(a)(1) initial disclosure provisions are amended to establish a nationally uniform practice. The scope of the disclosure obligation is narrowed to cover only information that the disclosing party may use to support its position. In addition, the rule exempts specified categories of proceedings from initial disclosure, and permits a party who contends that disclosure is not appropriate in the circumstances of the case to present its objections to the court, which must then determine whether disclosure should be made. Related changes are made in Rules 26(d) and (f). . . .

The Committee has discerned widespread support for national uniformity. Many lawyers have experienced difficulty in coping with divergent disclosure and other practices as they move from one district to another. Lawyers surveyed by the Federal Judicial Center ranked adoption of a uniform national disclosure rule second among proposed rule changes (behind increased availability of judges to resolve discovery disputes) as a means to reduce litigation expenses without interfering with fair outcomes. . . .

Subdivision (a)(1). . . . The initial disclosure obligation of subdivisions (a)(1)(A) and (B) has been narrowed to identification of witnesses and documents that the disclosing party may use to support its claims or defenses. "Use" includes any use at a pretrial conference, to support a motion, or at trial. The disclosure obligation is also triggered by intended use in discovery, apart from use to respond to a discovery request; use of a document to question a witness during a deposition is a common example. The disclosure obligation attaches both to witnesses and documents a party intends to use and also to witnesses and to documents the party intends to use if — in the language of Rule 26(a)(3) — "the need arises."

A party is no longer obligated to disclose witnesses or documents, whether favorable or unfavorable, that it does not intend to use. The obligation to disclose information the party may use connects directly to the exclusion sanction of Rule 37(c)(1). Because the disclosure obligation is limited to material that the party may use, it is no longer tied to particularized allegations in the pleadings. Subdivision (e)(1), which is unchanged, requires supplementation if information later acquired would have been subject to the disclosure requirement. As case preparation continues, a party must supplement its disclosures when it determines that it may use a witness or document that it did not previously intend to use.

The disclosure obligation applies to "claims and defenses," and therefore requires a party to disclose information it may use to support its denial or rebuttal of the allegations, claim, or defense of another party. It thereby bolsters the requirements of Rule 11(b)(4), which authorizes denials "warranted on the evidence," and disclosure should include the identity of any witness or document that the disclosing party may use to support such denials. . . .

New subdivision (a)(1)(E) excludes eight specified categories of proceedings from initial disclosure. The objective of this listing is to identify cases in which there is likely to be little or no discovery, or in which initial disclosure appears unlikely to contribute to the effective development of the case. The list was developed after a review of the categories excluded by local rules in various districts from the operation of Rule 16(b) and the conference requirements of subdivision (f). Subdivision (a)(1)(E) refers to categories of "proceedings" rather than categories of "actions" because some might not properly be labeled "actions." Case designations made by the parties or the clerk's office at the time of filing do not control application of the exemptions. The descriptions in the rule are generic and are intended to be administered by the parties — and, when needed, the courts — with the flexibility needed to adapt to gradual evolution in the types of proceedings that fall within these general categories. The exclusion of an action for review on an administrative record, for example, is intended to reach a proceeding that is framed as an "appeal" based solely on an administrative record. The exclusion should not apply to a proceeding in a form that commonly permits admission of new evidence to supplement the record. Item (vii), excluding a proceeding ancillary to proceedings in other courts, does not refer to bankruptcy proceedings; application of the Civil Rules to bankruptcy proceedings is determined by the Bankruptcy Rules.

Subdivision (a)(1)(E) is likely to exempt a substantial proportion of the cases in most districts from the initial disclosure requirement. Based on 1996 and 1997 case filing statistics, Federal Judicial Center staff estimate that, nationwide, these categories total approximately one-third of all civil filings. . . .

The time for initial disclosure is extended to 14 days after the subdivision (f) conference unless the court orders otherwise. This change is integrated with corresponding changes requiring that the subdivision (f) conference be held 21 days before the Rule 16(b) scheduling conference or scheduling order, and that the report on the subdivision (f) conference be submitted to the court 14 days after the meeting. These changes provide a more orderly opportunity for the parties to review the disclosures, and for the court to consider the report. In many instances, the subdivision (f) conference and the effective preparation of the case would benefit from disclosure before the conference, and earlier disclosure is encouraged.

Subdivision (b)(1). In 1978, the Committee published for comment a proposed amendment, suggested by the Section of Litigation of the American Bar Association, to refine the scope of discovery by deleting the "subject matter" language. This proposal was withdrawn, and the Committee has since then made other changes in the discovery rules to address concerns about overbroad discovery. Concerns about costs and delay of discovery have persisted nonetheless, and other bar groups have repeatedly renewed similar proposals for amendment to this subdivision to delete the "subject matter" language. Nearly one-third of the lawyers surveyed in 1997 by the Federal Judicial Center endorsed narrowing the scope of discovery as a means of reducing litigation expense without interfering with fair case resolutions. Discovery and Disclosure Practice, supra, at 44-45 (1997). The Committee has heard that in some instances, particularly cases involving large quantities of discovery, parties seek to justify discovery requests that sweep far beyond the claims and defenses of the parties on the ground that they nevertheless have a bearing on the "subject matter" involved in the action.

The amendments proposed for subdivision (b)(1) include one element of these earlier proposals but also differ from these proposals in significant ways. The similarity is that the amendments describe the scope of party-controlled discovery in terms of matter relevant to the claim or defense of any party. The court, however, retains authority to order discovery of any matter relevant to the subject matter involved in the action for good cause. The amendment is designed to involve the court more actively in regulating the breadth of sweeping or contentious discovery. The Committee has been informed repeatedly by lawyers that involvement of the court in managing discovery is an important method of controlling problems of inappropriately broad discovery. Increasing the availability of judicial officers to resolve discovery disputes and increasing court management of discovery were both strongly endorsed by the attorneys surveyed by the Federal Judicial Center. See Discovery and Disclosure Practice, supra, at 44. Under the amended provisions, if there is an objection that discovery goes beyond material relevant to the parties' claims or defenses, the court would become involved to determine whether the discovery is relevant to the claims or defenses and, if not, whether good cause exists for authorizing it so long as it is relevant to the subject matter of the action. The good-cause standard warranting broader discovery is meant to be flexible.

The Committee intends that the parties and the court focus on the actual claims and defenses involved in the action. The dividing line between information relevant to the claims and defenses and that relevant only to the subject matter of the action cannot be defined with precision. A variety of types of information not directly pertinent to the incident in suit could be relevant to the claims or defenses raised in a given action. For example, other incidents of the same type, or involving the same product, could be properly discoverable under the revised standard. Information about organizational arrangements or filing systems of a party could be discoverable if likely to yield or lead to the discovery of admissible information. Similarly, information that could be used to impeach a likely witness, although not otherwise relevant to the claims or defenses, might be properly discoverable. In each instance, the determination whether such information is discoverable because it is relevant to the claims or defenses depends on the circumstances of the pending action.

The rule change signals to the court that it has the authority to confine discovery to the claims and defenses asserted in the pleadings, and signals to the parties that they have no entitlement to discovery to develop new claims or defenses that are not already identified in the pleadings. In general, it is hoped that reasonable lawyers can cooperate to manage discovery without the need for judicial intervention. When judicial intervention is invoked, the actual scope of discovery should be determined according to the reasonable needs of the action. The court may permit broader discovery in a particular case depending on the circumstances of the case, the nature of the claims and defenses, and the scope of the discovery requested. . . .

The amendments also modify the provision regarding discovery of information not admissible in evidence. As added in 1946, this sentence was designed to make clear that otherwise relevant material could not be withheld because it was hearsay or otherwise inadmissible. The Committee was concerned that the "reasonably calculated to lead to the discovery of admissible evidence" standard set forth in this sentence might swallow any other limitation on the scope of discovery. Accordingly, this sentence has been amended to clarify that information must be relevant to be discoverable, even though inadmissible, and that discovery of such material is permitted if reasonably calculated to lead to the discovery of admissible evidence. As used here, "relevant" means within the scope of discovery as defined in this subdivision, and it would include information relevant to the subject matter involved in the action if the court has ordered discovery to that limit based on a showing of good cause.

Finally, a sentence has been added calling attention to the limitations of subdivision (b)(2)(i), (ii), and (iii). These limitations apply to discovery that is otherwise within the scope of subdivision (b)(1). The Committee has been told repeatedly that courts have not implemented these limitations with the vigor that was contemplated. See 8 Federal Practice & Procedure §2008.1 at 121. This otherwise redundant cross-reference has been added to emphasize the need for active judicial use of subdivision (b)(2) to control excessive discovery. Cf. Crawford-El v. Britton, 118 S. Ct. 1584, 1597 (1998) (quoting Rule 26(b)(2)(iii) and stating that "Rule 26 vests the trial judge with broad discretion to tailor discovery narrowly").

Subdivision (b)(2). Rules 30, 31, and 33 establish presumptive national limits on the numbers of depositions and interrogatories. New Rule 30(d)(2) establishes a presumptive limit on the length of depositions. Subdivision (b)(2) is amended to remove the previous permission for local rules that establish different presumptive limits on these discovery activities. There is no reason to believe that unique circumstances justify varying these nationally-applicable presumptive limits in certain districts. The limits can be modified by court order or agreement in an individual action, but "standing" orders imposing different presumptive limits are not authorized. Because there is no national rule limiting the number of Rule 36 requests for admissions, the rule continues to authorize local rules that impose numerical limits on them. This change is not intended to interfere with differentiated case management in districts that use this technique by case-specific order as part of their Rule 16 process. . . .

In any situation in which discovery requests are challenged as exceeding the limitations of subdivision (b)(2), the court may fashion an appropriate order including cost-bearing. Where appropriate it could, for example, order that some discovery requests be fully satisfied because they are not disproportionate, direct that certain requests not be answered at all, and condition responses to other requests on payment by the party seeking the discovery of part or all of the costs of complying with the request. In determining whether to order cost-bearing, the court should ensure that only reasonable costs are included, and (as suggested by limitation (iii)), it may take account of the parties' relative resources in determining whether it is appropriate for the party seeking discovery to shoulder part or all of the cost of responding to the discovery. . . .

Subdivision (f). As in subdivision (d), the amendments remove the prior authority to exempt cases by local rule from the conference requirement. The Committee has been informed that the addition of the conference was one of the most successful changes made in the 1993 amendments, and it therefore has determined to apply the conference requirement nationwide. The categories of proceedings exempted from initial disclosure under subdivision (a)(1)(E) are exempted from the conference requirement for the reasons that warrant exclusion from initial disclosure. The court may order that the conference need not occur in a case where otherwise required, or that it occur in a case otherwise exempted by subdivision (a)(1)(E). "Standing" orders altering the conference requirement for categories of cases are not authorized.

Rule 27. Depositions Before Action or Pending Appeal

(a) Before Action.

*(1) **Petition.*** A person who desires to perpetuate testimony regarding any matter that may be cognizable in any court of the United States may file a verified petition in the United States district court in the district of the residence of any expected adverse party. The petition shall be entitled in the name of the petitioner and shall show: 1, that the petitioner expects to be a party to an action cognizable in a court of the United States but is presently unable to bring it or cause it to be brought, 2, the subject matter of the expected action and the petitioner's interest therein, 3, the facts which the petitioner desires to establish by the proposed testimony and the reasons for desiring to perpetuate it, 4, the names or a description of the persons the petitioner expects will be adverse parties and their addresses so far as known, and 5, the names and addresses of the persons to be examined and the substance of the testimony which the petitioner expects to elicit from each, and shall ask for an order authorizing the petitioner to take the depositions of the persons to be examined named in the petition, for the purpose of perpetuating their testimony.

*(2) **Notice and Service.*** The petitioner shall thereafter serve a notice upon each person named in the petition as an expected adverse party, together with a copy of the petition, stating that the petitioner will apply to the court, at a time and place named therein, for the order described in the petition. At least 20 days before the date of hearing the notice shall be served either within or without the district or state in the manner provided in Rule 4(d) for service of summons; but if such service cannot with due diligence be made upon any expected adverse party named in the petition, the court may make such order as is just for service by publication or otherwise, and shall appoint, for persons not served in the manner provided in Rule 4(d), an attorney who shall represent them, and, in case they are not otherwise represented, shall cross-examine the deponent. If any expected adverse party is a minor or incompetent the provisions of Rule 17(c) apply.

*(3) **Order and Examination.*** If the court is satisfied that the perpetuation of the testimony may prevent a failure or delay of justice, it shall make an order designating or describing the persons whose depositions may be taken and specifying the subject matter of the examination and whether the depositions shall be taken upon oral examination or written interrogatories. The depositions may then be taken in accordance with these rules; and the court may make orders of the character provided for by Rules 34 and 35. For the purpose of applying these rules to depositions for perpetuating testimony, each reference

therein to the court in which the action is pending shall be deemed to refer to the court in which the petition for such deposition was filed.

(4) Use of Deposition. If a deposition to perpetuate testimony is taken under these rules or if, although not so taken, it would be admissible in evidence in the courts of the state in which it is taken, it may be used in any action involving the same subject matter subsequently brought in a United States district court, in accordance with the provisions of Rule 32(a).

(b) Pending Appeal. If an appeal has been taken from a judgment of a district court or before the taking of an appeal if the time therefor has not expired, the district court in which the judgment was rendered may allow the taking of the depositions of witnesses to perpetuate their testimony for use in the event of further proceedings in the district court. In such case the party who desires to perpetuate the testimony may make a motion in the district court for leave to take the depositions, upon the same notice and service thereof as if the action was pending in the district court. The motion shall show (1) the names and addresses of persons to be examined and the substance of the testimony which the party expects to elicit from each; (2) the reasons for perpetuating their testimony. If the court finds that the perpetuation of the testimony is proper to avoid a failure or delay of justice, it may make an order allowing the depositions to be taken and may make orders of the character provided for by Rules 34 and 35, and thereupon the depositions may be taken and used in the same manner and under the same conditions as are prescribed in these rules for depositions taken in actions pending in the district court.

(c) Perpetuation by Action. This rule does not limit the power of a court to entertain an action to perpetuate testimony.

As amended Dec. 27, 1946, eff. Mar. 19, 1948; Dec. 29, 1948, eff. Oct. 20, 1949; Mar. 1, 1971, eff. July 1, 1971; Mar. 2, 1987, eff. Aug. 1, 1987.

Rule 28. Persons Before Whom Depositions May Be Taken

(a) Within the United States. Within the United States or within a territory or insular possession subject to the jurisdiction of the United States, depositions shall be taken before an officer authorized to administer oaths by the laws of the United States or of the place where the examination is held, or before a person appointed by the court in which the action is pending. A person so appointed has power to administer oaths and take testimony. The term officer as used in Rules 30, 31, and 32 includes a person appointed by the court or designated by the parties under Rule 29.

(b) In Foreign Countries. Depositions may be taken in a foreign country (1) pursuant to any applicable treaty or convention, or (2) pursuant to a letter of request (whether or not captioned a letter rogatory), or (3) on notice before a person authorized to administer oaths in the place where the examination is held, either by the law thereof or by the law of the United States, or (4) before a person commissioned by the court, and a person so commissioned shall have the power by virtue of the commission to administer any necessary oath and take testimony. A commission or a letter of request shall be issued on application and notice and on terms that are just and appropriate. It is not requisite to the issuance of a commission or a letter of request that the taking of the deposition in any other manner is impracticable or inconvenient; and both a commission and a letter of request may be issued in proper cases. A notice or commission may designate the person before whom the deposition is to be taken either by name or descriptive title. A letter of request may be addressed "To the Appropriate Authority in [here name the country]." When a letter of request or any other device is used pursuant to any applicable treaty or convention, it shall be captioned in the form prescribed by that treaty or convention. Evidence obtained in response to a letter of request need not be excluded merely because it is not a verbatim transcript, because the testimony was not taken under oath, or because of any similar departure from the requirements for depositions taken within the United States under these rules.

(c) Disqualification for Interest. No deposition shall be taken before a person who is a relative or employee or attorney or counsel of any of the parties, or is a relative or employee of such attorney or counsel, or is financially interested in the action.

As amended Dec. 27, 1946, eff. Mar. 19, 1948; Jan. 21, 1963, eff. July 1, 1963; Mar. 2, 1987, eff. Aug. 1, 1987; Apr. 22, 1993, eff. Dec. 1, 1993.

Rule 29. Stipulations Regarding Discovery Procedure

Unless otherwise directed by the court, the parties may by written stipulation (1) provide that depositions may be taken before any person, at any time or place, upon any notice, and in any manner and when so taken may be used like other depositions, and (2) modify other procedures governing or limitations placed upon discovery, except that stipulations extending the time provided in Rules 33, 34, and 36 for responses to discovery may, if they would interfere with any time set for completion of discovery, for hearing of a motion, or for trial, be made only with the approval of the court.

As amended Mar. 30, 1970, eff. July 1, 1970; Apr. 22, 1993, eff. Dec. 1, 1993.

ADVISORY COMMITTEE NOTES, 1993 AMENDMENTS

This rule is revised to give greater opportunity for litigants to agree upon modifications to the procedures governing discovery or to limitations upon discovery. Counsel are encouraged to agree on less expensive and time-consuming methods to obtain information, as through voluntary exchange of documents, use of interviews in lieu of depositions, etc. Likewise, when more depositions or interrogatories are needed than allowed under these rules or when more time is needed to complete a deposition than allowed under a local rule, they can, by agreeing to the additional discovery, eliminate the need for a special motion addressed to the court.

Rule 30. Depositions upon Oral Examination

(a) When Depositions May Be Taken; When Leave Required.

(1) A party may take the testimony of any person, including a party, by deposition upon oral examination without leave of court except as provided inparagraph (2). The attendance of witnesses may be compelled by subpoena as provided in Rule 45.

(2) A party must obtain leave of court, which shall be granted to the extent consistent with the principles stated in Rule 26(b)(2), if the person to be examined is confined in prison or if, without the written stipulation of the parties,

(A) a proposed deposition would result in more than ten depositions being taken under this rule or Rule 31 by the plaintiffs, or by the defendants, or by third-party defendants;

(B) the person to be examined already has been deposed in the case; or

(C) a party seeks to take a deposition before the time specified in Rule 26(d) unless the notice contains a certification, with supporting facts, that the person to be examined is expected to leave the United States and be unavailable for examination in this country unless deposed before that time.

(b) Notice of Examination: General Requirements; Method of Recording; Production of Documents and Things; Deposition of Organization; Deposition by Telephone.

(1) A party desiring to take the deposition of any person upon oral examination shall give reasonable notice in writing to every other party to the action. The notice shall state the time and place for taking the deposition and the name and address of each person to be examined, if known, and, if the name is not known, a general description sufficient to identify the person or the particular class or group to which the person belongs. If a subpoena duces tecum is to be served on the person to be examined, the designation of the materials to be produced as set forth in the subpoena shall be attached to, or included in, the notice.

(2) The party taking the deposition shall state in the notice the method by which the testimony shall be recorded. Unless the court orders otherwise, it may be recorded by sound, sound-and-visual, or stenographic means, and the party

taking the deposition shall bear the cost of the recording. Any party may arrange for a transcription to be made from the recording of a deposition taken by nonstenographic means.

(3) With prior notice to the deponent and other parties, any party may designate another method to record the deponent's testimony in addition to the method specified by the person taking the deposition. The additional record or transcript shall be made at that party's expense unless the court otherwise orders.

(4) Unless otherwise agreed by the parties, a deposition shall be conducted before an officer appointed or designated under Rule 28 and shall begin with a statement on the record by the officer that includes (A) the officer's name and business address; (B) the date, time, and place of the deposition; (C) the name of the deponent; (D) the administration of the oath or affirmation to the deponent; and (E) an identification of all persons present. If the deposition is recorded other than stenographically, the officer shall repeat items (A) through (C) at the beginning of each unit of recorded tape or other recording medium. The appearance or demeanor of deponents or attorneys shall not be distorted through camera or sound-recording techniques. At the end of the deposition, the officer shall state on the record that the deposition is complete and shall set forth any stipulations made by counsel concerning the custody of the transcript or recording and the exhibits, or concerning other pertinent matters.

(5) The notice to a party deponent may be accompanied by a request made in compliance with Rule 34 for the production of documents and tangible things at the taking of the deposition. The procedure of Rule 34 shall apply to the request.

(6) A party may in the party's notice and in a subpoena name as the deponent a public or private corporation or a partnership or association or governmental agency and describe with reasonable particularity the matters on which examination is requested. In that event, the organization so named shall designate one or more officers, directors or managing agents, or other persons who consent to testify on its behalf, and may set forth, for each person designated, the matters on which the person will testify. A subpoena shall advise a non-party organization of its duty to make such a designation. The persons so designated shall testify as to matters known or reasonably available to the organization. This subdivision (b)(6) does not preclude taking a deposition by any other procedure authorized in these rules.

(7) The parties may stipulate in writing or the court may upon motion order that a deposition be taken by telephone or other remote electronic means. For the purposes of this rule and Rules 28(a), 37(a)(1), and 37(b)(1), a deposition taken by such means is taken in the district and at the place where the deponent is to answer questions.

(c) Examination and Cross-Examination; Record of Examination; Oath; Objections. Examination and cross-examination of witnesses may proceed as permitted at the trial under the provisions of the Federal Rules of Evidence except Rules 103 and 615. The officer before whom the deposition is to be taken shall put the witness on oath or affirmation and shall personally, or by someone acting under the officer's direction and in the officer's presence, record the testimony of the witness. The testimony shall be taken stenographically or recorded by any other method authorized by subdivision (b)(2) of this rule. All objections made at the time of the examination to the qualifications of the officer taking the deposition, to the manner of taking it, to the evidence presented, to the conduct of any party, or to any other aspect of the proceedings shall be noted by the officer upon the record of the deposition; but the examination shall proceed, with the testimony being taken subject to the objections. In lieu of participating in the oral examination, parties may serve written questions in a sealed envelope on the party taking the deposition and the party taking the deposition shall transmit them to the officer, who shall propound them to the witness and record the answers verbatim.

(d) Schedule and Duration; Motion to Terminate or Limit Examination.
(1) Any objection during a deposition must be stated concisely and in a non-argumentative and non-suggestive manner. A person may instruct a deponent not to answer only when necessary to preserve a privilege, to enforce a limitation directed by the court, or to present a motion under Rule 30(d)(4).

(2) Unless otherwise authorized by the court or stipulated by the parties, a deposition is limited to one day of seven hours. The court must allow additional time consistent with Rule 26(b)(2) if needed for a fair examination of the deponent or if the deponent or another person, or other circumstance, impedes or delays the examination.

(3) If the court finds that any impediment, delay, or other conduct has frustrated the fair examination of the deponent, it may impose upon the persons responsible an appropriate sanction, including the reasonable costs and attorney's fees incurred by any parties as a result thereof.

(4) At any time during a deposition, on motion of a party or of the deponent and upon a showing that the examination is being conducted in bad faith or in such manner as unreasonably to annoy, embarrass, or oppress the deponent or party, the court in which the action is pending or the court in the district where the deposition is being taken may order the officer conducting the examination to cease forthwith from taking the deposition, or may limit the scope and manner of the taking of the deposition as provided in Rule 26(c). If the order made terminates the examination, it may be resumed thereafter only upon the order of the court in which the action is pending. Upon demand of the objecting party or deponent, the taking of the deposition must be suspended for the time necessary to make a motion for an order. The provisions of Rule 37(a)(4) apply to the award of expenses incurred in relation to the motion.

(e) Review by Witness; Changes; Signing. If requested by the deponent or a party before completion of the deposition, the deponent shall have 30 days after being notified by the officer that the transcript or recording is available in which to review the transcript or recording and, if there are changes in form or substance, to sign a statement reciting such changes and the reasons given by the deponent for making them. The officer shall indicate in the certificate prescribed by subdivision (f)(1) whether any review was requested and, if so, shall append any changes made by the deponent during the period allowed.

(f) Certification and Delivery by Officer; Exhibits; Copies.

(1) The officer must certify that the witness was duly sworn by the officer and that the deposition is a true record of the testimony given by the witness. This certificate must be in writing and accompany the record of the deposition. Unless otherwise ordered by the court, the officer must securely seal the deposition in an envelope or package indorsed with the title of the action and marked "Deposition of [here insert name of witness]" and must promptly send it to the attorney who arranged for the transcript or recording, who must store it under conditions that will protect it against loss, destruction, tampering, or deterioration. Documents and things produced for inspection during the examination of the witness must, upon the request of a party, be marked for identification and annexed to the deposition and may be inspected and copied by any party, except that if the person producing the materials desires to retain them the person may (A) offer copies to be marked for identification and annexed to the deposition and to serve thereafter as originals if the person affords to all parties fair opportunity to verify the copies by comparison with the originals, or (B) offer the originals to be marked for identification, after giving to each party an opportunity to inspect and copy them, in which event the materials may then be used in the same manner as if annexed to the deposition. Any party may move for an order that the original be annexed to and returned with the deposition to the court, pending final disposition of the case.

(2) Unless otherwise ordered by the court or agreed by the parties, the officer shall retain stenographic notes of any deposition taken stenographically or a copy of the recording of any deposition taken by another method. Upon payment of reasonable charges therefor, the officer shall furnish a copy of the transcript or other recording of the deposition to any party or to the deponent.

(3) The party taking the deposition shall give prompt notice of its filing to all other parties.

(g) Failure to Attend or to Serve Subpoena; Expenses.

(1) If the party giving the notice of the taking of a deposition fails to attend and proceed therewith and another party attends in person or by attorney pursuant to the notice, the court may order the party giving the notice to pay to such other party the reasonable expenses incurred by that party and that party's attorney in attending, including reasonable attorney's fees.

(2) If the party giving the notice of the taking of a deposition of a witness fails to serve a subpoena upon the witness and the witness because of such failure

does not attend, and if another party attends in person or by attorney because that party expects the deposition of that witness to be taken, the court may order the party giving the notice to pay to such other party the reasonable expenses incurred by that party and that party's attorney in attending, including reasonable attorney's fees.

As amended Jan. 21, 1963, eff. July 1, 1963; Mar. 30, 1970, eff. July 1, 1970; Mar. 1, 1971, eff. July 1, 1971; Nov. 20, 1972, and expressly approved by P.L. 93-595, eff. July 1, 1975; Apr. 29, 1980, eff. Aug. 1, 1980; Mar. 2, 1987, eff. Aug. 1, 1987; Apr. 22, 1993, eff. Dec. 1, 1993; Apr. 17, 2000, eff. Dec. 1, 2000.

ADVISORY COMMITTEE NOTES, 1970, 1980, 1993, AND 2000 AMENDMENTS

1970 AMENDMENTS . . .

Subdivision (b)(6). A new provision is added, whereby a party may name a corporation, partnership, association, or governmental agency as the deponent and designate the matters on which he requests examination, and the organization shall then name one or more of its officers, directors, or managing agents, or other persons consenting to appear and testify on its behalf with respect to matters known or reasonably available to the organization. Cf. Alberta Sup. Ct. R. 255. The organization may designate persons other than officers, directors, and managing agents, but only with their consent. Thus, an employee or agent who has an independent or conflicting interest in the litigation — for example, in a personal injury case — can refuse to testify on behalf of the organization.

This procedure supplements the existing practice whereby the examining party designates the corporate official to be deposed. Thus, if the examining party believes that certain officials who have not testified pursuant to this subdivision have added information, he may depose them. On the other hand, a court's decision whether to issue a protective order may take account of the availability and use made of the procedures provided in this subdivision. . . .

1980 AMENDMENTS . . .

Subdivision (b)(7). Depositions by telephone are now authorized by Rule 29 upon stipulation of the parties. The amendment authorizes that method by order of the court. The final sentence is added to make it clear that when a deposition is taken by telephone it is taken in the district and at the place where the witness is to answer the questions rather than that where the questions are propounded.

1993 AMENDMENTS

Subdivision (a). . . .

Paragraph (2)(A) is new. It provides a limit on the number of depositions the parties may take, absent leave of court or stipulation with the other parties. One aim of this revision is to assure judicial review under the standards stated in Rule 26(b)(2) before any side will be allowed to take more than ten depositions in a case without agreement of the other parties. A second objective is to emphasize that counsel have a professional obligation to develop a mutual cost-effective plan for discovery in the case. Leave to take additional depositions should be granted when consistent with the principles of Rule 26(b)(2), and in some cases the ten-per-side limit should be reduced in accordance with those same principles. Consideration should ordinarily be given at the planning meeting of the parties under Rule 26(f) and at the time of a scheduling conference under Rule 16(b) as to enlargements or reductions in the number of depositions, eliminating the need for special motions.

Subdivision (d). . . .

Paragraph (3) authorizes appropriate sanctions not only when a deposition is unreasonably prolonged, but also when an attorney engages in other practices that improperly frustrate the fair examination of the deponent, such as making improper objections or giving directions not to answer prohibited by paragraph (1). In general, counsel should not engage in any conduct during a deposition that would not be allowed in the presence of a judicial officer. The making of an excessive number of unnecessary objections may itself constitute sanctionable conduct, as may the refusal of an attorney to agree with other counsel on a fair apportionment of the time allowed for examination of a deponent or a refusal to agree to a reasonable request for some additional time to complete a deposition, when that is permitted by the local rule or order.

2000 AMENDMENTS

Subdivision (d). . . . Paragraph (2) imposes a presumptive durational limitation of one day of seven hours for any deposition. The Committee has been informed that overlong depositions can result in undue costs and delays in some circumstances. This limitation contemplates that there will be reasonable breaks during the day for lunch and other reasons, and that the only time to be counted is the time occupied by the actual deposition. For purposes of this durational limit, the deposition of each person designated under Rule 30(b)(6) should be considered a separate deposition. The presumptive duration may be extended, or otherwise altered, by agreement. Absent agreement, a court order is needed. The party seeking a court order to extend the examination, or otherwise alter the limitations, is expected to show good cause to justify such an order.

Rule 31. Depositions upon Written Questions

(a) Serving Questions; Notice.

(1) A party may take the testimony of any person, including a party, by deposition upon written questions without leave of court except as provided in

paragraph (2). The attendance of witnesses may be compelled by the use of subpoena as provided in Rule 45.

(2) A party must obtain leave of court, which shall be granted to the extent consistent with the principles stated in Rule 26(b)(2), if the person to be examined is confined in prison or if, without the written stipulation of the parties,

(A) a proposed deposition would result in more than ten depositions being taken under this rule or Rule 30 by the plaintiffs, or by the defendants, or by third-party defendants;

(B) the person to be examined has already been deposed in the case; or

(C) a party seeks to take a deposition before the time specified in Rule 26(d).

(3) A party desiring to take a deposition upon written questions shall serve them upon every other party with a notice stating (1) the name and address of the person who is to answer them, if known, and if the name is not known, a general description sufficient to identify the person or the particular class or group to which the person belongs, and (2) the name or descriptive title and address of the officer before whom the deposition is to be taken. A deposition upon written questions may be taken of a public or private corporation or a partnership or association or governmental agency in accordance with the provisions of Rule 30(b)(6).

(4) Within 14 days after the notice and written questions are served, a party may serve cross questions upon all other parties. Within 7 days after being served with cross questions, a party may serve redirect questions upon all other parties. Within 7 days after being served with redirect questions, a party may serve recross questions upon all other parties. The court may for cause shown enlarge or shorten the time.

(b) Officer to Take Responses and Prepare Record. A copy of the notice and copies of all questions served shall be delivered by the party taking the deposition to the officer designated in the notice, who shall proceed promptly, in the manner provided by Rule 30(c), (e), and (f), to take the testimony of the witness in response to the questions and to prepare, certify, and file or mail the deposition, attaching thereto the copy of the notice and the questions received by the officer.

(c) Notice of Filing. When the deposition is filed the party taking it shall promptly give notice thereof to all other parties.

As amended Mar. 30, 1970, eff. July 1, 1970; Mar. 2, 1987, eff. Aug. 1, 1987; Apr. 22, 1993, eff. Dec. 1, 1993.

Rule 32. Use of Depositions in Court Proceedings

(a) Use of Depositions. At the trial or upon the hearing of a motion or an interlocutory proceeding, any part or all of a deposition, so far as admissible under the rules of evidence applied as though the witness were then present and testifying, may be used against any party who was present or represented at the taking of the deposition or who had reasonable notice thereof, in accordance with any of the following provisions:

(1) Any deposition may be used by any party for the purpose of contradicting or impeaching the testimony of deponent as a witness, or for any other purpose permitted by the Federal Rules of Evidence.

(2) The deposition of a party or of anyone who at the time of taking the deposition was an officer, director, or managing agent, or a person designated under Rule 30(b)(6) or 31(a) to testify on behalf of a public or private corporation, partnership or association or governmental agency which is a party may be used by an adverse party for any purpose.

(3) The deposition of a witness, whether or not a party, may be used by any party for any purpose if the court finds:

(A) that the witness is dead; or

(B) that the witness is at a greater distance than 100 miles from the place of trial or hearing, or is out of the United States, unless it appears that the absence of the witness was procured by the party offering the deposition; or

(C) that the witness is unable to attend or testify because of age, illness, infirmity, or imprisonment; or

(D) that the party offering the deposition has been unable to procure the attendance of the witness by subpoena; or

(E) upon application and notice, that such exceptional circumstances exist as to make it desirable, in the interest of justice and with due regard to the importance of presenting the testimony of witnesses orally in open court, to allow the deposition to be used.

A deposition taken without leave of court pursuant to a notice under Rule 30(a)(2)(C) shall not be used against a party who demonstrates that, when served with the notice, it was unable through the exercise of diligence to obtain counsel to represent it at the taking of the deposition; nor shall a deposition be used against a party who, having received less than 11 days notice of a deposition, has promptly upon receiving such notice filed a motion for a protective order under Rule 26(c)(2) requesting that the deposition not be held or be held at a different time or place and such motion is pending at the time the deposition is held.

(4) If only part of a deposition is offered in evidence by a party, an adverse party may require the offeror to introduce any other part which ought in fairness to be considered with the part introduced, and any party may introduce any other parts.

Substitution of parties pursuant to Rule 25 does not affect the right to use depositions previously taken; and when an action has been brought in any court of the United States or of any State and another action involving the same subject matter is afterward brought between the same parties or their representatives or successors in interest, all depositions lawfully taken and duly filed in the former action may be used in the latter as if originally taken therefor. A deposition previously taken may also be used as permitted by the Federal Rules of Evidence.

(b) Objection to Admissibility. Subject to the provisions of Rule 28(b) and subdivision (d)(3) of this rule, objection may be made at the trial or hearing to receiving in evidence any deposition or part thereof for any reason which would require the exclusion of the evidence if the witness were then present and testifying.

(c) Form of Presentation. Except as otherwise directed by the court, a party offering deposition testimony pursuant to this rule may offer it in stenographic or nonstenographic form, but, if in nonstenographic form, the party shall also provide the court with a transcript of the portions so offered. On request of any party in a case tried before a jury, deposition testimony offered other than for impeachment purposes shall be presented in nonstenographic form, if available, unless the court for good cause orders otherwise.

(d) Effect of Errors and Irregularities in Depositions.

(1) As to Notice. All errors and irregularities in the notice for taking a deposition are waived unless written objection is promptly served upon the party giving the notice.

(2) As to Disqualification of Officer. Objection to taking a deposition because of disqualification of the officer before whom it is to be taken is waived unless made before the taking of the deposition begins or as soon thereafter as the disqualification becomes known or could be discovered with reasonable diligence.

(3) As to Taking of Deposition.

(A) Objections to the competency of a witness or to the competency, relevancy, or materiality of testimony are not waived by failure to make them before or during the taking of the deposition, unless the ground of the objection is one which might have been obviated or removed if presented at that time.

(B) Errors and irregularities occurring at the oral examination in the manner of taking the deposition, in the form of the questions or answers, in the oath or affirmation, or in the conduct of parties, and errors of any kind which might be obviated, removed, or cured if promptly presented, are waived unless seasonable objection thereto is made at the taking of the deposition.

(C) Objections to the form of written questions submitted under Rule 31 are waived unless served in writing upon the party propounding them within the time allowed for serving the succeeding cross or other questions and within 5 days after service of the last questions authorized.

(4) As to Completion and Return of Deposition. Errors and irregularities in the manner in which the testimony is transcribed or the deposition is prepared, signed, certified, sealed, indorsed, transmitted, filed, or otherwise dealt with by the officer under Rules 30 and 31 are waived unless a motion to suppress the deposition or some part thereof is made with reasonable promptness after such defect is, or with due diligence might have been, ascertained.

As amended Mar. 30, 1970, eff. July 1, 1970; Nov. 20, 1972, and expressly approved by P.L. 93-595, eff. July 1, 1975; Apr. 29, 1980, eff. Aug. 1, 1980; Mar. 2, 1987, eff. Aug. 1, 1987; Apr. 22, 1993, eff. Dec. 1, 1993.

Rule 33. Interrogatories to Parties

(a) Availability. Without leave of court or written stipulation, any party may serve upon any other party written interrogatories, not exceeding 25 in number including all discrete subparts, to be answered by the party served or, if the party served is a public or private corporation or a partnership or association or governmental agency, by any officer or agent, who shall furnish such information as is available to the party. Leave to serve additional interrogatories shall be granted to the extent consistent with the principles of Rule 26(b)(2). Without leave of court or written stipulation, interrogatories may not be served before the time specified in Rule 26(d).

(b) Answers and Objections.

(1) Each interrogatory shall be answered separately and fully in writing under oath, unless it is objected to, in which event the objecting party shall state the reasons for objection and shall answer to the extent the interrogatory is not objectionable.

(2) The answers are to be signed by the person making them, and the objections signed by the attorney making them.

(3) The party upon whom the interrogatories have been served shall serve a copy of the answers, and objections if any, within 30 days after the service of the interrogatories. A shorter or longer time may be directed by the court or, in the absence of such an order, agreed to in writing by the parties subject to Rule 29.

(4) All grounds for an objection to an interrogatory shall be stated with specificity. Any ground not stated in a timely objection is waived unless the party's failure to object is excused by the court for good cause shown.

(5) The party submitting the interrogatories may move for an order under Rule 37(a) with respect to any objection to or other failure to answer an interrogatory.

(c) Scope; Use at Trial. Interrogatories may relate to any matters which can be inquired into under Rule 26(b)(1), and the answers may be used to the extent permitted by the rules of evidence.

An interrogatory otherwise proper is not necessarily objectionable merely because an answer to the interrogatory involves an opinion or contention that relates to fact or the application of law to fact, but the court may order that such an interrogatory need not be answered until after designated discovery has been completed or until a pre-trial conference or other later time.

(d) Option to Produce Business Records. Where the answer to an interrogatory may be derived or ascertained from the business records of the party upon whom the interrogatory has been served or from an examination, audit or inspection of such business records, including a compilation, abstract or summary thereof, and the burden of deriving or ascertaining the answer is substantially the same for the party serving the interrogatory as for the party served, it is a sufficient answer to such interrogatory to specify the records from which the answer may be derived or ascertained and to afford to the party serving the interrogatory reasonable opportunity to examine, audit or inspect such records and to make copies, compilations, abstracts or summaries. A specification shall be in sufficient detail to permit the interrogating party to locate and to identify, as readily as can the party served, the records from which the answer may be ascertained.

As amended Dec. 27, 1946, eff. Mar. 19, 1948; Mar. 30, 1970, eff. July 1, 1970; Apr. 29, 1980, eff. Aug. 1, 1980; Apr. 22, 1993, eff. Dec. 1, 1993.

Advisory Committee Notes, 1970 and 1980 Amendments

1970 amendments

. . . The amendment improves the procedure of Rule 33 in the following respects:

(1) The time allowed for response is increased to 30 days and this time period applies to both answers and objections, but a defendant need not respond in less than 45 days after service of the summons and complaint upon him. As is true under existing law, the responding party who believes that some parts or all of the interrogatories are objectionable may choose to seek a protective order under new Rule 26(c) or may serve objections under this rule. Unless he applies for a protective order, he is required to serve answers or objections in response to the interrogatories, subject to the sanctions provided in Rule 37(d). Answers and objections are served together, so that a response to each interrogatory is encouraged, and any failure to respond is easily noted.

(2) In view of the enlarged time permitted for response, it is no longer necessary to require leave of court for service of interrogatories. The purpose of this requirement — that defendant have time to obtain counsel before a response must be made — is adequately fulfilled by the requirement that interrogatories be served upon a party with or after service of the summons and complaint upon him. . . .

Subdivision (b). There are numerous and conflicting decisions on the question whether and to what extent interrogatories are limited to matters "of fact," or may elicit opinions, contentions, and legal conclusions. . . .

Rule 33 is amended to provide that an interrogatory is not objectionable merely because it calls for an opinion or contention that relates to fact or the application of law to fact. Efforts to draw sharp lines between facts and opinions have invariably been unsuccessful, and the clear trend of the cases is to permit "factual" opinions. As to requests for opinions or contentions that call for the application of law to fact, they can be most useful in narrowing and sharpening the issues, which is a major purpose of discovery. See Diversified Products Corp. v. Sports Center Co., 42 F.R.D. 3 (D. Md. 1967); [4 Moore's Federal Practice ¶233.17 (2d ed. 1966);] Field & McKusick, Maine Civil Practice §26.18 (1959). On the other hand, under the new language interrogatories may not extend to issues of "pure law," i.e., legal issues unrelated to the facts of the case. Cf. United States v. Maryland & Va. Milk Producers Assn., Inc., 22 F.R.D. 300 (D.D.C. 1958).

Since interrogatories involving mixed questions of law and fact may create disputes between the parties which are best resolved after much or all of the other discovery has been completed, the court is expressly authorized to defer an answer. Likewise, the court may delay determination until pretrial conference, if it believes that the dispute is best resolved in the presence of the judge. . . .

Subdivision (c). This is a new subdivision, adapted from Calif. Code Civ. Proc. §2030(c), relating especially to interrogatories which require a party to engage in burdensome or expensive research into his own business records in order to give an answer. The subdivision gives the party an option to make the records available and place the burden of research on the party who seeks the information. "This provision, without undermining the liberal scope of interrogatory discovery, places the burden of discovery upon its potential benefitee," Louisell, Modern California Discovery, 124-125 (1963), and alleviates a problem which in the past has troubled Federal courts. See Speck, The Use of Discovery in United States District Courts, 60 Yale L.J. 1132, 1142-1144 (1951). The interrogating party is protected against abusive use of this provision through the requirement that the burden of ascertaining the answer be substantially the same for both sides. A respondent may not impose on an interrogating party a mass of records as to which research is feasible only for one familiar with the records. At the same time, the respondent unable to invoke this subdivision does not on that account lose the protection available to him under new Rule 26(c) against oppressive or unduly burdensome or expensive interrogatories. And even when the respondent successfully invokes the subdivision, the court is not deprived of its usual power, in appropriate cases, to require that the interrogating party reimburse the respondent for the expense of assembling his records and making them intelligible.

1980 AMENDMENTS

Subdivision (c). The Committee is advised that parties upon whom interrogatories are served have occasionally responded by directing the interrogating party to a mass of business records or by offering to make all of their records available, justifying the response by the option provided by this subdivision. Such practices are an abuse of the option. A party who is permitted by the terms of this subdivision to offer records for inspection in lieu of answering an interrogatory should offer them in a manner that permits the same direct and economical access that is available to the party. If the information sought exists in the form of compilations, abstracts or summaries then available to the responding party, those should be made available to the interrogating party. The final sentence is added to make it clear that a responding party has the duty to specify, by category and location, the records from which answers to interrogatories can be derived.

Rule 34. Production of Documents and Things and Entry upon Land for Inspection and Other Purposes

(a) **Scope.** Any party may serve on any other party a request (1) to produce and permit the party making the request, or someone acting on the requestor's behalf, to inspect and copy, any designated documents (including writings, drawings, graphs, charts, photographs, phono-records, and other data compilations from which information can be obtained, translated, if necessary, by the respondent through detection devices into reasonably usable form), or to inspect and copy, test, or sample any tangible things which constitute or contain matters within the scope of Rule 26(b) and which are in the possession, custody or control of the party upon whom the request is served; or (2) to permit entry upon designated land or other property in the possession or control of the party upon whom the request is served for the purpose of inspection and measuring, surveying, photographing, testing, or sampling the property or any designated object or operation thereon, within the scope of Rule 26(b).

(b) **Procedure.** The request shall set forth, either by individual item or by category, the items to be inspected, and describe each with reasonable par ticularity. The request shall specify a reasonable time, place, and manner of making the inspection and performing the related acts. Without leave of court or written stipulation, a request may not be served before the time specified in Rule 26(d).

The party upon whom the request is served shall serve a written response within 30 days after the service of the request. A shorter or longer time may be directed by the court or, in the absence of such an order, agreed to in writing by the parties, subject to Rule 29. The response shall state, with respect to each item or category, that inspection and related activities will be permitted as requested, unless the request is objected to, in which event the reasons for the objection shall be stated. If objection is made to part of an item or category, the part shall be specified and inspection permitted of the remaining parts. The party submitting the request may move for an order under Rule 37(a) with respect to any objection to or other failure to respond to the request or any part thereof, or any failure to permit inspection as requested.

A party who produces documents for inspection shall produce them as they are kept in the usual course of business or shall organize and label them to correspond with the categories in the request.

(c) Persons Not Parties. A person not a party to the action may be compelled to produce documents and things or to submit to an inspection as provided in Rule 45.

As amended Dec. 27, 1946, eff. Mar. 19, 1948; Mar. 30, 1970, eff. July 1, 1970; Apr. 29, 1980, eff. Aug. 1, 1980; Mar. 2, 1987, eff. Aug. 1, 1987; Apr. 30, 1991, eff. Dec. 1, 1991; Apr. 22, 1993, eff. Dec. 1, 1993.

ADVISORY COMMITTEE NOTES, 1980 AMENDMENTS

Subdivision (b). The Committee is advised that, "It is apparently not rare for parties deliberately to mix critical documents with others in the hope of obscuring significance." Report of the Special Committee for the Study of Discovery Abuse, Section of Litigation of the American Bar Association (1977) 22. The sentence added by this subdivision follows the recommendation of the Report.

Rule 35. Physical and Mental Examination of Persons

(a) Order for Examination. When the mental or physical condition (including the blood group) of a party, or of a person in the custody or under the legal control of a party, is in controversy, the court in which the action is pending may order the party to submit to a physical or mental examination by a suitably licensed or certified examiner or to produce for examination the person in the party's custody or legal control. The order may be made only on motion for good cause shown and upon notice to the person to be examined and to all parties and shall specify the time, place, manner, conditions, and scope of the examination and the person or persons by whom it is to be made.

(b) Report of Examiner.

(1) If requested by the party against whom an order is made under Rule 35(a) or the person examined, the party causing the examination to be made shall deliver to the requesting party a copy of the detailed written report of the examiner setting out the examiner's findings, including results of all tests made, diagnoses and conclusions, together with like reports of all earlier examinations of the same condition. After delivery the party causing the examination shall be entitled upon request to receive from the party against whom the order is made a like report of any examination, previously or thereafter made, of the same condition, unless, in the case of a report of examination of a person not a party, the party shows that the party is unable to obtain it. The court on motion may make an order against a party requiring delivery of a report on such terms as are

just, and if an examiner fails or refuses to make a report the court may exclude the examiner's testimony if offered at trial.

(2) By requesting and obtaining a report of the examination so ordered or by taking the deposition of the examiner, the party examined waives any privilege the party may have in that action or any other involving the same controversy, regarding the testimony of every other person who has examined or may thereafter examine the party in respect of the same mental or physical condition.

(3) This subdivision applies to examinations made by agreement of the parties, unless the agreement expressly provides otherwise. This subdivision does not preclude discovery of a report of an examiner or the taking of a deposition of the examiner in accordance with the provisions of any other rule.

As amended Mar. 30, 1970, eff. July 1, 1970; Mar. 2, 1987, eff. Aug. 1, 1987; Nov. 18, 1988, Pub. L. 100-690, Title VII, §7047(b), 102 Stat. 4401; Apr. 30, 1991, eff. Dec. 1, 1991.

ADVISORY COMMITTEE NOTES, 1970 AMENDMENT

Subdivision (a). Rule 35(a) has hitherto provided only for an order requiring a party to submit to an examination. It is desirable to extend the rule to provide for an order against the party for examination of a person in his custody or under his legal control. As appears from the provisions of amended Rule 37(b) (2) and the comment under that rule, an order to "produce" the third person imposes only an obligation to use good faith efforts to produce the person.

The amendment will settle beyond doubt that a parent or guardian suing to recover for injuries to a minor may be ordered to produce the minor for examination. Further, the amendment expressly includes blood examination within the kinds of examinations that can be ordered under the rule.

Rule 36. Requests for Admission

(a) Request for Admission. A party may serve upon any other party a written request for the admission, for purposes of the pending action only, of the truth of any matters within the scope of Rule 26(b)(1) set forth in the request that relate to statements or opinions of fact or of the application of law to fact, including the genuineness of any documents described in the request. Copies of documents shall be served with the request unless they have been or are otherwise furnished or made available for inspection and copying. Without leave of court or written stipulation, requests for admission may not be served before the time specified in Rule 26(d).

Each matter of which an admission is requested shall be separately set forth. The matter is admitted unless, within 30 days after service of the request, or within such shorter or longer time as the court may allow, or as the parties may agree to in writing, subject to Rule 29, the party to whom the request is directed serves upon the party requesting the admission a written answer or objection addressed to the matter, signed by the party or by the party's attorney. If objection is made, the reasons therefor shall be stated. The answer shall specifically deny the matter or set forth in detail the reasons why the answering party cannot truthfully admit or deny the matter. A denial shall fairly meet the substance of the requested admission, and when good faith requires that a party qualify an answer or deny only a part of the matter of which an admission is requested, the party shall specify so much of it as is true and qualify or deny the remainder. An answering party may not give lack of information or knowledge as a reason for failure to admit or deny unless the party states that the party has made reasonable inquiry and that the information known or readily obtainable by the party is insufficient to enable the party to admit or deny. A party who considers that a matter of which an admission has been requested presents a genuine issue for trial may not, on that ground alone, object to the request; the party may, subject to the provisions of Rule 37(c), deny the matter or set forth reasons why the party cannot admit or deny it.

The party who has requested the admissions may move to determine the sufficiency of the answers or objections. Unless the court determines that an objection is justified, it shall order that an answer be served. If the court determines that an answer does not comply with the requirements of this rule, it may order either that the matter is admitted or that an amended answer be served. The court may, in lieu of these orders, determine that final disposition of the request be made at a pre-trial conference or at a designated time prior to trial. The provisions of Rule 37(a)(4) apply to the award of expenses incurred in relation to the motion.

(b) Effect of Admission. Any matter admitted under this rule is conclusively established unless the court on motion permits withdrawal or amendment of the admission. Subject to the provisions of Rule 16 governing amendment of a pre-trial order, the court may permit withdrawal or amendment when the presentation of the merits of the action will be subserved thereby and the party who obtained the admission fails to satisfy the court that withdrawal or amendment will prejudice that party in maintaining the action or defense on the merits. Any admission made by a party under this rule is for the purpose of the pending action only and is not an admission for any other purpose nor may it be used against the party in any other proceeding.

As amended Dec. 27, 1946, eff. Mar. 19, 1948; Mar. 30, 1970, eff. July 1, 1970; Mar. 2, 1987, eff. Aug. 1, 1987; Apr. 22, 1993, eff. Dec. 1, 1993.

Advisory Committee Notes, 1970 Amendments

Rule 36 serves two vital purposes, both of which are designed to reduce trial time. Admissions are sought, first to facilitate proof with respect to issues that cannot be eliminated from the case, and secondly, to narrow the issues by eliminating those that can be. The changes made in the rule are designed to serve these purposes more effectively. Certain disagreements in the courts about the proper scope of the rule are resolved. In addition, the procedural operation of the rule is brought into line with other discovery procedures, and the binding effect of an admission is clarified. See generally Finman, The Request for Admissions in Federal Civil Procedure, 71 Yale L.J. 371 (1962).

Subdivision (a). As revised, the subdivision provides that a request may be made to admit any matters within the scope of Rule 26(b) that relate to statements or opinions of fact or of the application of law to fact. It thereby eliminates the requirement that the matters be "of fact." This change resolves conflicts in the court decisions as to whether a request to admit matters of "opinion" and matters involving "mixed law and fact" is proper under the rule. . . .

Not only is it difficult as a practical matter to separate "fact" from "opinion," see 4 Moore's Federal Practice ¶236.04 (2d ed. 1966); cf. 2A Barron & Holtzoff, Federal Practice and Procedure 317 (Wright ed. 1961), but an admission on a matter of opinion may facilitate proof or narrow the issues or both. An admission of a matter involving the application of law to fact may, in a given case, even more clearly narrow the issues. For example, an admission that an employee acted in the scope of his employment may remove a major issue from the trial. In McSparran v. Hanigan, plaintiff admitted that "the premises on which said accident occurred, were occupied or under the control" of one of the defendants, 225 F. Supp. at 636. This admission, involving law as well as fact, removed one of the issues from the lawsuit and thereby reduced the proof required at trial. The amended provision does not authorize requests for admissions of law unrelated to the facts of the case.

Requests for admission involving the application of law to fact may create disputes between the parties which are best resolved in the presence of the judge after much or all of the other discovery has been completed. Power is therefore expressly conferred upon the court to defer decision until a pretrial conference is held or until a designated time prior to trial. On the other hand, the court should not automatically defer decision; in many instances, the importance of the admission lies in enabling the requesting party to avoid the burdensome accumulation of proof prior to the pretrial conference.

Courts have also divided on whether an answering party may properly object to request for admission as to matters which that party regards as "in dispute." Compare, e.g., Syracuse Broadcasting Corp. v. Newhouse, 271 F.2d 910, 917 (2d Cir. 1959); Driver v. Gindy Mfg. Corp., 24 F.R.D. 473 (E.D. Pa. 1959); with, e.g., McGonigle v. Baxter, 27 F.R.D. 504 (E.D. Pa. 1961); United States v. Ehbauer, 13 F.R.D. 462 (W.D. Mo. 1952). The proper response in such cases is an answer. The very purpose of the request is to ascertain whether the answering party is prepared to admit or regards the matter as presenting a genuine issue for trial. In his answer, the party may deny, or he may give as his reason for inability to admit or deny the existence of a genuine issue. The party runs no risk of sanctions if the matter is genuinely in issue, since Rule 37(c) provides a sanction of costs only when there are no good reasons for a failure to admit.

On the other hand, requests to admit may be so voluminous and so framed that the answering party finds the task of identifying what is in dispute and what is not unduly burdensome. If so, the responding party may obtain a protective order under Rule 26(c). Some of the decisions sustaining objections on "disputability" grounds could have been justified by the burdensome character of the requests. See, e.g., Syracuse Broadcasting Corp. v. Newhouse, supra.

Another sharp split of authority exists on the question whether a party may base his answer on lack of information or knowledge without seeking out additional information. . . .

The rule as revised adopts the majority view, as in keeping with a basic principle of the discovery rules that a reasonable burden may be imposed on the parties when its discharge will facilitate preparation for trial and ease the trial process. It has been argued against this view that one side should not have the burden of "proving" the other side's case. The revised rule requires only that the answering party make reasonable inquiry and secure such knowledge and information as are readily obtainable by him. In most instances, the investigation will be necessary either to his own case or to preparation for rebuttal. Even when it is not, the information may be close enough at hand to be "readily obtainable." Rule 36 requires only that the party state that he has taken these steps. The sanction for failure of a party to inform himself before he answers lies in the award of costs after trial, as provided in Rule 37(c). . . .

Rule 37. Failure to Make or Cooperate in Discovery: Sanctions

(a) Motion For Order Compelling Disclosure or Discovery. A party, upon reasonable notice to other parties and all persons affected thereby, may apply for an order compelling disclosure or discovery as follows:

(1) Appropriate Court. An application for an order to a party shall be made to the court in which the action is pending. An application for an order to a person who is not a party shall be made to the court in the district where the discovery is being, or is to be, taken.

(2) Motion.

(A) If a party fails to make a disclosure required by Rule 26(a), any other party may move to compel disclosure and for appropriate sanctions. The motion must include a certification that the movant has in good faith conferred or attempted to confer with the party not making the disclosure in an effort to secure the disclosure without court action.

(B) If a deponent fails to answer a question propounded or submitted under Rules 30 or 31, or a corporation or other entity fails to make a designation under Rule 30(b)(6) or 31(a), or a party fails to answer an interrogatory submitted under Rule 33, or if a party, in response to a request for inspection submitted under Rule 34, fails to respond that inspection will be permitted as requested or fails to permit inspection as requested, the discovering party may move for an order compelling an answer, or a designation, or an order compelling inspection in accordance with the request. The motion must include a certification that the movant has in good faith conferred or attempted to confer with the person or party failing to make the discovery in an effort to secure the information or material without court action. When taking a deposition on oral examination, the proponent of the question may complete or adjourn the examination before applying for an order.

(3) Evasive or Incomplete Disclosure, Answer, or Response. For purposes of this subdivision an evasive or incomplete disclosure, answer, or response is to be treated as a failure to disclose, answer, or respond.

(4) Expenses and Sanctions.

(A) If the motion is granted or if the disclosure or requested discovery is provided after the motion was filed, the court shall, after affording an opportunity to be heard, require the party or deponent whose conduct necessitated the motion or the party or attorney advising such conduct or both of them to pay to the moving party the reasonable expenses incurred in making the motion, including attorney's fees, unless the court finds that the motion was filed without the movant's first making a good faith effort to obtain the disclosure or discovery without court action, or that the opposing party's nondisclosure, response, or objection was substantially justified, or that other circumstances make an award of expenses unjust.

(B) If the motion is denied, the court may enter any protective order authorized under Rule 26(c) and shall, after affording an opportunity to be heard, require the moving party or the attorney filing the motion or both of them to pay to the party or deponent who opposed the motion the reasonable expenses incurred in opposing the motion, including attorney's fees, unless the court finds that the making of the motion was substantially justified or that other circumstances make an award of expenses unjust.

(C) If the motion is granted in part and denied in part, the court may enter any protective order authorized under Rule 26(c) and may, after affording an opportunity to be heard, apportion the reasonable expenses incurred in relation to the motion among the parties and persons in a just manner.

(b) Failure to Comply with Order.

(1) Sanctions by Court in District Where Deposition Is Taken. If a deponent fails to be sworn or to answer a question after being directed to do so by the court in the district in which the deposition is being taken, the failure may be considered a contempt of that court.

(2) Sanctions by Court in Which Action Is Pending. If a party or an officer, director, or managing agent of a party or a person designated under Rule 30(b)(6) or 31(a) to testify on behalf of a party fails to obey an order to provide or permit discovery, including an order made under subdivision (a) of this rule or Rule 35,

or if a party fails to obey an order entered under Rule 26(f), the court in which the action is pending may make such orders in regard to the failure as are just, and among others the following:

(A) An order that the matters regarding which the order was made or any other designated facts shall be taken to be established for the purposes of the action in accordance with the claim of the party obtaining the order;

(B) An order refusing to allow the disobedient party to support or oppose designated claims or defenses, or prohibiting that party from introducing designated matters in evidence;

(C) An order striking out pleadings or parts thereof, or staying further proceedings until the order is obeyed, or dismissing the action or proceeding or any part thereof, or rendering a judgment by default against the disobedient party;

(D) In lieu of any of the foregoing orders or in addition thereto, an order treating as a contempt of court the failure to obey any orders except an order to submit to a physical or mental examination;

(E) Where a party has failed to comply with an order under Rule 35(a) requiring that party to produce another for examination, such orders as are listed in paragraphs (A), (B), and (C) of this subdivision, unless the party failing to comply shows that that party is unable to produce such person for examination.

In lieu of any of the foregoing orders or in addition thereto, the court shall require the party failing to obey the order or the attorney advising that party or both to pay the reasonable expenses, including attorney's fees, caused by the failure, unless the court finds that the failure was substantially justified or that other circumstances make an award of expenses unjust.

(c) Failure to Disclose; False or Misleading Disclosure; Refusal to Admit.

(1) A party that without substantial justification fails to disclose information required by Rule 26(a) or 26(e)(1), or to amend a prior response to discovery as required by 26(e)(2) is not, unless such failure is harmless, permitted to use as evidence at a trial, at a hearing, or on a motion any witness or information not so disclosed. In addition to or in lieu of this sanction, the court, on motion and after affording an opportunity to be heard, may impose other appropriate sanctions. In addition to requiring payment of reasonable expenses, including attorney's fees, caused by the failure, these sanctions may include any of the actions authorized under Rule 37(b)(2) and may include informing the jury of the failure to make the disclosure.

(2) If a party fails to admit the genuineness of any document or the truth of any matter as requested under Rule 36, and if the party requesting the admissions thereafter proves the genuineness of the document or the truth of the matter, the requesting party may apply to the court for an order requiring the other party to pay the reasonable expenses incurred in making that proof, including reasonable attorney's fees. The court shall make the order unless it finds that (A) the request

was held objectionable pursuant to Rule 36(a), or (B) the admission sought was of no substantial importance, or (C) the party failing to admit had reasonable ground to believe that the party might prevail on the matter, or (D) there was other good reason for the failure to admit.

(d) Failure of Party to Attend at Own Deposition or Serve Answers to Interrogatories or Respond to Request for Inspection. If a party or an officer, director, or managing agent of a party or a person designated under Rule 30(b)(6) or 31(a) to testify on behalf of a party fails (1) to appear before the officer who is to take the deposition, after being served with a proper notice, or (2) to serve answers or objections to interrogatories submitted under Rule 33, after proper service of the interrogatories, or (3) to serve a written response to a request for inspection submitted under Rule 34, after proper service of the request, the court in which the action is pending on motion may make such orders in regard to the failure as are just, and among others it may take any action authorized under subparagraphs (A), (B), and (C) of subdivision (b)(2) of this rule. Any motion specifying a failure under clause (2) or (3) of this subdivision shall include a certification that the movant has in good faith conferred or attempted to confer with the party failing to answer or respond in an effort to obtain such answer or response without court action. In lieu of any order or in addition thereto, the court shall require the party failing to act or the attorney advising that party or both to pay the reasonable expenses, including attorney's fees, caused by the failure unless the court finds that the failure was substantially justified or that other circumstances make an award of expenses unjust.

The failure to act described in this subdivision may not be excused on the ground that the discovery sought is objectionable unless the party failing to act has a pending motion for a protective order as provided by Rule 26(c).

(e) Subpoena of Person in Foreign Country. [*Abrogated.*]

(f) Expenses Against United States. Repealed. Pub. L. 69-481, Title II, §205(a), eff. Oct. 1, 1981, 94 Stat. 2330.

(g) Failure to Participate in the Framing of a Discovery Plan. If a party or a party's attorney fails to participate in good faith in the development and submission of a proposed discovery plan as required by Rule 26(f), the court may, after opportunity for hearing, require such party or attorney to pay to any other party the reasonable expenses, including attorney's fees, caused by the failure.

As amended Dec. 29, 1948, eff. Oct. 20, 1949; Mar. 30, 1970, eff. July 1, 1970; Apr. 29, 1980, eff. Aug. 1, 1980; Pub. L. 96-481, Title II, §205(a), Oct 21, 1980, 94 Stat. 2330; Mar. 2, 1987, eff. Aug. 1, 1987; Apr. 22, 1993, eff. Dec. 1, 1993.

ADVISORY COMMITTEE NOTES, 1993 AMENDMENTS

Subdivision (a). . . .

Under revised paragraph (3), evasive or incomplete disclosures and responses to interrogatories and production requests are treated as failures to disclose or respond. Interrogatories and requests for production should not be read or interpreted in an artificially restrictive or hypertechnical manner to avoid disclosure of information fairly covered by the discovery request, and to do so is subject to appropriate sanctions under subdivision (a). . . .

Subdivision (c). The revision provides a self-executing sanction for failure to make a disclosure required by Rule 26(a), without need for a motion under subdivision (a)(2)(A).

Paragraph (1) prevents a party from using as evidence any witnesses or information that, without substantial justification, has not been disclosed as required by Rules 26(a) and 26(e)(1). This automatic sanction provides a strong inducement for disclosure of material that the disclosing party would expect to use as evidence, whether at a trial, at a hearing, or on a motion, such as one under Rule 56. As disclosure of evidence offered solely for impeachment purposes is not required under those rules, this preclusion sanction likewise does not apply to that evidence. . . .

VI. Trials

Rule 38. Jury Trial of Right

(a) Right Preserved. The right of trial by jury as declared by the Seventh Amendment to the Constitution or as given by a statute of the United States shall be preserved to the parties inviolate.

(b) Demand. Any party may demand a trial by jury of any issue triable of right by a jury by (1) serving upon the other parties a demand therefor in writing at any time after the commencement of the action and not later than 10 days after the service of the last pleading directed to such issue, and (2) filing and demand as required by Rule 5(d). Such demand may be indorsed upon a pleading of the party.

(c) Same: Specification of Issues. In the demand a party may specify the issues which the party wishes so tried; otherwise the party shall be deemed to have demanded trial by jury for all the issues so triable. If the party has demanded trial by jury for only some of the issues, any other party within 10 days after service of the demand or such lesser time as the court may order, may serve a demand for trial by jury of any other or all of the issues of fact in the action.

(d) Waiver. The failure of a party to serve and file a demand as required by this rule constitutes a waiver by the party of trial by jury. A demand for trial by jury made as herein provided may not be withdrawn without the consent of the parties.

(e) Admiralty and Maritime Claims. These rules shall not be construed to create a right to trial by jury of the issues in an admiralty or maritime claim within the meaning of Rule 9(h).

As amended Feb. 28, 1966, eff. July 1, 1966; Mar. 2, 1987, eff. Aug. 1, 1987; Apr. 22, 1993, eff. Dec. 1, 1993.

Rule 39. Trial by Jury or by the Court

(a) By Jury. When trial by jury has been demanded as provided in Rule 38, the action shall be designated upon the docket as a jury action. The trial of all issues so demanded shall be by jury, unless (1) the parties or their attorneys of record, by written stipulation filed with the court or by an oral stipulation made in open court and entered in the record, consent to trial by the court sitting without a jury or (2) the court upon motion or of its own initiative finds that a right of trial by jury of some or all of those issues does not exist under the Constitution or statutes of the United States.

(b) By the Court. Issues not demanded for trial by jury as provided in Rule 38 shall be tried by the court; but, notwithstanding the failure of a party to demand a jury in an action in which such a demand might have been made of right, the court in its discretion upon motion may order a trial by a jury of any or all issues.

(c) Advisory Jury and Trial by Consent. In all actions not triable of right by a jury the court upon motion or of its own initiative may try any issue with an advisory jury or, except in actions against the United States when a statute of the United States provides for trial without a jury, the court, with the consent of both parties, may order a trial with a jury whose verdict has the same effect as if trial by jury had been a matter of right.

Rule 40. Assignment of Cases for Trial

The district courts shall provide by rule for the placing of actions upon the trial calendar (1) without request of the parties or (2) upon request of a party and notice to the other parties or (3) in such other manner as the courts deem expedient. Precedence shall be given to actions entitled thereto by any statute of the United States.

Rule 41. Dismissal of Actions

(a) Voluntary Dismissal: Effect Thereof.

(1) By Plaintiff; by Stipulation. Subject to the provisions of Rule 23(e), of Rule 66, and of any statute of the United States, an action may be dismissed by the plaintiff without order of court (i) by filing a notice of dismissal at any time before service by the adverse party of an answer or of a motion for summary judgment, whichever first occurs, or (ii) by filing a stipulation of dismissal signed by all parties who have appeared in the action. Unless otherwise stated in the notice of dismissal or stipulation, the dismissal is without prejudice, except that a notice of dismissal operates as an adjudication upon the merits when filed by a plaintiff who has once dismissed in any court of the United States or of any state an action based on or including the same claim.

(2) By Order of Court. Except as provided in paragraph (1) of this subdivision of this rule, an action shall not be dismissed at the plaintiff's instance save upon order of the court and upon such terms and conditions as the court deems proper. If a counterclaim has been pleaded by a defendant prior to the service upon the defendant of the plaintiff's motion to dismiss, the action shall not be dismissed against the defendant's objection unless the counterclaim can remain pending for independent adjudication by the court. Unless otherwise specified in the order, a dismissal under this paragraph is without prejudice.

(b) Involuntary Dismissal: Effect Thereof. For failure of the plaintiff to prosecute or to comply with these rules or any order of court, a defendant may move for dismissal of an action or of any claim against the defendant. Unless the court in its order for dismissal otherwise specifies, a dismissal under this subdivision and any dismissal not provided for in this rule, other than a dismissal for lack of jurisdiction, for improper venue, or for failure to join a party under Rule 19, operates as an adjudication upon the merits.

(c) Dismissal of Counterclaim, Cross-Claim, or Third-Party Claim. The provisions of this rule apply to the dismissal of any counterclaim, cross-claim, or third-party claim. A voluntary dismissal by the claimant alone pursuant to paragraph (1) of subdivision (a) of this rule shall be made before a responsive pleading is served or, if there is none, before the introduction of evidence at the trial or hearing.

(d) Costs of Previously Dismissed Action. If a plaintiff who has once dismissed an action in any court commences an action based upon or including the same claim against the same defendant, the court may make such order for the payment of costs of the action previously dismissed as it may deem proper and may stay the proceedings in the action until the plaintiff has complied with the order. As amended Dec. 27, 1946, eff. Mar. 19, 1948; Jan. 21, 1963, eff. July

1, 1963; Feb. 28, 1966, eff. July 1, 1966; Dec. 4, 1967, eff. July 1, 1968; Mar 2, 1987, eff. Aug. 1, 1987; Apr. 30, 1991, eff. Dec. 1, 1991.

Rule 42. Consolidation; Separate Trials

(a) **Consolidation.** When actions involving a common question of law or fact are pending before the court, it may order a joint hearing or trial of any or all the matters in issue in the actions; it may order all the actions consolidated; and it may make such orders concerning proceedings therein as may tend to avoid unnecessary costs or delay.

(b) **Separate Trials.** The court, in furtherance of convenience or to avoid prejudice, or when separate trials will be conducive to expedition and economy, may order a separate trial of any claim, cross-claim, counterclaim, or third-party claim, or of any separate issue or of any number of claims, cross-claims, counterclaims, third-party claims, or issues, always preserving inviolate the right of trial by jury as declared by the Seventh Amendment to the Constitution or as given by a statute of the United States.

As amended Feb. 28, 1966, eff. July 1, 1966.

Rule 43. Taking of Testimony

(a) **Form.** In every trial, the testimony of witnesses shall be taken in open court unless a federal law, these rules, the Federal Rules of Evidence, or other rules adopted by the Supreme Court provide otherwise. The court may, for good cause shown in compelling circumstances and upon appropriate safeguards, permit presentation of testimony in open court by contemporaneous transmission from a different location.

(b) **Scope of Examination and Cross-Examination.** [*Abrogated.*]

(c) **Record of Excluded Evidence.** [*Abrogated.*]

(d) **Affirmation in Lieu of Oath.** Whenever under these rules an oath is required to be taken, a solemn affirmation may be accepted in lieu thereof.

(e) **Evidence on Motions.** When a motion is based on facts not appearing of record the court may hear the matter on affidavits presented by the respective parties, but the court may direct that the matter be heard wholly or partly on oral testimony or depositions.

(f) **Interpreters.** The court may appoint an interpreter of its own selection and may fix the interpreter's reasonable compensation. The compensation shall be paid out of funds provided by law or by one or more of the parties as the court may direct, and may be taxed ultimately as costs, in the discretion of the court.

As amended Feb. 28, 1966, eff. July 1, 1966; Nov. 20, 1972, eff. July 1, 1975; Dec. 18, 1972, eff. July 1, 1975; Mar. 2, 1987, eff. Aug. 1, 1987; Apr. 23, 1996, eff. Dec. 1, 1996.

Rule 44. Proof of Official Record

(a) **Authentication.**

(1) ***Domestic.*** An official record kept within the United States, or any state, district, or commonwealth, or within a territory subject to the administrative or judicial jurisdiction of the United States or an entry therein, when admissible for any purpose, may be evidenced by an official publication thereof or by a copy attested by the officer having the legal custody of the record, or by the officer's deputy, and accompanied by a certificate that such officer has the custody. The certificate may be made by a judge of a court of record of the district or political subdivision in which the record is kept, authenticated by the seal of the court, or may be made by any public officer having a seal of office and having official duties in the district or political subdivision in which the record is kept, authenticated by the seal of the officer's office.

(2) ***Foreign.*** A foreign official record, or an entry therein, when admissible for any purpose, may be evidenced by an official publication thereof; or a copy thereof, attested by a person authorized to make the attestation, and accompanied by a final certification as to the genuineness of the signature and official position (i) of the attesting person, or (ii) of any foreign official whose certificate of genuineness of signature and official position relates to the attestation or is in a chain of certificates of genuineness of signature and offical position relating to the attestation. A final certification may be made by a secretary of embassy or legation, consul general, consul, vice consul, or consular agent of the United States, or a diplomatic or consular official of the foreign country assigned or accredited to the United States. If reasonable opportunity has been given to all parties to investigate the authenticity and accuracy of the documents, the court may, for good cause shown, (i) admit an attested copy without final certification or (ii) permit the foreign official record to be evidenced by an attested summary with or without a final certification. The final certification is unnecessary if the record and the attestation are certified as provided in a treaty or convention to which the United States and the foreign country in which the official record is located are parties.

(b) Lack of Record. A written statement that after diligent search no record or entry of a specified tenor is found to exist in the records designated by the statement, authenticated as provided in subdivision (a)(1) of this rule in the case of a domestic record, or complying with the requirements of subdivision (a)(2) of this rule for a summary in the case of a foreign record, is admissible as evidence that the records contain no such record or entry.

(c) Other Proof. This rule does not prevent the proof of official records or of entry or lack of entry therein by any other method authorized by law.

As amended Feb. 28, 1966, eff. July 1, 1966; Mar. 2, 1987, eff. Aug. 1, 1987; Apr. 30, 1991, eff. Dec. 1, 1991.

Rule 44.1. Determination of Foreign Law

A party who intends to raise an issue concerning the law of a foreign country shall give notice by pleadings or other reasonable written notice. The court, in determining foreign law, may consider any relevant material or source, including testimony, whether or not submitted by a party or admissible under the Federal Rules of Evidence. The court's determination shall be treated as a ruling on a question of law.

Added Feb. 28, 1966, eff. July 1, 1966; as amended Nov. 20, 1972, and expressly approved by P.L. 93-595, eff. July 1, 1975; Mar. 2, 1987, eff. Aug. 1, 1987.

Rule 45. Subpoena

(a) Form; Issuance.

(1) Every subpoena shall

(A) state the name of the court from which it is issued; and

(B) state the title of the action, the name of the court in which it is pending, and its civil action number; and

(C) command each person to whom it is directed to attend and give testimony or to produce and permit inspection and copying of designated books, documents or tangible things in the possession, custody or control of that person, or to permit inspection of premises, at a time and place therein specified; and

(D) set forth the text of subdivisions (c) and (d) of this rule.

A command to produce evidence or to permit inspection may be joined with a command to appear at trial or hearing or at deposition, or may be issued separately.

(2) A subpoena commanding attendance at a trial or hearing shall issue from the court for the district in which the hearing or trial is to be held. A

subpoena for attendance at a deposition shall issue from the court for the district designated by the notice of deposition as the district in which the deposition is to be taken. If separate from a subpoena commanding the attendance of a person, a subpoena for production or inspection shall issue from the court for the district in which the production or inspection is to be made.

(3) The clerk shall issue a subpoena, signed but otherwise in blank, to a party requesting it, who shall complete it before service. An attorney as officer of the court may also issue and sign a subpoena on behalf of

(A) a court in which the attorney is authorized to practice; or

(B) a court for a district in which a deposition or production is compelled by the subpoena, if the deposition or production pertains to an action pending in a court in which the attorney is authorized to practice.

(b) Service.

(1) A subpoena may be served by any person who is not a party and is not less than 18 years of age. Service of a subpoena upon a person named therein shall be made by delivering a copy thereof to such person and, if the person's attendance is commanded, by tendering to that person the fees for one day's attendance and the mileage allowed by law. When the subpoena is issued on behalf of the United States or an officer or agency thereof, fees and mileage need not be tendered. Prior notice of any commanded production of documents and things or inspection of premises before trial shall be served on each party in the manner prescribed by Rule 5(b).

(2) Subject to the provisions of clause (ii) of subparagraph (c)(3)(A) of this rule, a subpoena may be served at any place within the district of the court by which it is issued, or at any place without the district that is within 100 miles of the place of the deposition, hearing, trial, production, or inspection specified in the subpoena or at any place within the state where a state statute or rule of court permits service of a subpoena issued by a state court of general jurisdiction sitting in the place of the deposition, hearing, trial, production, or inspection specified in the subpoena. When a statute of the United States provides therefor, the court upon proper application and cause shown may authorize the service of a subpoena at any other place. A subpoena directed to a witness in a foreign country who is a national or resident of the United States shall issue under the circumstances and in the manner and be served as provided in Title 28, U.S.C. §1783.

(3) Proof of service when necessary shall be made by filing with the clerk of the court by which the subpoena is issued a statement of the date and manner of service and of the names of the persons served, certified by the person who made the service.

(c) Protection of Persons Subject to Subpoenas.

(1) A party or an attorney responsible for the issuance and service of a subpoena shall take reasonable steps to avoid imposing undue burden or expense

on a person subject to that subpoena. The court on behalf of which the subpoena was issued shall enforce this duty and impose upon the party or attorney in breach of this duty an appropriate sanction, which may include, but is not limited to, lost earnings and a reasonable attorney's fee.

(2)(A) A person commanded to produce and permit inspection and copying of designated books, papers, documents or tangible things, or inspection of premises need not appear in person at the place of production or inspection unless commanded to appear for deposition, hearing or trial.

(B) Subject to paragraph (d)(2) of this rule, a person commanded to produce and permit inspection and copying may, within 14 days after service of the subpoena or before the time specified for compliance if such time is less than 14 days after service, serve upon the party or attorney designated in the subpoena written objection to inspection or copying of any or all of the designated materials or of the premises. If objection is made, the party serving the subpoena shall not be entitled to inspect and copy the materials or inspect the premises except pursuant to an order of the court by which the subpoena was issued. If objection has been made, the party serving the subpoena may, upon notice to the person commanded to produce, move at any time for an order to compel the production. Such an order to compel production shall protect any person who is not a party or an officer of a party from significant expense resulting from the inspection and copying commanded.

(3)(A) On timely motion, the court by which a subpoena was issued shall quash or modify the subpoena if it

(i) fails to allow reasonable time for compliance;

(ii) requires a person who is not a party or an officer of a party to travel to a place more than 100 miles from the place where that person resides, is employed or regularly transacts business in person, except that, subject to the provisions of clause (c)(3)(B)(iii) of this rule, such a person may in order to attend trial be commanded to travel from any such place within the state in which the trial is held, or

(iii) requires disclosure of privileged or other protected matter and no exception or waiver applies, or

(iv) subjects a person to undue burden.

(B) If a subpoena

(i) requires disclosure of a trade secret or other confidential research, development, or commercial information, or

(ii) requires disclosure of an unretained expert's opinion or information not describing specific events or occurrences in dispute and resulting from the expert's study made not at the request of any party, or

(iii) requires a person who is not a party or an officer of a party to incur substantial expense to travel more than 100 miles to attend trial,

The court may, to protect a person subject to or affected by the subpoena, quash or modify the subpoena or, if the party in whose behalf the subpoena is issued shows a substantial need for the testimony or material that cannot be otherwise met without undue hardship and assures that the person to whom the subpoena is addressed will be reasonably compensated, the court may order appearance or production only upon specified conditions.

(d) Duties in Responding to Subpoena.

(1) A person responding to a subpoena to produce documents shall produce them as they are kept in the usual course of business or shall organize and label them to correspond with the categories in the demand.

(2) When information subject to a subpoena is withheld on a claim that it is privileged or subject to protection as trial preparation materials, the claim shall be made expressly and shall be supported by a description of the nature of the documents, communications, or things not produced that is sufficient to enable the demanding party to contest the claim.

(e) Contempt. Failure by any person without adequate excuse to obey a subpoena served upon that person may be deemed a contempt of the court from which the subpoena issued. An adequate cause for failure to obey exists when a subpoena purports to require a non-party to attend or produce at a place not within the limits provided by clause (ii) of subparagraph (c)(3)(A)

As amended Dec. 27, 1946, eff. Mar. 19, 1948; Dec. 29, 1948, eff. Oct. 20, 1949; Mar. 30, 1970, eff. July 1, 1970; Apr. 29, 1980, eff. Aug. 1, 1980; Apr. 29, 1985, eff. Aug. 1, 1985; Mar. 2, 1987, eff. Aug. 1, 1987; Apr. 30, 1991, eff. Dec. 1, 1991.

ADVISORY COMMITTEE NOTES, 1991 AMENDMENTS

Purposes of Revision. The purposes of this revision are (1) to clarify and enlarge the protections afforded persons who are required to assist the court by giving information or evidence; (2) to facilitate access outside the deposition procedure provided by Rule 30 to documents and other information in the possession of persons who are not parties; (3) to facilitate service of subpoenas for depositions or productions of evidence at places distant from the district in which an action is proceeding; (4) to enable the court to compel a witness found within the state in which the court sits to attend trial; (5) to clarify the organizations of the text of the rule. . . .

Paragraph (a)(3) authorizes attorneys in distant districts to serve as officers authorized to issue commands in the name of the court. Any attorney permitted to represent a client in a federal court, even one admitted pro haec vice, has the same authority as a clerk to issue a subpoena from any federal court for the district in which the subpoena is served and enforced. In authorizing attorneys to issue subpoenas from distant courts, the amended rule effectively authorizes service of a subpoena anywhere in the United States by an attorney representing any party. This change is intended to ease the administrative burdens of inter-district law practice. The former rule resulted in delay and expense caused by the need to secure forms from clerks' offices some distance from the place at which the action proceeds. This change does not enlarge the burden on the witness. . . .

[T]he revised rule [also] authorizes the issuance of a subpoena to compel the inspection of premises in the possession of a non-party. Rule 34 has authorized such inspections of premises in the possession of a party as discovery compelled under Rule 37, but prior practice required an independent proceeding to secure such relief ancillary to the federal proceeding when the premises were not in the possession of a party. Practice in some states has long authorized such use of a subpoena for this purpose without apparent adverse consequence. . . .

Subparagraph (c)(3)(A) identifies those circumstances in which a subpoena must be quashed or modified. It restates the former provisions with respect to the limits of mandatory travel that are set forth in the former paragraphs (d)(2) and (e)(1), with one important change. Under the revised rule, a federal court can compel a witness to come from any place in the state to attend trial, whether or not the local state law so provides. This extension is subject to the qualification provided in the next paragraph, which authorizes the court to condition enforcement of a subpoena compelling a non-party witness to bear substantial expense to attend trial. The traveling non-party witness may be entitled to reasonable compensation for the time and effort entailed. . . .

Subdivision (c). . . .

A non-party required to produce documents or materials is protected against significant expense resulting from involuntary assistance to the court. This provision applies, for example, to a non-party required to provide a list of class members. The court is not required to fix the costs in advance of production, although this will often be the most satisfactory accommodation to protect the party seeking discovery from excessive costs. In some instances, it may be preferable to leave uncertain costs to be determined after the materials have been produced, provided that the risk of uncertainty is fully disclosed to the discovering party. See, e.g., United States v. Columbia Broadcasting Systems, Inc., 666 F.2d 364 (9th Cir. 1983). . . .

Clause (c)(3)(B)(ii) provides appropriate protection for the intellectual property of the non-party witness; it does not apply to the expert retained by the party, whose information is subject to the provisions of Rule 26(b)(4). A growing problem has been the use of subpoenas to compel the giving of evidence and information by unretained experts. Experts are not exempt from the duty to give evidence, even if they cannot be compelled to prepare themselves to give effective testimony, e.g., Carter-Wallace, Inc. v. Otte, 474 F.2d 529 (2d Cir. 1972), but compulsion to give evidence may threaten the intellectual property of experts denied the opportunity to bargain for the value of their [expertise] . . . Arguably the compulsion to testify can be regarded as a "taking" of intellectual property. The rule establishes the right of such persons to withhold their expertise, at least unless the party seeking it makes the kind of showing required for a conditional denial of a motion to quash as provided in the final sentence of subparagraph (c)(3)(B); that requirement is the same as that necessary to secure work product under rule 26(b)(3) and gives assurance of reasonable compensation. The Rule thus approves the accommodation of competing interests exemplified in United States v. Columbia Broadcasting

Systems, Inc., 666 F.2d 364 (9th Cir. 1982). See also Wright v. Jeep Corporation, 547 F. Supp. 871 (E.D. Mich. 1982). . . .

Subdivision (e). . . .

"Adequate cause" for a failure to obey a subpoena remains undefined. In at least some circumstances, a non-party might be guilty of contempt for refusing to obey a subpoena even though the subpoena manifestly overreaches the appropriate limits of the subpoena power. E.g., Walker v. City of Birmingham, 388 U.S. 307 (1967). But, because the command of the subpoena is not in fact one uttered by a judicial officer, contempt should be very sparingly applied when the non-party witness has been overborne by a party or attorney. The language added to subdivision (f) is intended to assure that result where a non-party has been commanded, on the signature of an attorney, to travel greater distances than can be compelled pursuant to this rule.

Rule 46. Exceptions Unnecessary

Formal exceptions to rulings or orders of the court are unnecessary; but for all purposes for which an exception has heretofore been necessary it is sufficient that a party, at the time the ruling or order of the court is made or sought, makes known to the court the action which the party desires the court to take or the party's objection to the action of the court and the grounds therefor; and, if a party has no opportunity to object to a ruling or order at the time it is made, the absence of an objection does not thereafter prejudice the party.

As amended Mar. 2, 1987, eff. Aug. 1, 1987.

Rule 47. Selection of Jurors

(a) **Examination of Jurors.** The court may permit the parties or their attorneys to conduct the examination of prospective jurors or may itself conduct the examination. In the latter event, the court shall permit the parties or their attorneys to supplement the examination by such further inquiry as it deems proper or shall itself submit to the prospective jurors such additional questions of the parties or their attorneys as it deems proper.

(b) **Peremptory Challenges.** The court shall allow the number of peremptory challenges provided by 28 U.S.C. §1870.

(c) **Excuse.** The court may for good cause excuse a juror from service during trial or deliberation.

As amended Feb. 28, 1966, eff. July 1, 1966; Apr. 30, 1991, eff. Dec. 1, 1991.

Rule 48. Number of Jurors — Participation in Verdict

The court shall seat a jury of not fewer than six and not more than twelve members and all jurors shall participate in the verdict unless excused from service by the court pursuant to Rule 47(c). Unless the parties otherwise stipulate, (1) the verdict shall be unanimous and (2) no verdict shall be taken from a jury reduced in size to fewer than six members.

As amended Apr. 30, 1991, eff. Dec. 1, 1991.

Advisory Committee Notes, 1991 Amendments

It appears that the minimum size of a jury consistent with the Seventh Amendment is six. Cf. Ballew v. Georgia, 435 U.S. 223 (1978) (holding that a conviction based on a jury of less than six is a denial of due process of law). If the parties agree to trial before a smaller jury, a verdict can be taken, but the parties should not other than in exceptional circumstances be encouraged to waive the right to a jury of six, not only because of the constitutional stature of the right, but also because smaller juries are more erratic and less effective in serving to distribute responsibility for the exercise of judicial power.

Because the institution of the alternate juror has been abolished by the proposed revision of Rule 47, it will ordinarily be prudent and necessary, in order to provide for sickness or disability among jurors, to seat more than six jurors. The use of jurors in excess of six increases the representativeness of the jury and harms no interest of a party. Ray v. Parkside Surgery Center, 13 F.R. Serv. 585 (6th cir. 1989).

If the court takes the precaution of seating a jury larger than six, an illness occurring during the deliberation period will not result in a mistrial, as it did formerly, because all seated jurors will participate in the verdict and a sufficient number will remain to render a unanimous verdict of six or more.

In exceptional circumstances, as where a jury suffers depletions during trial and deliberations that are greater than can reasonably be expected, the parties may agree to be bound by a verdict rendered by fewer than six jurors. The court should not, however, rely upon the availability of such an agreement, for the use of juries smaller than six is problematic for reasons fully explained in Ballew v. Georgia, supra.

Rule 49. Special Verdicts and Interrogatories

(a) Special Verdicts. The court may require a jury to return only a special verdict in the form of a special written finding upon each issue of fact. In that event the court may submit to the jury written questions susceptible of categorical or other brief answer or may submit written forms of the several special findings which might properly be made under the pleadings and evidence; or it may use such other method of submitting the issues and requiring the written findings thereon as it deems most appropriate. The court shall give to the jury such explanation and instruction concerning the matter thus submitted as may be necessary to enable the jury to make its findings upon each issue. If in so doing the court omits any issue of fact raised by the pleadings or by the evidence, each party waives the right to a trial by jury of the issue so omitted unless before the jury retires the party demands its submission to the jury. As to an issue omitted without such demand the court may make a finding; or, if it fails to do so, it shall be deemed to have made a finding in accord with the judgment on the special verdict.

(b) General Verdict Accompanied by Answer to Interrogatories. The court may submit to the jury, together with appropriate forms for a general verdict, written interrogatories upon one or more issues of fact the decision of which is necessary to a verdict. The court shall give such explanation or instruction as may be necessary to enable the jury both to make answers to the interrogatories and to render a general verdict, and the court shall direct the jury both to make written answers and to render a general verdict. When the general verdict and the answers are harmonious, the appropriate judgment upon the verdict and answers shall be entered pursuant to Rule 58. When the answers are consistent with each other but one or more is inconsistent with the general verdict, judgment may be entered pursuant to Rule 58 in accordance with the answers, notwithstanding the general verdict, or the court may return the jury for further consideration of its answers and verdict or may order a new trial. When the answers are inconsistent with each other and one or more is likewise inconsistent with the general verdict, judgment shall not be entered, but the court shall return the jury for further consideration of its answers and verdict or shall order a new trial.

As amended Jan. 21, 1963, eff. July 1, 1963; Mar. 2, 1987, eff. Aug. 1, 1987.

Rule 50. Judgment as a Matter of Law in Jury Trials; Alternative Motion for New Trial; Conditional Rulings

(a) Judgment as a Matter of Law.

(1) If during a trial by jury a party has been fully heard on an issue and there is no legally sufficient evidentiary basis for a reasonable jury to find for that party on that issue, the court may determine the issue against that party and may grant a motion for judgment as a matter of law against that party with respect to a claim or defense that cannot under the controlling law be maintained or defeated without a favorable finding on that issue.

(2) Motions for judgment as a matter of law may be made at any time before submission of the case to the jury. Such a motion shall specify the judgment sought and the law and the facts on which the moving party is entitled to the judgment.

(b) Renewing Motion for Judgment After Trial; Alternative Motion for New Trial. If, for any reason, the court does not grant a motion for a judgment as a matter of law made at the close of all the evidence, the court is considered to have submitted the action to the jury subject to the court's later deciding the legal questions raised by the motion. The movant may renew its request for judgment as a matter of law by filing a motion no later than 10 days after entry of judgment and may alternatively request a new trial or join a motion for a new trial under Rule 59. In ruling on a renewed motion, the court may:

(1) if a verdict was returned:
  (A) allow the judgment to stand,
  (B) order a new trial, or
  (C) direct entry of judgment as a matter of law; or
(2) if no verdict was returned:
  (A) order a new trial, or
  (B) direct entry of judgment as a matter of law.

(c) Granting Renewed Motion for Judgment as a Matter of Law; Conditional Rulings; New Trial Motion.

(1) If the renewed motion for judgment as a matter of law is granted, the court shall also rule on the motion for a new trial, if any, by determining whether it should be granted if the judgment is thereafter vacated or reversed, and shall specify the grounds for granting or denying the motion for the new trial. If the motion for a new trial is thus conditionally granted, the order thereon does not affect the finality of the judgment. In case the motion for a new trial has been conditionally granted and the judgment is reversed on appeal, the new trial shall proceed unless the appellate court has otherwise ordered. In case the motion for a new trial has been conditionally denied, the appellee on appeal may assert error in that denial; and if the judgment is reversed on appeal, subsequent proceedings shall be in accordance with the order of the appellate court.

(2) Any motion for a new trial under Rule 59 by a party against whom judgment as a matter of law is rendered shall be filed no later than 10 days after entry of the judgment.

(d) Same: Denial of Motion for Judgment as a Matter of Law. If the motion for judgment as a matter of law is denied, the party who prevailed on that motion may, as appellee, assert grounds entitling the party to a new trial in the event the appellate court concludes that the trial court erred in denying the motion for judgment. If the appellate court reverses the judgment, nothing in this rule precludes it from determining that the appellee is entitled to a new trial, or from directing the trial court to determine whether a new trial shall be granted.

As amended Jan. 21, 1963, eff. July 1, 1963; Mar. 2, 1987, eff. Aug. 1, 1987; Apr. 30, 1991, eff. Dec. 1, 1991; Apr. 22, 1993, eff. Dec. 1, 1993; Apr. 27, 1995, eff. Dec. 1, 1995.

ADVISORY COMMITTEE NOTES, 1963, 1991, AND 1995 AMENDMENTS

1963 AMENDMENTS . . .

Subdivision (c) deals with the situation where a party joins a motion for a new trial with his motion for judgment n.o.v., or prays for a new trial in the alternative, and the motion for judgment n.o.v. is granted. The procedure to be followed in making rulings on the motion for the new trial, and the consequences of the rulings thereon, were partly set out in Montgomery Ward & Co. v. Duncan, 311 U.S. 243, 253 (1940), and have been further elaborated in later cases. . . . However, courts as well as counsel have often misunderstood the procedure, and it will be helpful to summarize the proper practice in the text of the rule. The amendments do not alter the effects of a jury verdict or the scope of appellate review.

In the situation mentioned, subdivision (c)(1) requires that the court make a "conditional" ruling on the new-trial motion, i.e., a ruling which goes on the assumption that the motion for judgment n.o.v. was erroneously granted and will be reversed or vacated; and the court is required to state its grounds for the conditional ruling. Subdivision (c)(1) then spells out the consequences of a reversal of the judgment in the light of the conditional ruling on the new-trial motion.

If the motion for new trial has been conditionally granted, and the judgment is reversed, "the new trial shall proceed unless the appellate court has otherwise ordered." The party against whom the judgment n.o.v. was entered below may, as appellant, besides seeking to overthrow that judgment, also attack the conditional grant of the new trial. And the appellate court, if it reverses the judgment n.o.v., may in an appropriate case also reverse the conditional grant of the new trial and direct that judgment be entered on the verdict. . . .

If the motion for a new trial has been conditionally denied, and the judgment is reversed, "subsequent proceedings shall be in accordance with the order of the appellate court." The party in whose favor judgment n.o.v. was entered below may, as appellee, besides seeking to uphold that judgment, also urge on the appellate court that the trial court committed error in conditionally denying the new trial. The appellee may assert this error in his brief, without taking a cross-appeal. . . . If the appellate court concludes that the judgment cannot stand, but accepts the appellee's contention that there was error in the conditional denial of the new trial, it may order a new trial in lieu of directing the entry of judgment upon the verdict.

Subdivision (c)(2), which also deals with the situation where the trial court has granted the motion for judgment n.o.v., states that the verdict-winner may apply to the trial court for a new trial pursuant to Rule 59 after the judgment n.o.v. has been entered against him. In arguing to the trial court in opposition to the motion for judgment n.o.v., the verdict-winner may, and often will, contend that he is entitled, at the least, to a new trial, and the court has a range of discretion to grant a new trial or (where plaintiff won the verdict) to order a dismissal of the action without prejudice instead of granting judgment n.o.v. . . .

Subdivision (d) deals with the situation where judgment has been entered on the jury verdict, the motion for judgment n.o.v. and any motion for a new trial having been denied by the trial court. The verdict-winner, as appellee, besides seeking to uphold the judgment, may urge upon the appellate court that in case the trial court is found to have erred in entering judgment on the verdict, there are grounds for granting him a new trial instead of directing the entry of judgment for his opponent. In appropriate cases the appellate court is not precluded from itself directing that a new trial be had. . . .

1991 AMENDMENTS

Subdivision (a). . . .

The revision abandons the familiar terminology of direction of verdict for several reasons. The term is misleading as a description of the relationship between judge and jury. It is also freighted with anachronisms some of which are the subject of the text of former subdivision (a) of this rule that is deleted in this revision. Thus, it should not be necessary to state in the text of this rule that a motion made pursuant to it is not a waiver of the right to jury trial, and only the antiquities of directed verdict practice suggest that it might have been. The term "judgment as a matter of law" is an almost equally familiar term and appears in the text of Rule 56; its use in Rule 50 calls attention to the relationship between the two rules. Finally, the change enables the rule to refer to preverdict and post-verdict motions with a terminology that does not conceal the common identity of two motions made at different times in the proceeding.

If a motion is denominated a motion for directed verdict or for judgment notwithstanding the verdict, the party's error is merely formal. Such a motion should be treated as a motion for judgment as a matter of law in accordance with this rule.

Paragraph (a)(1) articulates the standard for the granting of a motion for judgment as a matter of law. It effects no change in the existing standard. That existing standard was not expressed in the former rule, but was articulated in long-standing case law. See generally Cooper, Directions for Directed Verdicts: A Compass for Federal Courts, 55 Minn. L. Rev. 903 (1971). The expressed standard makes clear that action taken under the rule is a performance of the court's duty to assure enforcement of the controlling law and is not an intrusion on any responsibility for factual determinations conferred on the jury by the Seventh Amendment or any other provision of federal law. Because this standard is also used as a reference point for entry of summary judgment under 56(a), it serves to link the two related provisions. . . .

The second sentence of paragraph (a)(2) does impose a requirement that the moving party articulate the basis on which a judgment as a matter of law might be rendered. The articulation is necessary to achieve the purpose of the requirement that the motion be made before the case is submitted to the jury, so that the responding party may seek to correct any overlooked deficiencies in the proof. The revision thus alters the result in cases in which courts have used various techniques to avoid the requirement that a motion for a directed verdict be made as a predicate to a motion for judgment notwithstanding the verdict. E.g., Benson v. Allphin, 788 F.2d 268 (7th cir. 1986) ("this circuit has allowed something less than a formal motion for directed verdict to preserve a party's right to move for judgment notwithstanding the verdict"). See generally 9 Wright & Miller, Federal Practice and Procedure §2537 (1971 and Supp.). The information required with the motion may be supplied by explicit reference to materials and argument previously supplied to the court. . . .

Often it appears to the court or to the moving party that a motion for judgment as a matter of law made at the close of the evidence should be reserved for a post-verdict decision. This is so because a jury verdict for the moving party moots the issue and because a preverdict ruling gambles that a reversal may result in a new trial that might have been avoided. For these reasons, the court may often wisely decline to rule on a motion for judgment as a matter of law made at the close of the evidence, and it is not inappropriate for the moving party to suggest such a postponement of the ruling until after the verdict has been rendered.

1995 AMENDMENTS

The only change, other than stylistic, intended by this revision is to prescribe a uniform explicit time for filing of post-judgment motions under this rule — no later than 10 days after entry of the judgment. Previously, there was an inconsistency in the wording of Rules 50, 52, and 59 with respect to whether certain post-judgment motions had to be filed, or merely served, during that period. This inconsistency caused special problems when motions for a new trial were joined with other post-judgment motions. These motions affect the finality of the judgment, a matter often of importance to third persons as well as the parties and the court. The Committee believes that each of these rules should be revised to require filing before end of the 10-day period. Filing is an event that can be determined with certainty from court records. The phrase "no later than" is used — rather than "within" — to include post-judgment motions that sometimes are filed before actual entry of the judgment by the clerk. It should be noted that under Rule 6(a) Saturdays, Sundays, and legal holidays are excluded in measuring the 10-day period, and that under Rule 5 the motions when filed are to contain a certificate of service on other parties.

Rule 51. Instructions to Jury: Objection

At the close of the evidence or at such earlier time during the trial as the court reasonably directs, any party may file written requests that the court instruct the jury on the law as set forth in the requests. The court shall inform counsel of its proposed action upon the requests prior to their arguments to the jury. The court, at its election, may instruct the jury before or after argument, or both. No party may assign as error the giving or the failure to give an instruction unless that party objects thereto before the jury retires to consider its verdict, stating distinctly the matter objected to and the grounds of the objection. Opportunity shall be given to make the objection out of the hearing of the jury.

As amended Mar. 2, 1987, eff. Aug. 1, 1987.

Rule 52. Findings by the Court; Judgment on Partial Findings

(a) Effect. In all actions tried upon the facts without a jury or with an advisory jury, the court shall find the facts specially and state separately its conclusions of law thereon, and judgment shall be entered pursuant to Rule 58; and in granting or refusing interlocutory injunctions the court shall similarly set forth the findings of fact and conclusions of law which constitute the grounds of its action. Requests for findings are not necessary for purposes of review. Findings of fact, whether based on oral or documentary evidence, shall not be set aside unless clearly erroneous, and due regard shall be given to the opportunity of the trial court to judge of the credibility of the witnesses. The findings of a master, to the extent that the court adopts them, shall be considered as the findings of the court. It will be sufficient if the findings of fact and conclusions of law are stated orally and recorded in open court following the close of the evidence or appear in an opinion or memorandum of decision filed by the court. Findings of fact and conclusions of law are unnecessary on decisions of motions under Rules 12 or 56 or any other motion except as provided in subdivision (c) of this rule.

(b) Amendment. On a party's motion filed no later than 10 days after entry of judgment, the court may amend its findings — or make additional findings — and may amend the judgment accordingly. The motion may accompany a motion for a new trial under Rule 59. When findings of fact are made in actions tried without a jury, the sufficiency of the evidence supporting the findings may be later questioned whether or not in the district court the party raising the question objected to the findings, moved to amend them, or moved for partial findings.

(c) Judgment on Partial Findings. If during a trial without a jury a party has been fully heard on an issue and the court finds against the party on that issue, the court may enter judgment as a matter of law against that party with respect to a claim or defense that cannot under the controlling law be maintained or defeated without a favorable finding on that issue, or the court may decline to render any judgment until the close of all the evidence. Such a judgment shall be supported by findings of fact and conclusions of law as required by subdivision (a) of this rule.

As amended Dec. 27, 1946, eff. Mar. 19, 1948; Jan. 21, 1963, eff. July 1, 1963; Apr. 28, 1983, eff. Aug. 1, 1983; Apr. 29, 1985, eff. Aug. 1, 1985; Apr. 30, 1991, eff. Dec. 1, 1991; Apr. 22, 1993, eff. Dec. 1, 1993; Apr. 27, 1995, eff. Dec. 1, 1995.

Advisory Committee Notes, 1983, 1985 and 1991 Amendments

1983 amendments

Rule 52(a) has been amended to revise its penultimate sentence to provide explicitly that the district judge may make the findings of fact and conclusions of law required in nonjury cases orally. Nothing in the prior text of the rule forbids this practice, which is widely utilized by district judges. See Christensen, A Modest Proposal for Immeasurable Improvement, 64 A.B.A.J. 693 (1978). The objective is to lighten the burden on the trial court in preparing findings in nonjury cases. In addition, the amendment should reduce the number of published district court opinions that embrace written findings.

1985 AMENDMENTS

Rule 52(a) has been amended (1) to avoid continued confusion and conflicts among the circuits as to the standard of appellate review of findings of fact by the court, (2) to eliminate the disparity between the standard of review as literally stated in Rule 52(a) and the practice of some courts of appeals, and (3) to promote nationwide uniformity. See Note, Rule 52(a): Appellate Review of Findings of Fact Based on Documentary or Undisputed Evidence, 49 Va. L. Rev. 506, 536 (1963).

Some courts of appeal have stated that when a trial court's findings do not rest on demeanor evidence and evaluation of a witness' credibility, there is no reason to defer to the trial court's findings and the appellate court more readily can find them to be clearly erroneous. . . .

The principal argument advanced in favor of a more searching appellate review of findings by the district court based solely on documentary evidence is that the rationale of Rule 52(a) does not apply when the findings do not rest on the trial court's assessment of credibility of the witnesses but on an evaluation of documentary proof and the drawing of inferences from it, thus eliminating the need for any special deference to the trial court's findings. These considerations are outweighed by the public interest in the stability and judicial economy that would be promoted by recognizing that the trial court, not the appellate tribunal, should be the finder of the facts. To permit courts of appeals to share more actively in the fact-finding function would tend to undermine the legitimacy of the district courts in the eyes of litigants, multiply appeals by encouraging appellate retrial of some factual issues, and needlessly reallocate judicial authority.

1991 AMENDMENTS

Subdivision (c) is added. It parallels the revised Rule 50)(a), but is applicable to non-jury trials. It authorizes the court to enter judgment at any time that it can appropriately make a dispositive finding of fact on the evidence. . . .

Judgment entered under this rule differs from a summary judgment under Rule 56 in the nature of the evaluation made by the court. A judgment on partial findings is made after the court has heard all the evidence bearing on the crucial issue of fact, and the finding is reversible only if the appellate court finds it to be "clearly erroneous." A summary judgment, in contrast, is made on the basis of facts established on account of the absence of contrary evidence or presumptions; such establishments of fact are rulings on questions of law as provided in Rule 56(a) and are not shielded by the "clear error" standard of review.

Rule 53. Masters

(a) **Appointment and Compensation.** The court in which any action is pending may appoint a special master therein. As used in these rules the word "master" includes a referee, an auditor, an examiner, and an assessor. The compensation to be allowed to a master shall be fixed by the court, and shall be charged upon such of the parties or paid out of any fund or subject matter of the action, which is in the custody and control of the court as the court may direct; provided that this provision for compensation shall not apply when a United States magistrate judge is designated to serve as a master. The master shall not retain the master's report as security for the master's compensation; but when the party ordered to pay the compensation allowed by the court does not pay it after notice and within the time prescribed by the court, the master is entitled to a writ of execution against the delinquent party.

(b) **Reference.** A reference to a master shall be the exception and not the rule. In actions to be tried by a jury, a reference shall be made only when the issues are complicated; in actions to be tried without a jury, save in matters of account and of difficult computation of damages, a reference shall be made only upon a showing that some exceptional condition requires it. Upon the consent of the parties, a magistrate judge may be designated to serve as a special master without regard to the provisions of this subdivision.

(c) **Powers.** The order of reference to the master may specify or limit the master's powers and may direct the master to report only upon particular issues or to do or perform particular acts or to receive and report evidence only and may fix the time and place for beginning and closing the hearings and for the filing of the master's report. Subject to the specifications and limitations stated in the order, the master has and shall exercise the power to regulate all proceedings in every hearing before the master and to do all acts and take all measures necessary or proper for the efficient performance of the master's duties under the order. The master may require the production before the master of evidence upon all matters embraced in the reference, including the production of all books, papers, vouchers, documents, and writings applicable thereto. The master may rule upon the admissibility of evidence unless otherwise directed by the order of reference and has the authority to put witnesses on oath and may examine them and may call the parties to the action and examine them upon oath. When a party so requests, the master shall make a record of the evidence offered and excluded in the same manner and subject to the same limitations as provided in the Federal Rules of Evidence for a court sitting without a jury.

(d) **Proceedings.**

(1) ***Meetings.*** When a reference is made, the clerk shall forthwith furnish the master with a copy of the order of reference. Upon receipt thereof unless

the order of reference otherwise provides, the master shall forthwith set a time and place for the first meeting of the parties or their attorneys to be held within 20 days after the date of the order of reference and shall notify the parties or their attorneys. It is the duty of the master to proceed with all reasonable diligence. Either party, on notice to the parties and master, may apply to the court for an order requiring the master to speed the proceedings and to make the report. If a party fails to appear at the time and place appointed, the master may proceed ex parte or, in the master's discretion, adjourn the proceedings to a future day, giving notice to the absent party of the adjournment.

(2) ***Witnesses.*** The parties may procure the attendance of witnesses before the master by the issuance and service of subpoenas as provided in Rule 45. If without adequate excuse a witness fails to appear or give evidence, the witness may be punished as for a contempt and be subjected to the consequences, penalties, and remedies provided in Rules 37 and 45.

(3) ***Statement of Accounts.*** When matters of accounting are in issue before the master, the master may prescribe the form in which the accounts shall be submitted and in any proper case may require or receive in evidence a statement by a certified public accountant who is called as a witness. Upon objection of a party to any of the items thus submitted or upon a showing that the form of statement is insufficient, the master may require a different form of statement to be furnished, or the accounts or specific items thereof to be proved by oral examination of the accounting parties or upon written interrogatories or in such other manner as the master directs.

(e) **Report.**

(1) ***Contents and Filing.*** The master shall prepare a report upon the matters submitted to the master by the order of reference and, if required to make findings of fact and conclusions of law, the master shall set them forth in the report. The master shall file the report with the clerk of the court and serve on all parties notice of the filing. In an action to be tried without a jury, unless otherwise directed by the order of reference, the master shall file with the report a transcript of the proceedings and of the evidence and the original exhibits. Unless otherwise directed by the order of reference, the master shall serve a copy of the report on each party.

(2) ***In Non-Jury Actions.*** In an action to be tried without a jury the court shall accept the master's findings of fact unless clearly erroneous. Within 10 days after being served with notice of the filing of the report any party may serve written objections thereto upon the other parties. Application to the court for action upon the report and upon objections thereto shall be by motion and upon notice as prescribed in Rule 6(d). The court after hearing may adopt the report or may modify it or may reject it in whole or in part or may receive further evidence or may recommit it with instructions.

*(3) **In Jury Actions.*** In an action to be tried by a jury the master shall not be directed to report the evidence. The master's findings upon the issues submitted to the master are admissible as evidence of the matters found and may be read to the jury, subject to the ruling of the court upon any objections in point of law which may be made to the report.

*(4) **Stipulation as to Findings.*** The effect of a master's report is the same whether or not the parties have consented to the reference; but, when the parties stipulate that a master's findings of fact shall be final, only questions of law arising upon the report shall thereafter be considered.

*(5) **Draft Report.*** Before filing the master's report a master may submit a draft thereof to counsel for all parties for the purpose of receiving their suggestions.

(f) Application to Magistrate Judge. A magistrate judge is subject to this rule only when the order referring a matter to the magistrate judge expressly provides that the reference is made under this Rule.

As amended Feb. 28, 1966, eff. July 1, 1966; Apr. 28, 1983, eff. Aug. 1, 1983; Mar. 2, 1987, eff. Aug. 1, 1987; Apr. 30, 1991, eff. Dec. 1, 1991; Apr. 22, 1993, eff. Dec. 1, 1993.

ADVISORY COMMITTEE NOTES, 1983 AMENDMENTS

Subdivision (a). The creation of full-time magistrates, who serve at government expense and have no nonjudicial duties competing for their time, eliminates the need to appoint standing masters. Thus the prior provision in Rule 53(a) authorizing the appointment of standing masters is deleted. Additionally, the definition of "master" in subdivision (a) now eliminates the superseded office of commissioner. . . .

Although the existence of magistrates may make the appointment of outside masters unnecessary in many instances, see, e.g., Gautreaux v. Chicago Housing Authority, 384 F. Supp. 37 (N.D. Ill. 1974), mandamus denied sub nom., Chicago Housing Authority v. Austin, 511 F.2d 82 (7th Cir. 1975); Avco Corp. v. American Tel. & Tel. Co., 68 F.R.D. 532 (S.D. Ohio 1975), such masters may prove useful when some special expertise is desired or when a magistrate is unavailable for lengthy and detailed supervision of a case.

Subdivision (b). The provisions of 28 U.S.C. §636(b)(2) not only permit magistrates to serve as masters under Rule 53(b) but also eliminate the exceptional condition requirement of Rule 53(b) when the reference is made with the consent of the parties. The amendment to subdivision (b) brings Rule 53 into harmony with the statute by exempting magistrates, appointed with the consent of the parties, from the general requirement that some exceptional condition requires the reference. It should be noted that subdivision (b) does not address the question, raised in recent decisional law and commentary, as to whether the exceptional condition requirement is applicable when private masters who are not magistrates are appointed with the consent of the parties. See Silberman, Masters and Magistrates Part II: The American Analogue, 50 N.Y.U.L. Rev. 1297, 1354 (1975). . . .

Subdivision (f). The new subdivision responds to confusion flowing from the dual authority for references of pretrial matters to magistrates. Such references can be made, with or without the consent of the parties, pursuant to Rule 53 or under 28 U.S.C. §636(b)(1)(A) and (b)(1)(B). There are a number of distinctions between references made under the statute and under the rule. For example, under the statute nondispositive pretrial matters may be referred to a magistrate, without consent, for final determination with reconsideration by the district judge if the magistrate's order is clearly erroneous or contrary to law. Under the rule, however, the appointment of a master, without consent of the parties, to supervise discovery would require some exceptional condition (Rule 53(b)) and would subject the proceedings to the report procedures of Rule 53(e). If an order of reference does not clearly articulate the source of the court's authority the resulting proceedings could be subject to attack on grounds of the magistrate's noncompliance with the provisions of Rule 53. This subdivision therefore establishes a presumption that the limitations of Rule 53 are not applicable unless the reference is specifically made subject to Rule 53.

A magistrate serving as a special master under 28 U.S.C. §636(b)(2) is governed by the provisions of Rule 53, with the exceptional condition requirement lifted in the case of a consensual reference.

VII. Judgment

Rule 54. Judgments; Costs

(a) Definition; Form. "Judgment" as used in these rules includes a decree and any order from which an appeal lies. A judgment shall not contain a recital of pleadings, the report of a master, or the record of prior proceedings.

(b) Judgment upon Multiple Claims or Involving Multiple Parties. When more than one claim for relief is presented in an action, whether as a claim, counterclaim, cross-claim, or third-party claim, or when multiple parties are involved, the court may direct the entry of a final judgment as to one or more but fewer than all of the claims or parties only upon an express determination that there is no just reason for delay and upon an express direction for the entry of judgment. In the absence of such determination and direction, any order or other form of decision, however designated, which adjudicates fewer than all the claims or the rights and liabilities of fewer than all the parties shall not terminate the action as to any of the claims or parties, and the order or other form of decision is subject to revision at any time before the entry of judgment adjudicating all the claims and the rights and liabilities of all the parties.

(c) Demand for Judgment. A judgment by default shall not be different in kind from or exceed in amount that prayed for in the demand for judgment. Except as to a party against whom a judgment is entered by default, every final judgment shall grant the relief to which the party in whose favor it is rendered is entitled, even if the party has not demanded such relief in the party's pleadings.

(d) Costs; Attorneys' Fees.

(1) Costs Other than Attorneys' Fees. Except when express provision therefor is made either in a statute of the United States or in these rules, costs other than attorneys' fees shall be allowed as of course to the prevailing party unless the court otherwise directs; but costs against the United States, its officers, and agencies shall be imposed only to the extent permitted by law. Such costs may be taxed by the clerk on one day's notice. On motion served within 5 days thereafter, the action of the clerk may be reviewed by the court.

(2) Attorneys' Fees.

(A) Claims for attorney's fees and related nontaxable expenses shall be made by motion unless the substantive law governing the action provides for the recovery of such fees as an element of damages to be proved at trial.

(B) Unless otherwise provided by statute or order of the court, the motion must be filed no later than 14 days after entry of judgment; must specify the judgment and the statute, rule, or other grounds entitling the moving party to the award; and must state the amount or provide a fair estimate of the amount sought. If directed by the court, the motion shall also disclose the terms of any agreement with respect to fees to be paid for the services for which claim is made.

(C) On request of a party or class member, the court shall afford an opportunity for adversary submissions with respect to the motion in accordance with Rule 43(e) or Rule 78. The court may determine issues of liability for fees before receiving submissions bearing on issues of evaluation of services for which liability is imposed by the court. The court shall find the facts and state its conclusions of law as provided in Rule 52(a).

(D) By local rule the court may establish special procedures by which issues relating to such fees may be resolved without extensive evidentiary hearings. In addition, the court may refer issues relating to the value of services to a special master under Rule 53 without regard to the provisions of subdivision (b) thereof and may refer a motion for attorneys' fees to a magistrate judge under Rule 72(b) as if it were a dispositive pretrial matter.

(E) The provisions of subparagraphs (A) through (D) do not apply to claims for fees and expenses as sanctions for violations of these rules or under 28 U.S.C. §1927.

As amended Dec. 27, 1946, eff. Mar. 19, 1948; Apr. 17, 1961, eff. July 19, 1961; Mar. 2, 1987, eff. Aug. 1, 1987; Apr. 22, 1993, eff. Dec. 1, 1993; Apr. 29, 2002, eff. Dec. 1, 2002.

Advisory Committee Notes, 1946, 1961, and 1993 Amendments

1946 amendments

The historic rule in the federal courts has always prohibited piecemeal disposal of litigation. . . . Rule 54(b) was originally adopted in view of the wide scope and possible content of the newly created "civil action" in order to avoid the possible injustice of a delay in judgment of a distinctly separate claim to await adjudication of the entire case. It was not designed to overturn the settled federal rule stated above. . . .

Unfortunately, this was not always understood, and some confusion ensued. Hence situations arose where district courts made a piecemeal disposition of an action and entered what the parties thought amounted to a judgment, although a trial remained to be had on other claims similar or identical with those disposed of. In the interim the parties did not know their ultimate rights, and accordingly took an appeal, thus putting the finality of the partial judgment in question. While most appellate courts have reached a result generally in accord with the intent of the rule, yet there have been divergent precedents and division of views which have served to render the issues more clouded to the parties appellant. It hardly seems a case where multiplicity of precedents will tend to remove the problem from debate. . . . After extended consideration, [the Committee] concluded that a retention of the older federal rule was desirable, and that this rule needed only the exercise of a discretionary power to afford a remedy in the infrequent harsh case to provide a simple, definite, workable rule. . . .

1961 amendments

A serious difficulty has . . . arisen because the rule speaks of claims but nowhere mentions parties. A line of cases has developed in the circuits consistently holding the rule to be inapplicable to the dismissal, even with the requisite trial court determination, of one or more but fewer than all defendants jointly charged in an action, i.e., charged with various forms of concerted or related wrongdoing or related liability. . . . For purposes of Rule 54(b) it was arguable that there were as many "claims" as there were parties defendant and that the rule in its present text applied where fewer than all of the parties were dismissed . . . but the Courts of Appeals are now committed to an opposite view. . . .

1993 amendments

Subdivision (d). . . .

The rule does not require that the motion be supported at the time of filing with the evidentiary material bearing on the fees. This material must of course be submitted in due course, according to such schedule as the court may direct in light of the circumstances of the case. What is required is the filing of a motion sufficient to alert the adversary and the court that there is a claim for fees and the amount of such fees (or a fair estimate).

If directed by the court, the moving party is also required to disclose any fee agreement, including those between attorney and client, between attorneys sharing a fee to be awarded, and between adversaries made in partial settlement of a dispute where the settlement must be implemented by court action as may be required by Rules 23(e) and 23.1 or other like provisions. With respect to the fee arrangements requiring court approval, the court may also by local rule require disclosure immediately after such arrangements are agreed to. E.g., Rule 5 of United States District Court for the Eastern District of New York; cf. In re "Agent Orange" Product Liability Litigation (MDL 381), 611 F. Supp. 1452, 1464 (E.D.N.Y. 1985).

In the settlement of class actions resulting in a common fund from which fees will be sought, courts frequently have required that claims for fees be presented in advance of hearings to consider approval of the proposed settlement. The rule does not affect this practice, as it permits the court to require submissions of fee claims in advance of entry of judgment.

Rule 55. Default

(a) **Entry.** When a party against whom a judgment for affirmative relief is sought has failed to plead or otherwise defend as provided by these rules and that fact is made to appear by affidavit or otherwise, the clerk shall enter the party's default.

(b) **Judgment.** Judgment by default may be entered as follows:

(1) ***By the Clerk.*** When the plaintiff's claim against a defendant is for a sum certain or for a sum which can by computation be made certain, the clerk upon request of the plaintiff and upon affidavit of the amount due shall enter judgment for that amount and costs against the defendant, if the defendant has been defaulted for failure to appear and is not an infant or incompetent person.

(2) ***By the Court.*** In all other cases the party entitled to a judgment by default shall apply to the court therefor; but no judgment by default shall be entered against an infant or incompetent person unless represented in the action by a general guardian, committee, conservator, or other such representative who has appeared therein. If the party against whom judgment by default is sought has appeared in the action, the party (or, if appearing by representative, the party's representative) shall be served with written notice of the application for judgment at least 3 days prior to the hearing on such application. If, in order to enable the court to enter judgment or to carry it into effect, it is necessary to take an account or to determine the amount of damages or to establish the truth of any averment by evidence or to make an investigation of any other matter, the court may conduct such hearings or order such references as it deems necessary and proper and shall accord a right of trial by jury to the parties when and as required by any statute of the United States.

(c) **Setting Aside Default.** For good cause shown the court may set aside an entry of default and, if a judgment by default has been entered, may likewise set it aside in accordance with Rule 60(b).

(d) **Plaintiffs, Counterclaimants, Cross-Claimants.** The provisions of this rule apply whether the party entitled to the judgment by default is a plaintiff, a third-party plaintiff, or a party who has pleaded a cross-claim or counterclaim. In all cases a judgment by default is subject to the limitations of Rule 54(c).

(e) **Judgment Against the United States.** No judgment by default shall be entered against the United States or an officer or agency thereof unless the claimant establishes a claim or right to relief by evidence satisfactory to the court.

As amended Mar. 2, 1987, eff. Aug. 1, 1987.

Rule 56. Summary Judgment

(a) **For Claimant.** A party seeking to recover upon a claim, counterclaim, or cross-claim or to obtain a declaratory judgment may, at any time after the expiration of 20 days from the commencement of the action or after service of a motion for summary judgment by the adverse party, move with or without supporting affidavits for a summary judgment in the party's favor upon all or any part thereof.

(b) **For Defending Party.** A party against whom a claim, counterclaim, or cross-claim is asserted or a declaratory judgment is sought may, at any time, move with or without supporting affidavits for a summary judgment in the party's favor as to all or any part thereof.

(c) **Motion and Proceedings Thereon.** The motion shall be served at least 10 days before the time fixed for the hearing. The adverse party prior to the day of hearing may serve opposing affidavits. The judgment sought shall be rendered forthwith if the pleadings, depositions, answers to interrogatories and admissions on file, together with the affidavits, if any, show that there is no genuine issue as to any material fact and that the moving party is entitled to a judgment as a matter of law. A summary judgment, interlocutory in character, may be rendered on the issue of liability alone although there is a genuine issue as to the amount of damages.

(d) **Case Not Fully Adjudicated on Motion.** If on motion under this rule judgment is not rendered upon the whole case or for all the relief asked and a trial is necessary, the court at the hearing of the motion, by examining the pleadings and the evidence before it and by interrogating counsel, shall if practicable ascertain what material facts exist without substantial controversy and what material facts are actually and in good faith controverted. It shall thereupon make an order specifying the facts that appear without substantial controversy, including the extent to which the amount of damages or other relief is not in controversy, and directing such further proceedings in the action as are just. Upon the trial of the action the facts so specified shall be deemed established, and the trial shall be conducted accordingly.

(e) **Form of Affidavits; Further Testimony; Defense Required.** Supporting and opposing affidavits shall be made on personal knowledge, shall set forth such facts as would be admissible in evidence, and shall show affirmatively that the affiant is competent to testify to the matters stated therein. Sworn or certified copies of all papers or parts thereof referred to in an affidavit shall be attached thereto or served therewith. The court may permit affidavits to be supplemented or opposed by depositions, answers to interrogatories, or further affidavits. When a motion for summary judgment is made and supported as provided in this rule, an adverse party may not rest upon the mere allegations or denials of the adverse party's pleading, but the adverse party's response, by affidavits or as otherwise provided in this rule, must set forth specific facts showing that there is a genuine issue for trial. If the adverse party does not so respond, summary judgment, if appropriate, shall be entered against the adverse party.

(f) **When Affidavits Are Unavailable.** Should it appear from the affidavits of a party opposing the motion that the party cannot for reasons stated present by affidavit facts essential to justify the party's opposition, the court may refuse the application for judgment or may order a continuance to permit affidavits to be obtained or depositions to be taken or discovery to be had or may make such other order as is just.

(g) **Affidavits Made in Bad Faith.** Should it appear to the satisfaction of the court at any time that any of the affidavits presented pursuant to this rule are presented in bad faith or solely for the purpose of delay, the court shall forthwith order the party employing them to pay to the other party the amount of the reasonable expenses which the filing of the affidavits caused the other party to incur, including reasonable attorney's fees, and any offending party or attorney may be adjudged guilty of contempt.

As amended Dec. 27, 1946, eff. Mar. 19, 1948; Jan. 21, 1963, eff. July 1, 1963; Mar. 2, 1987, eff. Aug. 1, 1987.

Rule 57. Declaratory Judgments

The procedure for obtaining a declaratory judgment pursuant to Title 28 U.S.C. §2201, shall be in accordance with these rules, and the right to trial by jury may be demanded under the circumstances and in the manner provided in Rules 38 and 39. The existence of another adequate remedy does not preclude a judgment for declaratory relief in cases where it is appropriate. The court may order a speedy hearing of an action for a declaratory judgment and may advance it on the calendar.

As amended Dec. 29, 1948, eff. Oct. 20, 1949.

Rule 58. Entry of Judgment

(a) Separate Document.

(1) Every judgment and amended judgment must be set forth on a separate document, but a separate document is not required for an order disposing of a motion:

(A) for judgment under Rule 50(b);

(B) to amend or make additional findings of fact under Rule 52(b);

(C) for attorney fees under Rule 54;

(D) for a new trial, or to alter or amend the judgment, under Rule 59; or

(E) for relief under Rule 60.

(2) Subject to Rule 54(b):

(A) unless the court orders otherwise, the clerk must, without awaiting the court's direction, promptly prepare, sign, and enter the judgment when:

(i) the jury returns a general verdict,

(ii) the court awards only costs or a sum certain, or

(iii) the court denies all relief;

(B) the court must promptly approve the form of the judgment, which the clerk must promptly enter, when:

(i) the jury returns a special verdict or a general verdict accompanied by interrogatories, or

(ii) the court grants other relief not described in Rule 58(a)(2).

(b) Time of Entry. Judgment is entered for purposes of these rules:

(1) if Rule 58(a)(1) does not require a separate document, when it is entered in the civil docket under Rule 79(a), and

(2) if Rule 58(a)(1) requires a separate document, when it is entered in the civil docket under Rule 79(a) and when the earlier of these events occurs:

(A) when it is set forth on a separate document, or

(B) when 150 days have run from entry in the civil docket under Rule 79(a).

(c) Cost or Fee Awards.

(1) Entry of judgment may not be delayed, nor the time for appeal extended, in order to tax costs or award fees, except as provided in Rule 58(c)(2).

(2) When a timely motion for attorney fees is made under Rule 54(d)(2),

the court may act before a notice of appeal has been filed and has become effective to order that the motion have the same effect under Federal Rule of Appellate Procedure 4(a)(4) as a timely motion under Rule 59.

(d) Request for Entry. A party may request that judgment be set forth on a separate document as required by Rule 58(a)(1).

As amended Dec. 27, 1946, eff. Mar. 19, 1948; Jan. 21, 1963, eff. July 1, 1963; Apr. 22, 1993, eff. Dec. 1, 1993; Apr. 29, 2002, eff. Dec. 1, 2002.

Advisory Committee Notes, 2002 Amendments

Rule 58 has provided that a judgment is effective only when set forth on a separate document and entered as provided in Rule 79(a). This simple separate document requirement has been ignored in many cases. The result of failure to enter judgment on a separate document is that the time for making motions under Rules 50, 52, 54(d)(2)(B), 59, and some motions under Rule 60, never begins to run. The time to appeal under Appellate Rule 4(a) also does not begin to run. There have been few visible problems with respect to Rule 50, 52, 54(d)(2)(B), 59, or 60 motions, but there have been many and horridly confused problems under Appellate Rule 4(a). These amendments are designed to work in conjunction with Appellate Rule 4(a) to ensure that appeal time does not linger on indefinitely, and to maintain the integration of the time periods set for Rules 50, 52, 54(d)(2)(B), 59, and 60 with Appellate Rule 4(a).

Rule 58(a) preserves the core of the present separate document requirement, both for the initial judgment and for any amended judgment. No attempt is made to sort through the confusion that some courts have found in addressing the elements of a separate document. It is easy to prepare a separate document that recites the terms of the judgment without offering additional explanation or citation of authority. Forms 31 and 32 provide examples.

Rule 58 is amended, however, to address a problem that arises under Appellate Rule 4(a). Some courts treat such orders as those that deny a motion for new trial as a "judgment," so that appeal time does not start to run until the order is entered on a separate document. Without attempting to address the question whether such orders are appealable, and thus judgments as defined by Rule 54(a), the amendment provides that entry on a separate document is not required for an order disposing of the motions listed in Appellate Rule 4(a). . . .

Rule 58(b) discards the attempt to define the time when a judgment becomes "effective." Taken in conjunction with the Rule 54(a) definition of a judgment to include "any order from which an appeal lies," the former Rule 58 definition of effectiveness could cause strange difficulties in implementing pretrial orders that are appealable under interlocutory appeal provisions or under expansive theories of finality. Rule 58(b) replaces the definition of effectiveness with a new provision that defines the time when judgment is entered. If judgment is promptly set forth on a separate document, as should be done when required by Rule 58(a)(1), the new provision will not change the effect of Rule 58. But in the cases in which court and clerk fail to comply with this simple requirement, the motion time periods set by Rules 50, 52, 54, 59, and 60 begin to run after expiration of 150 days from entry of the judgment in the civil docket as required by Rule 79(a).

A companion amendment of Appellate Rule 4(a)(7) integrates these changes with the time to appeal. . . .

Rule 59. New Trials; Amendment of Judgments

(a) **Grounds.** A new trial may be granted to all or any of the parties and on all or part of the issues (1) in an action in which there has been a trial by jury, for any of the reasons for which new trials have heretofore been granted in actions at law in the courts of the United States; and (2) in an action tried without a jury, for any of the reasons for which rehearings have heretofore been granted in suits in equity in the courts of the United States. On a motion for a new trial in an action tried without a jury, the court may open the judgment if one has been entered, take additional testimony, amend findings of fact and conclusions of law or make new findings and conclusions, and direct the entry of a new judgment.

(b) **Time for Motion.** Any motion for a new trial shall be filed no later than 10 days after entry of the judgment.

(c) **Time for Serving Affidavits.** When a motion for new trial is based on affidavits they shall be filed with the motion. The opposing party has 10 days after service to file opposing affidavits, but that period may be extended for up to 20 days, either by the court for good cause or by the parties' written stipulation. The court may permit reply affidavits.

(d) **On Court's Initiative; Notice; Specifying Grounds.** No later than 10 days after entry of judgment the court, on its own, may order a new trial for any reason that would justify granting one on a party's motion. After giving the parties notice and an opportunity to be heard, the court may grant a timely motion for a new trial for a reason not stated in the motion. When granting a new trial on its own initiative or for a reason not stated in a motion, the court shall specify the grounds in its order.

(e) **Motion to Alter or Amend a Judgment.** Any motion to alter or amend a judgment shall be filed no later than 10 days after entry of the judgment.

As amended Dec. 27, 1946, eff. Mar. 19, 1948; Feb. 28, 1966, eff. July 1, 1966; Apr. 27, 1995, eff. Dec. 1, 1995.

Rule 60. Relief from Judgment or Order

(a) **Clerical Mistakes.** Clerical mistakes in judgments, orders or other parts of the record and errors therein arising from oversight or omission may be corrected by the court at any time of its own initiative or on the motion of any party and after such notice, if any, as the court orders. During the pendency of an appeal, such mistakes may be so corrected before the appeal is docketed in the appellate court, and thereafter while the appeal is pending may be so corrected with leave of the appellate court.

(b) **Mistakes; Inadvertence; Excusable Neglect; Newly Discovered Evidence; Fraud, etc.** On motion and upon such terms as are just, the court may relieve a party or a party's legal representative from a final judgment, order, or proceeding for the following reasons: (1) mistake, inadvertence, surprise, or excusable neglect; (2) newly discovered evidence which by due diligence could not have been discovered in time to move for a new trial under Rule 59(b); (3) fraud (whether heretofore denominated intrinsic or extrinsic), misrepresentation, or other misconduct of an adverse party; (4) the judgment is void; (5) the judgment has been satisfied, released, or discharged, or a prior judgment upon which it is based has been reversed or otherwise vacated, or it is no longer equitable that the judgment should have prospective application; or (6) any other reason justifying relief from the operation of the judgment. The motion shall be made within a reasonable time, and for reasons (1), (2), and (3) not more than one year after the judgment, order, or proceeding was entered or taken. A motion under this subdivision (b) does not affect the finality of a judgment or suspend its operation. This rule does not limit the power of a court to entertain an independent action to relieve a party from a judgment, order, or proceeding, or to grant relief to a defendant not actually personally notified as provided in Title 28, U.S.C., §1655, or to set aside a judgment for fraud upon the court. Writs of coram nobis, coram vobis, audita querela, and bills of review and bills in the nature of a bill of review, are abolished, and the procedure for obtaining any relief from a judgment shall be by motion as prescribed in these rules or by any independent action.

As amended Dec. 27, 1946, eff. Mar. 19, 1948; Dec. 29, 1948, eff. Oct. 20, 1949; Mar. 2, 1987, eff. Aug. 1, 1987.

Rule 61. Harmless Error

No error in either the admission or the exclusion of evidence and no error or defect in any ruling or order or in anything done or omitted by the court or by any of the parties is ground for granting a new trial or for setting aside a verdict or for vacating, modifying or otherwise disturbing a judgment or order, unless refusal to take such action appears to the court inconsistent with substantial justice. The court at every stage of the proceeding must disregard any error or defect in the proceeding which does not affect the substantial rights of the parties.

Rule 62. Stay of Proceedings to Enforce a Judgment

(a) **Automatic Stay; Exceptions — Injunctions, Receiverships, and Patent Accountings.** Except as stated herein, no execution shall issue upon a judgment nor shall proceedings be taken for its enforcement until the expiration of 10 days after its entry. Unless otherwise ordered by the court, an interlocutory or final judgment in an action for an injunction or in a receivership action, or a judgment or order directing an accounting in an action for infringement of letters patent, shall not be stayed during the period after its entry and until an appeal is taken or during the pendency of an appeal. The provisions of subdivision (c) of this rule govern the suspending, modifying, restoring, or granting of an injunction during the pendency of an appeal.

(b) Stay on Motion for New Trial or for Judgment. In its discretion and on such conditions for the security of the adverse party as are proper, the court may stay the execution of or any proceedings to enforce a judgment pending the disposition of a motion for a new trial or to alter or amend a judgment made pursuant to Rule 59, or of a motion for relief from a judgment or order made pursuant to Rule 60, or of a motion for judgment in accordance with a motion for a directed verdict made pursuant to Rule 50, or of a motion for amendment to the findings or for additional findings made pursuant to Rule 52(b).

(c) **Injunction Pending Appeal.** When an appeal is taken from an interlocutory or final judgment granting, dissolving, or denying an injunction, the court in its discretion may suspend, modify, restore, or grant an injunction during the pendency of the appeal upon such terms as to bond or otherwise as it considers proper for the security of the rights of the adverse party. If the judgment appealed from is rendered by a district court of three judges specially constituted pursuant to a statute of the United States, no such order shall be made except (1) by such court sitting in open court or (2) by the assent of all the judges of such court evidenced by their signatures to the order.

(d) Stay upon Appeal. When an appeal is taken the appellant by giving a supersedeas bond may obtain a stay subject to the exceptions contained in subdivision (a) of this rule. The bond may be given at or after the time of filing the notice of appeal or of procuring the order allowing the appeal, as the case may be. The stay is effective when the supersedeas bond is approved by the court.

(e) **Stay in Favor of the United States or Agency Thereof.** When an appeal is taken by the United States or an officer or agency thereof or by direction of any department of the Government of the United States and the operation or enforcement of the judgment is stayed, no bond, obligation, or other security shall be required from the appellant.

(f) **Stay According to State Law.** In any state in which a judgment is a lien upon the property of the judgment debtor and in which the judgment debtor is entitled to a stay of execution, a judgment debtor is entitled, in the district court held therein, to such stay as would be accorded the judgment debtor had the action been maintained in the courts of that state.

(g) **Power of Appellate Court Not Limited.** The provisions in this rule do not limit any power of an appellate court or of a judge or justice thereof to stay proceedings during the pendency of an appeal or to suspend, modify, restore, or grant an injunction during the pendency of an appeal or to make any order appropriate to preserve the status quo or the effectiveness of the judgment subsequently to be entered.

(h) **Stay of Judgment as to Multiple Claims or Multiple Parties.** When a court has ordered a final judgment under the conditions stated in Rule 54(b), the court may stay enforcement of that judgment until the entering of a subsequent judgment or judgments and may prescribe such conditions as are necessary to secure the benefit thereof to the party in whose favor the judgment is entered.

As amended Dec. 27, 1946, eff. Mar. 19, 1948; Dec. 29, 1948, eff. Oct. 20, 1949; Apr. 17, 1961, eff. July 19, 1961; Mar. 2, 1987, eff. Aug. 1, 1987.

Rule 63. Inability of a Judge to Proceed

If a trial or hearing has been commenced and the judge is unable to proceed, any other judge may proceed with it upon certifying familiarity with the record and determining that the proceedings in the case may be completed without prejudice to the parties. In a hearing or trial without a jury, the successor judge shall at the request of a party recall any witness whose testimony is material and disputed and who is available to testify again without undue burden. The successor judge may also recall any other witness.

As amended Mar. 2, 1987, eff. Aug. 1, 1987; Apr. 30, 1991, eff. Dec. 1, 1991.

1991 Amendments

The revision substantially displaces the former rule. The former rule was limited to the disability of the judge, and made no provision for disqualification or possible other reasons for the withdrawal of the judge during proceedings. In making provision for other circumstances, the revision is not intended to encourage judges to discontinue participation in a trial for any but compelling reasons. Cf. United States v. Lane, 708 F.2d 1394, 1395-1397 (9th cir. 1983). Manifestly, a substitution should not be made for the personal convenience of the court, and the reasons for a substitution should be stated on the record.

VIII. Provisional and Final Remedies and Special Proceedings

Rule 64. Seizure of Person or Property

At the commencement of and during the course of an action, all remedies providing for seizure of person or property for the purpose of securing satisfaction of the judgment ultimately to be entered in the action are available under the circumstances and in the manner provided by the law of the state in which the district court is held, existing at the time the remedy is sought, subject to the following qualifications: (1) any existing statute of the United States governs to the extent to which it is applicable; (2) the action in which any of the foregoing remedies is used shall be commenced and prosecuted or, if removed from a state court, shall be prosecuted after removal, pursuant to these rules. The remedies thus available include arrest, attachment, garnishment, replevin, sequestration, and other corresponding or equivalent remedies, however designated and regardless of whether by state procedure the remedy is ancillary to an action or must be obtained by an independent action.

Rule 65. Injunctions

(a) Preliminary Injunction.

(1) Notice. No preliminary injunction shall be issued without notice to the adverse party.

(2) Consolidation of Hearing with Trial on Merits. Before or after the commencement of the hearing of an application for a preliminary injunction, the court may order the trial of the action on the merits to be advanced and consolidated with the hearing of the application. Even when this consolidation is not ordered, any evidence received upon an application for a preliminary injunction which would be admissible upon the trial on the merits becomes part of the record on the trial and need not be repeated upon the trial. This subdivision (a) (2) shall be so construed and applied as to save to the parties any rights they may have to trial by jury.

(b) Temporary Restraining Order; Notice; Hearing; Duration. A temporary restraining order may be granted without written or oral notice to the adverse party or that party's attorney only if (1) it clearly appears from specific facts shown by affidavit or by the verified complaint that immediate and irreparable injury loss or damage will result to the applicant before the adverse party or that party's attorney can be heard in opposition, and (2) the applicant's attorney certifies to the court in writing the efforts, if any, which have been made to give the notice and the reasons supporting the claim that notice should not be required. Every temporary restraining order granted without notice shall be indorsed with the date and hour of issuance; shall be filed forthwith in the clerk's office and entered of record; shall define the injury and state why it is irreparable and why the order was granted without notice; and shall expire by its terms within such time after entry, not to exceed 10 days, as the court fixes, unless within the time so fixed the order, for good cause shown, is extended for a like period or unless the party against whom the order is directed consents that it may be extended for a longer period. The reasons for the extension shall be entered of record. In case a temporary restraining order is granted without notice, the motion for a preliminary injunction shall be set down for hearing at the earliest possible time and takes precedence of all matters except older matters of the same character; and when the motion comes on for hearing the party who obtained the temporary restraining order shall proceed with the application for a preliminary injunction and, if the party does not do so, the court shall dissolve the temporary restraining order. On 2 days' notice to the party who obtained the temporary restraining order without notice or on such shorter notice to that party as the court may prescribe, the adverse party may appear and move its dissolution or modification and in that event the court shall proceed to hear and determine such motion as expeditiously as the ends of justice require.

(c) Security. No restraining order or preliminary injunction shall issue except upon the giving of security by the applicant, in such sum as the court deems proper, for the payment of such costs and damages as may be incurred or suffered by any party who is found to have been wrongfully enjoined or restrained. No such security shall be required of the United States or of an officer or agency thereof.

The provisions of Rule 65.1 apply to a surety upon a bond or undertaking under this rule.

(d) Form and Scope of Injunction or Restraining Order. Every order granting an injunction and every restraining order shall set forth the reasons for its issuance; shall be specific in terms; shall describe in reasonable detail, and not by reference to the complaint or other document, the act or acts sought to be restrained; and is binding only upon the parties to the action, their officers, agents, servants, employees, and attorneys, and upon those persons in active concert or participation with them who receive actual notice of the order by personal service or otherwise.

(e) Employer and Employee; Interpleader; Constitutional Cases. These rules do not modify any statute of the United States relating to temporary restraining orders and preliminary injunctions in actions affecting employer and employee; or the provisions of Title 28, U.S.C., §2361, relating to preliminary injunctions in actions of interpleader or in the nature of interpleader; or Title 28, U.S.C., §2284, relating to actions required by Act of Congress to be heard and determined by a district court of three judges.

(f) Copyright Impoundment. This rule applies to copyright impoundment proceedings.

As amended Dec. 27, 1946, eff. Mar. 19, 1948; Dec. 29, 1948, eff. Oct. 20, 1949; Feb 28, 1966, eff. July 1, 1966; Mar. 2, 1987, eff. Aug. 1, 1987; Apr. 23, 2001, eff. Dec. 1, 2001.

ADVISORY COMMITTEE NOTES, 1966 AMENDMENTS

Subdivision (b). In view of the possibly drastic consequences of a temporary restraining order, the opposition should be heard, if feasible, before the order is granted. Many judges have properly insisted that, when time does not permit of formal notice of the application to the adverse party, some expedient, such as telephonic notice to the attorney for the adverse party, be resorted to if this can reasonably be done. On occasion, however, temporary restraining orders have been issued without any notice when it was feasible for some fair, although informal, notice to be given. . . .

Heretofore the first sentence of subdivision (b), in referring to a notice "served" on the "adverse party" on which a "hearing" could be held, perhaps invited the interpretation that the order might be granted without notice if the circumstances did not permit of a formal hearing on the basis of a formal notice. The subdivision is amended to make it plain that informal notice, which may be communicated to the attorney rather than the adverse party, is to be preferred to no notice at all.

Before notice can be dispensed with, the applicant's counsel must give his certificate as to any efforts made to give notice and the reasons why notice should not be required. This certificate is in addition to the requirement of an affidavit or verified complaint setting forth the facts as to the irreparable injury which would result before the opposition could be heard. . . .

Rule 65.1. Security: Proceedings Against Sureties

Whenever these rules, including the Supplemental Rules for Certain Admiralty and Maritime Claims, require or permit the giving of security by a party, and security is given in the form of a bond or stipulation or other undertaking with one or more sureties, each surety submits to the jurisdiction of the court and irrevocably appoints the clerk of the court as the surety's agent upon whom any papers affecting the surety's liability on the bond or undertaking may be served. The surety's liability may be enforced on motion without the necessity of an independent action. The motion and such notice of the motion as the court prescribes may be served on the clerk of the court, who shall forthwith mail copies to the sureties if their addresses are known.

Added Feb. 28, 1966, eff. July 1, 1966; as amended Mar. 2, 1987, eff. Aug. 1, 1987.

Rule 66. Receivers Appointed by Federal Courts

An action wherein a receiver has been appointed shall not be dismissed except by order of the court. The practice in the administration of estates by receivers or by other similar officers appointed by the court shall be in accordance with the practice heretofore followed in the courts of the United States or as provided in rules promulgated by the district courts. In all other respects the action in which the appointment of a receiver is sought or which is brought by or against a receiver is governed by these rules.

As amended Dec. 27, 1946, eff. Mar. 19, 1948; Dec. 29, 1948, eff. Oct. 20, 1949.

Rule 67. Deposit in Court

In an action in which any part of the relief sought is a judgment for a sum of money or the disposition of a sum of money or the disposition of any other thing capable of delivery, a party, upon notice to every other party, and by leave of court, may deposit with the court all or any part of such sum or thing, whether or not that party claims all or any part of the sum or thing. The party making the deposit shall serve the order permitting deposit on the clerk of the court. Money paid into court under this rule shall be deposited and withdrawn in accordance with the provisions of Title 28, U.S.C., §§2041, and 2042; the Act of June 26, 1934, c. 756, §23, as amended (48 Stat. 1236, 58 Stat. 845), U.S.C., Title 31, §725v; or any like statute. The fund shall be deposited in an interest-bearing account or invested in an interest-bearing instrument approved by the court.

As amended Dec. 29, 1948, eff. Oct. 20, 1949; Apr. 28, 1983, eff. Aug. 1, 1983.

ADVISORY COMMITTEE NOTES, 1983 AMENDMENT

Rule 67 has been amended in three ways. The first change is the addition of the clause in the first sentence. Some courts have construed the present rule to permit deposit only when the party making it claims no interest in the fund or thing deposited. E.g., Blasin-Stern v. Beech-Nut Life Savings Corp., 429 F. Supp. 533 (D. Puerto Rico 1975); Dinkins v. General Aniline & Film Corp., 214 F. Supp. 281 (S.D.N.Y. 1963). However, there are situations in which a litigant may wish to be relieved of responsibility for a sum or thing, but continue to claim an interest in all or part of it. In these cases the deposit-in-court procedure should be available; in addition to the advantages to the party making the deposit, the procedure gives other litigants assurance that any judgment will be collectable. The amendment is intended to accomplish that.

The second change is the addition of a requirement that the order of deposit be served on the clerk of the court in which the sum or thing is to be deposited. This is simply to assure that the clerk knows what is being deposited and what his responsibilities are with respect to the deposit. The latter point is particularly important since the rule as amended contemplates that deposits will be placed in interest-bearing accounts; the clerk must know what treatment has been ordered for the particular deposit.

The third change is to require that any money be deposited in an interest-bearing account or instrument approved by the court.

Rule 68. Offer of Judgment

At any time more than 10 days before the trial begins, a party defending against a claim may serve upon the adverse party an offer to allow judgment to be taken against the defending party for the money or property or to the effect specified in the offer, with costs then accrued. If within 10 days after the service of the offer the adverse party serves written notice that the offer is accepted, either party may then file the offer and notice of acceptance together with proof of service thereof and thereupon the clerk shall enter judgment. An offer not accepted shall be deemed withdrawn and evidence thereof is not admissible except in a proceeding to determine costs. If the judgment finally obtained by the offeree is not more favorable than the offer, the offeree must pay the costs incurred after the making of the offer. The fact that an offer is made but not accepted does not preclude a subsequent offer. When the liability of one party to another has been determined by verdict or order or judgment, but the amount or extent of the liability remains to be determined by further proceedings, the party adjudged liable may make an offer of judgment, which shall have the same effect as an offer made before trial if it is served within a reasonable time not less than 10 days prior to the commencement of hearings to determine the amount or extent of liability.

As amended Dec. 27, 1946, eff. Mar. 19, 1948; Feb. 28, 1966, eff. July 1, 1966; Mar. 2, 1987, eff. Aug. 1, 1987.

Rule 69. Execution

(a) In General. Process to enforce a judgment for the payment of money shall be a writ of execution, unless the court directs otherwise. The procedure on execution, in proceedings supplementary to and in aid of a judgment, and in proceedings on and in aid of execution shall be in accordance with the practice and procedure of the state in which the district court is held, existing at the time the remedy is sought, except that any statute of the United States governs to the extent that it is applicable. In aid of the judgment or execution, the judgment creditor or a successor in interest when that interest appears of record, may obtain discovery from any person, including the judgment debtor, in the manner provided in these rules or in the manner provided by the practice of the state in which the district court is held.

(b) Against Certain Public Officers. When a judgment has been entered against a collector or other officer of revenue under the circumstances stated in Title 28, U.S.C., §2006, or against an officer of Congress in an action mentioned in the Act of March 3, 1875, ch. 130, §8 (18 Stat. 401), U.S.C., Title 2, §118, and when the court has given the certificate of probable cause for the officer's act as provided in those statutes, execution shall not issue against the officer or the officer's property but the final judgment shall be satisfied as provided in such statutes.

As amended Dec. 29, 1948, eff. Oct. 20, 1949; Mar. 30, 1970, eff. July 1, 1970; Mar. 2, 1987, eff. Aug. 1, 1987.

Rule 70. Judgment for Specific Acts; Vesting Title

If a judgment directs a party to execute a conveyance of land or to deliver deeds or other documents or to perform any other specific act and the party fails to comply within the time specified, the court may direct the act to be done at the cost of the disobedient party by some other person appointed by the court and the act when so done has like effect as if done by the party. On application of the party entitled to performance, the clerk shall issue a writ of attachment or sequestration against the property of the disobedient party to compel obedience to the judgment. The court may also in proper cases adjudge the party in contempt. If real or personal property is within the district, the court in lieu of directing a conveyance thereof may enter a judgment divesting the title of any party and vesting it in others and such judgment has the effect of a conveyance executed in due form of law. When any order or judgment is for the delivery of possession, the party in whose favor it is entered is entitled to a writ of execution or assistance upon application to the clerk.

Rule 71. Process in Behalf of and Against Persons Not Parties

When an order is made in favor of a person who is not a party to the action, that person may enforce obedience to the order by the same process as if a party;

and, when obedience to an order may be lawfully enforced against a person who is not a party, that person is liable to the same process for enforcing obedience to the order as if a party.

As amended Mar. 2, 1987, eff. Aug. 1, 1987.

Rule 71A. Condemnation of Property

(a) **Applicability of Other Rules.** The Rules of Civil Procedure for the United States District Courts govern the procedure for the condemnation of real and personal property under the power of eminent domain, except as otherwise provided in this rule.

(b) **Joinder of Properties.** The plaintiff may join in the same action one or more separate pieces of property, whether in the same or different ownership and whether or not sought for the same use.

(c) **Complaint.**

(1) Caption. The complaint shall contain a caption as provided in Rule 10(a), except that the plaintiff shall name as defendants the property, designated generally by kind, quantity, and location, and at least one of the owners of some part of or interest in the property.

(2) Contents. The complaint shall contain a short and plain statement of the authority for the taking, the use for which the property is to be taken, a description of the property sufficient for its identification, the interests to be acquired, and as to each separate piece of property a designation of the defendants who have been joined as owners thereof or of some interest therein. Upon the commencement of the action, the plaintiff need join as defendants only the persons having or claiming an interest in the property whose names are then known, but prior to any hearing involving the compensation to be paid for a piece of property, the plaintiff shall add as defendants all persons having or claiming an interest in that property whose names can be ascertained by a reasonably diligent search of the records, considering the character and value of the property involved and the interests to be acquired, and also those whose names have otherwise been learned. All others may be made defendants under the designation "Unknown Owners." Process shall be served as provided in subdivision (d) of this rule upon all defendants, whether named as defendants at the time of the commencement of the action or subsequently added, and a defendant may answer as provided in subdivision (e) of this rule. The court meanwhile may order such distribution of a deposit as the facts warrant.

*(3) **Filing.*** In addition to filing the complaint with the court, the plaintiff shall furnish to the clerk at least one copy thereof for the use of the defendants and additional copies at the request of the clerk or of a defendant.

(d) Process.

*(1) **Notice; Delivery.*** Upon the filing of the complaint the plaintiff shall forthwith deliver to the clerk joint or several notices directed to the defendants named or designated in the complaint. Additional notices directed to defendants subsequently added shall be so delivered. The delivery of the notice and its service have the same effect as the delivery and service of the summons under Rule 4.

*(2) **Same; Form.*** Each notice shall state the court, the title of the action, the name of the defendant to whom it is directed, that the action is to condemn property, a description of the defendant's property sufficient for its identification, the interest to be taken, the authority for the taking, the uses for which the property is to be taken, that the defendant may serve upon the plaintiff's attorney an answer within 20 days after service of the notice, and that the failure so to serve an answer constitutes a consent to the taking and to the authority of the court to proceed to hear the action and to fix the compensation. The notice shall conclude with the name of the plaintiff's attorney and an address within the district in which action is brought where the attorney may be served. The notice need contain a description of no other property than that to be taken from the defendants to whom it is directed.

*(3) **Service of Notice.***

(A) Personal Service. Personal service of the notice (but without copies of the complaint) shall be made in accordance with Rule 4 upon a defendant whose residence is known and who resides within the United States or a territory subject to the administrative or judicial jurisdiction of the United States.

(B) Service by Publication. Upon the filing of a certificate of the plaintiff's attorney stating that the attorney believes a defendant cannot be personally served, because after diligent inquiry within the state in which the complaint is filed the defendant's place of residence cannot be ascertained by the plaintiff or, if ascertained, that it is beyond the territorial limits of personal service as provided in this rule, service of the notice shall be made on this defendant by publication in a newspaper published in the county where the property is located, or if there is no such newspaper, then in a newspaper having a general circulation where the property is located, once a week for not less than three successive weeks. Prior to the last publication, a copy of the notice shall also be mailed to a defendant who cannot be personally served as provided in this rule but whose place of residence is then known. Unknown owners may be

served by publication in like manner by a notice addressed to "Unknown Owners."

Service by publication is complete upon the date of the last publication. Proof of publication and mailing shall be made by certificate of the plaintiff's attorney, to which shall be attached a printed copy of the published notice with the name and dates of the newspaper marked thereon.

(4) ***Return; Amendment.*** Proof of service of the notice shall be made and amendment of the notice or proof of its service allowed in the manner provided for the return and amendment of the summons under Rule 4.

(e) **Appearance or Answer.** If a defendant has no objection or defense to the taking of the defendant's property, the defendant may serve a notice of appearance designating the property in which the defendant claims to be interested. Thereafter the defendant shall receive notice of all proceedings affecting it. If a defendant has any objection or defense to the taking of the property, the defendant shall serve an answer within 20 days after the service of notice upon the defendant. The answer shall identify the property in which the defendant claims to have an interest, state the nature and extent of the interest claimed, and state all the defendant's objections and defenses to the taking of the property. A defendant waives all defenses and objections not so presented, but at the trial of the issue of just compensation, whether or not the defendant has previously appeared or answered, the defendant may present evidence as to the amount of the compensation to be paid for the property, and the defendant may share in the distribution of the award. No other pleading or motion asserting any additional defense or objection shall be allowed.

(f) **Amendment of Pleadings.** Without leave of court, the plaintiff may amend the complaint at any time before the trial of the issue of compensation and as many times as desired, but no amendment shall be made which will result in a dismissal forbidden by subdivision (i) of this rule. The plaintiff need not serve a copy of an amendment, but shall serve notice of the filing, as provided in Rule 5(b), upon any party affected thereby who has appeared and, in the manner provided in subdivision (d) of this rule, upon any party affected thereby who has not appeared. The plaintiff shall furnish to the clerk of the court for the use of the defendants at least one copy of each amendment, and he shall furnish additional copies on the request of the clerk or of a defendant. Within the time allowed by subdivision (e) of this rule a defendant may serve an answer to the amended pleading, in the form and manner and with the same effect as there provided.

(g) **Substitution of Parties.** If a defendant dies or becomes incompetent or transfers an interest after the defendant's joinder, the court may order substitution of the proper party upon motion and notice of hearing. If the motion and notice of hearing are to be served upon a person not already a party, service shall be made as provided in subdivision (d)(3) of this rule.

(h) Trial. If the action involves the exercise of the power of eminent domain under the law of the United States, any tribunal specially constituted by an Act of Congress governing the case for the trial of the issue of just compensation shall be the tribunal for the determination of that issue; but if there is no such specially constituted tribunal any party may have a trial by jury of the issue of just compensation by filing a demand therefor within the time allowed for answer or within such further time as the court may fix, unless the court in its discretion orders that, because of the character, location, or quantity of the property to be condemned, or for other reasons in the interest of justice, the issue of compensation shall be determined by a commission of three persons appointed by it.

In the event that a commission is appointed the court may direct that not more than two additional persons serve as alternate commissioners to hear the case and replace commissioners who, prior to the time when a decision is filed, are found by the court to be unable or disqualified to perform their duties. An alternate who does not replace a regular commissioner shall be discharged after the commission renders its final decision. Before appointing the members of the commission and alternates the court shall advise the parties of the identity and qualifications of each prospective commissioner and alternate and may permit the parties to examine each such designee. The parties shall not be permitted or required by the court to suggest nominees. Each party shall have the right to object for valid cause to the appointment of any person as a commissioner or alternate. If a commission is appointed it shall have the powers of a master provided in subdivision (c) of Rule 53 and proceedings before it shall be governed by the provisions of paragraphs (1) and (2) of subdivision (d) of Rule 53. Its action and report shall be determined by a majority and its findings and report shall have the effect, and be dealt with by the court in accordance with the practice, prescribed in paragraph (2) of subdivision (e) of Rule 53. Trial of all issues shall otherwise be by the court.

(i) Dismissal of Action.

(1) As of Right. If no hearing has begun to determine the compensation to be paid for a piece of property and the plaintiff has not acquired the title or a lesse interest in or taken possession, the plaintiff may dismiss the action as to that property, without an order of the court, by filing a notice of dismissal setting forth a brief description of the property as to which the action is dismissed.

(2) By Stipulation. Before the entry of any judgment vesting the plaintiff with title or a lesser interest in or possession of property, the action may be dismissed in whole or in part, without an order of the court, as to any property by filing a stipulation of dismissal by the plaintiff and the defendant affected

thereby; and, if the parties so stipulate, the court may vacate any judgment that has been entered.

*(3) **By Order of the Court.*** At any time before compensation for a piece of property has been determined and paid and after motion and hearing, the court may dismiss the action as to that property, except that it shall not dismiss the action as to any part of the property of which the plaintiff has taken possession or in which the plaintiff has taken title or a lesser interest, but shall award just compensation for the possession, title or lesser interest so taken. The court at any time may drop a defendant unnecessarily or improperly joined.

*(4) **Effect.*** Except as otherwise provided in the notice, or stipulation of dismissal, or order of the court, any dismissal is without prejudice.

(j) Deposit and Its Distribution. The plaintiff shall deposit with the court any money required by law as a condition to the exercise of the power of eminent domain; and, although not so required, may make a deposit when permitted by statute. In such cases the court and attorneys shall expedite the proceedings for the distribution of the money so deposited and for the ascertainment and payment of just compensation. If the compensation finally awarded to any defendant exceeds the amount which has been paid to the defendant on distribution of the deposit, the court shall enter judgment against the plaintiff and in favor of that defendant for the deficiency. If the compensation finally awarded to any defendant is less than the amount which has been paid to that defendant, the court shall enter judgment against that defendant and in favor of the plaintiff for the overpayment.

(k) Condemnation Under a State's Power of Eminent Domain. The practice as herein prescribed governs in actions involving the exercise of the power of eminent domain under the law of a state, provided that if the state law makes provision for trial of any issue by jury, or for trial of the issue of compensation by jury or commission or both, that provision shall be followed.

(l) Costs. Costs are not subject to Rule 54(d).

Added Apr. 30, 1951, eff. Aug. 1, 1951; amended Jan. 21, 1963, eff. July 1, 1963; Apr. 29, 1985, eff. Aug. 1, 1985; Mar. 2, 1987, eff. Aug. 1, 1987; Apr. 25, 1988, eff. Aug. 1, 1988; Nov. 18, 1988, Pub. L. 100-690, Title VII, §7050, 102 Stat. 4401; Apr. 22, 1993, eff. Dec. 1, 1993.

IX. Special Proceedings

Rule 72. Magistrate Judges; Pretrial Orders

(a) Nondispositive Matters. A magistrate judge to whom a pretrial matter not dispositive of a claim or defense of a party is referred to hear and determine shall promptly conduct such proceedings as are required and when appropriate enter into the record a written order setting forth the disposition of the matter. Within 10 days after being served with a copy of the magistrate judge's order, a party may serve and file objections to the order; a party may not thereafter assign as error a defect in the magistrate judge's order to which objection was not timely made. The district judge to whom the case is assigned shall consider such objections and shall modify or set aside any portion of the magistrate judge's order found to be clearly erroneous or contrary to law.

(b) Dispositive Motions and Prisoner Petitions. A magistrate judge assigned without consent of the parties to hear a pretrial matter dispositive of a claim or defense of a party or a prisoner petition challenging the conditions of confinement shall promptly conduct such proceedings as are required. A record shall be made of all evidentiary proceedings before the magistrate judge, and a record may be made of such other proceedings as the magistrate judge deems necessary. The magistrate judge shall enter into the record a recommendation for disposition of the matter, including proposed findings of fact when appropriate. The clerk shall forthwith mail copies to all parties.

A party objecting to the recommended disposition of the matter shall promptly arrange for the transcription of the record, or portions of it as all parties may agree upon or the magistrate judge deems sufficient, unless the district judge otherwise directs. Within 10 days after being served with a copy of the recommended disposition, a party may serve and file specific, written objections to the proposed findings and recommendations. A party may respond to another party's objections within 10 days after being served with a copy thereof. The district judge to whom the case is assigned shall make a de novo determination upon the record, or after additional evidence, of any portion of the magistrate judge's disposition to which specific written objection has been made in accordance with this rule. The district judge may accept, reject, or modify the recommended decision, receive further evidence, or recommit the matter to the magistrate judge with instructions.

Added Apr. 28, 1983, eff. Aug. 1, 1983; Apr. 30, 1991, eff. Dec. 1, 1991; Apr. 22, 1993, eff. Dec. 1, 1993.

ADVISORY COMMITTEE NOTES, 1983 ADDITION

Subdivision (a). This subdivision addresses court-ordered referrals of nondispositive matters under 28 U.S.C §636(b)(1)(A). The rule calls for a written order of the magistrate's disposition to preserve the record and facilitate review. An oral order read into the record by the magistrate will satisfy this requirement.

No specific procedures or timetables for raising objections to the magistrate's rulings on nondispositive matters are set forth in the Magistrates Act. The rule fixes a 10-day period in order to avoid uncertainty and provide uniformity that will eliminate the confusion that might arise if different periods were prescribed by local rule in different districts. It also contemplated that a party who is successful before the magistrate will be afforded an opportunity to respond to objections raised to the magistrate's ruling.

The last sentence of subdivision (a) specifies that reconsideration of a magistrate's order, as provided for in the Magistrates Act, shall be by the district judge to whom the case is assigned. This rule does not restrict experimentation by the district courts under 28 U.S.C. §636(b)(3) involving references of matters other than pretrial matters, such as appointment of counsel, taking of default judgments, and acceptance of jury verdicts when the judge is unavailable.

Subdivision (b). This subdivision governs court-ordered referrals of dispositive pretrial matters and prisoner petitions challenging conditions of confinement, pursuant to statutory authorization in 28 U.S.C. §636(b)(1)(B). This rule does not extend to habeas corpus petitions, which are covered by the specific rules relating to proceedings under Sections 2254 and 2255 of Title 28.

This rule implements the statutory procedures for making objections to the magistrate's proposed findings and recommendations. The 10-day period, as specified in the statute, is subject to Rule 6(e) which provides for an additional 3-day period when service is made by mail. Although no specific provision appears in the Magistrates Act, the rule specifies a 10-day period for a party to respond to objections to the magistrate's recommendation.

Implementing the statutory requirements, the rule requires the district judge to whom the case is assigned to make a de novo determination of those portions of the report, findings, or recommendations to which timely objection is made. The term "de novo" signifies that the magistrate's findings are not protected by the clearly erroneous doctrine, but does not indicate that a second evidentiary hearing is required. See United States v. Raddatz, 417 U.S. 667 (1980). See also Silberman, Masters and Magistrates Part II: The American Analogue, 50 N.Y.U. L. Rev. 1297, 1367 (1975). When no timely objection is filed, the court need only satisfy itself that there is no clear error on the face of the record in order to accept the recommendation. See Campbell v. United States Dist. Court, 501 F.2d 196, 206 (9th Cir. 1974), cert. denied, 419 U.S. 879, quoted in House Report No. 94-1609, 94th Cong. 2d Sess. (1976) at 3. Compare Park Motor Mart, Inc. v. Ford Motor Co., 616 F.2d 603 (1st Cir. 1980). Failure to make timely objection to the magistrate's report prior to its adoption by the district judge may constitute a waiver of appellate review of the district judge's order. See United States v. Walters, 638 F.2d 947 (6th Cir. 1981).

Rule 73. Magistrate Judges; Trial by Consent and Appeal Options

(a) Powers; Procedure. When specially designated to exercise such jurisdiction by local rule or order of the district court and when all parties consent thereto, a magistrate judge may exercise the authority provided by Title 28, U.S.C. §636(c) and may conduct any or all proceedings, including a jury or nonjury trial, in a civil case. A record of the proceedings shall be made in accordance with the requirements of Title 28, U.S.C. §636(c)(5).

(b) Consent. When a magistrate judge has been designated to exercise civil trial jurisdiction, the clerk shall give written notice to the parties of their opportunity to consent to the exercise by a magistrate judge of civil jurisdiction over the case, as authorized by Title 28, U.S.C. §636(c). If, within the period specified by local rule, the parties agree to a magistrate judge's exercise of such authority, they shall execute and file a joint form of consent or separate forms of consent setting forth such election.

A district judge, magistrate judge, or other court official may again advise the parties of the availability of the magistrate judge, but, in so doing, shall also advise the parties that they are free to withhold consent without adverse substantive consequences. A district judge or magistrate judge shall not be informed of a party's response to the clerk's notification, unless all parties have consented to the referral of the matter to a magistrate judge.

The district judge, for good cause shown on the judge's own initiative, or under extraordinary circumstances shown by a party, may vacate a reference of a civil matter to a magistrate judge under this subdivision.

(c) Appeal. In accordance with Title 28, U.S.C. §636(c)(3), appeal from a judgment entered upon direction of a magistrate judge in proceedings under this rule will lie to the court of appeals as it would from a judgment of the district court.

Added Apr. 28, 1983, eff. Aug. 1, 1983; amended Mar. 2, 1987, eff. Aug. 1, 1987; Apr. 22, 1993, eff. Dec. 1, 1993; Apr. 11, 1997, eff. Dec. 1, 1997.

ADVISORY COMMITTEE NOTES, 1983 ADDITION

Subdivision (a). This subdivision implements the broad authority of the 1979 amendments to the Magistrates Act, 28 U.S.C. §636(c), which permit a magistrate to sit in lieu of a district judge and exercise civil jurisdiction over a case, when the parties consent. See McCabe, The Federal Magistrate Act of 1979, 16 Harv. J. Legis. 343, 364-379 (1979). In order to exercise this jurisdiction, a magistrate must be specially designated under 28 U.S.C. §636(c)(1) by the district court or courts he serves. The only exception to a magistrate's exercise of civil jurisdiction, which includes the power to conduct jury and nonjury trials and decide dispositive motions, is the contempt power. A hearing on contempt is to be conducted by the district judge upon certification of the facts and an order to show cause by the magistrate. See 28 U.S.C. §639(e). In view of 28 U.S.C. §636(c)(1) and this rule, it is unnecessary to amend Rule 58 to provide that the decision of a magistrate is a "decision by the court" for the purposes of that rule and a "final decision of the district court" for purposes of 28 U.S.C. §1291 governing appeals.

Subdivision (b). This subdivision implements the blind consent provision of 28 U.S.C. §636(c)(2) and is designed to ensure that neither the judge nor the magistrate attempts to induce a party to consent to reference of a civil matter under this rule to a magistrate. See House Rep. No. 96-444, 96th Cong. 1st Sess. 8 (1979).

The rule opts for a uniform approach in implementing the consent provision by directing the clerk to notify the parties of their opportunity to elect to proceed before a magistrate and by requiring the execution and filing of a consent form or forms setting forth the election. However, flexibility at the local level is preserved in that local rules will determine how notice shall be communicated to the parties, and local rules will specify the time period within which an election must be made.

The last paragraph of subdivision (b) reiterates the provision in 28 U.S.C. §636(c)(6) for vacating a reference to the magistrate.

Subdivision (c). Under 28 U.S.C. §636(c)(3), the normal route of appeal from the judgment of a magistrate — the only route that will be available unless the parties otherwise agree in advance — is an appeal by the aggrieved party "directly to the appropriate United States court of appeals from the judgment of the magistrate in the same manner as an appeal from any other judgment of a district court." The quoted statutory language indicates Congress' intent that the same procedures and standards of appealability that govern appeals from district court judgments govern appeals from magistrates' judgments.

Rule 74. Method of Appeal from Magistrate Judge to District Judge Under Title 28, U.S.C. §636(c)(4) and Rule 73(d) [*Abrogated.*]

Rule 75. Proceedings on Appeal from Magistrate to District Judge Under Rule 73(d) [*Abrogated.*]

Rule 76. Judgment of the District Judge on the Appeal Under Rule 73(d) and Costs [*Abrogated.*]

X. District Courts and Clerks

Rule 77. District Courts and Clerks

(a) District Courts Always Open. The district courts shall be deemed always open for the purpose of filing any pleading or other proper paper, of issuing and returning mesne and final process, and of making and directing all interlocutory motions, orders, and rules.

(b) Trials and Hearings; Orders in Chambers. All trials upon the merits shall be conducted in open court and so far as convenient in a regular court room. All other acts or proceedings may be done or conducted by a judge in chambers, without the attendance of the clerk or other court officials and at any place either within or without the district; but no hearing, other than one ex parte, shall be conducted outside the district without the consent of all parties affected thereby.

(c) Clerk's Office and Orders by Clerk. The clerk's office with the clerk or a deputy in attendance shall be open during business hours on all days except Saturdays, Sundays, and legal holidays, but a district court may provide by local rule or order that its clerk's office shall be open for specified hours on Saturdays or particular legal holidays other than New Year's Day, Birthday of Martin Luther King, Jr., Washington's Birthday, Memorial Day, Independence Day, Labor Day, Columbus Day, Veterans Day, Thanksgiving Day, and Christmas Day. All motions and applications in the clerk's office for issuing mesne process, for issuing final process to enforce and execute judgments, for entering defaults or judgments by default, and for other proceedings which do not require allowance or order of the court are grantable of course by the clerk; but the clerk's action may be suspended or altered or rescinded by the court upon cause shown.

(d) Notice of Orders or Judgments. Immediately upon the entry of an order or judgment the clerk shall serve a notice of the entry in the manner provided for in Rule 5(b) upon each party who is not in default for failure to appear, and shall make a note in the docket of the service. Any party may in addition serve a notice of such entry in the manner provided in Rule 5(b) for the service of papers. Lack of notice of the entry by the clerk does not affect the time to appeal or relieve or authorize the court to relieve a party for failure to appeal within the time allowed, except as permitted in Rule 4(a) of the Federal Rules of Appellate Procedure.

As amended Dec. 27, 1946, eff. Mar. 19, 1948; Jan. 21, 1963, eff. July 1, 1963; Dec. 4, 1967, eff. July 1, 1968; Mar. 1, 1971, eff. July 1, 1971; Mar. 2, 1987, eff. Aug. 1, 1987; Apr. 30, 1991, eff. Dec. 1, 1991; Apr. 23, 2001, eff. Dec. 1, 2001.

Rule 78. Motion Day

Unless local conditions make it impracticable, each district court shall establish regular times and places, at intervals sufficiently frequent for the prompt dispatch of business, at which motions requiring notice and hearing may be heard and disposed of; but the judge at any time or place and on such notice, if any, as the judge considers reasonable may make orders for the advancement, conduct, and hearing of actions.

To expedite its business, the court may make provision by rule or order for the submission and determination of motions without oral hearing upon brief written statements of reasons in support and opposition.

As amended Mar. 2, 1987, eff. Aug. 1, 1987.

Rule 79. Books and Records Kept by the Clerk and Entries Therein

(a) Civil Docket. The clerk shall keep a book known as "civil docket" of such form and style as may be prescribed by the Director of the Administrative Office of the United States Courts with the approval of the Judicial Conference of the United States, and shall enter therein each civil action to which these rules are made applicable. Actions shall be assigned consecutive file numbers. The file number of each action shall be noted on the folio of the docket whereon the first entry of the action is made. All papers filed with the clerk, all process issued and returns made thereon, all appearances, orders, verdicts, and judgments shall be entered chronologically in the civil docket on the folio assigned to the action and shall be marked with its file number. These entries shall be brief but shall show the nature of each paper filed or writ issued and the substance of each order or judgment of the court and of the returns showing execution of process. The entry of an order or judgment shall show the date the entry is made. When in an action trial by jury has been properly demanded or ordered the clerk shall enter the word "jury" on the folio assigned to that action.

(b) Civil Judgments and Orders. The clerk shall keep, in such form and manner as the Director of the Administrative Office of the United States Courts with the approval of the Judicial Conference of the United States may prescribe, a correct copy of every final judgment or appealable order, or order affecting title to or lien upon real or personal property, and any other order which the court may direct to be kept.

(c) Indices; Calendars. Suitable indices of the civil docket and of every civil judgment and order referred to in subdivision (b) of this rule shall be kept by the clerk under the direction of the court. There shall be prepared under the direction of the court calendars of all actions ready for trial, which shall distinguish "jury actions" from "court actions."

(d) Other Books and Records of the Clerk. The clerk shall also keep such other books and records as may be required from time to time by the Director of the Administrative Office of the United States Courts with the approval of the Judicial Conference of the United States.

As amended Dec. 27, 1946, eff. Mar. 19, 1948; Dec. 29, 1948, eff. Oct. 20, 1949; Jan. 21, 1963, eff. July 1, 1963.

Rule 80. Stenographer; Stenographic Report or Transcript as Evidence

(a) **Stenographer.** [*Abrogated.*]

(b) **Official Stenographer.** [*Abrogated.*]

(c) **Stenographic Report or Transcript as Evidence.** Whenever the testimony of a witness at a trial or hearing which was stenographically reported is admissible in evidence at a later trial, it may be proved by the transcript thereof duly certified by the person who reported the testimony.

As amended Dec. 27, 1946, eff. Mar. 19, 1948.

XI. General Provisions

Rule 81. Applicability in General

(a) **Proceedings to Which the Rules Apply.**

(1) These rules do not apply to prize proceedings in admiralty governed by Title 10, U.S.C. §§7651-7681. They do apply to proceedings in bankruptcy to the extent provided by the Federal Rules of Bankruptcy Procedure.

(2) These rules are applicable to proceedings for admission to citizenship, habeas corpus, and quo warranto, to the extent that the practice in such proceedings is not set forth in statutes of the United States, the Rule Governing Section 2254 Cases, or the Rule Governing Section 2255 Proceedings, and has heretofore conformed to the practice in civil actions.

(3) In proceedings under Title 9, U.S.C., relating to arbitration, or under the Act of May 20, 1926, ch. 347, §9 (44 Stat. 585), U.S.C., Title 45, §159, relating to boards of arbitration of railway labor disputes, these rules apply only to the extent that matters of procedure are not provided for in those statutes. These rules apply to proceedings to compel the giving of testimony or production of documents in accordance with a subpoena issued by an officer or agency of the United States under any statute of the United States except as otherwise provided by statute or by rules of the district court or by order of the court in the proceedings.

(4) These rules do not alter the method prescribed by the Act of February 18, 1922, c. 57, §2 (42 Stat. 388), U.S.C., Title 7, §292; or by the Act of June 10, 1930, c. 436, §7 (46 Stat. 534), as amended, U.S.C., Title 7, §499g(c), for instituting proceedings in the United States district courts to review orders of the Secretary of Agriculture; or prescribed by the Act of June 25, 1934, c. 742, §2 (48 Stat. 1214), U.S.C., Title 15, §522, for instituting proceedings to review

orders of the Secretary of the Interior; or prescribed by the Act of February 22, 1935, c. 18, §5 (49 Stat. 31), U.S.C., Title 15, §715d(c), as extended, for instituting proceedings to review orders of petroleum control boards; but the conduct of such proceedings in the district courts shall be made to conform to these rules as far as applicable.

(5) These rules do not alter the practice in the United States district courts prescribed in the Act of July 5, 1935, c. 372, §§9 and 10 (49 Stat. 453), as amended, U.S.C., Title 29, §§159 and 160, for beginning and conducting proceedings to enforce orders of the National Labor Relations Board; and in respects not covered by those statutes, the practice in the district courts shall conform to these rules so far as applicable.

(6) These rules apply to proceedings for enforcement or review of compensation orders under the Longshoremen's and Harbor Workers' Compensation Act, Act of March 4, 1927, c. 509, §§18, 21 (44 Stat. 1434, 1436), as amended, U.S.C., Title 33, §§918, 921, except to the extent that matters of procedure are provided for in that Act. The provisions for service by publication and for answer in proceedings to cancel certificates of citizenship under the Act of June 27, 1952, c. 477, Title III, c. 2, §340 (66 Stat. 260), U.S.C., Title 8, §1451, remain in effect.

(7) *[Abrogated.]*

(b) Scire Facias and Mandamus. The writs of scire facias and mandamus are abolished. Relief heretofore available by mandamus or scire facias may be obtained by appropriate action or by appropriate motion under the practice prescribed in these rules.

(c) Removed Actions. These rules apply to civil actions removed to the United States district courts from the state courts and govern procedure after removal. Repleading is not necessary unless the court so orders. In a removed action in which the defendant has not answered, the defendant shall answer or present the other defenses or objections available under these rules within 20 days after the receipt through service or otherwise of a copy of the initial pleading setting forth the claim for relief upon which the action or proceeding is based, or within 20 days after the service of summons upon such initial pleading, then filed, or within 5 days after the filing of the petition for removal, whichever period is longest. If at the time of removal all necessary pleadings have been served, a party entitled to trial by jury under Rule 38 shall be accorded it, if the party's demand therefor is served within 10 days after the petition for removal is filed if the party is the petitioner, or if not the petitioner within 10 days after service on the party of the notice of filing the petition. A party who, prior to removal, has made an express demand for trial by jury in accordance with state law, need not make a demand after removal. If state law applicable in the court from which the case is removed does not require the parties to make express demands in order to claim trial by jury, they need not make demands after removal unless the court directs that they do so within a specified time if they desire to claim trial by jury. The court may make this direction on its own motion and shall do so as a matter of course at the request of any party. The failure of a party to make demand as directed constitutes a waiver by that party of trial by jury.

(d) District of Columbia; Courts and Judges. [*Abrogated.*]

(e) Law Applicable. Whenever in these rules the law of the state in which the district court is held is made applicable, the law applied in the District of Columbia governs proceedings in the United States District Court for the District of Columbia. When the word "state" is used, it includes, if appropriate, the District of Columbia. When the term "statute of the United States" is used, it includes, so far as concerns proceedings in the United States District Court for the District of Columbia, any Act of Congress locally applicable to and in force in the District of Columbia. When the law of a state is referred to, the word "law" includes the statutes of that state and the state judicial decisions construing them.

(f) References to Officer of the United States. Under any rule in which reference is made to an officer or agency of the United States, the term "officer" includes a district director of internal revenue, a former district director or collector of internal revenue, or the personal representative of a deceased district director or collector of internal revenue.

As amended Dec. 27, 1946, eff. Mar. 19, 1948; Dec. 29, 1948, eff. Oct. 20, 1948; Jan. 21, 1963, eff. July 1, 1963; Dec. 4, 1967, eff. July 1, 1968; Mar. 1, 1971, eff. July 1, 1971; Mar. 2, 1987, eff. Aug. 1, 1987; Apr. 23, 2001, eff. Dec. 1, 2001; Apr. 29, 2002, eff. Dec. 1, 2002.

Rule 82. Jurisdiction and Venue Unaffected

These rules shall not be construed to extend or limit the jurisdiction of the United States district courts or the venue of actions therein. An admiralty or maritime claim within the meaning of Rule 9(h) shall not be treated as a civil action for the purposes of Title 28, U.S.C. §§1391-93.

As amended Dec. 29, 1948, eff. Oct. 20, 1949; Feb. 28, 1966, eff. July 1, 1966.

Rule 83. Rules by District Courts; Judge's Directives

(a) Local Rules.

(1) Each district court, acting by a majority of its district judges, may after giving appropriate public notice and an opportunity for comment, make and

amend rules governing its practice. A local rule shall be consistent with — but not duplicative of — Acts of Congress and rules adopted under 28 U.S.C. §§2072 and 2075, and shall conform to any uniform numbering system prescribed by the Judicial Conference of the United States. A local rule takes effect on the date specified by the district court and remains in effect unless amended by the court or abrogated by the judicial council of the circuit. Copies of rules and amendments shall, upon their promulgation, be furnished to the judicial council and the Administrative Office of the United States Courts and be made available to the public.

(2) A local rule imposing a requirement of form shall not be enforced in a manner that causes a party to lose rights because of a nonwillful failure to comply with the requirement.

(b) Procedures When There Is No Controlling Law. A judge may regulate practice in any manner consistent with federal law, rules adopted under 28 U.S.C. §§2072 and 2075, and local rules of the district. No sanction or other disadvantage may be imposed for noncompliance with any requirement not in federal law, federal rules, or the local district rules unless the alleged violator has been furnished in the particular case with actual notice of the requirement.

As amended Apr. 29, 1985, eff. Aug. 1, 1985; Apr. 27, 1995, eff. Dec. 1, 1995.

ADVISORY COMMITTEE NOTES, 1985 AND 1995 AMENDMENTS

1985 AMENDMENT

Rule 83, which has not been amended since the Federal Rules were promulgated in 1938, permits each district to adopt local rules not inconsistent with the Federal Rules by a majority of the judges. . . .

The amended Rule attempts, without impairing the procedural validity of existing local rules, to enhance the local rulemaking process by requiring appropriate public notice of proposed rules and an opportunity to comment on them. Although some district courts apparently consult the local bar before promulgating rules, many do not, which has led to criticism of a process that has district judges consulting only with each other. See 12 C. Wright & A. Miller, supra, §3152, at 217; Blair, The New Local Rules for Federal Practice in Iowa, 23 Drake L. Rev. 517 (1974). The new language subjects local rulemaking to scrutiny similar to that accompanying the Federal Rules, administrative rulemaking, and legislation. It attempts to assure that the expert advice of practitioners and scholars is made available to the district court before local rules are promulgated. See Weinstein, Reform of Court Rule-Making Procedures 84-87, 127-137, 151 (1977).

. . . The expectation is that the judicial council will examine all local rules, including those currently in effect, with an eye toward determining whether they are valid and consistent with the Federal Rules, promote inter-district uniformity and efficiency, and do not undermine the basic objectives of the Federal Rules. . . .

The practice pursued by some judges of issuing standing orders has been controversial, particularly among members of the practicing bar. The last sentence in Rule 83 has been amended to make certain that standing orders are not inconsistent with the Federal Rules or any local district court rules. Beyond that, it is hoped that each district will adopt procedures, perhaps by local rule, for promulgating and reviewing single-judge standing orders.

1995 AMENDMENT

Subdivision (a). This rule is amended to reflect the requirement that local rules be consistent not only with the national rules but also with Acts of Congress. The amendment also states that local rules should not repeat Acts of Congress or local rules.

The amendment also requires that the numbering of local rules conform with any uniform numbering system that may be prescribed by the Judicial Conference. Lack of uniform numbering might create unnecessary traps for counsel and litigants. A uniform numbering system would make it easier for an increasingly national bar and for litigants to locate a local rule that applies to a particular procedural issue.

Paragraph (2) is new. Its aim is to protect against loss of rights in the enforcement of local rules relating to matters of form. For example, a party should not be deprived of a right to a jury trial because its attorney, unaware of — or forgetting — a local rule directing that jury demands be noted in the caption of the case, includes a jury demand only in the body of the pleading. . . .

Subdivision (b). This rule provides flexibility to the court in regulating practice when there is no controlling law. Specifically, it permits the court to regulate practice in any manner consistent with Acts of Congress, with rules adopted under 28 U.S.C. §§2072 and 2075, and with the district local rules.

This rule recognizes that courts rely on multiple directives to control practice. Some courts regulate practice through the published Federal Rules and the local rules of the court. Some courts also have used internal operating procedures, standing orders, and other internal directives. Although such directives continue to be authorized, they can lead to problems. Counsel or litigants may be unaware of various directives. In addition, the sheer volume of directives may impose an unreasonable barrier. For example, it may be difficult to obtain copies of the directives. Finally, counsel or litigants may be unfairly sanctioned for failing to comply with a directive. For these reasons, the amendment to this rule disapproves imposing any sanction or other disadvantage on a person for noncompliance with such an internal directive, unless the alleged violator has been furnished actual notice of the requirement in a particular case.

There should be no adverse consequence to a party or attorney for violating special requirements relating to practice before a particular court unless the party or attorney has actual notice of those requirements. Furnishing litigants with a copy outlining the judge's practices — or attaching instructions to a notice setting a case for conference or trial — would suffice to give actual notice, as would an order in a case specifically adopting by reference a judge's standing order and indicating how copies can be obtained.

Rule 84. Forms

The forms contained in the Appendix of Forms are sufficient under the rules and are intended to indicate the simplicity and brevity of statement which the rules contemplate.

As amended Dec. 27, 1946, eff. Mar. 19, 1948.

Rule 85. Title

These rules may be known and cited as the Federal Rules of Civil Procedure.

Rule 86. Effective Date

(a) [**Effective Date of Original Rules.**] These rules will take effect on the day which is 3 months subsequent to the adjournment of the second regular session of the 75th Congress, but if that day is prior to September 1, 1938, then these rules will take effect on September 1, 1938. They govern all proceedings in actions brought after they take effect and also all further proceedings in actions then pending, except to the extent that in the opinion of the court their application in a particular action pending when the rules take effect would not be feasible or would work injustice, in which event the former procedure applies.

(b) **Effective Date of Amendments.** The amendments adopted by the Supreme Court on December 27, 1946, and transmitted to the Attorney General on January 2, 1947, shall take effect on the day which is three months subsequent to the adjournment of the first regular session of the 80th Congress, but, if that day is prior to September 1, 1947, then these amendments shall take effect on September 1, 1947. They govern all proceedings in actions brought after they take effect and also all further proceedings in actions then pending, except to the extent that in the opinion of the court their application in a particular action pending when the amendments take effect would not be feasible or would work injustice, in which event the former procedure applies.

Added Dec. 27, 1946, eff. Mar. 19, 1948.

(c) **Effective Date of Amendments.** The amendments adopted by the Supreme Court on December 29, 1948, and transmitted to the Attorney General on December 31, 1948, shall take effect on the day following the adjournment of the first regular session of the 81st Congress.

Added Dec. 29, 1948, eff. Oct. 20, 1949.

(d) **Effective Date of Amendments.** The amendments adopted by the Supreme Court on April 17, 1961, and transmitted to the Congress on April 18,

1961, shall take effect on July 19, 1961. They govern all proceedings in actions brought after they take effect and also all further proceedings in actions then pending, except to the extent that in the opinion of the court their application in a particular action pending when the amendments take effect would not be feasible or would work injustice, in which event the former procedure applies.

Added Apr. 17, 1961, eff. July 19, 1961.

(e) **Effective Date of Amendments.** The amendments adopted by the Supreme Court on January 21, 1963, and transmitted to the Congress on January 21, 1963 shall take effect on July 1, 1963. They govern all proceedings in actions brought after they take effect and also all further proceedings in actions then pending, except to the extent that in the opinion of the court their application in a particular action pending when the amendments take effect would not be feasible or would work injustice, in which event the former procedure applies.

Added Jan. 21, 1963, eff. July 1, 1963.

[The practice of amending Rule 86 to show effective times of amendments was discontinued after the 1963 amendments. Adoption and effective dates of subsequent amendments are shown after the relevant change in the rule.]

APPENDIX OF FORMS

(See Rule 84)

TABLE OF FORMS

26. Allegation of Reason for Omitting Party
27. Notice of Appeal to Court of Appeals Under Rule 73(b)
28. Notice: Condemnation
29. Complaint: Condemnation
30. Suggestion of Death upon the Record Under Rule 25(a)(1)
31. Judgment on Jury Verdict
32. Judgment on Decision by the Court
33. Notice of Availability of a Magistrate Judge to Exercise Jurisdiction and Appeal Option
34. Consent to Exercise of Jurisdiction by a United States Magistrate Judge, Election of Appeal to a District Judge
34-A. Order of Reference
35. Report of Parties' Planning Meeting

Introductory Statement

1. The following forms are intended for illustration only. They are limited in number. No attempt is made to furnish a manual of forms. Each form assumes the action to be brought in the Southern District of New York. If the district in which an action is brought has divisions, the division should be indicated in the caption.

2. Except where otherwise indicated each pleading, motion, and other paper should have a caption similar to that of the summons, with the designation of the particular paper substituted for the word "Summons." In the caption of the summons and in the caption of the complaint all parties must be named but in other pleadings and papers, it is sufficient to state the name of the first party on either side, with an appropriate indication of other parties. See Rules 4(b), 7(b)(2), and 10(a).

3. In Form 3 and the forms following, the words, "Allegation of jurisdiction," are used to indicate the appropriate allegation in Form 2.

4. Each pleading, motion, and other paper is to be signed in his individual name by at least one attorney of record (Rule 11). The attorney's name is to be followed by his address as indicated in Form 3. In forms following Form 3 the signature and address are not indicated.

5. If a party is not represented by an attorney, the signature and address of the party are required in place of those of the attorney.

Form 1. Summons

United States District Court for the Southern District of New York

Civil Action, File Number ____

____

A. B., Plaintiff

v. SUMMONS

C. D., Defendant

To the above-named Defendant:

You are hereby summoned and required to serve upon ________, plaintiff's attorney, whose address is ________, an answer to the complaint which is herewith served upon you, within 20[1] days after service of this summons upon you, exclusive of the day of service. If you fail to do so, judgment by default will be taken against you for the relief demanded in the complaint.

____

Clerk of Court

[Seal of the U.S. District Court]
Dated ______________________

As amended Dec. 29, 1948, eff. Oct. 20, 1949.

(This summons is issued pursuant to Rule 4 of the Federal Rules of Civil Procedure.)

Form 1-A. Notice of Lawsuit and Request for Waiver of Service of Summons

To: ______(name of individual defendant or agent)______ [as ______(title)______ of ______(corporation)______]

A lawsuit has been commenced against you (or the entity on whose behalf you are addressed). A copy of the complaint is attached to this notice. It has been filed in the United States District Court for the ______(district)______ and has been assigned docket number ______.

1. If the United States or an officer or agency thereof is a defendant, the time to be inserted as to it is 60 days.

This is not a formal summons or notification from the court, but rather my request that you sign and return the enclosed waiver of service in order to save the cost of serving you with a judicial summons and an additional copy of the complaint. The cost of service will be avoided if I receive a signed copy of the waiver within 30 days[1] after the date designated below as the date on which this Notice and Request is sent. I enclose a stamped and addressed envelope (or other means of cost-free return) for your use. An extra copy of the waiver is also attached for your records.

If you comply with this request and return the signed waiver, it will be filed with the court and no summons will be served on you. The action will then proceed as if you had been served on the date the waiver is filed, except that you will not be obligated to answer the complaint before 60 days from the date designated below as the date on which this notice is sent (or before 90 days from the date if your address is not in any judicial district of the United States).

If you do not return the signed waiver within the time indicated, I will take appropriate steps to effect formal service in a manner authorized by the Federal Rules of Civil Procedure and will then, to the extent authorized by those Rules, ask the court to require you (or the party on whose behalf you are addressed) to pay the full costs of such service. In that connection, please read the statement concerning the duty of parties to waive the service of the summons, which is set forth on the reverse side (or at the foot) of the waiver form.

I affirm that this request is being sent to you on behalf of the plaintiff, this __ day of ______, ___.

____

Signature of Plaintiff's Attorney or Unrepresented Plaintiff

Added Apr. 22, 1993, eff. Dec. 1, 1993.

Form 1-B. Waiver of Service of Summons

To: (name of plaintiff's attorney or unrepresented plaintiff)

I acknowledge receipt of your request that I waive service of a summons in the action of ______(caption of action)______, which is case ___(docket number)___ in the United States District Court for the ______(district)______. I have also received a copy of

1. Addressee must be given at least 30 days (60 days if located in foreign country) in which to return waiver.

the complaint in the action, two copies of this instrument, and a means by which I can return the signed waiver to you without cost to me.

I agree to save the cost of service of a summons and an additional copy of the complaint in this lawsuit by not requiring that I (or the entity on whose behalf I am acting) be served with judicial process in the manner provided by Rule 4.

I (or the entity on whose behalf I am acting) will retain all defenses or objections to the lawsuit or to the jurisdiction or venue of the court except for objections based on a defect in the summons or in the service of the summons.

I understand that a judgment may be entered against me (or the party on whose behalf I am acting) if an answer or motion under Rule 12 is not served upon you within 60 days after __(date request was sent)__, or within 90 days after that date if the request was sent outside the United States.

__________ ____________________________

Date Signature

Printed/typed name:________________
[as ____________________]
[of ____________________]

To be printed on reverse side of the waiver form or set forth at the foot of the form:

Duty to Avoid Unnecessary Costs of Service of Summons

Rule 4 of the Federal Rules of Civil Procedure requires certain parties to cooperate in saving unnecessary costs of service of the summons and complaint. A defendant located in the United States who, after being notified of an action and asked by a plaintiff located in the United States to waive service of a summons, fails to do so will be required to bear the cost of such service unless good cause be shown for its failure to sign and return the waiver.

It is not good cause for a failure to waive service that a party believes that the complaint is unfounded, or that the action has been brought in an improper place or in a court that lacks jurisdiction over the subject matter of the action or over its person or property. A party who waives service of the summons retains all defenses and objections (except any relating to the summons or to the service of the summons), and may later object to the jurisdiction of the court or to the place where the action has been brought.

A defendant who waives service must within the time specified on the waiver form serve on the plaintiff's attorney (or unrepresented plaintiff) a response to the complaint and must also file a signed copy of the response with the court. If the answer or motion is not served within this time, a default judgment may be taken against that defendant. By waiving service, a defendant is allowed more time to answer than if the summons had been actually served when the request for waiver of service was received.

Added Apr. 22, 1993, eff. Dec. 1, 1993.

Form 2. Allegation of Jurisdiction

(a) Jurisdiction founded on diversity of citizenship and amount.

Plaintiff is a [citizen of the State of Connecticut][1] [corporation incorporated under the laws of the State of Connecticut having its principal place of business in the State of Connecticut] and defendant is a corporation incorporated under the laws of the State of New York having its principal place of business in a State other than the State of Connecticut. The matter in controversy exceeds, exclusive of interest and costs, the sum specified by 28 U.S.C. § 1332.

(b) Jurisdiction founded on the existence of a Federal question.

This action arises under [the Constitution of the United States, Article ____, Section ____]; [the ____ Amendment to the Constitution of the United States, Section ____]; [the Act of ____, ____ Stat. ____; U.S.C., Title ____, § ____]; [the Treaty of the United States (here describe the treaty)],[2] as hereinafter more fully appears.

(c) Jurisdiction founded on the existence of a question arising under particular statutes.

The action arises under the Act of ____, ____ Stat. ____; U.S.C., Title ____, § ____, as hereinafter more fully appears.

(d) Jurisdiction founded on the admiralty or maritime character of the claim.

This is a case of admiralty and maritime jurisdiction, as hereinafter more fully appears. [If the pleader wishes to invoke the distinctively maritime procedures referred to in Rule 9(h), add the following or its substantial equivalent: This is an admiralty or maritime claim within the meaning of Rule 9(h).]

As amended Apr. 17, 1961, eff. July 19, 1961; Feb. 28, 1966, eff. July 1, 1966; Apr. 22, 1993, eff. Dec. 1, 1993; April 29, 1999, eff. Dec. 1, 1999.

Form 3. Complaint on a Promissory Note

1. Allegation of jurisdiction.
2. Defendant on or about June 1, 1935, executed and delivered to plaintiff a promissory note [in the following words and figures: (here set out the note verbatim)]; [a copy of which is hereto annexed as Exhibit A]; [whereby defendant promised to pay to plaintiff or order on June 1, 1936 the sum of ____ dollars with interest thereon at the rate of six percent. per annum].
3. Defendant owes to plaintiff the amount of said note and interest.

1. Form for natural person.

2. Use the appropriate phrase or phrases. The general allegation of the existence of a Federal question is ineffective unless the matters constituting the claim for relief as set forth in the complaint raise a Federal question.

Wherefore plaintiff demands judgment against defendant for the sum of ______ dollars, interest, and costs.

Signed: ____________________
Attorney for Plaintiff
Address: ____________________

As amended Jan. 21, 1963, eff. July 1, 1963.

Form 4. Complaint on an Account

1. Allegation of jurisdiction.
2. Defendant owes plaintiff ______ dollars according to the account hereto annexed as Exhibit A.

Wherefore (etc. as in Form 3).

As amended Jan. 21, 1963, eff. July 1, 1963.

Form 5. Complaint for Goods Sold and Delivered

1. Allegation of jurisdiction.
2. Defendant owes plaintiff ______ dollars for goods sold and delivered by plaintiff to defendant between June 1, 1936 and December 1, 1936.

Wherefore (etc. as in Form 3).

As amended Jan. 21, 1963, eff. July 1, 1963.

Form 6. Complaint for Money Lent

1. Allegation of jurisdiction.
2. Defendant owes plaintiff ______ dollars for money lent by plaintiff to defendant on June 1, 1936.

Wherefore (etc. as in Form 3).

As amended Jan. 21, 1963, eff. July 1, 1963.

Form 7. Complaint for Money Paid by Mistake

1. Allegation of jurisdiction.
2. Defendant owes plaintiff ____ dollars for money paid by plaintiff to

defendant by mistake on June 1, 1936, under the following circumstances: [here state the circumstances with particularity — see Rule 9(b)].

Wherefore (etc. as in Form 3).

As amended Jan. 21, 1963, eff. July 1, 1963.

Form 8. Complaint for Money Had and Received

1. Allegation of jurisdiction.

2. Defendant owes plaintiff ______ dollars for money had and received from one G. H. on June 1, 1936, to be paid by defendant to plaintiff.

Wherefore (etc. as in Form 3).

As amended Jan. 21, 1963, eff. July 1, 1963.

Form 9. Complaint for Negligence

1. Allegation of jurisdiction.

2. On June 1, 1936, in a public highway called Boylston Street in Boston, Massachusetts, defendant negligently drove a motor vehicle against plaintiff who was then crossing said highway.

3. As a result plaintiff was thrown down and had his leg broken and was otherwise injured, was prevented from transacting his business, suffered great pain of body and mind, and incurred expenses for medical attention and hospitalization in the sum of one thousand dollars.

Wherefore plaintiff demands judgment against defendant in the sum of ______ dollars and costs.

As amended Jan. 21, 1963, eff. July 1, 1963.

Form 10. Complaint for Negligence Where Plaintiff Is Unable to Determine Definitely Whether the Person Responsible Is C. D. or E. F. or Whether Both Are Responsible Where His Evidence May Justify a Finding of Wilfulness or of Recklessness or of Negligence

A. B., Plaintiff
v.
C. D. and E. F., Defendants

COMPLAINT

1. Allegation of jurisdiction.

2. On June 1, 1936, in a public highway called Boylston Street in Boston,

Massachusetts, defendant C. D. or defendant E. F., or both defendants C. D. and E. F. wilfully or recklessly or negligently drove or caused to be driven a motor vehicle against plaintiff who was then crossing said highway.

3. As a result plaintiff was thrown down and had his leg broken and was otherwise injured, was prevented from transacting his business, suffered great pain of body and mind, and incurred expenses for medical attention and hospitalization in the sum of one thousand dollars.

Wherefore plaintiff demands judgment against C. D. or against E. F. or against both in the sum of ______ dollars and costs.

As amended Jan. 21, 1963, eff. July 1, 1963.

Form 11. Complaint for Conversion

1. Allegation of jurisdiction.

2. On or about December 1, 1936, defendant converted to his own use ten bonds of the ______ Company (here insert brief identification as by number and issue) of the value of ______ dollars, the property of plaintiff.

Wherefore plaintiff demands judgment against defendant in the sum of ______ dollars, interest, and costs.

As amended Jan. 21, 1963, eff. July 1, 1963.

Form 12. Complaint for Specific Performance of Contract to Convey Land

1. Allegation of jurisdiction.

2. On or about December 1, 1936, plaintiff and defendant entered into an agreement in writing a copy of which is hereto annexed as Exhibit A.

3. In accord with the provisions of said agreement plaintiff tendered to defendant the purchase price and requested a conveyance of the land, but defendant refused to accept the tender and refused to make the conveyance.

4. Plaintiff now offers to pay the purchase price.

Wherefore plaintiff demands (1) that defendant be required specifically to perform said agreement, (2) damages in the sum of one thousand dollars, and (3) that if specific performance is not granted plaintiff have judgment against defendant in the sum of ______ dollars.

As amended Jan. 21, 1963, eff. July 1, 1963.

Form 13. Complaint on Claim for Debt and to Set Aside Fraudulent Conveyance Under Rule 18(b)

A. B., Plaintiff

v. COMPLAINT

C. D. and E. F., Defendants

1. Allegation of jurisdiction.

2. Defendant C. D. on or about ____ executed and delivered to plaintiff a promissory note [in the following words and figures: (here set out the note verbatim)]; [a copy of which is hereto annexed as Exhibit A]; [whereby defendant C. D. promised to pay to plaintiff or order on ____ the sum of five thousand dollars with interest thereon at the rate of ____ percent. per annum].

3. Defendant C. D. owes to plaintiff the amount of said note and interest.

4. Defendant C. D. on or about ____ conveyed all his property, real and personal [or specify and describe] to defendant E. F. for the purpose of defrauding plaintiff and hindering and delaying the collection of the indebtedness evidenced by the note above referred to.

Wherefore plaintiff demands:

(1) That plaintiff have judgment against defendant C. D. for ______ dollars and interest; (2) that the aforesaid conveyance to defendant E. F. be declared void and the judgment herein be declared a lien on said property; (3) that plaintiff have judgment against the defendants for costs.

As amended Jan. 21, 1963, eff. July 1, 1963.

Form 14. Complaint for Negligence Under Federal Employers' Liability Act

1. Allegation of jurisdiction.

2. During all the times herein mentioned defendant owned and operated in interstate commerce a railroad which passed through a tunnel located at ____ and known as Tunnel No. ______ .

3. On or about June 1, 1936, defendant was repairing and enlarging the tunnel in order to protect interstate trains and passengers and freight from injury and in order to make the tunnel more conveniently usable for interstate commerce.

4. In the course of thus repairing and enlarging the tunnel on said day defendant employed plaintiff as one of its workmen, and negligently put plaintiff

to work in a portion of the tunnel which defendant had left unprotected and unsupported.

5. By reason of defendant's negligence in thus putting plaintiff to work in that portion of the tunnel, plaintiff was, while so working pursuant to defendant's orders, struck and crushed by a rock, which fell from the unsupported portion of the tunnel, and was (here describe plaintiff's injuries).

6. Prior to these injuries, plaintiff was a strong, able-bodied man, capable of earning and actually earning ______ dollars per day. By these injuries he has been made incapable of any gainful activity, has suffered great physical and mental pain, and has incurred expense in the amount of ______ dollars for medicine, medical attendance, and hospitalization.

Wherefore plaintiff demands judgment against defendant in the sum of ______ dollars and costs.

Form 15. Complaint for Damages Under Merchant Marine Act

1. Allegation of jurisdiction. [If the pleader wishes to invoke the distinctively maritime procedures referred to in Rule 9(h), add the following or its substantial equivalent: This is an admiralty or maritime claim within the meaning of Rule 9(h).]

2. During all the times herein mentioned defendant was the owner of the steamship ____ and used it in the transportation of freight for hire by water in interstate and foreign commerce.

3. During the first part of (month and year) at ____ plaintiff entered the employ of defendant as an able seaman on said steamship under seamen's articles of customary form for a voyage from ____ ports to the Orient and return at a wage of ______ dollars per month and found, which is equal to a wage of ______ dollars per month as a shore worker.

4. On June 1, 1936, said steamship was about ____ days out of the port of ____ and was being navigated by the master and crew on the return voyage of ____ ports. (Here describe weather conditions and the condition of the ship and state as in an ordinary complaint for personal injuries the negligent conduct of defendant.)

5. By reason of defendant's negligence in thus (brief statement of defendant's negligent conduct) and the unseaworthiness of said steamship, plaintiff was (here describe plaintiff's injuries).

6. Prior to these injuries, plaintiff was a strong, able-bodied man, capable of earning and actually earning ____ dollars per day. By these injuries he has been made incapable of any gainful activity; has suffered great physical and mental pain, and has incurred expense in the amount of ______ dollars for medicine, medical attendance, and hospitalization.

Wherefore plaintiff demands judgment against defendant in the sum of ______ dollars and costs.

As amended Feb. 28, 1966, eff. July 1, 1966.

Form 16. Complaint for Infringement of Patent

1. Allegation of jurisdiction.

2. On May 16, 1934, United States Letters Patent No. ______ were duly and legally issued to plaintiff for an invention in an electric motor; and since that date plaintiff has been and still is the owner of those Letters Patent.

3. Defendant has for a long time past been and still is infringing those Letters Patent by making, selling, and using electric motors embodying the patented invention, and will continue to do so unless enjoined by this court.

4. Plaintiff has placed the required statutory notice on all electric motors manufactured and sold by him under said Letters Patent, and has given written notice to defendant of his said infringement.

Wherefore plaintiff demands a preliminary and final injunction against continued infringement, an accounting for damages, and an assessment of interest and costs against defendant.

As amended Jan. 21, 1963, eff. July 1, 1963.

Form 17. Complaint for Infringement of Copyright and Unfair Competition

1. Allegation of jurisdiction.

2. Prior to March, 1936, plaintiff, who then was and ever since has been a citizen of the United States, created and wrote an original book, entitled __________.

3. This book contains a large amount of material wholly original with plaintiff and is copyrightable subject matter under the laws of the United States.

4. Between March 2, 1936, and March 10, 1936, plaintiff complied in all respects with the Act of (give citation) and all other laws governing copyright, and secured the exclusive rights and privileges in and to the copyright of said book, and received from the Register of Copyrights a certificate of registration, dated and identified as follows: "March 10, 1936, Class ______, No. ____."

5. Since March 10, 1936, said book has been published by plaintiff and all copies of it made by plaintiff or under his authority or license have been printed, bound, and published in strict conformity with the provisions of the Act of __________ and all other laws governing copyright.

6. Since March 10, 1936, plaintiff has been and still is the sole proprietor of all rights, title, and interest in and to the copyright in said book.

7. After March 10, 1936, defendant infringed said copyright by publishing and placing upon the market a book entitled __________, which was copied largely from plaintiff's copyrighted book, entitled __________.

8. A copy of plaintiff's copyrighted book is hereto attached as "Exhibit 1"; and a copy of defendant's infringing book is hereto attached as "Exhibit 2."

9. Plaintiff has notified defendant that defendant has infringed the copyright of plaintiff, and defendant has continued to infringe the copyright.

10. After March 10, 1936, and continuously since about __________, defendant has been publishing, selling and otherwise marketing the book entitled __________, and has thereby been engaging in unfair trade practices and unfair competition against plaintiff to plaintiff's irreparable damage.

Wherefore plaintiff demands:

(1) That defendant, his agents, and servants be enjoined during the pendency of this action and permanently from infringing said copyright of said plaintiff in any manner, and from publishing, selling, marketing or otherwise disposing of any copies of the book entitled __________.

(2) That defendant be required to pay to plaintiff such damages as plaintiff has sustained in consequence of defendant's infringement of said copyright and said unfair trade practices and unfair competition and to account for

(a) all gains, profits and advantages derived by defendant by said trade practices and unfair competition and

(b) all gains, profits, and advantages derived by defendant by his infringement of plaintiff's copyright or such damages as to the court shall appear proper within the provisions of the copyright statutes, but not less than two hundred and fifty dollars.

(3) That defendant be required to deliver up to be impounded during the pendency of this action all copies of said book entitled __________ in his possession or under his control and to deliver up for destruction all infringing copies and all plates, molds, and other matter for making such infringing copies.

(4) That defendant pay to plaintiff the costs of this action and reasonable attorney's fees to be allowed to the plaintiff by the court.

(5) That plaintiff have such other and further relief as is just.

As amended Dec. 27, 1946, eff. Mar. 19, 1948.

Form 18. Complaint for Interpleader and Declaratory Relief

1. Allegation of jurisdiction.

2. On or about June 1, 1935, plaintiff issued to G. H. a policy of life insurance whereby plaintiff promised to pay to K. L. as beneficiary the sum of ______ dollars upon the death of G. H. The policy required the payment by G. H. of a stipulated premium on June 1, 1936, and annually thereafter as a condition precedent to its continuance in force.

3. No part of the premium due June 1, 1936, was ever paid and the policy ceased to have any force or effect on July 1, 1936.

4. Thereafter, on September 1, 1936, G. H. and K. L. died as the result of a collision between a locomotive and the automobile in which G. H. and K. L. were riding.

Defendant C. D. is the duly appointed and acting executor of the will of G. H.; defendant E. F. is the duly appointed and acting executor of the will of K. L.; defendant X. Y. claims to have been duly designated as beneficiary of said policy in place of K. L.

6. Each of defendants, C. D., E. F., and X. Y., is claiming that the above-mentioned policy was in full force and effect at the time of the death of G. H.; each of them is claiming to be the only person entitled to receive payment of the amount of the policy and has made demand for payment thereof.

7. By reason of these conflicting claims of the defendants, plaintiff is in great doubt as to which defendant is entitled to be paid the amount of the policy, if it was in force at the death of G. H.

Wherefore plaintiff demands that the court adjudge:

(1) That none of the defendants is entitled to recover from plaintiff the amount of said policy or any part thereof.

(2) That each of the defendants be restrained from instituting any action against plaintiff for the recovery of the amount of said policy or any part thereof.

(3) That, if the court shall determine that said policy was in force at the death of G. H., the defendants be required to interplead and settle between themselves their rights to the money due under said policy, and that plaintiff be discharged from all liability in the premises except to the person whom the court shall adjudge entitled to the amount of said policy.

(4) That plaintiff recover its costs.

As amended Jan. 21, 1963, eff. July 1, 1963.

Form 18-A. Notice and Acknowledgment for Service by Mail [*Abrogated.*]

Form 19. Motion to Dismiss, Presenting Defenses of Failure to State a Claim, of Lack of Service of Process, of Improper Venue, and of Lack of Jurisdiction Under Rule 12(b)

The defendant moves the court as follows:

1. To dismiss the action because the complaint fails to state a claim against defendant upon which relief can be granted.

2. To dismiss the action or in lieu thereof to quash the return of service of

summons on the grounds (a) that the defendant is a corporation organized under the laws of Delaware and was not and is not subject to service of process within the Southern District of New York, and (b) that the defendant has not been properly served with process in this action, all of which more clearly appears in the affidavits of M. N. and X. Y. hereto annexed as Exhibit A and Exhibit B respectively.

3. To dismiss the action on the ground that it is in the wrong district because (a) the jurisdiction of this court is invoked solely on the ground that the action arises under the Constitution and laws of the United States and (b) the defendant is a corporation incorporated under the laws of the State of Delaware and is not licensed to do or doing business in the Southern District of New York, all of which more clearly appears in the affidavits of K. L. and V. W. hereto annexed as Exhibit C and D respectively.

4. To dismiss the action on the ground that the court lacks jurisdiction because the amount actually in controversy is less than ten thousand dollars exclusive of interest and costs.

Signed: ____________________
Attorney for Defendant
Address: ____________________

Notice of Motion

To: ____________________
Attorney for Plaintiff
____

Please take notice, that the undersigned will bring the above motion on for hearing before this Court at Room ____, United States Court House, Foley Square, City of New York, on the ____ day of ______, 193____, at 10 o'clock in the forenoon of that day or as soon thereafter as counsel can be heard.

Signed: ____________________
Attorney for Defendant
Address: ____________________

As amended Dec. 29, 1948, eff. Oct. 20, 1949; Apr. 17, 1961, eff. July 19, 1961.

Form 20. Answer Presenting Defenses Under Rule 12(b)

First Defense

The complaint fails to state a claim against defendant upon which relief can be granted.

Second Defense

If defendant is indebted to plaintiffs for the goods mentioned in the complaint, he is indebted to them jointly with G. H. G. H. is alive; is a citizen of the State of New York and a resident of this district, is subject to the jurisdiction of this court, as to both service of process and venue; can be made a party without depriving this court of jurisdiction of the present parties, and has not been made a party.

Third Defense

Defendant admits the allegation contained in paragraphs 1 and 4 of the complaint; alleges that he is without knowledge or information sufficient to form a belief as to the truth of the allegations contained in paragraph 2 of the complaint; and denies each and every other allegation contained in the complaint.

Fourth Defense

The right of action set forth in the complaint did not accrue within six years next before the commencement of this action.

Counterclaim

(Here set forth any claim as a counterclaim in the manner in which a claim is pleaded in a complaint. No statement of the grounds on which the court's jurisdiction depends need be made unless the counterclaim requires independent grounds of jurisdiction.)

Cross-Claim Against Defendant M. N.

(Here set forth the claim constituting a cross-claim against defendant M. N. in the manner in which a claim is pleaded in a complaint. The statement of grounds upon which the court's jurisdiction depends need not be made unless the cross-claim requires independent grounds of jurisdiction.)

Form 21. Answer to Complaint Set Forth in Form 8, with Counterclaim for Interpleader

Defense

Defendant admits the allegations stated in paragraph 1 of the complaint; and denies the allegations stated in paragraph 2 to the extent set forth in the counterclaim herein.

Counterclaim for Interpleader

1. Defendant received the sum of ______ dollars as a deposit from E. F.
2. Plaintiff has demanded the payment of such deposit to him by virtue of an assignment of it which he claims to have received from E. F.

3. E.F. has notified the defendant that he claims such deposit, that the purported assignment is not valid, and that he holds the defendant responsible for the deposit.

Wherefore defendant demands:

(1) That the court order E. F. to be made a party defendant to respond to the complaint and to this counterclaim.[1]

(2) That the court order the plaintiff and E. F. to interplead their respective claims.

(3) That the court adjudge whether the plaintiff or E. F. is entitled to the sum of money.

(4) That the court discharge defendant from all liability in the premises except to the person it shall adjudge entitled to the sum of money.

(5) That the court award to the defendant its costs and attorney's fees.

As amended Jan. 21, 1963, eff. July 1, 1963.

Form 22-A. Summons and Complaint Against Third-Party Defendant

United States District Court for the Southern District of New York

Civil Action, File Number ____

A.B., Plaintiff

v.

C. D., Defendant and Third-Party Plaintiff — SUMMONS

v.

E. F., Third-Party Defendant

To the above-named Third-Party Defendant:

You are hereby summoned and required to serve upon ______, plaintiff's attorney whose address is __________, and upon __________, who is attorney for C. D., defendant and third-party plaintiff, and whose address is ________, an answer to the third-party complaint which is herewith served upon you within 20 days after the service of this summons upon you exclusive of the day of service.

1. Rule 13(h) provides for the court ordering parties to a counterclaim, but who are not parties to the original action, to be brought in as defendants.

If you fail to do so, judgment by default will be taken against you for the relief demanded in the third-party complaint. There is also served upon you herewith a copy of the complaint of the plaintiff which you may but are not required to answer.

____
Clerk of Court

[Seal of District Court]
Dated ____________________

United States District Court for the Southern District of New York

Civil Action, File Number ____

A.B., Plaintiff

v.

C. D., Defendant and Third-Party Plaintiff — THIRD-PARTY COMPLAINT

v.

E. F., Third-Party Defendant

1. Plaintiff A. B. has filed against defendant C. D. a complaint, a copy of which is hereto attached as "Exhibit A."

2. (Here state the grounds upon which C. D. is entitled to recover from E. F., all or part of what A. B. may recover from C. D. The statement should be framed as in an original complaint.)

Wherefore C. D. demands judgment against third-party defendant E. F. for all sums[1] that may be adjudged against defendant C. D. in favor of plaintiff A. B.

Signed: ____________________
Attorney for C. D.,
Third-Party Plaintiff

Address: ____________________

Added Jan. 21, 1963, eff. July 1, 1963.

1. Make appropriate change where C. D. is entitled to only partial recovery-over against E. F.

Form 22-B. Motion to Bring In Third-Party Defendant

Defendant moves for leave, as third-party plaintiff, to cause to be served upon E. F. a summons and third-party complaint, copies of which are hereto attached as Exhibit X.

Signed: ______________________
Attorney for Defendant C. D.

Address: ______________________

Notice of Motion

(Contents the same as in Form 19. The notice should be addressed to all parties to the action.)

EXHIBIT X

(Contents the same as in Form 22-A.)

Added Jan. 21, 1963, eff. July 1, 1963.

Form 23. Motion to Intervene as a Defendant Under Rule 24

(Based upon the complaint, Form 16)

United States District Court for the Southern District of New York

Civil Action, File Number ____

A.B., Plaintiff v. C. D., Defendant E. F., Applicant for Intervention	MOTION TO INTERVENE AS A DEFENDANT

E. F. moves for leave to intervene as a defendant in this action, in order to assert the defenses set forth in his proposed answer, of which a copy is hereto attached, on the ground that he is the manufacturer and vendor to the defendant, as well as to others, of the articles alleged in the complaint to be an infringement of plaintiff's patent, and as such has a defense to plaintiff's claim presenting both questions of law and of fact which are common to the main action.[1]

Signed: ______________________
Attorney for E. F.
Applicant for Intervention

Address: ______________________

Notice of Motion

(Contents the same as in Form 19)

United States District Court for the Southern District of New York

Civil Action, File Number ____

A.B., Plaintiff

v

C. D., Defendant
E. F., Intervener

INTERVENER'S ANSWER

First Defense

Intervener admits the allegations stated in paragraphs 1 and 4 of the complaint; denies the allegations in paragraph 3, and denies the allegations in paragraph 2 in so far as they assert the legality of the issuance of the Letters Patent to plaintiff.

Second Defense

Plaintiff is not the first inventor of the articles covered by the Letters Patent specified in his complaint, since articles substantially identical in character were previously patented in Letters Patent granted to intervener on January 5, 1920.

Signed: ______________________
Attorney for E. F.,
Intervener

Address: ______________________

As amended Dec. 29, 1948, eff. Oct. 20, 1949.

1. For other grounds of intervention, either of right or in the discretion of the court, see Rule 24(a) and (b).

Form 24. Request for Production of Documents, etc., Under Rule 34

Plaintiff A. B. requests defendant C. D. to respond within ______ days to the following requests:

(1) That defendant produce and permit plaintiff to inspect and to copy each of the following documents:

(Here list the documents either individually or by category and describe each of them.)

(Here state the time, place, and manner of making the inspection and performance of any related acts.)

(2) That defendant produce and permit plaintiff to inspect and to copy, test, or sample each of the following objects:

(Here list the objects either individually or by category and describe each of them.)

(Here state the time, place, and manner of making the inspection and performance of any related acts.)

(3) That defendant permit plaintiff to enter (here describe property to be entered) and to inspect and to photograph, test or sample (here describe the portion of the real property and the objects to be inspected).

(Here state the time, place, and manner of making the inspection and performance of any related acts.)

Signed: ______________________________
Attorney for Plaintiff

Address: ______________________________

As amended Mar. 30, 1970, eff. July 1, 1970.

Form 25. Request for Admission Under Rule 36

Plaintiff A. B. requests defendant C. D. within ____ days after service of this request to make the following admissions for the purpose of this action only and subject to all pertinent objections to admissibility which may be interposed at the trial:

1. That each of the following documents, exhibited with this request, is genuine.

(Here list the documents and describe each document.)

2. That each of the following statements is true.
(Here list the statements.)

Signed: ______________________
Attorney for Plaintiff

Address: ______________________

As amended Dec. 27, 1946, eff. Mar. 19, 1948.

Form 26. Allegation of Reason for Omitting Party

When it is necessary, under Rule 19(c), for the pleader to set forth in his pleading the names of persons who ought to be made parties, but who are not so made, there should be an allegation such as the one set out below:

John Doe named in this complaint is not made a party to this action [because he is not subject to the jurisdiction of this court]; [because he cannot be made a party to this action without depriving this court of jurisdiction].

Form 27. Notice of Appeal to Court of Appeals Under Rule 73(b)

Abrogated Dec. 4, 1967, eff. July 1, 1968.

Form 28. Notice: Condemnation

United States District Court for the Southern District of New York

Civil Action, File Number ____

United States of America, Plaintiff

v.

1,000 Acres of Land in [here insert a general location as "City of __________ " or "County of __________"], John Doe, et al., and Unknown Owners, Defendants

NOTICE

To (here insert the names of the defendants to whom the notice is directed):

You are hereby notified that a complaint in condemnation has heretofore been filed in the office of the clerk of the United States District Court for the

Southern District of New York, in the United States Court House in New York City, New York, for the taking (here state the interest to be acquired, as "an estate in fee simple") for use (here state briefly the use, "as a site for a post-office building") of the following described property in which you have or claim an interest.

(Here insert brief description of the property in which the defendants to whom the notice is directed, have or claim an interest.)

The authority for the taking is (here state briefly, as "the Act of ______, ____ Stat. ____, U.S.C.A., Title ____, § ____").[1]

You are further notified that if you desire to present any objection or defense to the taking of your property you are required to serve your answer on the plaintiff's attorney at the address herein designated within twenty days after __________.[2]

Your answer shall identify the property in which you claim to have an interest, state the nature and extent of the interest you claim, and state all of your objections and defenses to the taking of your property. All defenses and objections not so presented are waived. And in case of your failure so to answer the complaint, judgment of condemnation of that part of the above-described property in which you have or claim an interest will be rendered.

But without answering, you may serve on the plaintiff's attorney a notice of appearance designating the property in which you claim to be interested. Thereafter you will receive notice of all proceedings affecting it. At the trial of the issue of just compensation, whether or not you have previously appeared or answered, you may present evidence as to the amount of the compensation to be paid for your property, and you may share in the distribution of the award.

____

United States Attorney

Address: ______________________

(Here state an address within the district where the United States Attorney may be served, as "United States Court House, New York, N.Y.")

Dated __________

Added May 1, 1951, eff. Aug. 1, 1951.

1. And where appropriate add a citation to any applicable Executive Order.

2. Here insert the words "personal service of this notice upon you," if personal service is to be made pursuant to subdivision (d)(3)(i) of this rule [Rule 71A]; or, insert the date of the last publication of notice, if service by publication is to be made pursuant to subdivision (d)(3)(ii) of this rule.

Form 29. Complaint: Condemnation

United States District Court for the Southern District of New York

Civil Action, File Number ____

United States of America, Plaintiff

v.

1,000 Acres of Land in [here insert a general location as "City of ________ ________" or "County of ________"], John Doe, et al., and Unknown Owners, Defendants

COMPLAINT

1. This is an action of a civil nature brought by the United States of America for the taking of property under the power of eminent domain and for the ascertainment and award of just compensation to the owners and parties in interest.[1]

2. The authority for the taking is (here state briefly, as "the Act of ____, ____ Stat. ____, U.S.C.A., Title ____, § ____").[2]

3. The use for which the property is to be taken is (here state briefly the use, "as a site for a post-office building").

4. The interest to be acquired in the property is (here state the interest as "an estate in fee simple").

5. The property so to be taken is (here set forth a description of the property sufficient for its identification) or (described in Exhibit A hereto attached and made a part hereof).

6. The persons known to the plaintiff to have or claim an interest in the property[3] are:

1. If the plaintiff is not the United States, but is, for example, a corporation invoking the power of eminent domain delegated to it by the state, then this paragraph 1 of the complaint should be appropriately modified and should be preceded by a paragraph appropriately alleging federal jurisdiction for the action, such as diversity. See Form 2.

2. And where appropriate add a citation to any applicable Executive Order.

3. At the commencement of the action the plaintiff need name as defendants only the persons having or claiming an interest in the property whose names are then known, but prior to any hearing involving the compensation to be paid for a particular piece of property the plaintiff must add as defendants all persons having or claiming an interest in that property whose names can be ascertained by an appropriate search of the records and also those whose names have otherwise been learned. See Rule 71A(c)(2).

(Here set forth the names of such persons and the interests claimed.)[4]

7. In addition to the persons named, there are or may be others who have or may claim some interest in the property to be taken, whose names are unknown to the plaintiff and on diligent inquiry have not been ascertained. They are made parties to the action under the designation "Unknown Owners."

Wherefore the plaintiff demands judgment that the property be condemned and that just compensation for the taking be ascertained and awarded and for such other relief as may be lawful and proper.

____

United States Attorney

Address: ________________________

(Here state an address within the district where the United States Attorney may be served, as "United States Court House, New York, N.Y.")

Added May 1, 1951, eff. Aug. 1, 1951.

Form 30. Suggestion of Death upon the Record Under Rule 25(a)(1)

A. B. [describe as a party, or as executor, administrator, or other representative or successor of C. D., the deceased party] suggests upon the record, pursuant to Rule 25(a)(1), the death of C. D. [describe as party] during the pendency of this action.

Added Jan. 21, 1963, eff. July 1, 1963.

4. The plaintiff should designate, as to each separate piece of property, the defendants who have been joined as owners thereof or of some interest therein. See Rule 71A(c)(2).

Form 31. Judgment on Jury Verdict

United States District Court for the Southern District of New York

Civil Action, File Number ____

____

B., Plaintiff

v.

JUDGMENT

C. D., Defendant

This action came on for trial before the Court and a jury, Honorable John Marshall, District Judge, presiding, and the issues having been duly tried and the jury having duly rendered its verdict,

It is Ordered and Adjudged

[that the plaintiff A. B. recover of the defendant C. D. the sum of _____, with interest thereon at the rate of ____ per cent as provided by law, and his costs of action.]

[that the plaintiff take nothing, that the action be dismissed on the merits, and that the defendant C. D. recover of the plaintiff A. B. his costs of action.]

Dated at New York, New York, this ____ day of ______, 19.

____

Clerk of Court

Added Jan. 21, 1963, eff. July 1, 1963.

Form 32. Judgment on Decision by the Court

United States District Court for the Southern District of New York

Civil Action, File Number ____

____

JUDGMENT

B., Plaintiff

v.

C. D., Defendant

This action came on for [trial] [hearing] before the Court, Honorable John Marshall, District Judge, presiding, and the issues having been duly [tried] [heard] and a decision having been duly rendered,

It is Ordered and Adjudged

[that the plaintiff A. B. recover of the defendant C. D. the sum of ____, with interest thereon at the rate of ____ per cent as provided by law, and his costs of action.]

[that the plaintiff take nothing, that the action be dismissed on the merits, and that the defendant C. D. recover of the plaintiff A. B. his costs of action.]

Dated at New York, New York, this ____ day of ______, 19______.

____

Clerk of Court

Added Jan. 21, 1963, eff. July 1, 1963.

Form 33. Notice of Availability of a Magistrate Judge to Exercise Jurisdiction

In accordance with the provisions of Title 28, U.S.C. §636(c), you are hereby notified that a United States magistrate judge of this district court is available to exercise the court's jurisdiction and to conduct any or all proceedings in this case including a jury or nonjury trial, and entry of a final judgment. Exercise of this jurisdiction by a magistrate judge is, however, permitted only if all parties voluntarily consent.

You may, without adverse substantive consequences, withhold your consent, but this will prevent the court's jurisdiction from being exercised by a magistrate judge. If any party withholds consent, the identity of the parties consenting or withholding consent will not be communicated to any magistrate judge or to the district judge to whom the case has been assigned.

An appeal from a judgment entered by a magistrate judge may be taken directly to the United States court of appeals for this judicial circuit in the same manner as an appeal from any other judgment of a district court.

Copies of the Form for the "Consent to Jurisdiction by a United States Magistrate Judge" are available from the clerk of the court.

Added Apr. 28, 1983, eff. Aug. 1, 1983; amended Apr. 22, 1993, eff. Dec. 1, 1993; Apr. 11, 1997, eff. Dec. 1, 1997.

Form 34. Consent to Exercise of Jurisdiction by a United States Magistrate Judge

United States District Court
__________ District of __________

Plaintiff	Docket No. ____
v.	
Defendant	

CONSENT TO JURISDICTION BY A UNITED STATES MAGISTRATE JUDGE

In accordance with the provisions of Title 28, U.S.C. §636(c), the undersigned party or parties to the above-captioned civil matter hereby voluntarily consent to have a United States magistrate judge conduct any and all further proceedings in the case, including trial, and order the entry of a final judgment.

__________ ____________________

Date Signature

Note: Return this form to the Clerk of the Court if you consent to jurisdiction by a magistrate judge. Do not send a copy of this form to any district judge or magistrate judge.

Added Apr. 28, 1983, eff. Aug. 1, 1983; amended Apr. 22, 1993, eff. Dec. 1, 1993; Apr. 11, 1997, eff. Dec. 1, 1997.

Form 34-A. Order of Reference

United States District Court
__________ District of __________

Plaintiff	Docket No. ____
v.	
Defendant	

Order of Reference

IT IS HEREBY ORDERED that the above-captioned matter be referred to United States Magistrate Judge ________________ for all further proceedings and entry of judgment in accordance with Title 28, U.S.C. §636(c) and the consent of the parties.

____
U.S. District Judge

Added Apr. 22, 1993, eff. Dec. 1, 1993.

Form 35. Report of Parties' Planning Meeting

[Caption and Names of Parties]

1. Pursuant to Fed. R. Civ. P. 26(f), a meeting was held of ___(date)___ ___(place)___ and was attended by:
___(name)___ for plaintiff(s)
___*(name)*___ *for defendant(s)* ___*(party name)*___
___*(name)*___ *for defendant(s)* ___*(party name)*___

2. Pre-Discovery Disclosures. The parties [have exchanged] [will exchange by ___(date)___ the information required by [Fed. R. Civ. P. 26(a)(1)] [local rule.

3. Discovery Plan. The parties jointly propose to the court the following discovery plan: [Use separate paragraphs or subparagraphs as necessary if parties disagree.]

Discovery will be needed on the following subjects:
___(brief description of subjects on which discovery will be needed)___
All discovery commenced in time to be completed by ___(date)___.
[Discovery on ___(issue for early discovery)___ to be completed by ___(date)___.]
Maximum of __ interrogatories by each party to any other party. [Responses due __ days after service.]
Maximum of __ requests for admission by each party to any other party. [Responses due __ days after service.]
Maximum of __ depositions by plaintiff(s) and __ by defendant(s).
Each deposition [other than of ______] limited to maximum of __ hours unless extended by agreement of parties.
Reports from retained experts under Rule 26(a)(2) due:
from plaintiff(s) by ___(date)___
from defendant(s) by ___(date)___
Supplementations under Rule 26(e) due ___(time(s) or interval(s))___.

4. Other Items. [Use separate paragraphs or subparagraphs as necessary if parties disagree.]

The parties [request] [do not request] a conference with the court before entry of the scheduling order.

The parties request a pretrial conference in ____(month and year)____. Plaintiff(s) should be allowed until ____(date)____ to join additional parties and until ____(date)____ to amend the pleadings.

Defendant(s) should be allowed until ____(date)____ to join additional parties and until ____(date)____ to amend the pleadings.

All potentially dispositive motions should be filed by ____(date)____.

Settlement [is likely] [is unlikely] [cannot be evaluated prior to ____(date)____] [may be enhanced by use of the following alternative dispute resolution procedure: [____________].

Final lists of witnesses and exhibits under Rule 26(a)(3) should be due
from plaintiff(s) ____(date)____.
from defendant(s) by ____(date)____.

Parties should have days after service of final lists of witnesses and exhibits to list objections under Rule 26(a)(3).

The case should be ready for trial by ____(date)____ [and at this time is expected to take approximately ____(length of time)____.]

[Other matters.]

Date: ____________

Added Apr. 22, 1993, eff. Dec. 1, 1993.

SUPPLEMENTAL RULES FOR CERTAIN ADMIRALTY AND MARITIME CLAIMS

Adopted February 28, 1966, eff. July 1, 1966; as amended April 29, 1985, eff. August 1, 1985; March 2, 1987, eff. August 1, 1987; April 30, 1991, eff. December 1, 1991; April 17, 2000, eff. Dec. 1, 2000; April 29, 2002, eff. December 1, 2002.

TABLE OF RULES

(d) Direction with Respect to Property in Custody
(e) Expenses of Seizing and Keeping Property; Deposit
(f) Procedures for Release from Arrest or Attachment
(5) Release of Property
(a) Special Bond
(b) General Bond
(c) Release by Consent or Stipulation; Order of Court or Clerk; Costs
(d) Possessory, Petitory, and Partition Actions
(6) Reduction or Impairment of Security;
(7) Security on Counterclaim;
(8) Restricted Appearance
(9) Disposition of Property; Sales
(a) Actions for Forfeitures
(b) Interlocutory Sales
(c) Sales; Proceeds
F. Limitation of Liability
(1) Time for Filing Complaint; Security
(2) Complaint
(3) Claims Against Owner; Injunction
(4) Notice to Claimants
(5) Claims and Answer
(6) Information to Be Given Claimants
(7) Insufficiency of Fund or Security
(8) Objections to Claims: Distribution of Fund
(9) Venue; Transfer

Advisory Committee's Explanatory Statement to 1985 Amendments

Since their promulgation in 1966, the Supplemental Rules for Certain Admiralty and Maritime Claims have preserved the special procedures of arrest and attachment unique to admiralty law. In recent years, however, these Rules have been challenged as violating the principles of procedural due process enunciated in the United States Supreme Court's decision in Sniadach v. Family Finance Corp., 395 U.S. 337 (1969), and later developed in Fuentes v. Shevin, 407 U.S. 67 (1972), Mitchell v. W. T. Grant Co., 416 U.S. 600 (1974), and North Georgia Finishing, Inc. v. Di-Chem, Inc., 419 U.S. 601 (1975). These Supreme Court decisions provide five basic criteria for a constitutional seizure of property: (1) effective notice to persons having interests in the property seized, (2) judicial review prior to attachment, (3) avoidance of conclusory allegations in the complaint, (4) security posted by the plaintiff to protect the owner of the property under attachment, and (5) a meaningful and timely hearing after attachment. . . .

Advisory Committee's Explanatory Statement to 2000 Amendments

The Admiralty Rules proposals published in August 1998 were prompted by two primary goals. The first was to reflect the growing use of Admiralty procedure in civil forfeiture proceedings; the most important change in this area appears in Rule

C(6), which for the first time establishes separate provisions for civil forfeiture proceedings. The second goal was to adjust for the 1993 amendments of Civil Rule 4. Civil Rule 14 is changed only to reflect the change of nomenclature in Admiralty Rule C(6).

Rule A. Scope of Rules

These Supplemental Rules apply to the procedure in admiralty and maritime claims within the meaning of Rule 9(h) with respect to the following remedies:

(1) Maritime attachment and garnishment;

(2) Actions in rem;

(3) Possessory, petitory, and partition actions;

(4) Actions for exoneration from or limitation of liability.

These rules also apply to the procedure in statutory condemnation proceedings analogous to maritime actions in rem, whether within the admiralty and maritime jurisdiction or not. Except as otherwise provided, references in these Supplemental Rules to actions in rem include such analogous statutory condemnation proceedings.

The general Rules of Civil Procedure for the United States District Courts are also applicable to the foregoing proceedings except to the extent that they are inconsistent with these Supplemental Rules.

Rule B. In Personam Actions: Attachment and Garnishment

(1) When Available; Complaint, Affidavit, Judicial Authorization, and Process. In an in personam action:

(a) If a defendant is not found within the district, a verified complaint may contain a prayer for process to attach the defendant's tangible or intangible personal property — up to the amount sued for — in the hands of garnishees named in the process.

(b) The plaintiff or the plaintiff's attorney must sign and file with the complaint an affidavit stating that, to the affiant's knowledge, or on information and belief, the defendant cannot be found within the district. The court must review the complaint and affidavit and, if the conditions of this Rule B appear to exist, enter an order so stating and authorizing process of attachment and garnishment. The clerk may issue supplemental process enforcing the court's order upon application without further court order.

(c) If the plaintiff or the plaintiff's attorney certifies that exigent circumstances make court review impracticable, the clerk must issue the summons and process of attachment and garnishment. The plaintiff has the burden in any post-attachment hearing under Rule E(4)(f) to show that exigent circumstances existed.

(d)(i) If the property is a vessel or tangible property on board a vessel, the summons, process, and any supplemental process must be delivered to the marshal for service.

(ii) If the property is other tangible or intangible property, the summons, process, and any supplemental process must be delivered to a person or organization authorized to serve it, who may be (A) a marshal; (B) someone under contract with the United States; (C) someone specially appointed by the court for that purpose; or, (D) in an action brought by the United States, any officer or employee of the United States.

(e) The plaintiff may invoke state-law remedies under Rule 64 for seizure of person or property for the purpose of securing satisfaction of the judgment.

(2) Notice to Defendant. No default judgment may be entered except upon proof — which may be by affidavit — that:

(a) the complaint, summons, and process of attachment or garnishment have been served on the defendant in a manner authorized by Rule 4;

(b) the plaintiff or the garnishee has mailed to the defendant the complaint, summons, and process of attachment or garnishment, using any form of mail requiring a return receipt; or

(c) the plaintiff or the garnishee has tried diligently to give notice of the action to the defendant but could not do so.

(3) Answer.

(a) By Garnishee. The garnishee shall serve an answer, together with answers to any interrogatories served with the complaint, within 20 days after service of process upon the garnishee. Interrogatories to the garnishee may be served with the complaint without leave of court. If the garnishee refuses or neglects to answer on oath as to the debts, credits, or effects of the defendant in the garnishee's hands, or any interrogatories concerning such debts, credits, and effects that may be propounded by the plaintiff, the court may award compulsory process against the garnishee. If the garnishee admits any debts, credits, or effects, they shall be held in the garnishee's hands or paid into the registry of the court, and shall be held in either case subject to the further order of the court.

(b) By Defendant. The defendant shall serve an answer within 30 days after process has been executed, whether by attachment of property or service on the garnishee.

As amended Apr. 29, 1985, eff. Aug. 1, 1985; Mar. 2, 1987, eff. Aug. 1, 1987; Apr. 17, 2000, eff. Dec. 1, 2000.

Advisory Committee Notes to 1985 Amendment

Rule B(1) has been amended to provide for judicial scrutiny before the issuance of any attachment or garnishment process. Its purpose is to eliminate doubts as to whether the rule is consistent with the principles of procedural due process enunciated by the Supreme Court in Sniadach v. Family Finance Corp., 395 U.S. 337

(1969), and later developed in Fuentes v. Shevin, 407 U.S. 67 (1972), Mitchell v. W. T. Grant Co., 416 U.S. 600 (1974), and North Georgia Finishing, Inc. v. Di-Chem, Inc., 419 U.S. 601 (1975). . . .

The rule envisions that the order will issue when the plaintiff makes a prima facie showing that he has a maritime claim against the defendant in the amount sued for and the defendant is not present in the district. A simple order with conclusory findings is contemplated. The reference to review by the "court" is broad enough to embrace review by a magistrate as well as by a district judge.

The new provision recognizes that in some situations, such as when the judge is unavailable and the ship is about to depart from the jurisdiction, it will be impracticable, if not impossible, to secure the judicial review contemplated by Rule B(1). When "exigent circumstances" exist, the rule enables the plaintiff to secure the issuance of the summons and process of attachment and garnishment, subject to a later showing that the necessary circumstances actually existed. This provision is intended to provide a safety valve without undermining the requirement of preattachment scrutiny. Thus, every effort to secure judicial review, including conducting a hearing by telephone, should be pursued before resorting to the exigent circumstances procedure.

ADVISORY COMMITTEE NOTES, 2000 AMENDMENTS

Rule B(1) is amended in two ways, and style changes have been made. The service provisions of Rule C(3) are adopted in paragraph (d), providing alternatives to service by a marshal if the property to be seized is not a vessel or tangible property on board a vessel. The provision that allows the plaintiff to invoke state attachment and garnishment remedies is amended to reflect the 1993 amendments of Civil Rule 4. Former Civil Rule 4(e), incorporated in Rule B(1), allowed general use of state quasi-in-rem jurisdiction if the defendant was not an inhabitant of, or found within, the state. Rule 4(e) was replaced in 1993 by Rule 4(n)(2), which permits use of state law to seize a defendant's assets only if personal jurisdiction over the defendant cannot be obtained in the district where the action is brought.

Little purpose would be served by incorporating Rule 4(n)(2) in Rule B, since maritime attachment and garnishment are available whenever the defendant is not found within the district, a concept that allows attachment or garnishment even in some circumstances in which personal jurisdiction also can be asserted. In order to protect against any possibility that elimination of the reference to state quasi-in-rem jurisdiction remedies might seem to defeat continued use of state security devices, paragraph (e) expressly incorporates Civil Rule 64. Because Rule 64 looks only to security, not jurisdiction, the former reference to Rule E(8) is deleted as no longer relevant. . . .

Rule C. In Rem Actions: Special Provisions

(1) When Available. An action in rem may be brought:

(a) To enforce any maritime lien;

(b) Whenever a statute of the United States provides for a maritime action in rem or a proceeding analogous thereto.

Except as otherwise provided by law a party who may proceed in rem may also, or in the alternative, proceed in personam against any person who may be liable.

Statutory provisions exempting vessels or other property owned or possessed by or operated by or for the United States from arrest or seizure are not affected by this rule. When a statute so provides, an action against the United States or an instrumentality thereof may proceed on in rem principles.

(2) Complaint. In an action in rem the complaint must:

(a) be verified;

(b) describe with reasonable particularity the property that is the subject of the action;

(c) in an admiralty and maritime proceeding, state that the property is within the district or will be within the district while the action is pending;

(d) in a forfeiture proceeding for violation of a federal statute, state:

(i) the place of seizure and whether it was on land or on navigable waters;

(ii) whether the property is within the district, and if the property is not within the district the statutory basis for the court's exercise of jurisdiction over the property; and

(iii) all allegations required by the statute under which the action is brought.

(3) Judicial Authorization and Process.

(a) Arrest Warrant.

(i) When the United States files a complaint demanding a forfeiture for violation of a federal statute, the clerk must promptly issue a summons and a warrant for the arrest of the vessel or other property without requiring a certification of exigent circumstances, but if the property is real property the United States must proceed under applicable statutory procedures.

(ii)(A) In other actions, the court must review the complaint and any supporting papers. If the conditions for an in rem action appear to exist, the court must issue an order directing the clerk to issue a warrant for the arrest of the vessel or other property that is the subject of the action.

(B) If the plaintiff or the plaintiff's attorney certifies that exigent circumstances make court review impracticable, the clerk must promptly issue a summons and a warrant for the arrest of the vessel or other property that is the subject of the action. The plaintiff has the burden in any post-arrest hearing under Rule E(4)(f) to show that exigent circumstances existed.

(b) Service.

(i) If the property that is the subject of the action is a vessel or tangible property on board a vessel, the warrant and any supplemental process must be delivered to the marshal for service.

(ii) If the property that is the subject of the action is other property, tangible or intangible, the warrant and any supplemental process must be delivered to a person or organization authorized to enforce it, who may be: (A) a marshal; (B) someone under contract with the United States; (C) someone specially appointed by the court for that purpose; or, (D) in an action brought by the United States, any officer or employee of the United States.

*(c) **Deposit in Court.*** If the property that is the subject of the action consists in whole or in part of freight, the proceeds of property sold, or other intangible property, the clerk must issue — in addition to the warrant — a summons directing any person controlling the property to show cause why it should not be deposited in court to abide the judgment.

*(d) **Supplemental Process.*** The clerk may upon application issue supplemental process to enforce the court's order without further court order.

(4) Notice. No notice other than execution of process is required when the property that is the subject of the action has been released under Rule E(5). If the property is not released within 10 days after execution, the plaintiff must promptly — or within the time that the court allows — give public notice of the action and arrest in a newspaper designated by court order and having general circulation in the district, but publication may be terminated if the property is released before publication is completed. The notice must specify the time under Rule C(6) to file a statement of interest in or right against the seized property and to answer. This rule does not affect the notice requirements in an action to foreclose a preferred ship mortgage under 46 U.S.C. §§31301 et seq., as amended.

(5) Ancillary Process. In any action in rem in which process has been served as provided by this rule, if any part of the property that is the subject of the action has not been brought within the control of the court because it has been removed or sold, or because it is intangible property in the hands of a person who has not been served with process, the court may, on motion, order any person having possession or control of such property or its proceeds to show cause why it should not be delivered into the custody of the marshal or other person or organization having a warrant for the arrest of the property, or paid into court to abide the judgment; and, after hearing, the court may enter such judgment as law and justice may require.

(6) Responsive Pleading; Interrogatories.

*(a) **Civil Forfeiture.*** In an in rem forfeiture action for violation of a federal statute:

(i) a person who asserts an interest in or right against the property that is the subject of the action must file a verified statement identifying the interest or right:

(A) within 30 days after the earlier of (1) the date of service of the Government's complaint, or (2) completed publication of notice under Rule C(4), or

(B) within the time that the court allows;

(ii) an agent, bailee, or attorney must state the authority to file a statement of interest in or right against the property on behalf of another; and

(iii) a person who files a statement of interest in or right against the property must serve and file an answer within 20 days after filing the statement.

(b) Maritime Arrests and Other Proceedings. In an in rem action not governed by Rule C(6)(a):

(i) A person who asserts a right of possession or any ownership interest in the property that is the subject of the action must file a verified statement of right or interest:

(A) within 10 days after the earlier of (1) the execution of process, or (2) completed publication of notice under Rule C(4), or

(B) within the time that the court allows.

(ii) the statement of right or interest must describe the interest in the property that supports the person's demand for its restitution or right to defend the action;

(iii) an agent, bailee, or attorney must state the authority to file a statement of right or interest on behalf of another; and

(iv) a person who asserts a right of possession or any ownership interest must serve an answer within 20 days after filing the statement of interest or right.

(c) Interrogatories. Interrogatories may be served with the complaint in an in rem action without leave of court. Answers to the interrogatories must be served with the answer to the complaint.

As amended Apr. 29, 1985, eff. Aug. 1, 1985; Mar. 2, 1987, eff. Aug. 1, 1987; Apr. 30, 1991, eff. Dec. 1, 1991; Apr. 17, 2000, eff. Dec. 1, 2000; Apr. 29, 2002, eff. Dec. 1, 2002.

Advisory Committee Notes to 1985 Amendment

Rule C(3) has been amended to provide for judicial scrutiny before the issuance of any warrant of arrest. Its purpose is to eliminate any doubt as to the rule's constitutionality under the Sniadach line of cases. Sniadach v. Family Finance Corp., 395 U.S. 337 (1969), Fuentes v. Shevin, 407 U.S. 67 (1972), Mitchell v. W. T. Grant Co., 416 U.S. 600 (1974), and North Georgia Finishing, Inc. v. Di-Chem, Inc., 419 U.S. 601 (1975). . . .

The new provision recognizes that in some situations, such as when the judge is unavailable and the ship is about to depart from the jurisdiction, it will be impracticable, if not impossible to secure the judicial review contemplated by Rule C(3). When "exigent circumstances" exist, the rule enables the plaintiff to secure the issuance of the summons and warrant of arrest, subject to a later showing that the necessary circumstances actually existed. This provision is intended to provide a safety valve without undermining the requirement of pre-arrest scrutiny. Thus, every effort to secure judicial review, including conducting a hearing by telephone, should be pursued before invoking the exigent circumstances procedure.

Advisory Committee Notes, 2000 Amendments

Subdivision 2. In rem jurisdiction originally extended only to property within the judicial district. Since 1986, Congress has enacted a number of jurisdictional and venue statutes for forfeiture and criminal matters that in some circumstances permit a court to exercise authority over property outside the district. 28 U.S.C. §1355(b)(1) allows a forfeiture action in the district where an act or omission giving rise to forfeiture occurred, or in any other district where venue is established by §1395 or by any other statute. Section 1355(b)(2) allows an action to be brought as provided in (b)(1) or in the United States District Court for the District of Columbia when the forfeiture property is located in a foreign country or has been seized by authority of a foreign government. Section 1355(d) allows a court with jurisdiction under §1355(b) to cause service in any other district of process required to bring the forfeiture property before the court. Section 1395 establishes venue of a civil proceeding for forfeiture in the district where the forfeiture accrues or the defendant is found; in any district where the property is found; in any district into which the property is brought, if the property initially is outside any judicial district; or in any district where the vessel is arrested if the proceeding is an admiralty proceeding to forfeit a vessel. Section 1395(e) deals with a vessel or cargo entering a port of entry closed by the President, and transportation to or from a state or section declared to be in insurrection. 18 U.S.C. §981(h) creates expanded jurisdiction and venue over property located elsewhere that is related to a criminal prosecution pending in the district. These amendments, and related amendments of Rule E(3), bring these Rules into step with the new statutes. No change is made as to admiralty and maritime proceedings that do not involve a forfeiture governed by one of the new statutes.

Rule D. Possessory, Petitory, and Partition Actions

In all actions for possession, partition, and to try title maintainable according to the course of the admiralty practice with respect to a vessel, in all actions so maintainable with respect to the possession of cargo or other maritime property, and in all actions by one or more part owners against the others to obtain security for the return of the vessel from any voyage undertaken without their consent, or by one or more part owners against the others to obtain possession of the vessel for any voyage on giving security for its safe return, the process shall be by a warrant of arrest of the vessel, cargo, or other property, and by notice in the manner provided by Rule B(2) to the adverse party or parties.

Rule E. Actions in Rem and Quasi in Rem: General Provisions

(1) Applicability. Except as otherwise provided, this rule applies to actions in personam with process of maritime attachment and garnishment, actions in rem, and petitory, possessory, and partition actions, supplementing Rules B, C, and D.

(2) Complaint; Security.

(a) Complaint. In actions to which this rule is applicable the complaint shall state the circumstances from which the claim arises with such particularity that the defendant or claimant will be able, without moving for a more definite statement, to commence an investigation of the facts and to frame a responsive pleading.

(b) Security for Costs. Subject to the provisions of Rule 54(d) and of relevant statutes, the court may, on the filing of the complaint or on the appearance of any defendant, claimant, or any other party, or at any later time, require the plaintiff, defendant, claimant, or other party to give security, or additional security, in such sum as the court shall direct to pay all costs and expenses that shall be awarded against the party by any interlocutory order or by the final judgment, or on appeal by any appellate court.

(3) Process.

(a) In admiralty and maritime proceedings process in rem or of maritime attachment and garnishment may be served only within the district.

(b) In forfeiture cases process in rem may be served within the district or outside the district when authorized by statute.

(c) Issuance and Delivery. Issuance and delivery of process in rem, or of maritime attachment and garnishment, shall be held in abeyance if the plaintiff so requests.

(4) Execution of Process; Marshal's Return; Custody of Property; Procedures for Release.

(a) In General. Upon issuance and delivery of the process, or, in the case of summons with process of attachment and garnishment, when it appears that the defendant cannot be found within the district, the marshal or other person or organization having a warrant shall forthwith execute the process in accordance with this subdivision (4), making due and prompt return.

(b) Tangible Property. If tangible property is to be attached or arrested, the marshal or other person or organization having the warrant shall take it into the marshal's possession for safe custody. If the character or situation of the property is such that the taking of actual possession is impracticable, the marshal or other person executing the process shall affix a copy thereof to the property in a conspicuous place and leave a copy of the complaint and process with the person having possession or the person's agent. In furtherance of the marshal's custody of any vessel the marshal is authorized to make a written request to the collector of customs not to grant clearance to such vessel until notified by the marshal or deputy marshal or by the clerk that the vessel has been released in accordance with these rules.

(c) Intangible Property. If intangible property is to be attached or arrested the marshal or other person or organization having the warrant shall execute the process by leaving with the garnishee or other obligor a copy of the complaint and process requiring the garnishee or other obligor to answer as provided in Rules B(3)(a) and C(6); or the marshal may accept for payment into the registry of the court the amount owed to the extent of the amount claimed by the plaintiff with interest and costs, in which event the garnishee or other obligor shall not be required to answer unless alias process shall be served.

(d) Directions with Respect to Property in Custody. The marshal or other person or organization having the warrant may at any time apply to the court for directions with respect to property that has been attached or arrested, and shall give notice of such application to any or all of the parties as the court may direct.

(e) Expenses of Seizing and Keeping Property; Deposit. These rules do not alter the provisions of Title 28, U.S.C. §1921, as amended, relative to the expenses of seizing and keeping property attached or arrested and to the requirement of deposits to cover such expenses.

(f) Procedure for Release from Arrest or Attachment. Whenever property is arrested or attached, any person claiming an interest in it shall be entitled to a prompt hearing at which the plaintiff shall be required to show why the arrest or attachment should not be vacated or other relief granted consistent with these rules. This subdivision shall have no application to suits for seamen's wages when process is issued upon a certification of sufficient cause filed pursuant to Title 46, U.S.C. §§603 and 604 or to actions by the United States for forfeitures for violation of any statutes of the United States.

(5) Release of Property.

(a) Special Bond. Except in cases of seizures for forfeiture under any law of the United States, whenever process of maritime attachment and garnishment or process in rem is issued the execution of such process shall be stayed, or the property released, on the giving of security, to be approved by the court or clerk, or by stipulation of the parties, conditioned to answer the judgment of the court or of any appellate court. The parties may stipulate the amount and nature of such security. In the event of the inability or refusal of the parties so to stipulate the court shall fix the principal sum of the bond or stipulation at an amount sufficient to cover the amount of the plaintiff's claim fairly stated with accrued interest and costs; but the principal sum shall in no event exceed (i) twice the amount of the plaintiff's claim or (ii) the value of the property on due appraisement, whichever is smaller. The bond or stipulation shall be conditioned for the payment of the principal sum and interest thereon at 6 percent per annum.

(b) General Bond. The owner of any vessel may file a general bond or stipulation, with sufficient surety, to be approved by the court, conditioned to answer the judgment of such court in all or any actions that may be brought thereafter in such court in which the vessel is attached or arrested. Thereupon the execution of all such process against such vessel shall be stayed so long as the amount secured by such bond or stipulation is at least double the aggregate amount claimed by plaintiffs in all actions begun and pending in which such vessel has been attached or arrested. Judgments and remedies may be had on such bond or stipulation as if a special bond or stipulation had been filed in each of such actions. The district court may make necessary orders to carry this rule into effect, particularly as to the giving of proper notice of any action against or attachment of a vessel for which a general bond has been filed. Such bond or stipulation shall be indorsed by the clerk with a minute of the actions wherein process is so stayed. Further security may be required by the court at any time.

If a special bond or stipulation is given in a particular case, the liability on the general bond or stipulation shall cease as to that case.

(c) Release by Consent or Stipulation; Order of Court or Clerk; Costs. Any vessel, cargo, or other property in the custody of the marshal or other person or organization having the warrant may be released forthwith upon the marshal's acceptance and approval of a stipulation, bond, or other security, signed by the party on whose behalf the property is detained or the party's attorney and expressly authorizing such release, if all costs and charges of the court and its officers shall have first been paid. Otherwise no property in the custody of the marshal, other person or organization having the warrant, or other officer of the court shall be released without an order of the court; but such order may be entered as of course by the clerk, upon the giving of approved security as provided by law and these rules, or upon the dismissal or discontinuance of the action; but the marshal or other person or organization having the warrant shall not deliver any property so released until the costs and charges of the officers of the court shall first have been paid.

(d) Possessory, Petitory, and Partition Actions. The foregoing provisions of this subdivision (5) do not apply to petitory, possessory, and partition actions. In such cases the property arrested shall be released only by order of the court, on such terms and conditions and on the giving of such security as the court may require.

(6) Reduction or Impairment of Security. Whenever security is taken the court may, on motion and hearing, for good cause shown, reduce the amount of security given; and if the surety shall be or become insufficient, new or additional sureties may be required on motion and hearing.

(7) Security on Counterclaim.

(a) When a person who has given security for damages in the original action asserts a counterclaim that arises from the transaction or occurrence that is the subject of the original action, a plaintiff for whose benefit the security has been given must give security for damages demanded in the counterclaim unless the court, for cause shown, directs otherwise. Proceedings on the original claim must be stayed until this security is given, unless the court directs otherwise.

(b) The plaintiff is required to give security under Rule E(7)(a) when the United States or its corporate instrumentality counterclaims and would have been required to give security to respond in damages if a private party but is relieved by law from giving security.

(8) Restricted Appearance. An appearance to defend against an admiralty and maritime claim with respect to which there has issued process in rem, or process of attachment and garnishment, may be expressly restricted to the defense of such claim, and in that event is not an appearance for the purposes of any other claim with respect to which such process is not available or has not been served.

(9) Disposition of Property; Sales.

(a) Actions for Forfeitures. In any action in rem to enforce a forfeiture for violation of a statute of the United States the property shall be disposed of as provided by statute.

(b) Interlocutory Sales; Delivery.

(i) On application of a party, the marshal, or other person having custody of the property, the court may order all or part of the property sold — with the sales proceeds, or as much of them as will satisfy the judgment, paid into court to await further orders of the court — if:

(A) the attached or arrested property is perishable, or liable to deterioration, decay, or injury by being detained in custody pending the action;

(B) the expense of keeping the property is excessive or disproportionate; or

(C) there is an unreasonable delay in securing release of the property.

(ii) In the circumstances described in Rule E(9)(b)(i), the court, on motion by a defendant or a person filing a statement of interest or right under Rule C(6) , may order that the property, rather than being sold, be delivered to the movant upon giving security under these rules.

(c) Sales; Proceeds. All sales of property shall be made by the marshal or a deputy marshal, or by other person or organization having the warrant, or by any other person assigned by the court where the marshal or other person or organization having the warrant is a party in interest; and the proceeds of sale shall be forthwith paid into the registry of the court to be disposed of according to law.

(10) Preservation of Property. When the owner or another person remains in possession of property attached or arrested under the provisions of Rule E(4)(b) that permit execution of process without taking actual possession, the court, on a party's motion or on its own, may enter any order necessary to preserve the property and to prevent its removal.

As amended Apr. 29, 1985, eff. Aug. 1, 1985; Mar. 2, 1987, eff. Aug. 1, 1987; Apr. 30, 1991, eff. Dec. 1, 1991; Apr. 17, 2000, eff. Dec. 1, 2000.

ADVISORY COMMITTEE NOTES TO 1985 AMENDMENT

Rule E(4)(f) makes available the type of prompt post-seizure hearing in proceedings under Supplemental Rules B and C that the Supreme Court has called for in a number of cases arising in other contexts. See North Georgia Finishing, Inc. v. Di-Chem, Inc., 419 U.S. 601 (1975); Mitchell v. W. T. Grant Co., 416 U.S. 600 (1974). Although post-attachment and post-arrest hearings always have been available on motion, an explicit statement emphasizing promptness and elaborating the procedure has been lacking in the Supplemental Rules. Rule E(4)(f) is designed to satisfy the constitutional requirement of due process by guaranteeing to the shipowner a prompt post-seizure hearing at which he can attack the complaint, the arrest, the security demanded, or any other alleged deficiency in the proceedings up to that point. The amendment also is intended to eliminate the previously disparate treatment under local rules of defendants whose property has been seized pursuant to Supplemental Rules B and C. . . .

Rule F. Limitation of Liability

(1) Time for Filing Complaint; Security. Not later than six months after his receipt of a claim in writing, any vessel owner may file a complaint in the appropriate district court, as provided in subdivision (9) of this rule, for limitation of liability pursuant to statute. The owner (a) shall deposit with the court, for the benefit of claimants, a sum equal to the amount or value of the owner's interest in the vessel and pending freight, or approved security therefor, and in addition such sums, or approved security therefor, as the court may from time to time fix as necessary to carry out the provisions of the statutes as amended; or (b) at the owner's option shall transfer to a trustee to be appointed by the court, for the benefit of claimants, the owner's interest in the vessel and pending freight, together with such sums, or approved security therefor, as the court may from time to time fix as necessary to carry out the provisions of the statutes as amended. The plaintiff shall also give security for costs and, if the plaintiff elects to give security, for interest at the rate of 6 per cent per annum from the date of the security.

(2) **Complaint.** The complaint shall set forth the facts on the basis of which the right to limit liability is asserted, and all facts necessary to enable the court to determine the amount to which the owner's liability shall be limited. The complaint may demand exoneration from as well as limitation of liability. It shall state the voyage, if any, on which the demands sought to be limited arose, with the date and place of its termination; the amount of all demands including all unsatisfied liens or claims of lien, in contract or in tort or otherwise, arising on that voyage, so far as known to the plaintiff, and what actions and proceedings, if any, are pending thereon; whether the vessel was damaged, lost, or abandoned, and, if so, when and where; the value of the vessel at the close of the voyage or, in case of wreck, the value of her wreckage, strippings, or proceeds, if any, and where and in whose possession they are; and the amount of any pending freight recovered or recoverable. If the plaintiff elects to transfer the plaintiff's interest in the vessel to a trustee, the complaint must further show any prior paramount liens thereon, and what voyages or trips, if any, she has made since the voyage or trip on which the claims sought to be limited arose, and any existing liens arising upon any such subsequent voyage or trip, with the amounts and causes thereof, and the names and addresses of the lienors, so far as known; and whether the vessel sustained any injury upon or by reason of such subsequent voyage or trip.

(3) **Claims Against Owner; Injunction.** Upon compliance by the owner with the requirements of subdivision (1) of this rule all claims and proceedings against the owner or the owner's property with respect to the matter in question shall cease. On application of the plaintiff the court shall enjoin the further prosecution of any action or proceeding against the plaintiff or the plaintiff's property with respect to any claim subject to limitation in the action.

(4) **Notice to Claimants.** Upon the owner's compliance with subdivision (1) of this rule the court shall issue a notice to all persons asserting claims with respect to which the complaint seeks limitation, admonishing them to file their respective claims with the clerk of the court and to serve on the attorneys for the plaintiff a copy thereof on or before a date to be named in the notice. The date so fixed shall not be less than 30 days after issuance of the notice. For cause shown, the court may enlarge the time within which claims may be filed. The notice shall be published in such newspaper or newspapers as the court may direct once a week for four successive weeks prior to the date fixed for the filing of claims. The plaintiff not later than the day of second publication shall also mail a copy of the notice to every person known to have made any claim against

the vessel or the plaintiff arising out of the voyage or trip on which the claims sought to be limited arose. In cases involving death a copy of such notice shall be mailed to the decedent at the decedent's last known address, and also to any person who shall be known to have made any claim on account of such death.

(5) **Claims and Answer.** Claims shall be filed and served on or before the date specified in the notice provided for in subdivision (4) of this rule. Each claim shall specify the facts upon which the claimant relies in support of the claim, the items thereof, and the dates on which the same accrued. If a claimant desires to contest either the right to exoneration from or the right to limitation of liability the claimant shall file and serve an answer to the complaint unless the claim has included an answer.

(6) **Information to Be Given Claimants.** Within 30 days after the date specified in the notice for filing claims, or within such time as the court thereafter may allow, the plaintiff shall mail to the attorney for each claimant (or if the claimant has no attorney to the claimant) a list setting forth (a) the name of each claimant, (b) the name and address of the claimant's attorney (if the claimant is known to have one), (c) the nature of the claim, i.e., whether property loss, property damage, death, personal injury, etc., and (d) the amount thereof.

(7) **Insufficiency of Fund or Security.** Any claimant may by motion demand that the funds deposited in court or the security given by the plaintiff be increased on the ground that they are less than the value of the plaintiff's interest in the vessel and pending freight. Thereupon the court shall cause due appraisement to be made of the value of the plaintiff's interest in the vessel and pending freight; and if the court finds that the deposit or security is either insufficient or excessive it shall order its increase or reduction. In like manner any claimant may demand that the deposit or security be increased on the ground that it is insufficient to carry out the provisions of the statutes relating to claims in respect of loss of life or bodily injury; and, after notice and hearing, the court may similarly order that the deposit or security be increased or reduced.

(8) **Objections to Claims: Distribution of Fund.** Any interested party may question or controvert any claim without filing an objection thereto. Upon determination of liability the fund deposited or secured, or the proceeds of the vessel and pending freight, shall be divided pro rata, subject to all relevant provisions of law, among the several claimants in proportion to the amounts of their respective claims, duly proved, saving, however, to all parties any priority to which they may be legally entitled.

(9) **Venue; Transfer.** The complaint shall be filed in any district in which the vessel has been attached or arrested to answer for any claim with respect to which the plaintiff seeks to limit liability; or, if the vessel has not been attached

or arrested, then in any district in which the owner has been sued with respect to any such claim. When the vessel has not been attached or arrested to answer the matters aforesaid, and suit has not been commenced against the owner, the proceedings may be had in the district in which the vessel may be, but if the vessel is not within any district and no suit has been commenced in any district, then the complaint may be filed in any district. For the convenience of parties and witnesses, in the interest of justice, the court may transfer the action to any district; if venue is wrongly laid the court shall dismiss or, if it be in the interest of justice, transfer the action to any district in which it could have been brought. If the vessel shall have been sold, the proceeds shall represent the vessel for the purposes of these rules.

As amended Mar. 2, 1987, eff. Aug. 1, 1987.

SELECTED FEDERAL RULES OF APPELLATE PROCEDURE

As Amended Through December 1, 2002

TABLE OF RULES

VII. General Provisions

Title I. Applicability of Rules

Rule 1. Scope of Rules; Title

(a) Scope of Rules.

(1) These rules govern procedure in the United States courts of appeals.

(2) When these rules provide for filing a motion or other document in the district court, the procedure must comply with the practice of the district court.

(b) [*Abrogated.*]

(c) **Title.** These rules are to be known as the Federal Rules of Appellate Procedure.

As amended Apr. 30, 1979, eff. Aug. 1, 1979; Apr. 25, 1989, eff. Dec. 1, 1989; Apr. 29, 1994, eff. Dec. 1, 1994; Apr. 24, 1998, eff. Dec. 1, 1998; Apr. 29, 2002, eff. Dec. 1, 2002.

Rule 2. Suspension of Rules

On its own or a party's motion, a court of appeals may — to expedite its decision or for other good cause — suspend any provision of these rules in a particular case and order proceedings as it directs, except as otherwise provided in Rule 26(b).

As amended Apr. 24, 1998, eff. Dec. 1, 1998.

Title II. Appeal from a Judgment or Order of a District Court

Rule 3. Appeal as of Right — How Taken

(a) **Filing the Notice of Appeal.**

(1) An appeal permitted by law as of right from a district court to a court of appeals may be taken only by filing a notice of appeal with the district clerk within the time allowed by Rule 4. At the time of filing, the appellant must furnish the clerk with enough copies of the notice to enable the clerk to comply with Rule 3(d).

(2) An appellant's failure to take any step other than the timely filing of a notice of appeal does not affect the validity of the appeal, but is ground only for the court of appeals to act as it considers appropriate, including dismissing the appeal.

(3) An appeal from a judgment by a magistrate judge in a civil case is taken in the same way as an appeal from any other district court judgment.

(4) An appeal by permission under 28 U.S.C. §1292(b) or an appeal in a bankruptcy case may be taken only in the manner prescribed by Rules 5 and 6, respectively.

(b) **Joint or Consolidated Appeals.**

(1) When two or more parties are entitled to appeal from a district-court judgment or order, and their interests make joinder practicable, they may file a joint notice of appeal. They may then proceed on appeal as a single appellant.

(2) When the parties have filed separate timely notices of appeal, the appeals may be joined or consolidated by the court of appeals.

(c) Contents of the Notice of Appeal.

(1) The notice of appeal must:

(A) specify the party or parties taking the appeal by naming each one in the caption or body of the notice, but an attorney representing more than one party may describe those parties with such terms as "all plaintiffs," "the defendants," "the plaintiffs A, B, et al.," or "all defendants except X";

(B) designate the judgment, order, or part thereof being appealed; and

(C) name the court to which the appeal is taken.

(2) A pro se notice of appeal is considered filed on behalf of the signer and the signer's spouse and minor children (if they are parties), unless the notice clearly indicates otherwise.

(3) In a class action, whether or not the class has been certified, the notice of appeal is sufficient if it names one person qualified to bring the appeal as representative of the class.

(4) An appeal must not be dismissed for informality of form or title of the notice of appeal, or for failure to name a party whose intent to appeal is otherwise clear from the notice.

(5) Form 1 in the Appendix of Forms is a suggested form of a notice of appeal.

(d) Serving the Notice of Appeal.

(1) The district clerk must serve notice of the filing of a notice of appeal by mailing a copy to each party's counsel of record — excluding the appellant's — or, if a party is proceeding pro se, to the party's last known address. When a defendant in a criminal case appeals, the clerk must also serve a copy of the notice of appeal on the defendant, either by personal service or by mail addressed to the defendant. The clerk must promptly send a copy of the notice of appeal and of the docket entries — and any later docket entries — to the clerk of the court of appeals named in the notice. The district clerk must note, on each copy, the date when the notice of appeal was filed.

(2) If an inmate confined in an institution files a notice of appeal in the manner provided by Rule 4(c), the district clerk must also note the date when the clerk docketed the notice.

(3) The district clerk's failure to serve notice does not affect the validity of the appeal. The clerk must note on the docket the names of the parties to whom the clerk mails copies, with the date of mailing. Service is sufficient despite the death of a party or the party's counsel.

(e) Payment of Fees. Upon filing a notice of appeal, the appellant must pay the district clerk all required fees. The district clerk receives the appellate docket fee on behalf of the court of appeals.

As amended Apr. 30, 1979, eff. Aug. 1, 1979; Mar. 10, 1986, eff. July 1, 1986; Apr. 25, 1989, eff. Dec. 1, 1989; Apr. 22, 1993, eff. Dec. 1, 1993; Apr. 29, 1994, eff. Dec. 1, 1994; Apr. 24, 1998, eff. Dec. 1, 1998.

Rule 3.1 Appeal from a Judgment of a Magistrate Judge in a Civil Case [*Abrogated.*]

Rule 4. Appeal as of Right — When Taken

(a) Appeal in a Civil Case.

(1) *Time for Filing a Notice of Appeal.*

(A) In a civil case, except as provided in Rules 4(a)(1)(B), 4(a)(4), and 4(c), the notice of appeal required by Rule 3 must be filed with the district clerk within 30 days after the judgment or order appealed from is entered.

(B) When the United States or its officer or agency is a party, the notice of appeal may be filed by any party within 60 days after the judgment or order appealed from is entered.

(C) An appeal from an order granting or denying an application for a writ of error coram nobis is an appeal in a civil case for purposes of Rule 4(a).

(2) *Filing Before Entry of Judgment.* A notice of appeal filed after the court announces a decision or order — but before the entry of the judgment or order — is treated as filed on the date of and after the entry.

(3) *Multiple Appeals.* If one party timely files a notice of appeal, any other party may file a notice of appeal within 14 days after the date when the first notice was filed, or within the time otherwise prescribed by this Rule 4(a), whichever period ends later.

(4) *Effect of a Motion on a Notice of Appeal.*

(A) If a party timely files in the district court any of the following motions under the Federal Rules of Civil Procedure, the time to file an appeal runs for all parties from the entry of the order disposing of the last such remaining motion:

(i) for judgment under Rule 50(b);

(ii) to amend or make additional factual findings under Rule 52(b), whether or not granting the motion would alter the judgment;

(iii) for attorney's fees under Rule 54 if the district court extends the time to appeal under Rule 58;

(iv) to alter or amend the judgment under Rule 59;

(v) for a new trial under Rule 59; or

(vi) for relief under Rule 60 if the motion is filed no later than 10 days after the judgment is entered.

(B)(i) If a party files a notice of appeal after the court announces or enters a judgment — but before it disposes of any motion listed in Rule 4(a)(4)(A) — the notice becomes effective to appeal a judgment or order, in whole or in part, when the order disposing of the last such remaining motion is entered.

(ii) A party intending to challenge an order disposing of any motion listed in Rule 4(a)(4)(A), or a judgment altered or amended upon such a motion, must file a notice of appeal, or an amended notice of appeal — in compliance with Rule 3(c) — within the time prescribed by this Rule measured from the entry of the order disposing of the last such remaining motion.

(iii) No additional fee is required to file an amended notice.

(5) *Motion for Extension of Time.*

(A) The district court may extend the time to file a notice of appeal if:

(i) a party so moves no later than 30 days after the time prescribed by this Rule 4(a) expires; and

(ii) regardless of whether its motion is filed before or during the 30 days after the time prescribed by this Rule 4(a) expires, that party shows excusable neglect or good cause.

(B) A motion filed before the expiration of the time prescribed in Rule 4(a)(1) or (3) may be ex parte unless the court requires otherwise. If the motion is filed after the expiration of the prescribed time, notice must be given to the other parties in accordance with local rules.

(C) No extension under this Rule 4(a)(5) may exceed 30 days after the prescribed time or 10 days after the date when the order granting the motion is entered, whichever is later.

(6) *Reopening the Time to File an Appeal.* The district court may reopen the time to file an appeal for a period of 14 days after the date when its order to reopen is entered, but only if all the following conditions are satisfied:

(A) the motion is filed within 180 days after the judgment or order is entered or within 7 days after the moving party receives notice of the entry, whichever is earlier;

(B) the court finds that the moving party was entitled to notice of the entry of the judgment or order sought to be appealed but did not receive the notice from the district court or any party within 21 days after entry; and

(C) the court finds that no party would be prejudiced.

(7) *Entry Defined.*

(A) A judgment or order is entered for purposes of this Rule 4(a):

(i) if Federal Rule of Civil Procedure 58(a)(1) does not require a separate document, when the judgment or order is entered in the civil docket under Federal Rule of Civil Procedure 79(a); or

(ii) if Federal Rule of Civil Procedure 58(a)(1) requires a separate document, when the judgment or order is entered in the civil docket under Federal Rule of Civil Procedure 79(a) and when the earlier of these events occurs:

- the judgment or order is set forth on a separate document, or
- 150 days have run from entry of the judgment or order in the civil docket under Federal Rule of Civil Procedure 79(a).

(B) A failure to set forth a judgment or order on a separate document when required by Federal Rule of Civil Procedure 58(a)(1) does not affect the validity of an appeal from that judgment or order.

(b) Appeal in a Criminal Case.

(1) *Time for Filing a Notice of Appeal.*

(A) In a criminal case, a defendant's notice of appeal must be filed in the district court within 10 days after the later of:

(i) the entry of either the judgment or the order being appealed; or

(ii) the filing of the government's notice of appeal.

(B) When the government is entitled to appeal, its notice of appeal must be filed in the district court within 30 days after the later of:

(i) the entry of the judgment or order being appealed; or

(ii) the filing of a notice of appeal by any defendant.

(2) *Filing Before Entry of Judgment.* A notice of appeal filed after the court announces a decision, sentence, or order — but before the entry of the judgment or order — is treated as filed on the date of and after the entry.

(3) *Effect of a Motion on a Notice of Appeal.*

(A) If a defendant timely makes any of the following motions under the Federal Rules of Criminal Procedure, the notice of appeal from a judgment of conviction must be filed within 10 days after the entry of the order disposing of the last such remaining motion, or within 10 days after the entry of the judgment of conviction, whichever period ends later. This provision applies to a timely motion:

(i) for judgment of acquittal under Rule 29;

(ii) for a new trial under Rule 33, but if based on newly discovered evidence, only if the motion is made no later than 10 days after the entry of the judgment; or

(iii) for arrest of judgment under Rule 34.

(B) A notice of appeal filed after the court announces a decision, sentence, or order — but before it disposes of any of the motions referred to in Rule 4(b)(3)(A) — becomes effective upon the later of the following:

(i) the entry of the order disposing of the last such remaining motion; or

(ii) the entry of the judgment of conviction.

(C) A valid notice of appeal is effective — without amendment — to appeal from an order disposing of any of the motions referred to in Rule 4(b)(3)(A).

(4) *Motion for Extension of Time.* Upon a finding of excusable neglect or good cause, the district court may — before or after the time has expired, with

or without motion and notice — extend the time to file a notice of appeal for a period not to exceed 30 days from the expiration of the time otherwise prescribed by this Rule 4(b).

(5) *Jurisdiction.* The filing of a notice of appeal under this Rule 4(b) does not divest a district court of jurisdiction to correct a sentence under Federal Rule of Criminal Procedure 35(a), nor does the filing of a motion under 35(a) affect the validity of a notice of appeal filed before entry of the order disposing of the motion. The filing of a motion under Federal Rule of Criminal Procedure 35(a) does not suspend the time for filing a notice of appeal from a judgment of conviction.

(6) *Entry Defined.* A judgment or order is entered for purposes of this Rule 4(b) when it is entered on the criminal docket.

(c) Appeal by an Inmate Confined in an Institution.

(1) If an inmate confined in an institution files a notice of appeal in either a civil or a criminal case, the notice is timely if it is deposited in the institution's internal mail system on or before the last day for filing. If an institution has a system designed for legal mail, the inmate must use that system to receive the benefit of this rule. Timely filing may be shown by a declaration in compliance with 28 U.S.C. §1746 or by a notarized statement, either of which must set forth the date of deposit and state that first-class postage has been prepaid.

(2) If an inmate files the first notice of appeal in a civil case under this Rule 4(c), the 14-day period provided in Rule 4(a)(3) for another party to file a notice of appeal runs from the date when the district court dockets the first notice.

(3) When a defendant in a criminal case files a notice of appeal under this Rule 4(c), the 30-day period for the government to file its notice of appeal runs from the entry of the judgment or order appealed from or from the district court's docketing of the defendant's notice of appeal, whichever is later.

(d) Mistaken Filing in the Court of Appeals. If a notice of appeal in either a civil or a criminal case is mistakenly filed in the court of appeals, the clerk of that court must note on the notice the date when it was received and send it to the district clerk. The notice is then considered filed in the district court on the date so noted.

As amended Apr. 30,, 1979, eff. Aug. 1, 1979; Nov. 18, 1988, Pub. L. 100-690, Title VII, §7111, 102 Stat. 4419; Apr. 30, 1991, eff. Dec. 1, 1991; Apr. 22, 1993, eff. Dec. 1, 1993; Apr. 27, 1995, eff. Dec. 1, 1995; Apr. 24, 1998, eff. Dec. 1, 1998; Apr. 29, 2002, eff. Dec. 1, 2002.

Rule 5. Appeal by Permission

(a) Petition for Permission to Appeal.

(1) To request permission to appeal when an appeal is within the court of appeals' discretion, a party must file a petition for permission to appeal. The

petition must be filed with the circuit clerk with proof of service on all other parties to the district-court action.

(2) The petition must be filed within the time specified by the statute or rule authorizing the appeal or, if no such time is specified, within the time provided by Rule 4(a) for filing a notice of appeal.

(3) If a party cannot petition for appeal unless the district court first enters an order granting permission to do so or stating that the necessary conditions are met, the district court may amend its order, either on its own or in response to a party's motion, to include the required permission or statement. In that event, the time to petition runs from entry of the amended order.

(b) Contents of the Petition; Answer or Cross-Petition; Oral Argument.

(1) The petition must include the following:

(A) the facts necessary to understand the question presented;

(B) the question itself;

(C) the relief sought;

(D) the reasons why the appeal should be allowed and is authorized by a statute or rule; and

(E) an attached copy of:

(i) the order, decree, or judgment complained of and any related opinion or memorandum, and

(ii) any order stating the district court's permission to appeal or finding that the necessary conditions are met.

(2) A party may file an answer in opposition or a cross-petition within 7 days after the petition is served.

(3) The petition and answer will be submitted without oral argument unless the court of appeals orders otherwise.

(c) Form of Papers; Number of Copies. All papers must conform to Rule 32(c)(2). Except by the court's permission, a paper must not exceed 20 pages, exclusive of the disclosure statement, the proof of service, and the accompanying documents required by Rule 5(b)(1)(E). An original and 3 copies must be filed unless the court requires a different number by local rule or by order in a particular case.

(d) Grant of Permission; Fees; Cost Bond; Filing the Record.

(1) Within 10 days after the entry of the order granting permission to appeal, the appellant must:

(A) pay the district clerk all required fees; and

(B) file a cost bond if required under Rule 7.

(2) A notice of appeal need not be filed. The date when the order granting permission to appeal is entered serves as the date of the notice of appeal for calculating time under these rules.

(3) The district clerk must notify the circuit clerk once the petitioner has

paid the fees. Upon receiving this notice, the circuit clerk must enter the appeal on the docket. The record must be forwarded and filed in accordance with Rules 11 and 12(c).

As amended Apr. 30, 1979, eff. Aug. 1, 1979; Apr. 29, 1994, eff. Dec. 1, 1994; Apr. 24, 1998, eff. Dec. 1, 1998; Apr. 29, 2002, eff. Dec. 1, 2002.

Rule 5.1 Appeal by Leave Under 28 U.S.C. §636(c)(5) [*Abrogated.*]

Rule 6. Appeal in a Bankruptcy Case from a Final Judgment, Order, or Decree of a District Court or Bankruptcy Appellate Panel [Omitted]

Rule 7. Bond for Costs on Appeal in a Civil Case

In a civil case, the district court may require an appellant to file a bond or provide other security in any form and amount necessary to ensure payment of costs on appeal. Rule 8(b) applies to a surety on a bond given under this rule.

As amended Apr. 30, 1979, eff. Aug. 1, 1979; Apr. 24, 1998, eff. Dec. 1, 1998.

Rule 8. Stay or Injunction Pending Appeal

(a) Motion for Stay.

(1) *Initial Motion in the District Court.* A party must ordinarily move first in the district court for the following relief:

(A) a stay of the judgment or order of a district court pending appeal;

(B) approval of a supersedeas bond; or

(C) an order suspending, modifying, restoring, or granting an injunction while an appeal is pending.

(2) *Motion in the Court of Appeals; Conditions on Relief.* A motion for the relief mentioned in Rule 8(a)(1) may be made to the court of appeals or to one of its judges.

(A) The motion must:

(i) show that moving first in the district court would be impracticable; or

(ii) state that, a motion having been made, the district court denied the motion or failed to afford the relief requested and state any reasons given by the district court for its action.

(B) The motion must also include:

(i) the reasons for granting the relief requested and the facts relied on;

(ii) originals or copies of affidavits or other sworn statements supporting facts subject to dispute; and

(iii) relevant parts of the record.

(C) The moving party must give reasonable notice of the motion to all parties.

(D) A motion under this Rule 8(a)(2) must be filed with the circuit clerk and normally will be considered by a panel of the court. But in an exceptional case in which time requirements make that procedure impracticable, the motion may be made to and considered by a single judge.

(E) The court may condition relief on a party's filing a bond or other appropriate security in the district court.

(b) Proceeding Against a Surety. If a party gives security in the form of a bond or stipulation or other undertaking with one or more sureties, each surety submits to the jurisdiction of the district court and irrevocably appoints the district clerk as the surety's agent on whom any papers affecting the surety's liability on the bond or undertaking may be served. On motion, a surety's liability may be enforced in the district court without the necessity of an independent action. The motion and any notice that the district court prescribes may be served on the district clerk, who must promptly mail a copy to each surety whose address is known.

(c) Stay in a Criminal Case. Rule 38 of the Federal Rules of Criminal Procedure governs a stay in a criminal case.

As amended Mar. 10, 1986, eff. July 1, 1986; Apr. 27, 1995, eff. Dec. 1, 1995; Apr. 24, 1998, eff. Dec. 1, 1998.

Rule 9. Release in a Criminal Case [Omitted]

Rule 10. The Record on Appeal

(a) Composition of the Record on Appeal. The following items constitute the record on appeal:

(1) the original papers and exhibits filed in the district court;

(2) the transcript of proceedings, if any; and

(3) a certified copy of the docket entries prepared by the district clerk.

(b) The Transcript of Proceedings.

(1) *Appellant's Duty to Order.* Within 10 days after filing the notice of appeal or entry of an order disposing of the last timely remaining motion of a type specified in Rule 4(a)(4)(A), whichever is later, the appellant must do either of the following:

(A) order from the reporter a transcript of such parts of the proceedings not already on file as the appellant considers necessary, subject to a local rule of the court of appeals and with the following qualifications:

(i) the order must be in writing;

(ii) if the cost of the transcript is to be paid by the United States under the Criminal Justice Act, the order must so state; and

(iii) the appellant must, within the same period, file a copy of the order with the district clerk; or

(B) file a certificate stating that no transcript will be ordered.

(2) *Unsupported Finding or Conclusion.* If the appellant intends to urge on appeal that a finding or conclusion is unsupported by the evidence or is contrary to the evidence, the appellant must include in the record a transcript of all evidence relevant to that finding or conclusion.

(3) *Partial Transcript.* Unless the entire transcript is ordered:

(A) the appellant must — within the 10 days provided in Rule 10(b)(1) — file a statement of the issues that the appellant intends to present on the appeal and must serve on the appellee a copy of both the order or certificate and the statement;

(B) if the appellee considers it necessary to have a transcript of other parts of the proceedings, the appellee must, within 10 days after the service of the order or certificate and the statement of the issues, file and serve on the appellant a designation of additional parts to be ordered; and

(C) unless within 10 days after service of that designation the appellant has ordered all such parts, and has so notified the appellee, the appellee may within the following 10 days either order the parts or move in the district court for an order requiring the appellant to do so.

(4) *Payment.* At the time of ordering, a party must make satisfactory arrangements with the reporter for paying the cost of the transcript.

(c) Statement of the Evidence When the Proceedings Were Not Recorded or When a Transcript Is Unavailable. If the transcript of a hearing or trial is unavailable, the appellant may prepare a statement of the evidence or proceedings from the best available means, including the appellant's recollection. The statement must be served on the appellee, who may serve objections or proposed amendments within 10 days after being served. Thereupon the statement and any objections or proposed amendments must then be submitted to the district court for settlement and approval. As settled and approved, the statement must be included by the district clerk in the record on appeal.

(d) Agreed Statement as the Record on Appeal. In place of the record on appeal as defined in Rule 10 (a), the parties may prepare, sign, and submit to the district court a statement of the case showing how the issues presented by the appeal arose and were decided in the district court. The statement must set forth only those facts averred and proved or sought to be proved that are essential to the court's resolution of the issues. If the statement is truthful, it — together with any additions that the district court may consider necessary to a full presentation of the issues on appeal — must be approved by the district court and must then be certified to the court of appeals as the record on appeal. The district clerk must then send it to the circuit clerk within the time provided by Rule 11. A copy of the agreed statement may be filed in place of the appendix required by Rule 30.

(e) Correction or Modification of the Record.

(1) If any difference arises about whether the record truly discloses what occurred in the district court, the difference must be submitted to and settled by that court and the record conformed accordingly.

(2) If anything material to either party is omitted from or misstated in the record by error or accident, the omission or misstatement may be corrected and a supplemental record may be certified and forwarded:

(A) on stipulation of the parties;

(B) by the district court before or after the record has been forwarded; or

(C) by the court of appeals.

(3) All other questions as to the form and content of the record must be presented to the court of appeals.

As amended Apr. 30, 1979, eff. Aug. 1, 1979; Mar. 10, 1986, eff. July 1, 1986; Apr. 30, 1991, eff. Dec. 1, 1991; Apr. 22, 1993, eff. Dec. 1, 1993; Apr. 29, 1994, eff. Dec. 1, 1994; Apr. 27, 1995, eff. Dec. 1, 1995; Apr. 24, 1998, eff. Dec. 1, 1998.

Rule 11. Forwarding the Record

(a) Appellant's Duty. An appellant filing a notice of appeal must comply with Rule 10(b) and must do whatever else is necessary to enable the clerk to assemble and forward the record. If there are multiple appeals from a judgment or order, the clerk must forward a single record.

(b) Duties of Reporter and District Clerk.

(1) *Reporter's Duty to Prepare and File a Transcript.* The reporter must prepare and file a transcript as follows:

(A) Upon receiving an order for a transcript, the reporter must enter at the foot of the order the date of its receipt and the expected completion date and send a copy, so endorsed, to the circuit clerk.

(B) If the transcript cannot be completed within 30 days of the reporter's receipt of the order, the reporter may request the circuit clerk to grant additional time to complete it. The clerk must note on the docket the action taken and notify the parties.

(C) When a transcript is complete, the reporter must file it with the district clerk and notify the circuit clerk of the filing.

(D) If the reporter fails to file the transcript on time, the circuit clerk must notify the district judge and do whatever else the court of appeals directs.

(2) *District Clerk's Duty to Forward.* When the record is complete, the district clerk must number the documents constituting the record and send them promptly to the circuit clerk together with a list of the documents correspondingly numbered and reasonably identified. Unless directed to do so by a party or the circuit clerk, the district clerk will not send to the court of appeals documents of unusual bulk or weight, physical exhibits other than documents, or other parts of the record designated for omission by local rule of the court of appeals. If the exhibits are unusually bulky or heavy, a party must arrange with the clerks in advance for their transportation and receipt.

(c) Retaining the Record Temporarily in the District Court for Use in Preparing the Appeal. The parties may stipulate, or the district court on motion may order, that the district clerk retain the record temporarily for the parties to use in preparing the papers on appeal. In that event the district clerk must certify to the circuit clerk that the record on appeal is complete. Upon receipt of the appellee's brief, or earlier if the court orders or the parties agree, the appellant must request the district clerk to forward the record.

(d) [***Abrogated.***]

(e) Retaining the Record by Court Order.

(1) The court of appeals may, by order or local rule, provide that a certified copy of the docket entries be forwarded instead of the entire record. But a party may at any time during the appeal request that designated parts of the record be forwarded.

(2) The district court may order the record or some part of it retained if the court needs it while the appeal is pending, subject, however, to call by the court of appeals.

(3) If part or all of the record is ordered retained, the district clerk must send to the court of appeals a copy of the order and the docket entries together with the parts of the original record allowed by the district court and copies of any parts of the record designated by the parties.

(f) Retaining Parts of the Record in the District Court by Stipulation of the Parties. The parties may agree by written stipulation filed in the district court that designated parts of the record be retained in the district court subject to call by the court of appeals or request by a party. The parts of the record so designated remain a part of the record on appeal.

(g) Record for a Preliminary Motion in the Court of Appeals. If, before the record is forwarded, a party makes any of the following motions in the court of appeals:

- for dismissal;
- for release;
- for a stay pending appeal;
- for additional security on the bond on appeal or on a supersedeas bond; or
- for any other intermediate order —

the district clerk must send the court of appeals any parts of the record designated by any party.

As amended Apr. 30, 1979, eff. Aug. 1, 1979; Mar. 10, 1986, eff. July 1, 1986; Apr. 24, 1998, eff. Dec. 1, 1998.

Rule 12. Docketing the Appeal; Filing a Representation Statement; Filing the Record

(a) **Docketing the Appeal.** Upon receipt of the copy of the notice of appeal and the docket entries from the district clerk under Rule 3(d), the circuit clerk must docket the appeal under the title of the district court action and must identify the appellant, adding the appellant's name if necessary.

(b) **Filing a Representation Statement.** Unless the court of appeals designates another time, the attorney who filed the notice of appeal must, within 10 days after filing the notice, file a statement with the circuit clerk naming the parties that the attorney represents on appeal.

(c) **Filing the Record, Partial Record, or Certificate.** Upon receiving the record, partial record, or district clerk's certificate provided in Rule 11, the circuit clerk must file it and immediately notify all parties of the filing date.

As amended April 30, 1979, eff. Aug. 1, 1979; Mar. 10, 1986, eff. July 1, 1986; Apr. 22, 1993, eff. Dec. 1, 1993; Apr. 24, 1998, eff. Dec. 1, 1998.

Title III. Review of a Decision of the United States Tax Court [Omitted]

Title IV. Review or Enforcement of an Order of an Administrative Agency, Board, Commission, or Officer [Omitted]

Title V. Extraordinary Writs

Rule 21. Writs of Mandamus and Prohibition, and Other Extraordinary Writs

(a) Mandamus or Prohibition to a Court: Petition, Filing, Service, and Docketing.

(1) A party petitioning for a writ of mandamus or prohibition directed to a court must file a petition with the circuit clerk with proof of service on all parties to the proceeding in the trial-court. The party shall also provide a copy to the trial-court judge. All parties to the proceeding in the trial-court other than the petitioner are respondents for all purposes.

(2)(A) The petition shall be titled "In re [name of petitioner]."

(B) The petition shall state:

(i) the relief sought;

(ii) the issues presented;

(iii) the facts necessary to understand the issue presented by the petition; and

(iv) the reasons why the writ should issue.

(C) The petition must include a copy of any order or opinion or parts of the record that may be essential to understand the matters set forth in the petition.

(3) Upon receiving the prescribed docket fee, the clerk must docket the petition and submit it to the court.

(b) Denial; Order Directing Answer; Briefs; Precedence.

(1) The court may deny the petition without an answer. Otherwise, it must order the respondent, if any, to answer within a fixed time.

(2) The clerk must serve the order to respond on all persons directed to respond.

(3) Two or more respondents may answer jointly.

(4) The court of appeals may invite or order the trial-court judge to address the petition or may invite an amicus curiae to do so. The trial-court judge may request permission to address the petition but may not do so unless invited or ordered to do so by the court of appeals.

(5) If briefing or oral argument is required, the clerk must advise the parties, and when appropriate, the trial-court judge or amicus curiae.

(6) The proceeding must be given preference over ordinary civil cases.

(7) The circuit clerk must send a copy of the final disposition to the trial-court judge.

(c) Other Extraordinary Writs. An application for an extraordinary writ other than one provided for in Rule 21(a) must be made by filing a petition with the circuit clerk with proof of service on the respondents. Proceedings on the application must conform, so far as is practicable, to the procedures prescribed in Rule 21(a) and (b).

(d) Form of Papers; Number of Copies. All papers may conform to Rule 32(c)(2). Except by the court's permission, a paper must not exceed 30 pages, exclusive of the disclosure statement, the proof of service, and the accompanying documents required by Rule 21(a)(2)(C). An original and 3 copies must be filed unless the court requires the filing of a different number by local rule or by order in a particular case.

As amended Apr. 29, 1994, eff. Dec. 1, 1994, Apr. 23, 1996, eff. Dec. 1, 1996; Apr. 24, 1998, eff. Dec. 1, 1998; Apr. 29, 2002, eff. Dec. 1, 2002.

Title VI. Habeas Corpus; Proceedings in Forma Pauperis

[Rules 22 and 23 Omitted]

Rule 24. Proceeding in Forma Pauperis

(a) Leave to Proceed in Forma Pauperis.

(1) *Motion in the District Court.* Except as stated in Rule 24(a)(3), a party to a district-court action who desires to appeal in forma pauperis must file a motion in the district court. The party must attach an affidavit that:

(A) shows in the detail prescribed by Form 4 of the Appendix of Forms, the party's inability to pay or to give security for fees and costs;

(B) claims an entitlement to redress; and

(C) states the issues that the party intends to present on appeal.

(2) *Action on the Motion.* If the district court grants the motion, the party may proceed on appeal without prepaying or giving security for fees and costs, unless a statute provides otherwise. If the district court denies the motion, it must state its reasons in writing.

(3) *Prior Approval.* A party who was permitted to proceed in forma pauperis in the district-court action, or who was determined to be financially unable to obtain an adequate defense in a criminal case, may proceed on appeal in forma pauperis without further authorization, unless:

(A) the district court—before or after the notice of appeal is filed— certifies that the appeal is not taken in good faith or finds that the party is not otherwise entitled to proceed in forma pauperis and states in writing its reasons for the certification or finding; or

(B) a statute provides otherwise.

(4) *Notice of District Court's Denial.* The district clerk must immediately notify the parties and the court of appeals when the district court does any of the following:

(A) denies a motion to proceed on appeal in forma pauperis;

(B) certifies that the appeal is not taken in good faith; or

(C) finds that the party is not otherwise entitled to proceed in forma pauperis.

(5) *Motion in the Court of Appeals.* A party may file a motion to proceed on appeal in forma pauperis in the court of appeals within 30 days after service of the notice prescribed in Rule 24(a)(4). The motion must include a copy of the affidavit filed in the district court and the district court's statement of reasons for its actions. If no affidavit was filed in the district court, the party must include the affidavit prescribed by Rule 24(a)(1).

(b) Leave to Proceed in Forma Pauperis on Appeal or Review of an Administrative-Agency Proceeding. When an appeal or review of a proceeding before an administrative agency, board, commission, or officer (including, for the purpose of this rule the United States Tax Court) proceeds directly in a court of appeals, a party may file in the court of appeals a motion for leave to proceed on appeal in forma pauperis with an affidavit prescribed by Rule 24(a)(1).

(c) Leave to Use Original Record. A party allowed to proceed on appeal in forma pauperis may request that the appeal be heard on the original record without reproducing any part.

As amended Apr. 30, 1979, eff. Aug. 1, 1979; Mar. 10, 1986, eff. July 1, 1986; Apr. 24, 1998, eff. Dec. 1, 1998; Apr. 29, 2002, eff. Dec. 1, 2002.

Title VII. General Provisions

Rule 25. Filing and Service

(a) Filing.

(1) *Filing with the Clerk.* A paper required or permitted to be filed in a court of appeals must be filed with the clerk.

(2) *Filing: Method and Timeliness.*

(A) *In General.* Filing may be accomplished by mail addressed to the clerk, but filing is not timely unless the clerk receives the papers within the time fixed for filing.

(B) A *Brief or Appendix.* A brief or appendix is timely filed, however, if on or before the last day for filing, it is:

(i) mailed to the clerk by First-Class Mail, or other class of mail that is at least as expeditious, postage prepaid; or

(ii) dispatched to a third-party commercial carrier for delivery to the clerk within 3 calendar days.

(C) *Inmate Filing.* A paper filed by an inmate confined in an institution is timely filed if deposited in the institution's internal mailing system on or before the last day for filing. If an institution has a system designed for legal mail, the inmate must use that system to receive the benefit of this rule. Timely filing may be shown by a declaration in compliance with 28 U.S.C. §1746 or by a notarized statement, either of which must set forth the date of deposit and state that first-class postage has been prepaid.

(D) *Electronic Filing.* A court of appeals may by local rule permit papers to be filed, signed, or verified by electronic means that are consistent with technical standards, if any, that the Judicial Conference of the United States establishes. A paper filed by electronic means in compliance with a local rule constitutes a written paper for the purpose of applying these rules.

(3) *Filing a Motion with a Judge.* If a motion requests relief that may be granted by a single judge, the judge may permit the motion to be filed with the judge; the judge must note the filing date on the motion and give it to the clerk.

(4) *Clerk's Refusal of Documents.* The clerk must not refuse to accept for filing any paper presented for that purpose solely because it is not presented in proper form as required by these rules or by any local rules or practice.

(b) Service of All Papers Required. Unless a rule requires service by the clerk, a party must, at or before the time of filing a paper serve a copy on the other parties to the appeal or review. Service on a party represented by counsel must be made on the party's counsel.

(c) Manner of Service.

(1) Service may be any of the following:

(A) personal, including delivery to a responsible person at the office of counsel;

(B) by mail;

(C) by third-party commercial carrier for delivery within 3 calendar days; or

(D) by electronic means, if the party being served consents in writing.

(2) If authorized by local rule, a party may use the court's transmission equipment to make electronic service under Rule 25(c)(1)(D).

(3) When reasonable considering such factors as the immediacy of the relief sought, distance, and cost, service on a party must be by a manner at least as expeditious as the manner used to file the paper with the court.

(4) Service by mail or by commercial carrier is complete on mailing or delivery to the carrier. Service by electronic means is complete on transmission,

unless the party making service is notified that the paper was not received by the party served.

(d) Proof of Service.

(1) A paper presented for filing must contain either of the following:

(A) an acknowledgment of service by the person served; or

(B) proof of service consisting of a statement by the person who made service certifying:

(i) the date and manner of service;

(ii) the names of the persons served; and

(iii) their mail or electronic addresses, facsimile numbers, or the addresses of the places of delivery, as appropriate for the manner of service.

(2) When a brief or appendix is filed by mailing or dispatch in accordance with Rule 25(a)(2)(B), the proof of service must also state the date and manner by which the document was mailed or dispatched to the clerk.

(3) Proof of service may appear on or be affixed to the papers filed.

(e) Number of Copies. When these rules require the filing or furnishing of a number of copies, a court may require a different number by local rule or by order in a particular case.

As amended Mar. 10, 1986, eff. July 1, 1986; Apr. 30, 1991, eff. Dec. 1, 1991; Apr. 22, 1993, eff. Dec. 1, 1993; Apr. 29, 1994, eff. Dec. 1, 1994; Apr. 23, 1996, eff. Dec. 1, 1996; Apr. 24, 1998, eff. Dec. 1, 1998; Apr. 29, 2002, eff. Dec. 1, 2002.

Rule 26. Computing and Extending Time

(a) Computing Time. The following rules apply in computing any period of time specified in these rules or in any local rule, court order, or applicable statute:

(1) Exclude the day of the act, event, or default that begins the period.

(2) Exclude intermediate Saturdays, Sundays, and legal holidays when the period is less than 11 days, unless stated in calendar days.

(3) Include the last day of the period unless it is a Saturday, Sunday, legal holiday, or — if the act to be done is filing a paper in court — a day on which the weather or other conditions make the clerk's office inaccessible.

(4) As used in this rule, "legal holiday" means New Year's Day, Martin Luther King, Jr.'s Birthday, Presidents' Day, Memorial Day, Independence Day, Labor Day, Columbus Day, Veterans' Day, Thanksgiving Day, Christmas Day, and any other day declared a holiday by the President, Congress, or the state in which is located either the district court that rendered the challenged judgment or order, or the circuit clerk's principal office.

(b) Extending Time. For good cause, the court may extend the time prescribed by these rules or by its orders to perform any act, or may permit an act to be done after that time expires. But the court may not extend the time to file:

(1) a notice of appeal (except as authorized in Rule 4) or a petition for permission to appeal; or

(2) a notice of appeal from or a petition to enjoin, set aside, suspend, modify, enforce, or otherwise review an order of an administrative agency, board, commission, or officer of the United States, unless specifically authorized by law.

(c) Additional Time After Service. When a party is required or permitted to act within a prescribed period after a paper is served on that party, 3 calendar days are added to the prescribed period unless the paper is delivered on the date of service stated in the proof of service. For purposes of this Rule 26(c), a paper that is served electronically is not treated as delivered on the date of service stated in the proof of service.

As amended Mar. 1, 1971, eff. July 1, 1971; Mar. 10, 1986, eff. July 1, 1986; Apr. 25, 1989, eff. Dec. 1, 1989; Apr. 30, 1991, eff. Dec. 1, 1991; Apr. 23, 1996, eff. Dec. 1, 1996; Apr. 24, 1998, eff. Dec. 1, 1998; Apr. 29, 2002, eff. Dec. 1, 2002.

Rule 26.1 Corporate Disclosure Statement [Omitted]

Rule 27. Motions

(a) In General.

(1) *Application for Relief.* An application for an order or other relief is made by motion unless these rules prescribe another form. A motion must be in writing unless the court permits otherwise.

(2) *Contents of a Motion.*

(A) *Grounds and Relief Sought.* A motion must state with particularity the grounds for the motion, the relief sought, and the legal argument necessary to support it.

(B) *Accompanying Documents.*

(i) Any affidavit or other paper necessary to support a motion must be served and filed with the motion.

(ii) An affidavit must contain only factual information, not legal argument.

(iii) A motion seeking substantive relief must include a copy of the trial court's opinion or agency's decision as a separate exhibit.

(C) *Documents Barred or not Required.*

(i) A separate brief supporting or responding to a motion must not be filed.

(ii) A notice of motion is not required.

(iii) A proposed order is not required.

(3) *Response.*

(A) *Time to File.* Any party may file a response to a motion; Rule 27(a)(2) governs its contents. The response must be filed within 8 days after service of the motion unless the court shortens or extends the time. A motion authorized by Rules 8, 9, 18, or 41 may be granted before the 8-day period runs only if the court gives reasonable notice to the parties that it intends to act sooner.

(B) *Request for Affirmative Relief.* A response may include a motion for affirmative relief. The time to respond to the new motion, and to reply to that response, are governed by Rule 27(a)(3)(A) and (a)(4). The title of the response must alert the court to the request for relief.

(4) *Reply to Response.* Any reply to a response must be filed within 5 days after service of the response. A reply must not present matters that do not relate to the response.

(b) Disposition of a Motion for a Procedural Order. The court may act on a motion for a procedural order — including a motion under Rule 26(b) — at any time without awaiting a response, and may, by rule or by order in a particular case, authorize its clerk to act on specified types of procedural motions. A party adversely affected by the court's, or the clerk's, action may file a motion to reconsider, vacate, or modify that action. Timely opposition filed after the motion is granted in whole or in part does not constitute a request to reconsider, vacate, or modify the disposition; a motion requesting that relief must be filed.

(c) Power of a Single Judge to Entertain a Motion. A circuit judge may act alone on any motion, but may not dismiss or otherwise determine an appeal or other proceeding. A court of appeals may provide by rule or by order in a particular case that only the court may act on any motion or class of motions. The court may review the action of a single judge.

(d) Form of Papers; Page Limits; and Number of Copies.

(1) *Format.*

(A) *Reproduction.* A motion, response, or reply may be reproduced by any process that yields a clear black image on light paper. The paper must be opaque and unglazed. Only one side of the paper may be used.

(B) *Cover.* A cover is not required, but there must be a caption that includes the case number, the name of the court, the title of the case, and a brief descriptive title indicating the purpose of the motion and identifying the party or parties for whom it is filed. If a cover is used, it must be white.

(C) *Binding.* The document must be bound in any manner that is secure, does not obscure the text, and permits the document to lie reasonably flat when open.

(D) *Paper Size, Line Spacing, and Margins.* The document must be on

8½ by 11 inch paper. The text must be double-spaced, but quotations more than two lines long may be indented and single-spaced. Headings and footnotes may be single-spaced. Margins must be at least one inch on all four sides. Page numbers may be placed in the margins, but no text may appear there.

(2) *Page Limits.* A motion or a response to a motion must not exceed 20 pages, exclusive of the corporate disclosure statement and accompanying documents authorized by Rule 27(a)(2)(B), unless the court permits or directs otherwise. A reply to a response must not exceed 10 pages.

(3) *Number of Copies.* An original and 3 copies must be filed unless the court requires a different number by local rule or by order in a particular case.

(e) Oral Argument. A motion will be decided without oral argument unless the court orders otherwise.

As amended Apr. 30, 1979, eff. Aug. 1, 1979; Apr. 25, 1989, eff. Dec. 1, 1989; Apr. 29, 1994, eff. Dec. 1, 1994; Apr. 24, 1998, eff. Dec. 1, 1998; Apr. 29, 2002, eff. Dec. 1, 2002.

Rule 28. Briefs

(a) Appellant's Brief. The brief of the appellant must contain, under appropriate headings and in the order here indicated:

(1) a corporate disclosure statement if required by Rule 26.1;

(2) a table of contents, with page references;

(3) a table of authorities — ases (alphabetically arranged), statutes, and other authorities — with references to the pages of the brief where they are cited;

(4) a jurisdictional statement, including:

(A) the basis for the district court's or agency's subject-matter jurisdiction, with citations to applicable statutory provisions and stating relevant facts establishing jurisdiction;

(B) the basis for the court of appeals' jurisdiction, with citations to applicable statutory provisions and stating relevant facts establishing jurisdiction;

(C) the filing dates establishing the timelines of the appeal or petition for review; and

(D) an assertion that the appeal is from a final order or judgment that disposes of all parties' claims, or information establishing the court of appeals' jurisdiction on some other basis;

(5) a statement of the issues presented for review;

(6) a statement of the case briefly indicating the nature of the case, the course of proceedings, and the disposition below;

(7) a statement of facts relevant to the issues submitted for review with appropriate references to the record (see Rule 28(e));

(8) a summary of the argument, which must contain a succinct, clear, and

accurate statement of the arguments made in the body of the brief, and which must not merely repeat the argument headings;

(9) the argument, which must contain:

(A) appellant's contentions and the reasons for them, with citations to the authorities and parts of the record on which the appellant relies; and

(B) for each issue, a concise statement of the applicable standard of review (which may appear in the discussion of the issue or under a separate heading placed before the discussion of the issues);

(10) a short conclusion stating the precise relief sought; and

(11) the certificate of compliance, if required by Rule 32(a)(7).

(b) Appellee's Brief. The appellee's brief must conform to the requirements of Rule 28(a)(1)-(9) and (11), except that none of the following need appear unless the appellee is dissatisfied with the appellant's statement:

(1) the jurisdictional statement;

(2) the statement of the issues;

(3) the statement of the case;

(4) the statement of the facts; and

(5) the statement of the standard of review.

(c) Reply Brief. The appellant may file a brief in reply to the appellee's brief. An appellee who has cross-appealed may file a brief in reply to the appellant's response to the issues presented by the cross appeal. Unless the court permits, no further briefs may be filed. A reply brief must contain a table of contents, with page references, and a table of authorities — ases (alphabetically arranged), statutes and other authorities — with references to the pages of the reply brief where they are cited.

(d) References to Parties. In briefs and at oral arguments, counsel should minimize use of the terms "appellant" and "appellee." To make briefs clear, counsel should use the parties' actual names or the designations used in the lower court or in the agency proceedings, or such descriptive terms as "the employee," "the injured person," "the taxpayer," "the ship," "the stevedore."

(e) References to the Record. References to the parts of the record contained in the appendix filed with the appellant's brief must be to the pages of the appendix. If the appendix is prepared after the briefs are filed, a party referring to the record must follow one of the methods detailed in Rule 30(c). If the original record is used under Rule 30(f) and is not consecutively paginated, or if the brief refers to an unreproduced part of the record, any reference must be to the page of the original document. For example:

- Answer p. 7;
- Motion for Judgment p. 2;

- Transcript p. 231.

Only clear abbreviations may be used. A party referring to evidence whose admissibility is in controversy must cite the pages of the appendix or of the transcript at which the evidence was identified, offered, and received or rejected.

(f) **Reproduction of Statutes, Rules, Regulations, etc.** If the court's determination of the issues presented requires the study of statutes, rules, regulations, etc., the relevant parts must be set out in the brief or in an addendum at the end, or may be supplied to the court in pamphlet form.

(g) **[Reserved]**

(h) **Briefs in a Case Involving a Cross-Appeal.** If a cross-appeal is filed, the party who files a notice of appeal first is the appellant for the purposes of this rule and Rules 30, 31, and 34. If notices are filed on the same day, the plaintiff in the proceeding below is the appellant. These designations may be modified by agreement of the parties or by court order. With respect to appellee's cross-appeal and response to appellant's brief, appellee's brief must conform to the requirements of Rule 28(a)(1)-(11). But an appellee who is satisfied with appellant's statement need not include a statement of the case or of the facts.

(i) **Briefs in Cases Involving Multiple Appellants or Appellees.** In a case involving more than one appellant or appellee, including consolidated cases, any number of appellants or appellees may join in a brief, and any party may adopt by reference a part of another's brief. Parties may also join in reply briefs.

(j) **Citation of Supplemental Authorities.** If pertinent and significant authorities come to a party's attention after the party's brief has been filed — or after oral argument but before decision — a party may promptly advise the circuit clerk by letter, with a copy to all other parties, setting forth the citations. The letter must state the reasons for the supplemental citations, referring either to the page of the brief or to a point argued orally. The body of the letter must not exceed 350 words. Any response must be made promptly and must be similarly limited.

As amended Apr. 30, 1979, eff. Aug. 1, 1979; Mar. 10, 1986, eff. July 1, 1986; Apr. 25, 1989, eff. Dec. 1, 1989; Apr. 30, 1991, eff. Dec. 1, 1991; Apr. 22, 1993, eff. Dec. 1, 1993; Apr. 29, 1994, eff. Dec. 1, 1994; Apr. 24, 1998, eff. Dec. 1, 1998; Apr. 29, 2002, eff. Dec. 1, 2002.

Rule 29. Brief of an Amicus Curiae

(a) **When Permitted.** The United States or its officer or agency, or a State, Territory, Commonwealth, or the District of Columbia may file an amicus-curiae brief without the consent of the parties or leave of court. Any other amicus curiae may file a brief only by leave of court or if the brief states that all parties have consented to its filing.

(b) Motion for Leave to File. The motion must be accompanied by the proposed brief and state:

(1) the movant's interest; and

(2) the reason why an amicus brief is desirable and why the matters asserted are relevant to the disposition of the case.

(c) Contents and Form. An amicus brief must comply with Rule 32. In addition to the requirements of Rule 32, the cover must identify the party or parties supported and indicate whether the brief supports affirmance or reversal. If an amicus curiae is a corporation, the brief must include a disclosure statement like that required of parties by Rule 26.1. An amicus brief need not comply with Rule 28, but must include the following:

(1) a table of contents, with page references;

(2) a table of authorities — ase (alphabetically arranged), statutes and other authorities — with references to the pages of the brief where they are cited;

(3) a concise statement of the identity of the amicus curiae, its interest in the case, and the source of its authority to file;

(4) an argument, which may be preceded by a summary and which need not include a statement of the applicable standard of review; and

(5) a certificate of compliance, if required by Rule 32(a)(7).

(d) Length. Except by the court's permission, an amicus brief may be no more than one-half the maximum length authorized by these rules for a party's principal brief. If the court grants a party permission to file a longer brief, that extension does not affect the length of an amicus brief.

(e) Time for Filing. An amicus curiae must file its brief, accompanied by a motion for filing when necessary, no later than 7 days after the principal brief of the party being supported is filed. An amicux curiae that does not support either party must file its brief no later than 7 days after the appellant's or petitioner's principal brief is filed. A court may grant leave for later filing, specifying the time within which an opposing party may answer.

(f) Reply Brief. Except by the court's permission, an amicus curiae may not file a reply brief.

(g) Oral Argument. An amicus curiae may participate in oral argument only with the court's permission.

As amended Apr. 24, 1998, eff. Dec. 1, 1998.

Rule 30. Appendix to the Briefs

(a) Appellant's Responsibility.

(1) *Contents of the Appendix.* The appellant must prepare and file an appendix to the briefs containing:

(A) the relevant docket entries in the proceeding below;

(B) the relevant portions of the pleadings, charge, findings, or opinion;

(C) the judgment, order, or decision in question; and

(D) other parts of the record to which the parties wish to direct the court's attention.

(2) *Excluded Material.* Memoranda of law in the district court should not be included in the appendix unless they have independent relevance. Parts of the record may be relied on by the court or the parties even though not included in the appendix.

(3) *Time to File; Number of Copies.* Unless filing is deferred under Rule 30(c), the appellant must file 10 copies of the appendix with the brief and must serve one copy on counsel for each party separately represented. An unrepresented party proceeding in forma pauperis must file 4 legible copies with the clerk, and one copy must be served on counsel for each separately represented party. The court may by local rule or by order in a particular case require the filing or service of a different number.

(b) All Parties' Responsibilities.

(1) *Determining the Contents of the Appendix.* The parties are encouraged to agree on the contents of the appendix. In the absence of an agreement, the appellant must, within 10 days after the record is filed, serve on the appellee a designation of the parts of the record the appellant intends to include in the appendix and a statement of the issues the appellant intends to present for review. The appellee may, within 10 days after receiving the designation, serve on the appellant a designation of additional parts to which it wishes to direct the court's attention. The appellant must include the designated parts in the appendix. The parties must not engage in unnecessary designation of parts of the record, because the entire record is available to the court. This paragraph applies also to a cross-appellant and a cross-appellee.

(2) *Costs of Appendix.* Unless the parties agree otherwise, the appellant must pay the cost of the appendix. If the appellant considers parts of the record designated by the appellee to be unnecessary, the appellant may advise the appellee, who must then advance the cost of including those parts. The cost of the appendix is a taxable cost. But if any party causes unnecessary parts of the record to be included in the appendix, the court may impose the cost of those parts on that party. Each circuit must, by local rule, provide for sanctions against attorneys who unreasonably and vexatiously increase litigation costs by including unnecessary material in the appendix.

(c) Deferred Appendix.

(1) *Deferral Until After Briefs Are Filed.* The court may provide by rule for classes of cases or by order in a particular case that preparation of the appendix may be deferred until after the briefs have been filed and that the appendix may be filed 21 days after the appellee's brief is served. Even though the filing of the appendix may be deferred, Rule 30(b) applies; except that a party must designate the parts of the record it wants included in the appendix when it serves its brief, and need not include a statement of the issues presented.

(2) *References to the Record.*

(A) If the deferred appendix is used, the parties may cite in their briefs the pertinent pages of the record. When the appendix is prepared, the record pages cited in the briefs must be indicated by inserting record page numbers, in brackets, at places in the appendix where those pages of the record appear.

(B) A party who wants to refer directly to pages of the appendix may serve and file copies of the brief within the time required by Rule 31(a), containing appropriate references to pertinent pages of the record. In that event, within 14 days after the appendix is filed, the party must serve and file copies of the brief, containing references to the pages of the appendix in place of or in addition to the references to the pertinent pages of the record. Except for the correction of typographical errors, no other changes may be made to the brief.

(d) Format of the Appendix. The appendix must begin with a table of contents identifying the page at which each part begins. The relevant docket entries must follow the table of contents. Other parts of the record must follow chronologically. When pages from the transcript of proceedings are placed in the appendix, the transcript page numbers must be shown in brackets immediately before the included pages. Omissions in the text of papers or of the transcript must be indicated by asterisks. Immaterial formal matters (captions, subscriptions, acknowledgments, etc.) should be omitted.

(e) Reproduction of Exhibits. Exhibits designated for inclusion in the appendix may be reproduced in a separate volume, or volumes, suitably indexed. Four copies must be filed with the appendix, and one copy must be served on counsel for each separately represented party. If a transcript of a proceeding before an administrative agency, board, commission, or officer was used in a district-court action and has been designated for inclusion in the appendix, the transcript must be placed in the appendix as an exhibit.

(f) Appeal on the Original Record Without an Appendix. The court may, either by rule for all cases or classes of cases or by order in a particular case, dispense with the appendix and permit an appeal to proceed on the original record with any copies of the record, or relevant parts, that the court may order the parties to file.

As amended Mar. 30, 1970, eff. July 1, 1970; Mar. 10, 1986, eff. July 1,

1986; Apr. 30, 1991, eff. Dec. 1, 1991; Apr. 29, 1994, eff. Dec. 1, 1994; Apr. 24, 1998, eff. Dec. 1, 1998.

Rule 31. Serving and Filing Briefs

(a) Time to Serve and File a Brief.

(1) The appellant must serve and file a brief within 40 days after the record is filed. The appellee must serve and file a brief within 30 days after the appellant's brief is served. The appellant may serve and file a reply brief within 14 days after service of the appellee's brief but a reply brief must be filed at least 3 days before argument, unless the court, for good cause, allows a later filing.

(2) A court of appeals that routinely considers cases on the merits promptly after the briefs are filed may shorten the time to serve and file briefs, either by local rule or by order in a particular case.

(b) Number of Copies. Twenty-five copies of each brief must be filed with the clerk and 2 copies must be served on each unrepresented party and on counsel for each separately represented party. An unrepresented party proceeding in forma pauperis must file 4 legible copies with the clerk, and one copy must be served on each unrepresented party and on counsel for each separately represented party. The court may by local rule or by order in a particular case require the filing or service of a different number.

(c) Consequence of Failure to File. If an appellant fails to file a brief within the time provided by this rule, or within an extended time, an appellee may move to dismiss the appeal. An appellee who fails to file a brief will not be heard at oral argument unless the court grants permission.

As amended Mar. 30, 1970, eff. July 1, 1970; Mar. 10, 1986, eff. July 1, 1986; Apr. 29, 1994, eff. Dec. 1, 1994; Apr. 24, 1998, eff. Dec. 1, 1998; Apr. 29, 2002, eff. Dec. 1, 2002.

Rule 32. Form of Briefs, Appendices, and Other Papers [Omitted]

Rule 33. Appeal Conferences

The court may direct the attorneys — and, when appropriate, the parties — to participate in one or more conferences to address any matter that may aid in disposing of the proceedings, including simplifying the issues and discussing settlement. A judge or other person designated by the court may preside over the conference, which may be conducted in person or by telephone. Before a settlement conference, the attorneys must consult with their clients and obtain as much authority as feasible to settle the case. The court may, as a result of the conference, enter an order controlling the course of the proceedings or implementing any settlement agreement.

As amended Apr. 29, 1994, eff. Dec. 1, 1994; Apr. 24, 1998, eff. Dec. 1, 1998.

Rule 34. Oral Argument

(a) In General.

(1) *Party's Statement.* Any party may file, or a court may require by local rule, a statement explaining why oral argument should, or need not, be permitted.

(2) *Standards.* Oral argument must be allowed in every case unless a panel of three judges who have examined the briefs and record unanimously agrees that oral argument is unnecessary for any of the following reasons:

(A) the appeal is frivolous;

(B) the dispositive issue or issues have been authoritatively decided; or

(C) the facts and legal arguments are adequately presented in the briefs and record, and the decisional process would not be significantly aided by oral argument.

(b) Notice of Argument; Postponement. The clerk must advise all parties whether oral argument will be scheduled, and if so, the date, time, and place for it, and the time allowed for each side. A motion to postpone the argument or to allow longer argument must be filed reasonably in advance of the hearing date.

(c) Order and Contents of Argument. The appellant opens and concludes the argument. Counsel must not read at length from briefs, records, or authorities.

(d) Cross-Appeals and Separate Appeals. If there is a cross-appeal, Rule 28(h) determines which party is the appellant and which is the appellee for purposes of oral argument. Unless the court directs otherwise, a cross or separate appeal must be argued when the initial appeal is argued. Separate parties should avoid duplicative argument.

(e) Non Appearance of a Party. If the appellee fails to appear for argument, the court must hear appellant's argument. If the appellant fails to appear for argument, the court may hear the appellee's argument. If neither party appears, the case will be decided on the briefs, unless the court orders otherwise.

(f) Submission on Briefs. The parties may agree to submit a case for decision on the briefs, but the court may direct that the case be argued.

(g) **Use of Physical Exhibits at Argument; Removal.** Counsel intending to use physical exhibits other than documents at the argument must arrange to place them in the courtroom on the day of the argument before the court convenes. After the argument, counsel must remove the exhibits from the courtroom, unless the court directs otherwise. The clerk may destroy or dispose of the exhibits if counsel does not reclaim them within a reasonable time after the clerk gives notice to remove them.

As amended Apr. 30, 1979, eff. Aug. 1, 1979; Mar. 10, 1986, eff. July 1, 1986; Apr. 30, 1991, eff. Dec. 1, 1991; Apr. 22, 1993, eff. Dec. 1, 1993; Apr. 24, 1998, eff. Dec. 1, 1998.

Rule 35. En Banc Determination

(a) **When Hearing or Rehearing En Banc May Be Ordered.** A majority of the circuit judges who are in regular active service may order that an appeal or other proceeding be heard or reheard by the court of appeals en banc. An en banc hearing or rehearing is not favored and ordinarily will not be ordered unless:

(1) en banc consideration is necessary to secure or maintain uniformity of the court's decisions; or

(2) the proceeding involves a question of exceptional importance.

(b) **Petition for Hearing or Rehearing En Banc.** A party may petition for a hearing or rehearing en banc.

(1) The petition must begin with a statement that either:

(A) the panel decision conflicts with a decision of the United States Supreme Court or of the court to which the petition is addressed (with citation to the conflicting case or cases) and consideration by the full court is therefore necessary to secure and maintain uniformity of the court's decisions; or

(B) the proceeding involves one or more questions of exceptional importance, each of which must be concisely stated; for example, a petition may assert that a proceeding presents a question of exceptional importance if it involves an issue on which the panel decision conflicts with the authoritative decisions of other United States Courts of Appeals that have addressed the issue.

(2) Except by the court's permission, a petition for an en banc hearing or rehearing must not exceed 15 pages, excluding material not counted under Rule 32.

(3) For purposes of the page limit in Rule 35(b)(2), if a party files both a petition for panel rehearing and a petition for rehearing en banc, they are considered a single document even if they are filed separately, unless separate filing is required by local rule.

(c) Time for Petition for Hearing or Rehearing En Banc. A petition that an appeal be heard initially en banc must be filed by the date when the appellee's brief is due. A petition for a rehearing en banc must be filed within the time prescribed by Rule 40 for filing a petition for rehearing.

(d) Number of Copies. The number of copies to be filed must be prescribed by local rule and may be altered by order in a particular case.

(e) Response. No response may be filed to a petition for an en banc consideration unless the court orders a response.

(f) Call for a Vote. A vote need not be taken to determine whether the case will be heard or reheard en banc unless a judge calls for a vote.

As amended Apr. 30, 1979, eff. Aug. 1, 1979; Apr. 29, 1994, eff. Dec. 1, 1994; Apr. 24, 1998, eff. Dec. 1, 1998.

Rule 36. Entry of Judgment; Notice

(a) Entry. A judgment is entered when it is noted on the docket. The clerk must prepare, sign, and enter the judgment:

(1) after receiving the court's opinion — but if settlement of the judgment's form is required, after final settlement; or

(2) if a judgment is rendered without an opinion, as the court instructs.

(b) Notice. On the date when judgment is entered, the clerk must serve on all parties a copy of the opinion — or the judgment, if no opinion was written — and a notice of the date when the judgment was entered.

As amended Apr. 24, 1998, eff. Dec. 1, 1998; Apr. 29, 2002, eff. Dec. 1, 2002.

Rule 37. Interest on Judgment

(a) When the Court Affirms. Unless the law provides otherwise, if a money judgment in a civil case is affirmed, whatever interest is allowed by law is payable from the date when the district court's judgment was entered.

(b) When the Court Reverses. If the court modifies or reverses a judgment with a direction that a money judgment be entered in the district court, the mandate must contain instructions about the allowance of interest.

As amended Apr. 24, 1998, eff. Dec. 1, 1998.

Rule 38. Frivolous Appeal — Damages and Costs

If a court of appeals determines that an appeal is frivolous, it may, after a separately filed motion or notice from the court and reasonable opportunity to respond, award just damages and single or double costs to the appellee.

As amended Apr. 29, 1994, eff. Dec. 1, 1994; Apr. 24, 1998, eff. Dec. 1, 1998.

Rule 39. Costs

(a) **Against Whom Assessed.** The following rules apply unless the law provides or the court orders otherwise:

(1) if an appeal is dismissed, costs are taxed against the appellant, unless the parties agree otherwise;

(2) if a judgment is affirmed, costs are taxed against the appellant;

(3) if a judgment is reversed, costs are taxed against the appellee;

(4) if a judgment is affirmed in part, reversed in part, modified, or vacated, costs are taxed only as the court orders.

(b) **Costs For and Against the United States.** Costs for or against the United States, its agency, or officer will be assessed under Rule 39(a) only if authorized by law.

(c) **Costs Copies.** Each court of appeals must, by local rule, fix the maximum rate at for taxing the cost of producing necessary copies of a brief or appendix, or copies of records authorized by Rule 30(f). The rate must not exceed that generally charged for such work in the area where the clerk's office is located and should encourage economical methods of copying.

(d) **Bill of Costs; Objections; Insertion in Mandate.**

(1) A party who wants costs taxed must — within 14 days after entry of judgment — file with the circuit clerk, with proof of service, an itemized and verified bill of costs.

(2) Objections must be filed within 10 days after service of the bill of costs, unless the court extends the time.

(3) The clerk must prepare and certify an itemized statement of costs for insertion in the mandate, but issuance of the mandate must not be delayed for taxing costs. If the mandate issues before costs are finally determined, the district clerk must — upon the circuit clerk's request — add the statement of costs, or any amendment of it, to the mandate.

(e) Costs on Appeal Taxable in the District Court. The following costs on appeal are taxable in the district court for the benefit of the party entitled to costs under this rule:

(1) the preparation and transmission of the record;

(2) the reporter's transcript, if needed to determine the appeal;

(3) premiums paid for a supersedeas bond or other bond to preserve rights pending appeal; and

(4) the fee for filing the notice of appeal.

As amended Apr. 30, 1979, eff. Aug. 1, 1979; Mar. 10, 1986, eff. July 1, 1986; Apr. 24, 1998, eff. Dec. 1, 1998.

Rule 40. Petition for Panel Rehearing

(a) Time to File; Contents; Answer; Action by the Court if Granted.

(1) *Time.* Unless the time is shortened or extended by order or local rule, a petition for panel rehearing may be filed within 14 days after entry of judgment. But in a civil case, if the United States or its officer or agency is a party, the time within which any party may seek rehearing is 45 days after entry of judgment, unless an order shortens or extends the time.

(2) *Contents.* The petition must state with particularity each point of law or fact that the petitioner believes the court has overlooked or misapprehended and must argue in support of the petition. Oral argument is not permitted.

(3) *Answer.* Unless the court requests, no answer to a petition for panel rehearing is permitted. But ordinarily rehearing will not be granted in the absence of such a request.

(4) *Action by the Court.* If a petition for panel rehearing is granted, the court may do any of the following:

(A) make a final disposition of the case without reargument;

(B) restore the case to the calendar for reargument or resubmission; or

(C) issue any other appropriate order.

(b) Form of Petition; Length. The petition must comply in form with Rule 32. Copies must be served and filed as Rule 31 prescribes. Unless the court permits or a local rule provides otherwise, a petition for panel rehearing must not exceed 15 pages.

As amended Apr. 30, 1979, eff. Aug. 1, 1979; Apr. 29, 1994, eff. Dec. 1, 1994; Apr. 24, 1998, eff. Dec. 1, 1998.

Rule 41. Mandate: Contents; Issuance and Effective Date; Stay

(a) Contents. Unless the court directs that a formal mandate issue, the mandate consists of a certified copy of the judgment, a copy of the court's opinion, if any, and any direction about costs.

(b) When Issued. The court's mandate must issue 7 calendar days after the time to file a petition for rehearing expires, or 7 calendar days after entry of an order denying a timely petition for panel rehearing, rehearing en banc, or motion for stay of mandate, whichever is later. The court may shorten or extend the time.

(c) Effective Date. The mandate is effective when issued.

(d) Staying the Mandate.

(1) *On Petition for Reharing or Motion.* The timely filing of a petition for panel rehearing, petition for rehearing en banc, or motion for stay of mandate, stays the mandate until disposition of the petition or motion, unless the court orders otherwise.

(2) *Pending Petition for Certiorari.*

(A) A party may move to stay the mandate pending the filing of a petition for a writ of certiorari in the Supreme Court. The motion must be served on all parties and must show that the certiorari petiton would present a substantial question and that there is good cause for a stay.

(B) The stay must not exceed 90 days, unless the period is extended for good cause or unless the party who obtained the stay files a petition for the writ and so notifies the circuit clerk in writing within the period of the stay. In that case, the stay continues until the Supreme Court's final disposition.

(C) The court may require a bond or other security as a condition to granting or continuing a stay of the mandate.

(D) The court of appeals must issue the mandate immediately when a copy of a Supreme Court order denying the petition for writ of certiorari is filed.

As amended Apr. 29, 1994, eff. Dec. 1, 1994; Apr. 24, 1998, eff. Dec. 1, 1998; Apr. 29, 2002, eff. Dec. 1, 2002.

Rule 42. Voluntary Dismissal

(a) Dismissal in the District Court. Before an appeal has been docketed by the circuit clerk, the district court may dismiss the appeal on the filing of a stipulation signed by all parties or on the appellant's motion with notice to all parties.

(b) Dismissal in the Court of Appeals. The circuit clerk may dismiss a docketed appeal if the parties file a signed dismissal agreement specifying how costs are to be paid and pay any fees that are due. But no mandate or other process may issue without a court order. An appeal may be dismissed on the appellant's motion on terms agreed to by the parties or fixed by the court.

As amended Apr. 24, 1998, eff. Dec. 1, 1998.

Rule 43. Substitution of Parties

(a) Death of a Party.

(1) *After Notice of Appeal Is Filed.* If a party dies after a notice of appeal has been filed or while a proceeding is pending in the court of appeals, the decedent's personal representative may be substituted as a party on motion filed with the circuit clerk by the representative or by any party. A party's motion must be served on the representative in accordance with Rule 25. If the decedent has no representative, any party may suggest the death on the record, and the court of appeals may then direct appropriate proceedings.

(2) *Before Notice of Appeal Is Filed — Potential Appellant.* If a party entitled to appeal dies before filing a notice of appeal, the decedent's personal representative — or, if there is no personal representative, the decedent's attorney of record — may file a notice of appeal within the time prescribed by these rules. After the notice of appeal is filed, substitution must be in accordance with Rule 43(a)(1).

(3) *Before Notice of Appeal Is Filed — Potential Appellee.* If a party against whom an appeal may be taken dies after entry of a judgment or order in the district court, but before a notice of appeal is filed, an appellant may proceed as if the death had not occurred. After the notice of appeal is filed, substitution must be in accordance with Rule 43(a)(1).

(b) Substitution for a Reason Other Than Death. If a party needs to be substituted for any reason other than death, the procedure prescribed in Rule 43(a) applies.

(c) Public Officer: Identification; Substitution.

(1) *Identification of Party.* A public officer who is a party to an appeal or other proceeding in an official capacity may be described as a party by the public officer's official title rather than by name. But the court may require the public officer's name to be added.

(2) *Automatic Substitution of Officeholder.* When a public officer who is a party to an appeal or other proceeding in an official capacity dies, resigns, or otherwise ceases to hold office, the action does not abate. The public officer's successor is automatically substituted as a party. Proceedings following the substitution are to be in the name of the substituted party, but any misnomer that does not affect the substantial rights of the parties may be disregarded. An order of substitution may be entered at any time, but failure to enter an order does not affect the substitution.

As amended Mar. 10, 1986, eff. July 1, 1986; Apr. 24, 1998, eff. Dec. 1, 1998.

Rule 44. Case Involving a Constitutional Question When the United States or the Relevant State Is Not a Party

(a) Constitutional Challenge to Federal Statute. If a party questions the constitutionality of an Act of Congress in a proceeding in which the United

States or its agency, officer, or employee is not a party in an official capacity, the questioning party must give written notice to the circuit clerk immediately upon the filing of the record or as soon as the question is raised in the court of appeals. The clerk must then certify that fact to the Attorney General.

(b) Constitutional Challenge to State Statute. If a party questions the constitutionality of a statute of a State in a proceeding in which that State or its agency, officer, or employee is not a party in an official capacity, the questioning party must give written notice to the circuit clerk immediately upon the filing of the record or as soon as the question is raised in the court of appeals. The clerk must then certify that fact to the attorney general of the State.

As amended Apr. 24, 1998, eff. Dec. 1, 1998; Apr. 29, 2002, eff. Dec. 1, 2002.

Rule 45. Clerk's Duties

(a) General Provisions. [Omitted]

(b) Records. [Omitted]

(c) Notice of an Order or Judgment. Upon the entry of an order or judgment, the circuit clerk must immediately serve a notice of entry on each party, with a copy of any opinion, and must note the date of service on the docket. Service on a party represented by counsel must be made on counsel.

(d) Custody of Records and Papers. [Omitted]

As amended Mar. 1, 1971, eff. July 1, 1971; Mar. 10, 1986, eff. July 1, 1986; Apr. 24, 1998, eff. Dec. 1, 1998; Apr. 29, 2002, eff. Dec. 1, 2002.

Rule 46. Attorneys

(a) Admission to the Bar.

(1) *Eligibility.* An attorney is eligible for admission to the bar of a court of appeals if that attorney is of good moral and professional character and is admitted to practice before the Supreme Court of the United States, the highest court of a state, another United States court of appeals, or a United States district court (including the district courts for Guam, the Northern Mariana Islands, and the Virgin Islands).

(2) *Application.* An applicant must file an application for admission, on a form approved by the court that contains the applicant's personal statement showing eligibility for membership. The applicant must subscribe to the following oath or affirmation:

I, ___________, do solemnly swear [or affirm] that I will conduct myself as an attorney and counselor of this court, uprightly and according to law; and that I will support the Constitution of the United States.

(3) *Admission Procedures.* On written or oral motion of a member of the court's bar, the court will act on the application. An applicant may be admitted by oral motion in open court. But, unless the court orders otherwise, an applicant need not appear before the court to be admitted. Upon admission, an applicant must pay the clerk the fee prescribed by local rule or court order.

(b) Suspension or Disbarment.

(1) *Standard.* A member of the court's bar is subject to suspension or disbarment by the court if the member:

(A) has been suspended or disbarred from practice in any other court; or

(B) is guilty of conduct unbecoming a member of the court's bar.

(2) *Procedure.* The member must be given an opportunity to show good cause, within the time prescribed by the court, why the member should not be suspended or disbarred.

(3) *Order.* The court must enter an appropriate order after the member responds and a hearing is held, if requested, or after the time prescribed for a response expires, if no response is made.

(c) Discipline. A court of appeals may discipline an attorney who practices before it for conduct unbecoming a member of the bar or for failure to comply with any court rule. First, however, the court must afford the attorney reasonable notice, an opportunity to show cause to the contrary, and, if requested, a hearing.

As amended Mar. 10, 1986, eff. July 1, 1986; Apr. 24, 1998, eff. Dec. 1, 1998.

Rule 47. Local Rules by Courts of Appeals

(a) Local Rules.

(1) Each court of appeals acting by a majority of its judges in regular active service may, after giving appropriate public notice and opportunity for comment, make and amend rules governing its practice. A generally applicable direction to parties or lawyers regarding practice before a court must be in a local rule rather than an internal operating procedure or standing order. A local rule must be consistent with — but not duplicative of — Acts of Congress and rules adopted under 28 U.S.C. §2072 and must conform to any uniform numbering system prescribed by the Judicial Conference of the United States. Each circuit clerk must send the Administrative Office of the United States Courts a copy of each local rule and internal operating procedure when it is promulgated or amended.

(2) A local rule imposing a requirement of form must not be enforced in

a manner that causes a party to lose rights because of a nonwillful failure to comply with the requirement.

(b) Procedure When There Is No Controlling Law. A court of appeals may regulate practice in a particular case in any manner consistent with federal law, these rules, and local rules of the circuit. No sanction or other disadvantage may be imposed for noncompliance with any requirement not in federal law, federal rules, or the local circuit rules unless the alleged violator has been furnished in the particular case with actual notice of the requirement.

As amended Apr. 27, 1995, eff. Dec. 1, 1995; Apr. 24, 1998, eff. Dec. 1, 1998.

Rule 48. Masters

(a) Appointment; Powers. A court of appeals may appoint a special master to hold hearings, if necessary, and to recommend factual findings and disposition in matters ancillary to proceedings in the court. Unless the order referring a matter to a master specifies or limits the master's powers, those powers include, but are not limited to, the following:

(1) regulating all aspects of a hearing;

(2) taking all appropriate action for the effective performance of the master's duties under the order;

(3) requiring the production of evidence on all matters embraced in the reference; and

(4) administering oaths and examining witnesses and parties.

(b) Compensation. If the master is not a judge or court employee, the court must determine the master's compensation and whether the cost is to be charged to any party.

As amended Apr. 29, 1994, eff. Dec. 1, 1994; Apr. 24, 1998, eff. Dec. 1, 1998.

[The Federal Rules of Appellate Procedure were adopted December 4, 1967, effective July 1, 1968. The effective dates of amendments to rules included above are indicated there.]

THE CONSTITUTION OF THE UNITED STATES

We the People of the United States, in Order to form a more perfect Union, establish Justice, insure domestic Tranquility, provide for the common defence, promote the general Welfare, and secure the Blessings of Liberty to ourselves and our Posterity, do ordain and establish this Constitution for the United States of America.

Article I

Section 1. All legislative Powers herein granted shall be vested in a Congress of the United States, which shall consist of a Senate and House of Representatives.

Section 2. The House of Representatives shall be composed of Members chosen every second Year by the People of the several States, and the Electors in each State shall have the Qualifications requisite for Electors of the most numerous Branch of the State Legislature.

No Person shall be a Representative who shall not have attained to the Age of twenty-five Years, and been seven Years a Citizen of the United States, and who shall not, when elected, be an Inhabitant of that State in which he shall be chosen.

Representatives and direct Taxes shall be apportioned among the several States which may be included within this Union, according to their respective Numbers, which shall be determined by adding to the whole Number of free Persons, including those bound to Service for a Term of Years, and excluding Indians not taxed, three-fifths of all other Persons.* The actual Enumeration shall be made within three Years after the first Meeting of the Congress of the United States, and within every subsequent Term of ten Years, in such Manner as they shall by Law direct. The Number of Representatives shall not exceed one for every thirty thousand, but each State shall have at least one Representative; and until such Enumeration shall be made, the State of New Hampshire shall be entitled to chuse three, Massachusetts eight, Rhode Island and Providence Plantations one, Connecticut five, New York six, New Jersey four, Pennsylvania

*[Changed by Section 2 of the Fourteenth Amendment. — ED.]

eight, Delaware one, Maryland six, Virginia ten, North Carolina five, South Carolina five, and Georgia three.

When Vacancies happen in the Representation from any State, the executive Authority thereof shall issue Writs of Election to fill such Vacancies.

The House of Representatives shall chuse their Speaker and other Officers; and shall have the sole Power of Impeachment.

Section 3. The Senate of the United States shall be composed of two Senators from each State, chosen by the Legislature thereof,* for six Years; and each Senator shall have one Vote.

Immediately after they shall be assembled in Consequence of the first Election, they shall be divided as equally as may be into three Classes. The Seats of the Senators of the first Class shall be vacated at the Expiration of the second Year, of the second Class at the Expiration of the fourth Year, and of the third Class at the Expiration of the sixth Year, so that one-third may be chosen every second Year; and if Vacancies happen by Resignation, or otherwise, during the Recess of the Legislature of any State, the Executive thereof may make temporary Appointments until the next Meeting of the Legislature, which shall then fill such Vacancies.**

No Person shall be a Senator who shall not have attained to the Age of thirty Years, and been nine Years a Citizen of the United States, and who shall not, when elected, be an Inhabitant of that State for which he shall be chosen.

The Vice President of the United States shall be President of the Senate, but shall have no Vote, unless they be equally divided.

The Senate shall chuse their other Officers, and also a President pro tempore, in the Absence of the Vice President, or when he shall exercise the Office of President of the United States.

The Senate shall have the sole Power to try all Impeachments. When sitting for that Purpose, they shall be on Oath or Affirmation. When the President of the United States is tried, the Chief Justice shall preside: And no Person shall be convicted without the Concurrence of two-thirds of the Members present.

Judgment in Cases of Impeachment shall not extend further than to Removal from Office, and Disqualification to hold and enjoy any Office of Honor, Trust or Profit under the United States: but the Party convicted shall nevertheless be liable and subject to Indictment, Trial, Judgment and Punishment, according to Law.

Section 4. The Times, Places and Manner of holding Elections for Senators and Representatives, shall be prescribed in each State by the Legislature thereof; but the Congress may at any time by Law make or alter such Regulations, except as to the Places of chusing Senators.

The Congress shall assemble at least once in every Year, and such Meeting

*[Changed by Section 1 of the Seventeenth Amendment. — Ed.]
**[Changed by Section 2 of the Seventeenth Amendment. — Ed.]

shall be on the first Monday in December,* unless they shall by Law appoint a different Day.

***Section* 5.** Each House shall be the Judge of the Elections, Returns and Qualifications of its own Members, and a Majority of each shall constitute a Quorum to do Business; but a smaller Number may adjourn from Day to Day, and may be authorized to compel the Attendance of absent Members, in such Manner, and under such Penalties as each House may provide.

Each House may determine the Rules of its Proceedings, punish its Members for disorderly Behavior, and, with the Concurrence of two-thirds, expel a Member.

Each House shall keep a Journal of its Proceedings, and from Time to Time publish the Same, excepting such Parts as may in their Judgment require Secrecy; and the Yeas and Nays of the Members of either House on any Questions shall, at the Desire of one-fifth of those Present, be entered on the Journal.

Neither House, during the Session of Congress, shall, without the Consent of the Other, adjourn for more than three Days, nor to any other Place than that in which the two Houses shall be sitting.

***Section* 6.** The Senators and Representatives shall receive a Compensation for their Services, to be ascertained by Law, and paid out of the Treasury of the United States. They shall in all Cases, except Treason, Felony and Breach of the Peace, be privileged from Arrest during their Attendance at the Session of their respective Houses; and in going to and returning from the Same; and for any Speech or Debate in either House, they shall not be questioned in any other Place.

No Senator or Representative shall, during the Time for which he was elected, be appointed to any civil Office under the Authority of the United States, which shall have been created, or the Emoluments whereof shall have been encreased during such Time; and no Person holding any Office under the United States, shall be a Member of either House during his Continuance in Office.

***Section* 7.** All Bills for raising Revenue shall originate in the House of Representatives; but the Senate may propose or concur with Amendments as on other Bills.

Every Bill which shall have passed the House of Representatives and the Senate, shall, before it become a Law, be presented to the President of the United States; if he approve he shall sign it, but if not he shall return it, with his Objections to that House in which it shall have originated, who shall enter the Objections at large on their Journal, and proceed to reconsider it. If after such Reconsideration two-thirds of that House shall agree to pass the Bill, it shall be sent, together with the Objections, to the other House, by which it shall likewise be reconsidered, and if approved by two-thirds of that House, it shall become a Law. But in all such Cases the Votes of both Houses shall be determined by Yeas

*[Changed by Section 2 of the Twentieth Amendment. — Ed.]

and Nays, and the Names of the Persons voting for and against the Bill shall be entered on the Journal of each House respectively. If any Bill shall not be returned by the President within ten Days (Sundays excepted) after it shall have been presented to him, the Same shall be a Law, in like Manner as if he had signed it, unless the Congress by their Adjournment prevent its Return, in which Case it shall not be a Law.

Every Order, Resolution, or Vote to which the Concurrence of the Senate and House of Representatives may be necessary (except on a Question of Adjournment) shall be presented to the President of the United States; and before the Same shall take Effect, shall be approved by him, or, being disapproved by him, shall be repassed by two-thirds of the Senate and House of Representatives, according to the Rules and Limitations prescribed in the Case of a Bill.

***Section** 8.* The Congress shall have Power To lay and collect Taxes, Duties, Imposts and Excises, to pay the Debts and provide for the common Defence and general Welfare of the United States; but all Duties, Imposts and Excises shall be uniform throughout the United States;

To borrow Money on the credit of the United States;

To regulate Commerce with foreign Nations, and among the several States, and with the Indian Tribes;

To establish an uniform Rule of Naturalization, and uniform Laws on the subject of Bankruptcies throughout the United States;

To coin Money, regulate the Value thereof, and of foreign Coin, and fix the Standard of Weights and Measures;

To provide for the Punishment of counterfeiting the Securities and current Coin of the United States;

To establish Post Offices and post Roads;

To promote the Progress of Science and useful Arts, by securing for limited Times to Authors and Inventors the exclusive Right to their respective Writings and Discoveries;

To constitute Tribunals inferior to the supreme Court;

To define and punish Piracies and Felonies committed on the high Seas, and Offences against the Law of Nations;

To declare War, grant Letters of Marque and Reprisal, and make Rules concerning Captures on Land and Water;

To raise and support Armies, but no Appropriation of Money to that Use shall be for a longer Term than two Years;

To provide and maintain a Navy;

To make Rules for the Government and Regulation of the land and naval Forces;

To provide for calling forth the Militia to execute the Laws of the Union, suppress Insurrections and repel Invasions;

To provide for organizing, arming, and disciplining, the Militia, and for governing such Part of them as may be employed in the Service of the United

States, reserving to the States respectively, the Appointment of the Officers, and the Authority of training the Militia according to the discipline prescribed by Congress;

To exercise exclusive Legislation in all Cases whatsoever, over such District (not exceeding ten Miles square) as may, by Cession of Particular States, and the Acceptance of Congress, become the Seat of the Government of the United States, and to exercise like Authority over all Places purchased by the Consent of the Legislature of the State in which the Same shall be, for the Erection of Forts, Magazines, Arsenals, dock-Yards, and other needful Buildings; — And

To make all Laws which shall be necessary and proper for carrying into Execution the foregoing Powers, and all other Powers vested by this Constitution in the Government of the United States, or in any Department or Officer thereof.

Section 9. The Migration or Importation of such Persons as any of the States now existing shall think proper to admit, shall not be prohibited by the Congress prior to the Year one thousand eight hundred and eight, but a Tax or Duty may be imposed on such Importation, not exceeding ten Dollars for each Person.

The Privilege of the Writ of Habeas Corpus shall not be suspended, unless when in Cases of Rebellion or Invasion the public Safety may require it.

No Bill of Attainder or ex post fact Law shall be passed.

No Capitation, or other direct, Tax shall be laid, unless in Proportion to the Census or Enumeration herein before directed to be taken.

No Tax or Duty shall be laid on Articles exported from any State.

No Preference shall be given by any Regulation of Commerce or Revenue to the Ports of one State over those of another: nor shall Vessels bound to, or from, one State, be obliged to enter, clear, or pay Duties in another.

No Money shall be drawn from the Treasury, but in Consequence of Appropriations made by Law; and a regular Statement and Account of the Receipts and Expenditures of all public Money shall be published from Time to Time.

No Title of Nobility shall be granted by the United States; and no Person holding any Office of Profit or Trust under them, shall, without the Consent of the Congress, accept of any Present, Emolument, Office, or Title, of any Kind whatever, from any King, Prince, or foreign State.

Section 10. No State shall enter into any Treaty, Alliance, or Confederation; grant Letters of Marque and Reprisal; coin Money; emit Bills of Credit; make any Thing but gold and silver Coin a Tender in Payment of Debts; pass any Bill of Attainder, ex post facto Law, or Law impairing the Obligation of Contracts, or grant any Title of Nobility.

No State shall, without the Consent of the Congress, lay any Imposts or Duties on Imports or Exports, except what may be absolutely necessary for executing its inspection Laws: and the net Produce of all Duties and Imposts, laid by any State on Imports or Exports, shall be for the Use of the Treasury of the United States; and all such Laws shall be subject to the Revision and Controul of the Congress.

No State shall, without the Consent of Congress, lay any Duty of Tonnage, keep Troops, or Ships of War in Time of Peace, enter into any Agreement or Compact with another State, or with a foreign Power, or engage in War, unless actually invaded, or in such imminent Danger as will not admit of Delay.

Article II

Section 1. The executive Power shall be vested in a President of the United States of America. He shall hold his Office during the Term of four Years, and, together with the Vice President, chosen for the same Term, be elected, as follows:

Each State shall appoint, in such Manner as the Legislature thereof may direct, a Number of Electors, equal to the whole Number of Senators and Representatives to which the state may be entitled in the Congress: but no Senator or Representative or Person holding an Office of Trust or Profit under the United States, shall be appointed an Elector.

The Electors shall meet in their respective States and vote by Ballot for two Persons, of whom one at least shall not be an Inhabitant of the same State with themselves. And they shall make a List of all the Persons voted for, and of the Number of Votes for each; which List they shall sign and certify, and transmit sealed to the Seat of the Government of the United States, directed to the President of the Senate. The President of the Senate shall, in the Presence of the Senate and House of Representatives, open all of the Certificates, and the Votes shall then be counted. The Person having the greatest Number of Votes shall be the President, if such Number be a Majority of the whole Number of Electors appointed; and if there be more than one who have such Majority, and have an equal Number of Votes, then the House of Representatives shall immediately chuse by Ballot one of them for President; and if no Person have a Majority, then from the five highest on the List the said House shall in like Manner chuse the President. But in chusing the President, the Votes shall be taken by States, the Representation from each State having one Vote; a Quorum for this Purpose shall consist of a Member or Members from two-thirds of the States, and a Majority of all the States shall be necessary to a Choice. In every Case, after the Choice of the President, the Person having the greatest Number of Votes of the Electors shall be the Vice President. But if there should remain two or more who have equal Votes, the Senate shall chuse from them by Ballot the Vice President.*

The Congress may determine the Time of chusing the Electors, and the Day on which they shall give their Votes; which Day shall be the Same throughout the United States.

No Person except a natural born Citizen, or a Citizen of the United States,

*[Superseded by the Twelfth Amendment. — ED.]

at the Time of the Adoption of this Constitution, shall be eligible to the Office of President; neither shall any Person be eligible to that Office who shall not have attained to the Age of thirty-five Years, and been fourteen Years a Resident within the United States.

In Case of the Removal of the President from Office, or of his Death, Resignation, or Inability to discharge the Powers and Duties of the said Office, the Same shall devolve on the Vice President, and the Congress may by Law provide for the Case of Removal, Death, Resignation or Inability, both of the President and Vice President, declaring what Officer shall then act as President, and such Officer shall act accordingly, until the Disability be removed, or a President shall be elected.*

The President shall, at stated Times, receive for his Services a Compensation, which shall neither be encreased nor diminished during the Period for which he shall have been elected, and he shall not receive within that Period any other Emolument from the United States, or any of them.

Before he enter on the Execution of his Office, he shall take the following Oath or Affirmation: — "I do solemnly swear (or affirm) that I will faithfully execute the Office of President of the United States, and will to the best of my Ability, preserve, protect and defend the Constitution of the United States."

***Section** 2.* The President shall be Commander in Chief of the Army and Navy of the United States, and of the Militia of the several States, when called into the actual Service of the United States; he may require the Opinion, in writing, of the principal Officer in each of the executive Departments, upon any Subjects relating to the Duties of their respective Offices, and he shall have Power to grant Reprieves and Pardons for Offences against the United States, except in Cases of Impeachment.

He shall have Power, by and with the Advice and Consent of the Senate, to make Treaties, provided two-thirds of the Senators present concur; and he shall nominate, and by and with the Advice and Consent of the Senate, shall appoint Ambassadors, other public Ministers and Consuls, Judges of the supreme Court, and all other Officers of the United States, whose Appointments are not herein otherwise provided for, and which shall be established by Law: but the Congress may by Law vest the Appointment of such inferior Officers, as they think proper, in the President alone, in the Courts of Law, or in the Heads of Departments.

The President shall have Power to fill up all Vacancies that may happen during the Recess of the Senate, by granting Commissions which shall expire at the End of their next Session.

***Section** 3.* He shall from Time to Time give to the Congress Information on the State of the Union, and recommend to their Consideration such Measures as he shall judge necessary and expedient; he may, on extraordinary Occasions,

*[Modified by the Twenty-Fifth Amendment. — ED.]

convene both Houses, or either of them, and in Case of Disagreement between them, with Respect to the Time of Adjournment, he may adjourn them to such Time as he shall think proper; he shall receive Ambassadors and other public Ministers; he shall take Care that the Laws be faithfully executed, and shall Commission all the Officers of the United States.

Section 4. The President, Vice President and all civil Officers of the United States, shall be removed from Office on Impeachment for, and Conviction of, Treason, Bribery, or other high Crimes and Misdemeanors.

Article III

Section 1. The judicial Power of the United States, shall be vested in one supreme Court, and in such inferior Courts as the Congress may from time to time ordain and establish. The Judges, both of the supreme and inferior Courts, shall hold their Offices during good Behaviour, and shall, at stated Times, receive for their Services, a Compensation, which shall not be diminished during their Continuance in Office.

Section 2. The judicial Power shall extend to all Cases, in Law and Equity, arising under this Constitution, the Laws of the United States, and Treaties made, or which shall be made, under their Authority — to all Cases affecting Ambassadors, other public Ministers and Consuls — to all Cases of admiralty and maritime Jurisdiction — to Controversies to which the United States shall be a Party — to Controversies between two or more States — between a State and Citizens of another State — between Citizens of different States;;m1between Citizens of the same State claiming Lands under Grants of different States, and between a State, or the Citizens thereof, and foreign States, Citizens or Subjects.

In all Cases affecting Ambassadors, other public Ministers and Consuls, and those in which a State shall be Party, the supreme Court shall have original Jurisdiction. In all the other Cases before mentioned, the supreme Court shall have appellate Jurisdiction, both as to Law and Fact, with such Exceptions, and under such Regulations as the Congress shall make.

The Trial of all Crimes, except in Cases of Impeachment, shall be by Jury; and such Trial shall be held in the State where the said Crimes shall have been committed; but when not committed within any State, the Trial shall be at such Place or Places as the Congress may by Law have directed.

Section 3. Treason against the United States, shall consist only in levying War against them, or in adhering to their Enemies, giving them Aid and Comfort. No Person shall be convicted of Treason unless on the Testimony of two Witnesses to the same overt Act or on Confession in open Court.

The Congress shall have Power to declare the Punishment of Treason, but no Attainder of Treason shall work Corruption of Blood, or Forfeiture except during the Life of the Person attained.

Article IV

Section 1. Full Faith and Credit shall be given in each State to the public Acts, Records, and judicial Proceedings of every other State. And the Congress may by general Laws prescribe the Manner in which such Acts, Records and Proceedings shall be proved, and the Effect thereof.

Section 2. The Citizens of each State shall be entitled to all Privileges and Immunities of Citizens in the several States.

A Person charged in any State with Treason, Felony, or other Crime, who shall flee from Justice, and be found in another State, shall on Demand of the executive Authority of the State from which he fled, be delivered up, to be removed to the State having Jurisdiction of the Crime.

No Person held to Service or Labour in one State, under the Laws thereof, escaping into another, shall, in Consequence of any Law or Regulation therein, be discharged from such Service or Labour, but shall be delivered up on Claim of the Party to whom such Service or Labour may be due.

Section 3. New States may be admitted by the Congress into this Union; but no new State shall be formed or erected within the Jurisdiction of any other State; nor any State by formed by the Junction of two or more States, or Parts of States, without the Consent of the Legislatures of the States concerned as well as of the Congress.

The Congress shall have Power to dispose of and make all needful Rules and Regulations respecting the Territory or other Property belonging to the United States; and nothing in this Constitution shall be so construed as to Prejudice any Claims of the United States, or of any particular State.

Section 4. The United States shall guarantee to every State in this Union a Republican of Government, and shall protect each of them against Invasion; and on Application of the Legislature, or of the Executive (when the Legislature cannot be convened) against domestic Violence.

Article V

The Congress, whenever two-thirds of both Houses shall deem it necessary, shall propose Amendments to this Constitution, or, on the Application of the

Legislatures of two-thirds of the several States, shall call a Convention for proposing Amendments, which, in either Case, shall be valid to all Intents and Purposes, as Part of this Constitution, when ratified by the Legislatures of three-fourths of the several States, or by Conventions in three-fourths thereof, as the one or the other Mode of Ratification may be proposed by the Congress; provided that no Amendment which may be made prior to the Year one thousand eight hundred and eight shall in any Manner affect the first and fourth Clauses in the ninth Section of the first Article; and that no State, without its Consent, shall be deprived of its equal Suffrage in the Senate.

Article VI

All Debts contracted and Engagements entered into, before the Adoption of this Constitution, shall be as valid against the United States under this Constitution, as under the Confederation.

This Constitution, and the Laws of the United States which shall be made in Pursuance thereof; and all Treaties made, or which shall be made, under the Authority of the United States, shall be the supreme Law of the Land; and the Judges in every State shall be bound thereby, any Thing in the Constitution or Laws of any State to the Contrary notwithstanding.

The Senators and Representatives before mentioned, and the Members of the several State Legislatures, and all executive and judicial Officers, both of the United States and of the several States, shall be bound by Oath or Affirmation, to support this Constitution; but no religious Test shall ever be required as a Qualification to any Office or public Trust under the United States.

Article VII

The Ratification of the Conventions of nine States, shall be sufficient for the Establishment of this Constitution between the States so ratifying the Same.

Amendment I

Congress shall make no law respecting an establishment of religion, or prohibiting the free exercise thereof; or abridging the freedom of speech, or of the press; or the right of the people peaceably to assemble, and to petition the Government for a redress of grievances.

Amendment II

A well regulated militia, being necessary to the security of a free State, the right of the people to keep and bear arms, shall not be infringed.

Amendment III

No soldier shall, in time of peace be quartered in any house, without the consent of the owner, nor in time of war, but in a manner to be prescribed by law.

Amendment IV

The right of the people to be secure in their persons, houses, papers, and effects, against unreasonable searches and seizures, shall not be violated, and no Warrants shall issue, but upon probable cause, supported by Oath or affirmation, and particularly describing the place to be searched, and the persons or things to be seized.

Amendment V

No person shall be held to answer for a capital, or otherwise infamous crime, unless on a presentment or indictment of a Grand Jury, except in cases arising in the land or naval forces, or in the Militia, when in actual service in time of War or public danger; nor shall any person be subject for the same offence to be twice put in jeopardy of life or limb; nor shall be compelled in any criminal case to be a witness against himself, nor be deprived of life, liberty, or property, without due process of law; nor shall private property be taken for public use, without just compensation.

Amendment VI

In all criminal prosecutions, the accused shall enjoy the right to a speedy and public trial, by an impartial jury of the State and district wherein the crime shall have been committed, which district shall have been previously ascertained by law, and to be informed of the nature and cause of the accusation; to be confronted with the witnesses against him; to have compulsory process for obtaining witnesses in his favor, and to have the Assistance of Counsel for his defence.

Amendment VII

In Suits at common law, where the value in controversy shall exceed twenty dollars, the right of trial by jury shall be preserved, and no fact tried by a jury, shall be otherwise reexamined in any Court of the United States, than according to the rules of the common law.

Amendment VIII

Excessive bail shall not be required, nor excessive fines imposed, nor cruel and unusual punishments inflicted.

Amendment IX

The enumeration in the Constitution, of certain rights, shall not be construed to deny or disparage others retained by the people.

Amendment X

The powers not delegated to the United States by the Constitution, nor prohibited by it to the States, are reserved to the States respectively, or to the people.

Amendment XI

The Judicial power of the United States shall not be construed to extend to any suit in law or equity, commenced or prosecuted against one of the United States by Citizens of another State, or by Citizens or Subjects of any Foreign State.

Amendment XII

The electors shall meet in their respective States, and vote by ballot for President and Vice President, one of whom, at least, shall not be an inhabitant of the same State with themselves; they shall name in their ballots the person voted for as President, and in distinct ballots, the person voted for as Vice President, and they shall make distinct lists of all persons voted for as President, and of all persons voted for as Vice President, and of the number of votes for each, which lists they shall sign and certify, and transmit sealed to the seat of the government of the United States, directed to the President of the Senate; — The President of the Senate shall, in the presence of the Senate and House of Representatives, open all the certificates and the votes shall then be counted; — The person having the greatest number of votes for President, shall be the President, if such number be a majority of the whole number of electors appointed; and if no person have such majority, then from the persons having the highest numbers not exceeding three on the list of those voted for as President, the House of Representatives shall choose immediately, by ballot, the President. But in choosing the President, the votes shall be taken by States, the representation from each State having one vote; a quorum for this purpose shall consist of a member or members from two-thirds of the States, and a majority of all the States shall be necessary to a choice. And if the House of Representatives shall not choose a President whenever the right of choice shall devolve upon them, before the fourth day of March next following, then the Vice President shall act as President, as in the case of the death or other constitutional disability of the President.*

The person having the greatest number of votes as Vice President, shall be the Vice President, if such number be a majority of the whole number of electors appointed, and if no person have a majority, then from the two highest numbers on the list, the Senate shall choose the Vice President; a quorum for the purpose shall consist of two-thirds of the whole number of Senators, and a majority of the whole number shall be necessary to a choice. But no person constitutionally ineligible to the office of President shall be eligible to that of Vice President of the United States.

Amendment XIII

Section 1. Neither slavery nor involuntary servitude, except as a punishment for crime whereof the party shall have been duly convicted, shall exist within the United States, or any place subject to their jurisdiction.

Section 2. Congress shall have power to enforce this article by appropriate legislation.

*[Superseded by Section 3 of the Twentieth Amendment. — Ed.]

mendment XIV

Section 1. All persons born or naturalized in the United States and subject to the jurisdiction thereof, are citizens of the United States and of the State wherein they reside. No State shall make or enforce any law which shall abridge the privileges or immunities of citizens of the United States; nor shall any State deprive any person of life, liberty, or property, without due process of law; nor deny to any person within its jurisdiction the equal protection of the laws.

Section 2. Representatives shall be apportioned among the several States according to their respective numbers, counting the whole number of persons in each State, excluding Indians not taxed. But when the right to vote at any election for the choice of electors for President and Vice President of the United States, Representatives in Congress, the executive and judicial officers of a State, or the members of the legislature thereof, is denied to any of the male inhabitants of such State, being twenty-one years of age, and citizens of the United States, or in any way abridged, except for participation in rebellion or other crime, the basis of representation therein shall be reduced in the proportion which the number of such male citizens shall bear to the whole number of male citizens twenty-one years of age in such State.

Section 3. No person shall be a Senator or Representative in Congress, or elector of President and Vice President, or hold any office, civil or military, under the United States, or under any State, who, having previously taken an oath, as a member of Congress, or as an officer of the United States, or as a member of any State legislature, or as an executive or judicial officer of any State, to support the Constitution of the United States, shall have engaged in insurrection or rebellion against the same, or given aid or comfort to the enemies thereof. But Congress may by a vote of two-thirds of each House, remove such disability.

Section 4. The validity of the public debt of the United States, authorized by law, including debts incurred for payment of pensions and bounties for services in suppressing insurrection or rebellion, shall not be questioned. But neither the United States nor any State shall assume or pay any debt or obligation incurred in aid of insurrection or rebellion against the United States, or any claim for the loss or emancipation of any slave; but all such debts, obligations and claims shall be held illegal and void.

Section 5. The Congress shall have power to enforce, by appropriate legislation, the provisions of this article.

Amendment XV

Section 1. The right of citizens of the United States to vote shall not be denied or abridged by the United States or by any State on account of race, color, or previous condition of servitude.

Section 2. The Congress shall have power to enforce this article by appropriate legislation.

Amendment XVI

The Congress shall have power to lay and collect taxes on incomes, from whatever source derived, without apportionment among the several States, and without regard to any census or enumeration.

Amendment XVII

The Senate of the United States shall be composed of two Senators from each State, elected by the people thereof, for six years; and each Senator shall have one vote. The electors in each State shall have the qualifications requisite for electors of the most numerous branch of the State legislatures.

When vacancies happen in the representation of any State in the Senate, the executive authority of such State shall issue writs of election to fill such vacancies: *Provided*, That the legislature of any State may empower the executive thereof to make temporary appointments until the people fill the vacancies by election as the legislature may direct.

This amendment shall not be so construed as to affect the election or term of any Senator chosen before it becomes valid as part of the Constitution.

Amendment XVIII*

Section 1. After one year from the ratification of this article the manufacture, sale, or transportation of intoxicating liquors within, the importation thereof into, or the exportation thereof from the United States and all territory subject to the jurisdiction thereof for beverage purposes is hereby prohibited.

Section 2. The Congress and the several States shall have concurrent power to enforce this article by appropriate legislation.

Section 3. This article shall be inoperative unless it shall have been ratified as an amendment to the Constitution by the legislatures of the several States, as provided in the Constitution, within seven years from the date of the submission hereof to the States by the Congress.

*[Repealed by the Twenty-First Amendment. — ED.]

Amendment XIX

The right of citizens of the United States to vote shall not be denied or abridged by the United States or by any State on account of sex.

Congress shall have power to enforce this article by appropriate legislation.

Amendment XX

Section 1. The terms of the President and Vice President shall end at noon on the 20th day of January, and the terms of Senators and Representatives at noon on the 3d day of January, of the years in which such terms would have ended if this article had not been ratified; and the terms of their successors shall then begin.

Section 2. The Congress shall assemble at least once in every year, and such meeting shall begin at noon on the 3d day of January, unless they shall by law appoint a different day.

Section 3. If, at the time fixed for the beginning of the term of the President, the President-elect shall have died, the Vice President-elect shall become President. If a President shall not have been chosen before the time fixed for the beginning of his term, or if the President-elect shall have failed to qualify, then the Vice President-elect shall act as President until a President shall have qualified; and the Congress may by law provide for the case wherein neither a President-elect nor a Vice President-elect shall have qualified, declaring who shall then act as President, or the manner in which one who is to act shall be selected, and such person shall act accordingly until a President or Vice President shall have qualified.

Section 4. The Congress may by law provide for the case of the death of any of the persons from whom the House of Representatives may choose a President whenever the right of choice shall have devolved upon them, and for the case of the death of any of the persons from whom the Senate may choose a Vice President whenever the right of choice shall have devolved upon them.

Section 5. Sections 1 and 2 shall take effect on the 15th day of October following the ratification of this article.

Section 6. This article shall be inoperative unless it shall have been ratified as an amendment to the Constitution by the legislatures of three-fourths of the several States within seven years from the date of its submission.

Amendment XXI

Section 1. The eighteenth article of amendment to the Constitution of the United States is hereby repealed.

Section 2. The transportation or importation into any State, Territory, or possession of the United States for delivery or use therein of intoxicating liquors, in violation of the laws thereof, is hereby prohibited.

Section 3. This article shall be inoperative unless it shall have been ratified as an amendment to the Constitution by conventions in the several States, as provided in the Constitution, within seven years from the date of the submission hereof to the States by the Congress.

Amendment XXII

Section 1. No person shall be elected to the office of the President more than twice, and no person who has held the office of President, or acted as President, for more than two years of a term to which some other person was elected President shall be elected to the office of the President more than once.

But this article shall not apply to any person holding the office of President when this article was proposed by the Congress, and shall not prevent any person who may be holding the office of President, or acting as President, during the term within which this article becomes operative from holding the office of President or acting as President during the remainder of such term.

Section 2. This article shall be inoperative unless it shall have been ratified as an amendment to the Constitution by the legislatures of three-fourths of the several States within seven years from the date of its submission to the States by the Congress.

Amendment XXIII

Section 1. The District constituting the seat of government of the United States shall appoint in such manner as the Congress may direct:

A number of electors of President and Vice President equal to the whole number of Senators and Representatives in Congress to which the District would be entitled if it were a State, but in no event more than the least populous State; they shall be in addition to those appointed by the States, but they shall be considered, for the purposes of the election of President and Vice President, to be electors appointed by a State; and they shall meet in the District and perform such duties as provided by the twelfth article of amendment.

Section 2. The Congress shall have power to enforce this article by appropriate legislation.

Amendment XXIV

Section 1. The right of citizens of the United States to vote in any primary or other election for President or Vice President, for electors for President or Vice President, or for Senator or Representative in Congress, shall not be denied or abridged by the United States or any State by reason of failure to pay any poll tax or other tax.

Section 2. The Congress shall have the power to enforce this article by appropriate legislation.

Amendment XXV

Section 1. In case of the removal of the President from office or of his death or resignation, the Vice President shall become President.

Section 2. Whenever there is a vacancy in the office of the Vice President, the President shall nominate a Vice President who shall take office upon confirmation by a majority vote of both Houses of Congress.

Section 3. Whenever the President transmits to the President pro tempore of the Senate and the Speaker of the House of Representatives his written declaration that he is unable to discharge the powers and duties of his office, and until he transmits to them a written declaration to the contrary, such powers and duties shall be discharged by the Vice President as Acting President.

Section 4. Whenever the Vice President and a majority of either the principal officers of the executive departments or of such other body as Congress may by law provide, transmit to the President pro tempore of the Senate and the Speaker of the House of Representatives their written declaration that the President is unable to discharge the powers and duties of his office, the Vice President shall immediately assume the powers and duties of the office as Acting President.

Thereafter, when the President transmits to the President pro tempore of the Senate and the Speaker of the House of Representatives his written declaration that no inability exists, he shall resume the powers and duties of his office unless the Vice President and a majority of either the principal officers of the executive department or of such other body as Congress may by law provide, transmit within four days to the President pro tempore of the Senate and the Speaker of the House of Representatives their written declaration that the President is unable to discharge the powers and duties of his office. Thereupon Congress shall decide the issue, assembling within forty-eight hours for that purpose if not in session. If the Congress, within twenty-one days after receipt of the latter written declaration, or, if Congress is not in session, within twenty-one days after Congress is required to assemble, determines by two-thirds vote of both Houses that the President is unable to discharge the powers and duties of his office, the Vice President shall continue to discharge the same as Acting President; otherwise, the President shall resume the powers and duties of his office.

Amendment XXVI

Section 1. The right of citizens of the United States, who are eighteen years of age or older, to vote shall not be denied, or abridged by the United States or by any State on account of age.

Section 2. The Congress shall have power to enforce this article by appropriate legislation.

Amendment XXVII*

No law, varying the compensation for the services of the Senators and Representatives, shall take effect, until an election of Representatives shall have intervened.

*[This amendment, first proposed in 1789, had been ratified by 39 states by May 1992. Although there is a controversy over its validity, the Archivist of the United States certified it on May 19, 1992. — Ed.]

SELECTED PROVISIONS FROM UNITED STATES CODE, TITLE 28

Judiciary and Judicial Procedure

TABLE OF PROVISIONS

Part I. Organization of Courts

Chapter 1. Supreme Court

§1. Number of justices; quorum

The Supreme Court of the United States shall consist of a Chief Justice of the United States and eight associate justices, any six of whom shall constitute a quorum.

§2. Terms of court

The Supreme Court shall hold at the seat of government a term of court commencing on the first Monday in October of each year and may hold such adjourned or special terms as may be necessary.

§3. Vacancy in office of Chief Justice; disability

Whenever the Chief Justice is unable to perform the duties of his office or the office is vacant, his powers and duties shall devolve upon the associate justice next in precedence who is able to act, until such disability is removed or another Chief Justice is appointed and duly qualified.

§4. Precedence of associate justices

Associate justices shall have precedence according to the seniority of their commissions. Justices whose commissions bear the same date shall have precedence according to seniority in age.

§5. SALARIES OF JUSTICES

The Chief Justice and each associate justice shall each receive a salary at annual rates determined under section 225 of the Federal Salary Act of 1967 (2 U.S.C. 351-361), as adjusted by section 461 of this title.

Chapter 3. Court of Appeals

§41. NUMBER AND COMPOSITION OF CIRCUITS

The thirteen judicial circuits of the United States are constituted as follows:

Circuits	*Composition*
District of Columbia	District of Columbia.
First	Maine, Massachusetts, New Hampshire, Puerto Rico, Rhode Island.
Second	Connecticut, New York, Vermont.
Third	Delaware, New Jersey, Pennsylvania, Virgin Islands.
Fourth	Maryland, North Carolina, South Carolina, Virginia, West Virginia.
Fifth	District of the Canal Zone, Louisiana, Mississippi, Texas.
Sixth	Kentucky, Michigan, Ohio, Tennessee.
Seventh	Illinois, Indiana, Wisconsin.
Eighth	Arkansas, Iowa, Minnesota, Missouri, Nebraska, North Dakota, South Dakota.
Ninth	Alaska, Arizona, California, Idaho, Montana, Nevada, Oregon, Washington, Guam, Hawaii.
Tenth	Colorado, Kansas, New Mexico, Oklahoma, Utah, Wyoming.
Eleventh	Alabama, Florida, Georgia.
Federal	All Federal judicial districts.

§43. CREATION AND COMPOSITION OF COURTS

(a) There shall be in each circuit a court of appeals, which shall be a court of record, known as the United States Court of Appeals for the circuit.

(b) Each court of appeals shall consist of the circuit judges of the circuit in regular active service. The circuit justice and justices or judges designated or assigned shall also be competent to sit as judges of the court.

§44. APPOINTMENT, TENURE, RESIDENCE AND SALARY OF CIRCUIT JUDGES

(a) The President shall appoint, by and with the advice and consent of the Senate, circuit judges for the several circuits as follows:

Circuits	*Number of Judges*
District of Columbia	12
First	6
Second	13
Third	14
Fourth	15
Fifth	17
Sixth	16
Seventh	11
Eighth	11
Ninth	28
Tenth	12
Eleventh	12
Federal	12

(b) Circuit judges shall hold office during good behavior.

(c) Except in the District of Columbia, each circuit judge shall be a resident of the circuit for which appointed at the time of his appointment and thereafter while in active service. While in active service, each circuit judge of the Federal judicial circuit appointed after the effective date of the Federal Courts Improvement Act of 1982, and the chief judge of the Federal Judicial Circuit, whenever appointed, shall reside within fifty miles of the District of Columbia. In each circuit (other than the Federal Judicial Circuit) there shall be at least one circuit judge in regular active service appointed from the residents of each state in that circuit.

(d) Each circuit judge shall receive a salary at an annual rate determined under section 225 of the Federal Salary Act of 1967 (2 U.S.C. 351-361), as adjusted by section 461 of this title.

§45. Chief judges; precedence of judges

(a)(1) The chief judge of the circuit shall be the circuit judge in regular active service who is senior in commission of those judges who —

(A) are sixty-four years of age or under;

(B) have served for one year or more as a circuit judge; and

(C) have not served previously as chief judge.

(2)(A) In any case in which no circuit judge meets the qualifications of paragraph (1), the youngest circuit judge in regular active service who is sixty-five years of age or over and who has served as circuit judge for one year or more shall act as the chief judge.

(B) In any case under subparagraph (A) in which there is no circuit judge in regular active service who has served as a circuit judge for one year or more, the circuit judge in regular active service who is senior in commission and who has not served previously as chief judge shall act as the chief judge.

(3)(A) Except as provided in subparagraph (C), the chief judge of the circuit appointed under paragraph (1) shall serve for a term of seven years and shall serve after expiration of such term until another judge is eligible under paragraph (1) to serve as chief judge of the circuit.

(B) Except as provided in subparagraph (C), a circuit judge acting as chief judge under subparagraph (A) or (B) of paragraph (2) shall serve until a judge has been appointed who meets the qualifications under paragraph (1).

(C) No circuit judge may serve or act as chief judge of the circuit after attaining the age of seventy years unless no other circuit judge is qualified to serve as chief judge of the circuit under paragraph (1) or is qualified to act as chief judge under paragraph (2).

(b) The chief judge shall have precedence and preside at any session of the court which he attends. Other circuit judges of the court in regular active service shall have precedence and preside according to the seniority of their commissions. Judges whose commissions bear the same date shall have precedence according to seniority in age. The circuit justice, however, shall have precedence over all the circuit judges and shall preside at any session which he attends.

(c) If the chief judge desires to be relieved of his duties as chief judge while retaining his active status as circuit judge, he may so certify to the Chief Justice of the United States, and thereafter the chief judge of the circuit shall be such other circuit judge who is qualified to serve or act as chief judge under subsection (a).

(d) If a chief judge is temporarily unable to perform his duties as such, they shall be performed by the circuit judge in active service, present in the circuit and able and qualified to act, who is next in precedence.

§46. ASSIGNMENT OF JUDGES; PANELS; HEARINGS; QUORUM

(a) Circuit judges shall sit on the court and its panels in such order and at such times as the court directs.

(b) In each circuit the court may authorize the hearing and determination of cases and controversies by separate panels, each consisting of three judges at least a majority of whom shall be judges of that court, unless such judges cannot sit because recused or disqualified, or unless the chief judge of that court certifies that there is an emergency including, but not limited to, the unavailability of a judge of the court because of illness. Such panels shall sit at the times and places and hear the cases and controversies assigned as the court directs. The United States Court of Appeals for the Federal Circuit shall determine by rule a procedure for the rotation of judges from panel to panel to ensure that all of the judges sit on a representative cross section of the cases heard and, notwithstanding the first sentence of this subsection, may determine by rule the number of judges, not less than three, who constitute a panel.

(c) Cases and controversies shall be heard and determined by a court or panel of not more than three judges (except that the United States Court of Appeals for the Federal Circuit may sit in panels of more than three judges if its rules so provide), unless a hearing or rehearing before the court in banc is ordered by a majority of the circuit judges of the circuit who are in regular active service. A court in banc shall consist of all circuit judges in regular active service, or such number of judges as may be prescribed in accordance with section 6 of Public Law 95-486 (92 Stat. 1633), except that any senior circuit judge of the circuit shall be eligible (1) to participate, at his election and upon designation and assignment pursuant to section 294(c) of this title and the rules of the circuit, as a member of an in banc court reviewing a decision of a panel of which such judge was a member, or (2) to continue to participate in the decision of a case or controversy that was heard or reheard by the court in banc at a time when such judge was in regular active service.

(d) A majority of the number of judges authorized to constitute a court or panel thereof, as provided in paragraph (c), shall constitute a quorum.

§47. Disqualification of trial judge to hear appeal

No judge shall hear or determine an appeal from the decision of a case or issue tried by him.

§48. Terms of court

(a) The courts of appeals shall hold regular sessions at the places listed below, and at such other places within the respective circuit as each court may designate by rule.

Circuits	*Places*
District of Columbia	Washington
First	Boston
Second	New York
Third	Philadelphia
Fourth	Richmond, Asheville
Fifth	New Orleans, Fort Worth, Jackson
Sixth	Cincinnati
Seventh	Chicago
Eighth	St. Louis, Kansas City, Omaha, St. Paul
Ninth	San Francisco, Los Angeles, Portland, Seattle
Tenth	Denver, Wichita, Oklahoma City
Eleventh	Atlanta, Jacksonville, Montgomery
Federal	District of Columbia, and in any other place listed above as the court by rule direct

(b) Each court of appeals may hold special sessions at any place within its circuit as the nature of the business may require, and upon such notice as the court orders. The court may transact any business at a special session which it might transact at a regular session.

(c) Any court of appeals may pretermit, with the consent of the Judicial Conference of the United States, any regular session of court at any place for insufficient business or other good cause.

(d) The times and places of the sessions of the Court of Appeals for the Federal Circuit shall be prescribed with a view to securing reasonable opportunity to citizens to appear before the court with as little inconvenience and expense to citizens as is practicable.

Chapter 5. District Courts

§132. Creation and Composition of District Courts

(a) There shall be in each judicial district a district court which shall be a court of record known as the United States District Court for the district.

(b) Each district court shall consist of the district judge or judges for the district in regular active service. Justices or judges designated or assigned shall be competent to sit as judges of the court.

(c) Except as otherwise provided by law, or rule or order of court, the judicial power of a district court with respect to any action, suit or proceeding may be exercised by a single judge, who may preside alone and hold a regular or special session of court at the same time other sessions are held by other judges.

§133. Appointment and Number of District Judges

(a) The President shall appoint, by and with the advice and consent of the Senate, district judges for the several judicial districts, as follows:*

Districts	*Judges*
Alabama:	
Northern	7
Middle	3
Southern	3
Alaska	3
Arizona	12
Arkansas:	
Eastern	5
Western	3

*[In the case of the districts below bearing a dagger (†), the allocation of judges indicated in parentheses becomes effective on July 15, 2003. Until that date, the allocation appearing outside the parentheses is in effect — Ed.]

Districts	*Judges*
California:	
Northern	14
Eastern	6
Central	27
Southern	8 (13)†
Colorado	7
Connecticut	8
Delaware	4
District of Columbia	15
Florida:	
Northern	4
Middle	11
Southern	17
Georgia:	
Northern	11
Middle	4
Southern	3
Hawaii	3
Idaho	2
Illinois:	
Northern	22
Central	3 (4)†
Southern	3 (4)†
Indiana:	
Northern	5
Southern	5
Iowa:	
Northern	2
Southern	3
Kansas	5
Kentucky:	
Eastern	5
Western	4
Eastern and Western	1
Louisiana:	
Eastern	12
Middle	3
Western	7
Maine	3
Maryland	10
Massachusetts	13

Districts	*Judges*
Michigan:	
Eastern	15
Western	4
Minnesota	7
Mississippi:	
Northern	3
Southern	6
Missouri:	
Eastern	6
Western	5
Eastern and Western	2
Montana	3
Nebraska	3
Nevada	7
New Hampshire	3
New Jersey	17
New Mexico	6
New York:	
Northern	4
Southern	28
Eastern	15
Western	4
North Carolina:	
Eastern	4
Middle	4
Western	3 (4)†
North Dakota	2
Ohio:	
Northern	11
Southern	8
Oklahoma:	
Northern	3
Eastern	1
Western	6
Northern, Eastern, and Western	1
Oregon	6
Pennsylvania:	
Eastern	22
Middle	6
Western	10
Puerto Rico	7
Rhode Island	3
South Carolina	10

Districts	*Judges*
South Dakota	3
Tennessee:	
Eastern	5
Middle	4
Western	5
Texas:	
Northern	12
Southern	19
Eastern	7
Western	10 (13)[†]
Utah	5
Vermont	2
Virginia:	
Eastern	10 (11)[†]
Western	4
Washington:	
Eastern	4
Western	7
West Virginia:	
Northern	3
Southern	5
Wisconsin:	
Eastern	5
Western	2
Wyoming	3

(b)(1) In any case in which a judge of the United States (other than a senior judge) assumes the duties of a full-time office of Federal judicial administration, the President shall appoint, by and with the advice and consent of the Senate, an additional judge for the court on which such judge serves. If the judge who assumes the duties of such full-time office leaves that office and resumes the duties as an active judge of the court, then the President shall not appoint a judge to fill the first vacancy which occurs thereafter in that court.

(2) For purposes of paragraph (1), the term "office of Federal judicial administration" means a position as Director of the Federal Judicial Center, Director of the Administrative Office of the United States Courts, or administrative assistant to the Chief Justice.

§136. CHIEF JUDGES; PRECEDENCE OF DISTRICT JUDGES

(a)(1) In any district having more than one district judge, the chief judge of the district shall be the district judge in regular active service who is senior in commission of those judges who —

(A) are sixty-four years of age or under;
(B) have served for one year or more as a district judge; and
(C) have not served previously as chief judge.

(2)(A) In any case in which no district judge meets the qualifications of paragraph (1), the youngest district judge in regular active service who is sixty-five years of age or over and who has served as district judge for one year or more shall act as the chief judge.

(B) In any case under subparagraph (A) in which there is no district judge in regular active service who has served as a district judge for one year or more, the district judge in regular active service who is senior in commission and who has not served previously as chief judge shall act as the chief judge.

(3)(A) Except as provided in subparagraph (C), the chief judge of the district appointed under paragraph (1) shall serve for a term of seven years and shall serve after expiration of such term until another judge is eligible under paragraph (1) to serve as chief judge of the district.

(B) Except as provided in subparagraph (C), a district judge acting as chief judge under subparagraph (A) or (B) of paragraph (2) shall serve until a judge has been appointed who meets the qualifications under paragraph (1).

(C) No district judge may serve or act as chief judge of the district after attaining the age of seventy years unless no other district judge is qualified to serve as chief judge of the district under paragraph (1) or is qualified to act as chief judge under paragraph (2).

(b) The chief judge shall have precedence and preside at any session which he attends.

Other district judges shall have precedence and preside according to the seniority of their commissions. Judges whose commissions bear the same date shall have precedence according to seniority in age.

(c) A judge whose commission extends over more than one district shall be junior to all district judges except in the district in which he resided at the time he entered upon the duties of his office.

(d) If the chief judge desires to be relieved of his duties as chief judge while retaining his active status as district judge, he may so certify to the Chief Justice of the United States, and thereafter the chief judge of the district shall be such other district judge who is qualified to serve or act as chief judge under subsection (a).

(e) If a chief judge is temporarily unable to perform his duties as such, they shall be performed by the district judge in active service, present in the district and able and qualified to act, who is next in precedence.

§137. Division of business among district judges

The business of a court having more than one judge shall be divided among the judges as provided by the rules and orders of the court.

The chief judge of the district court shall be responsible for the observance of such rules and orders, and shall divide the business and assign the cases so far as such rules and orders do not otherwise prescribe.

If the district judges in any district are unable to agree upon the adoption of rules or orders for that purpose the judicial of the circuit shall make.

§143. Vacant judgeship as affecting proceedings

When the office of a district judge becomes vacant, all pending process, pleadings and proceedings shall, when necessary, be continued by the clerk until a judge is appointed or designated to hold such court.

§144. Bias or prejudice of judge

Whenever a party to any proceeding in a district court makes and files a timely and sufficient affidavit that the judge before whom the matter is pending has a personal bias or prejudice either against him or in favor of any adverse party, such judge shall proceed no further therein, but another judge shall be assigned to hear such proceeding.

The affidavit shall state the facts and the reasons for the belief that bias or prejudice exists, and shall be filed not less than ten days before the beginning of the term at which the proceeding is to be heard, or good cause shall be shown for failure to file it within such time. A party may file only one such affidavit in any case. It shall be accompanied by a certificate of counsel of record stating that it is made in good faith.

Chapter 15. Conferences and Councils of Judges

§331. Judicial Conference of the United States

The Chief Justice of the United States shall summon annually the chief judge of each judicial circuit, the chief judge of the Court of International Trade, and a district judge from each judicial circuit to a conference at such time and place in the United States as he may designate. He shall preside at such conference which shall be known as the Judicial Conference of the United States. Special sessions of the conference may be called by the Chief Justice at such times and places as he may designate.

The district judge to be summoned from each judicial circuit shall be chosen by the circuit and district judges of the circuit and shall serve as a member of the Judicial Conference of the United States for a term of not less than 3 successive years not for more than five successive years, as established by majority vote of all circuit and district judges of the circuit. A district judge serving as a member of the Judicial Conference may be either a judge in regular active service or a judge retired from regular active service under section 371(b) of this title.

If the chief judge of any circuit, the chief judge of the Court of International Trade, or the district judge chosen by the judges of the circuit is unable to attend, the Chief Justice may summon any other circuit or district judge from such circuit or any other judge of the Court of International Trade, as the case may be. Every judge summoned shall attend and, unless excused by the Chief Justice, shall remain throughout the sessions of the conference and advise as to the needs of his circuit or court and as to any matters in respect of which the administration of justice in the courts of the United States may be improved.

The Conference shall make a comprehensive survey of the condition of business in the courts of the United States and prepare plans for assignment of judges to or from circuits or districts where necessary. It shall also submit suggestions and recommendations to the various courts to promote uniformity of management procedures and the expeditious conduct of court business. The Conference is authorized to exercise the authority provided in chapter 16 of this title as the Conference, or through a standing committee. If the Conference elects to establish a standing committee, it shall be appointed by the Chief Justice and all petitions for review shall be reviewed by that committee. The Conference or the standing committee may hold hearings, take sworn testimony, issue subpoenas and subpoenas duces tecum, and make necessary and appropriate orders in the exercise of its authority. Subpoenas and subpoenas duces tecum shall be issued by the clerk of the Supreme Court or by the clerk of any court of appeals, at the direction of the Chief Justice or his designee and under the seal of the court, and shall be served in the manner provided in rule 45(c) of the Federal Rules of Civil Procedure for subpoenas and subpoenas duces tecum issued on behalf of the United States or an officer or any agency thereof. The Conference may also prescribe and modify rules for the exercise of the authority provided in chapter 16 of this title. All judicial officers and employees of the United States shall promptly carry into effect all orders of the Judicial Conference or the standing committee established pursuant to this section.

The Conference shall also carry on a continuous study of the operation and effect of the general rules of practice and procedure now or hereafter in use as prescribed by the Supreme Court for the other courts of the United States pursuant to law. Such changes in and addition to those rules as the Conference may deem desirable to promote simplicity in procedure, fairness in administration, the just determination of litigation, and the elimination of unjustifiable expense and delay shall be recommended by the Conference from time to time to the Supreme Court for its consideration and adoption, modification or rejection, in accordance with law.

The Judicial Conference shall review rules prescribed under section 2071 of this title by the courts, other than the Supreme Court and the district courts, for consistency with Federal law. The Judicial Conference may modify or abrogate any such rule so reviewed found inconsistent in the course of such a review.

The Attorney General shall, upon request of the Chief Justice, report to such conference on matters relating to the business of the several courts of the United States, with particular reference to cases to which the United States is a party.

The Chief Justice shall submit to Congress an annual report of the proceedings of the Judicial Conference and its recommendations for legislation.

Chapter 17. Resignation and Retirement of Justices and Judges

§372. RETIREMENT FOR DISABILITY; SUBSTITUTE JUDGE ON FAILURE TO RETIRE; JUDICIAL DISCIPLINE

(a) Any justice or judge of the United States appointed to hold office during good behavior who becomes permanently disabled from performing his duties may retire from regular active service, and the President shall, by and with the advice and consent of the Senate, appoint a successor.

Any justice or judge of the United States desiring to retire under this section shall certify to the President his disability in writing.

Whenever an associate judge of the Supreme Court, a chief judge of a circuit or the chief judge of the Court of International Trade, desires to retire under this section, he shall furnish to the President a certificate of disability signed by the Chief Justice of the United States.

A circuit or district judge, desiring to retire under this section, shall furnish to the President a certificate of disability signed by the chief judge of his circuit.

A judge of the Court of International Trade desiring to retire under this section, shall furnish to the President a certificate of disability signed by the chief judge of his court.

Each justice or judge retiring under this section after serving ten years continuously or otherwise shall, during the remainder of his lifetime, receive the salary of the office. A justice or judge retiring under this section who has served less than ten years in all shall, during the remainder of his lifetime, receive one-half the salary of the office.

(b) Whenever any judge of the United States appointed to hold office during good behavior who is eligible to retire under this section does not do so and a certificate of his disability signed by a majority of the members of the Judicial Council of his circuit in the case of a circuit or district judge, or by the Chief Justice of the United States in the case of the Chief Judge of the Court of International Trade, or by the chief judge of his court in the case of a judge of the Court of International Trade, is presented to the President and the President finds that such judge is unable to discharge efficiently all the duties of his office by reason of permanent mental or physical disability and that the appointment of an additional judge is necessary for the efficient dispatch of business, the

President may make such appointment by and with the advice and consent of the Senate. Whenever any such additional judge is appointed, the vacancy subsequently caused by the death, resignation, or retirement of the disabled judge shall not be filled. Any judge whose disability causes the appointment of an additional judge shall, for purpose of precedence, service as chief judge, or temporary performance of the duties of that office, be treated as junior in commission to the other judges of the circuit, district, or court.

(c)(1) Any person alleging that a circuit, district, or bankruptcy judge, or a magistrate, has engaged in conduct prejudicial to the effective and expeditious administration of the business of the courts, or alleging that such a judge or magistrate is unable to discharge all the duties of office by reason of mental or physical disability, may file with the clerk of the court of appeals for the circuit a written complaint containing a brief statement of the facts constituting such conduct. In the interests of the effective and expeditious administration of the business of the courts and on the basis of information available to the chief judge of the circuit, the chief judge may, by written order stating reasons therefor, identify a complaint for purposes of this subsection and thereby dispense with filing of a written complaint.

(2) Upon receipt of a complaint filed under paragraph (1) of this subsection, the clerk shall promptly transmit such complaint to the chief judge of the circuit, or, if the conduct complained of is that of the chief judge, to that circuit judge in regular active service next senior in date of commission (hereafter, for purposes of this subsection only, included in the term "chief judge"). The clerk shall simultaneously transmit a copy of the complaint to the judge or magistrate whose conduct is the subject of the complaint.

(3) After expeditiously reviewing a complaint, the chief judge, by written order stating his reasons, may —

(A) dismiss the complaint, if he finds it to be (i) not in conformity with paragraph (1) of this subsection, (ii) directly related to the merits of a decision or procedural ruling, or (iii) frivolous; or

(B) conclude the proceeding if he finds that appropriate corrective action has been taken or that action on the complaint is no longer necessary because of intervening events.

The chief judge shall transmit copies of his written order to the complainant and to the judge or magistrate whose conduct is the subject of the complaint.

(4) If the chief judge does not enter an order under paragraph (3) of this subsection, such judge shall promptly —

(A) appoint himself and equal numbers of circuit and district judges of the circuit to a special committee to investigate the facts and allegations contained in the complaint;

(B) certify the complaint and any other documents pertaining thereto to each member of such committee; and

(C) provide written notice to the complainant and the judge or magistrate whose conduct is the subject of the complaint of the action taken under this paragraph.

A judge appointed to a special committee under this paragraph may continue to serve on that committee after becoming a senior judge or, in the case of the chief judge of the circuit, after his term as chief judge terminates under subsection (a)(3) or (c) of section 45 of this title. If a judge appointed to a committee under this paragraph dies, or retires from office under section 371(a) of this title, while serving on the committee, the chief judge of the circuit may appoint another circuit or district judge, as the case may be, to the committee.

(5) Each committee appointed under paragraph (4) of this subsection shall conduct an investigation as extensive as it considers necessary, and shall expeditiously file a comprehensive written report thereon with the judicial council of the circuit. Such report shall present both the findings of the investigation and the committee's recommendations for necessary and appropriate action by the judicial council of the circuit.

(6) Upon receipt of a report filed under paragraph (5) of this subsection, the judicial council —

(A) may conduct any additional investigation which it considers to be necessary;

(B) shall take such action as is appropriate to assure the effective and expeditious administration of the business of the courts within the circuit, including, but not limited to, any of the following actions:

(i) directing the chief judge of the district of the magistrate whose conduct is the subject of the complaint to take such action as the judicial council considers appropriate;

(ii) certifying disability of a judge appointed to hold office during good behavior whose conduct is the subject of the complaint, pursuant to the procedures and standards provided under subsection (b) of this section;

(iii) requesting that any such judge appointed to hold office during good behavior voluntarily retire, with the provision that the length of service requirements under section 371 of this title shall not apply;

(iv) ordering that, on a temporary basis for a time certain, no further cases be assigned to any judge or magistrate whose conduct is the subject of a complaint;

(v) censuring or reprimanding such judge or magistrate by means of private communication;

(vi) censuring or reprimanding such judge or magistrate by means of public announcement; or

(vii) ordering such other action as it considers appropriate under the circumstances, except that (I) in no circumstances may the council order removal from office of any judge appointed to hold office during good behavior, and (II) any removal of a magistrate shall be in accordance with section 631 of this title and any removal of a bankruptcy judge shall be in accordance with section 152 of this title;

(C) may dismiss the complaint; and

(D) shall immediately provide written notice to the complainant and to such judge or magistrate of the action taken under this paragraph.

(7)(A) In addition to the authority granted under paragraph (6) of this subsection, the judicial council may, in its discretion, refer any complaint under this subsection, together with the record of any associated proceedings and its recommendations for appropriate action, to the Judicial Conference of the United States.

(B) In any case in which the judicial council determines, on the basis of a complaint and an investigation under this subsection, or on the basis of information otherwise available to the council, that a judge appointed to hold office during good behavior may have engaged in conduct —

(i) which might constitute one or more grounds for impeachment under article II of the Constitution; or

(ii) which, in the interest of justice, is not amenable to resolution by the judicial council,

the judicial council shall promptly certify such determination, together with any complaint and a record of any associated proceedings, to the Judicial Conference of the United States.

(C) A judicial council acting under authority of this paragraph shall, unless contrary to the interests of justice, immediately submit written notice to the complainant and to the judge or magistrate whose conduct is the subject of the action taken under this paragraph.

(8)(A) Upon referral or certification of any matter under paragraph (7) of this subsection, the Judicial Conference, after consideration of the prior proceedings and such additional investigation as it considers appropriate, shall by majority vote take such action, as described in paragraph (6)(B) of this subsection, as it considers appropriate. If the Judicial Conference concurs in the determination of the council, or makes its own determination, that consideration of impeachment may be warranted, it shall so certify and transmit the determination and the record of proceedings to the House of Representatives for whatever action the House of Representatives considers to be necessary. Upon receipt of the determination and record of proceedings in the House of Representatives, the Clerk of the House of Representatives shall make available to the public the determination and any reasons for the determination.

(B) If a judge or magistrate has been convicted a felony and has exhausted all means of obtaining direct review of the conviction, or the time for seeking further direct review of the conviction has passed and no such review has been sought, the Judicial Conference may, by majority vote and without referral or certification under paragraph (7), transmit to the House of Representatives a determination that consideration of impeachment may be warranted, together with appropriate court records, for whatever action the House of Representatives considers to be necessary.

(9)(A) In conducting any investigation under this subsection, the judicial council, or a special committee appointed under paragraph (4) of this subsection, shall have full subpoena powers as provided in section 332 (d) of this title.

(B) In conducting any investigation under this subsection, the Judicial Conference, or a standing committee appointed by the Chief Justice under section 331 of this title, shall have full subpoena powers as provided in that section.

(10) A complainant, judge, or magistrate aggrieved by a final order of the chief judge under paragraph (3) of this subsection may petition the judicial council for review thereof. A complainant, judge, or magistrate aggrieved by an action of the judicial council under paragraph (6) of this subsection may petition the Judicial Conference of the United States for review thereof. The Judicial Conference, or the standing committee established under section 331 of this title, may grant a petition filed by a complainant, judge, or magistrate under this paragraph. Except as expressly provided in this paragraph, all orders and determinations, including denials of petitions for review, shall be final and conclusive and shall not be judicially reviewable on appeal or otherwise.

(11) Each judicial council and the Judicial Conference may prescribe such rules for the conduct of proceedings under this subsection, including the processing of petitions for review, as each considers to be appropriate. Such rules shall contain provisions requiring that —

(A) adequate prior notice of any investigation be given in writing to the judge or magistrate whose conduct is the subject of the complaint;

(B) the judge or magistrate whose conduct is the subject of the complaint be afforded an opportunity to appear (in person or by counsel) at proceedings conducted by the investigating panel, to present oral and documentary evidence, to compel the attendance of witnesses or the production of documents, to cross-examine witnesses, and to present argument orally or in writing; and

(C) the complainant be afforded an opportunity to appear at proceedings conducted by the investigating panel, if the panel concludes that the complainant could offer substantial information.

Any such rule shall be made or amended only after giving appropriate public notice and an opportunity for comment.

Any rule promulgated under this subsection shall be a matter of public record, and any such rule promulgated by a judicial council may be modified by the Judicial Conference. No rule promulgated under this subsection may limit the period time within which a person may file a complaint under this subsection.

(12) No judge or magistrate whose conduct is the subject of an investigation under this subsection shall serve upon a special committee appointed under paragraph (4) of this subsection, upon a judicial council, upon the Judicial

Conference, or upon the standing committee established under section 331 of this title, until all related proceedings under this subsection have been finally terminated.

(13) No person shall be granted the right to intervene or to appear as amicus curiae in any proceeding before a judicial council or the Judicial Conference under this subsection.

(14) Except as provided in paragraph (8), all papers, documents, and records of proceedings related to investigations conducted under this subsection shall be confidential and shall not be disclosed by any person in any proceeding except to the extent that —

(A) the judicial council of the circuit in its discretion releases a copy of a report of a special investigative committee under paragraph (5) to the complainant whose complaint initiated the investigation by that special committee and to the judge or magistrate whose conduct is the subject of the complaint;

(B) the judicial council of the circuit, the Judicial Conference of the United States, or the Senate or the House of Representatives by resolution, releases any such material which is believed necessary to an impeachment investigation or trial of a judge under article I of the Constitution; or

(C) such disclosure is authorized in writing by the judge or magistrate who is the subject of the complaint and by the chief judge of the circuit, the Chief Justice, or the chairman of the standing committee established under section 331 of this title.

(15) Each written order to implement any action under paragraph (6)(B) of this subsection, which is issued by a judicial council, the Judicial Conference, or the standing committee established under section 331 of this title, shall be made available to the public through the appropriate clerk's office of the court of appeals for the circuit. Unless contrary to the interests of justice, each such order issued under this paragraph shall be accompanied by written reasons therefor.

(16) Upon the request of a judge or magistrate whose conduct is the subject of a complaint under this subsection, the judicial council may, if the complaint has been finally dismissed under paragraph (6)(C), recommend that the Director of the Administrative Office of the United States Courts award reimbursement, from funds appropriated to the Federal judiciary, for those reasonable expenses, including attorneys' fees, incurred by that judge or magistrate during the investigation which would not have been incurred but for the requirements of this subsection.

(17) Except as expressly provided in this subsection, nothing in this subsection shall be construed to affect any other provision of this title, the Federal Rules of Civil Procedure, the Federal Rules of Criminal Procedure, the Federal Rules of Appellate Procedure, or the Federal Rules of Evidence.

(18) The United States Court of Federal Claims, the Court of International Trade, and the Court of Appeals for the Federal Circuit shall each prescribe

rules, consistent with the foregoing provisions of this subsection, establishing procedures for the filing of complaints with respect to the conduct of any judge of such court and for the investigation and resolution of such complaints. In investigating and taking action with respect to any such complaint, each such court shall have the powers granted to a judicial council under this subsection.

Chapter 21. General Provisions Applicable to Courts and Judges

§454. PRACTICE OF LAW BY JUSTICES AND JUDGES

Any justice or judge appointed under the authority of the United States who engages in the practice of law is guilty of a high misdemeanor.

§455. DISQUALIFICATION OF JUSTICE, JUDGE, MAGISTRATE, OR REFEREE IN BANKRUPTCY

(a) Any justice, judge or magistrate of the United States shall disqualify himself in any proceeding in which his impartiality might reasonably be questioned.

(b) He shall also disqualify himself in the following circumstances:

(1) Where he has a personal bias or prejudice concerning a party, or personal knowledge of disputed evidentiary facts concerning the proceeding;

(2) Where in private practice he served as lawyer in the matter in controversy, or a lawyer with whom he previously practiced law served during such association as a lawyer concerning the matter, or the judge or such lawyer has been a material witness concerning it;

(3) Where he has served in governmental employment and in such capacity participated as counsel, adviser or material witness concerning the proceeding or expressed an opinion concerning the merits of the particular case in controversy;

(4) He knows that he, individually or as a fiduciary, or his spouse or minor child residing in his household, has a financial interest in the subject matter in controversy or in a party to the proceeding, or any other interest that could be substantially affected by the outcome of the proceeding;

(5) He or his spouse, or a person within the third degree of relationship to either of them, or the spouse of such a person:

(i) Is a party to the proceeding, or an officer, director, or trustee of a party;

(ii) Is acting as a lawyer in the proceeding;

(iii) Is known by the judge to have an interest that could be substantially affected by the outcome of the proceeding;

(iv) Is to the judge's knowledge likely to be a material witness in the proceeding.

(c) A judge should inform himself about his personal and fiduciary financial interests, and make a reasonable effort to inform himself about the personal financial interests of his spouse and minor children residing in his household.

(d) For the purposes of this section the following words or phrases shall have the meaning indicated:

(1) "proceeding" includes pretrial, trial, appellate review, or other stages of litigation;

(2) the degree of relationship is calculated according to the civil law system;

(3) "fiduciary" includes such relationships as executor, administrator, trustee, and guardian;

(4) "financial interest" means ownership of a legal or equitable interest, however small, or a relationship as director, adviser, or other active participant in the affairs of a party, except that:

(i) Ownership in a mutual or common investment fund that holds securities is not a "financial interest" in such securities unless the judge participates in the management of the fund;

(ii) An office in an educational, religious, charitable, fraternal, or civic organization is not a "financial interest" in securities held by the organization;

(iii) The proprietary interest of a policyholder in a mutual insurance company, of a depositor in a mutual savings association, or a similar proprietary interest, is a "financial interest" in the organization only if the outcome of the proceeding could substantially affect the value of the interest;

(iv) Ownership of government securities is a "financial interest" in the issuer only if the outcome of the proceeding could substantially affect the value of the securities.

(e) No justice, judge, magistrate, or referee in bankruptcy shall accept from the parties to the proceedings a waiver of any ground for disqualification enumerated in subsection (b). Where the ground for disqualification arises only under subsection (a), waiver may be accepted provided it is preceded by a full disclosure on the record of the basis for disqualification.

(f) Notwithstanding the preceding provisions of this section, if any justice, judge, magistrate, or bankruptcy judge to whom a matter has been assigned would be disqualified, after substantial judicial time has been devoted to the matter, because of the appearance or discovery, after the matter was assigned to him or her, that he or she individually or as a fiduciary, or his or her spouse or minor child residing in his or her household, has a financial interest in a party (other than an interest that could be substantially affected by the outcome), disqualification is not required if the justice, judge, magistrate, bankruptcy judge, spouse or minor child, as the case may be, divests himself or herself of the interest that provides the grounds for the disqualification.

Chapter 23. Civil Justice Expense and Delay Reduction Plans

§471. Requirement for a District Court Civil Justice Expense and Delay Reduction Plan

There shall be implemented by each United States district court, in accordance with this chapter, a civil justice expense and delay reduction plan. The plan may be a plan developed by such district court or a model plan developed by the Judicial Conference of the United States. The purposes of each plan are to facilitate deliberate adjudication of civil cases on the merits, monitor discovery, improve litigation management, and ensure just, speedy, and inexpensive resolutions of civil disputes.

§473. Content of Civil Justice Expense and Delay Reduction Plans

(a) In formulating the provisions of its civil justice expense and delay reduction plan, each United States district court, in consultation with an advisory group appointed under section 478 of this title, shall consider and may include the following principles and guidelines of litigation management and cost and delay reduction:

(1) systematic, differential treatment of civil cases that tailors the level of individualized and case specific management to such criteria as case complexity, the amount of time reasonably needed to prepare the case for trial, and the judicial and other resources required and available for the preparation and disposition of the case;

(2) early and ongoing control of the pretrial process through involvement of a judicial officer in —

(A) assessing and planning the progress of a case;

(B) setting early, firm trial dates, such that the trial is scheduled to occur within eighteen months of the filing of the complaint, unless a judicial officer certifies that —

(i) the demands of the case and its complexity make such a trial date incompatible with serving the ends of justice; or

(ii) the trial cannot reasonably be held within such time because of the complexity of the case or the number or complexity of pending criminal cases;

(C) controlling the extent of discovery and the time for completion of discovery, and ensuring compliance with appropriate requested discovery in a timely fashion; and

(D) setting, at the earliest practicable time, deadlines for filing motions and a time framework for their disposition;

(3) for all cases that the court or an individual judicial officer determines are complex and any other appropriate cases, careful and deliberate monitoring

through a discovery-case management conference or a series of such conferences at which the presiding judicial officer —

(A) explores the parties' receptivity to, and the propriety of, settlement or proceeding with the litigation;

(B) identifies or formulates the principal issues in contention and, in appropriate cases, provides for the staged resolution or bifurcation of issues for trial consistent with Rule 42(b) of the Federal Rules of Civil Procedure;

(C) prepares a discovery schedule and plan consistent with any presumptive time limits that a district court may set for the completion of discovery and with any procedures a district court may develop to —

(i) identify and limit the volume of discovery available to avoid unnecessary or unduly burdensome or expensive discovery; and

(ii) phase discovery into two or more stages; and

(D) sets, at the earliest practicable time, deadlines for filing motions and a time framework for their disposition;

(4) encouragement of cost-effective discovery through voluntary exchange of information among litigants and their attorneys and through the use of cooperative discovery devices;

(5) conservation of judicial resources by prohibiting the consideration of discovery motions unless accompanied by a certification that the moving party has made a reasonable and good faith effort to reach agreement with opposing counsel on the matters set forth in the motion; and

(6) authorization to refer appropriate cases to alternative dispute resolution programs that —

(A) have been designated for use in a district court; or

(B) the court may make available, including mediation, minitrial, and summary jury trial.

(b) In formulating the provisions of its civil justice expense and delay reduction plan, each United States district court, in consultation with an advisory group appointed under section 478 of this title, shall consider and may include the following litigation management and cost and delay reduction techniques:

(1) a requirement that counsel for each party to a case jointly present a discovery-case management plan for the case at the initial pretrial conference, or explain the reasons for their failure to do so;

(2) a requirement that each party be represented at each pretrial conference by an attorney who has the authority to bind that party regarding all matters previously identified by the court for discussion at the conference and all reasonably related matters;

(3) a requirement that all requests for extensions of deadlines for completion of discovery or for postponement of the trial be signed by the attorney and the party making the request;

(4) a neutral evaluation program for the presentation of the legal and factual basis of a case to a neutral court representative selected by the court at a nonbinding conference conducted early in the litigation;

(5) a requirement that, upon notice by the court, representatives of the parties with authority to bind them in settlement discussions be present or available by telephone during any settlement conference; and

(6) such other features as the district court considers appropriate after considering the recommendations of the advisory group referred to in section 472(a) of this title.

(c) Nothing in a civil justice expense and delay reduction plan relating to the settlement authority provisions of this section shall alter or conflict with the authority of the Attorney General to conduct litigation on behalf of the United States, or any delegation of the Attorney General.

Part III. Court Officers and Employees

Chapter 43. United States Magistrates

§631. Appointment and tenure

(a) The judges of each United States district court and the district courts of the Virgin Islands, Guam, and the Northern Mariana Islands shall appoint United States magistrate judges in such numbers and to serve at such locations within the judicial districts as the Judicial Conference may determine under this chapter. In the case of a magistrate judge appointed by the district court of the Virgin Islands, Guam, or the Northern Mariana Islands, this chapter shall apply as though the court appointing such a magistrate judge were a United States district court. Where there is more than one judge of a district court, the appointment, whether an original appointment or a reappointment, shall be by the concurrence of a majority of all the judges of such district court, and when there is no such concurrence, then by the chief judge. Where the conference deems it desirable, a magistrate may be designated to serve in one or more districts adjoining the district for which he is appointed. Such a designation shall be made by the concurrence of a majority of the judges of each of the district courts involved and shall specify the duties to be performed by the magistrate in the adjoining district or districts.

(b) No individual may be appointed or reappointed to serve as a magistrate under this chapter unless:

(1) He has been for at least 5 years a member in good standing of the bar of the highest court of a State, the District of Columbia, the Commonwealth of Puerto Rico, the Territory of Guam, the Commonwealth of the Northern Mariana Islands, or the Virgin Islands of the United States, except that an individual who does not meet the bar membership requirements of this paragraph may be appointed and serve as a part-time magistrate if the appointing

court or courts and the conference find that no qualified individual who is a member of the bar is available to serve at a specific location;

(2) He is determined by the appointing district court or courts to be competent to perform the duties of the office;

(3) In the case of an individual appointed to serve in a national park, he resides within the exterior boundaries of that park, or at some place reasonably adjacent thereto;

(4) He is not related by blood or marriage to a judge of the appointing court or courts at the time of his initial appointment; and

(5) He is selected pursuant to standards and procedures promulgated by the Judicial Conference of the United States. Such standards and procedures shall contain provision for public notice of all vacancies in magistrate positions and for the establishment by the district courts of merit selection panels, composed of residents of the individual judicial districts, to assist the courts in identifying and recommending persons who are best qualified to fill such positions.

(c) A magistrate may hold no other civil or military office or employment under the United States: *Provided, however,* That, with the approval of the conference, a part-time referee in bankruptcy or a clerk or deputy clerk of a court of the United States may be appointed and serve as a part-time United States magistrate, but the conference shall fix the aggregate amount of compensation to be received for performing the duties of part-time magistrate and part-time referee in bankruptcy, clerk or deputy clerk: *And provided further,* That retired officers and retired enlisted personnel of the Regular and Reserve components of the Army, Navy, Air Force, Marine Corps, and Coast Guard, members of the Reserve components of the Army, Navy, Air Force, Marine Corps, and Coast Guard, and members of the Army National Guard of the United States, the Air National Guard of the United States, and the Naval Militia and of the National Guard of a State, territory, or the District of Columbia, except the National Guard disbursing officers who are on a full-time salary basis, may be appointed and serve as United States magistrates.

(d) Except as otherwise provided in sections 375 and 636(h) of this title, no individual may serve under this chapter after having attained the age of seventy years: *Provided, however,* That upon a majority vote of all the judges of the appointing court or courts, which is taken upon the magistrate's attaining age seventy and upon each subsequent anniversary thereof, a magistrate who has attained the age of seventy years may continue to serve and may be reappointed under this chapter.

(e) The appointment of any individual as a full-time magistrate shall be for a term of eight years, and the appointment of any individuals as a part-time magistrate shall be for a term of four years, except that the term of a full-time or part-time magistrate appointed under subsection (k) shall expire upon —

(1) the expiration of the absent magistrate's term,

(2) the reinstatement of the absent magistrate in regular service in office as a magistrate,

(3) the failure of the absent magistrate to make timely application under subsection (j) of this section for reinstatement in regular service in office as a magistrate after discharge or release from military service,

(4) the death or resignation of the absent magistrate, or

(5) the removal from office of the absent magistrate pursuant to subsection (i) of this section, whichever may first occur.

(f) Upon the expiration of his term, a magistrate may, by a majority vote of the judges of the appointing district court or courts and with the approval of the judicial council of the circuit, continue to perform the duties of his office until his successor is appointed, or for 180 days after the date of the expiration of the magistrate's term, whichever is earlier.

(g) Each individual appointed as a magistrate under this section shall take the oath or affirmation prescribed by section 453 of this title before performing the duties of his office.

(h) Each appointment made by a judge or judges of a district court shall be entered of record in such court, and notice of such appointment shall be given at once by the clerk of that court to the Director.

(i) Removal of a magistrate during the term for which he is appointed shall be only for incompetency, misconduct, neglect of duty, or physical or mental disability, but a magistrate's office shall be terminated if the conference determines that the services performed by his office are no longer needed. Removal shall be by the judges of the district court for the judicial district in which the magistrate serves; where there is more than one judge of a district court, removal shall not occur unless a majority of all the judges of such court concur in the order of removal; and when there is a tie vote of the judges of the district court on the question of the removal or retention in office of a magistrate, then removal shall be only by a concurrence of a majority of all the judges of the council. In the case of a magistrate appointed under the third sentence of subsection (a) of this section, removal shall not occur unless a majority of all the judges of the appointing district courts concur in the order of removal; and where there is a tie vote on the question of the removal or retention in office of a magistrate, then removal shall be only by a concurrence of a majority of all the judges of the council or councils. Before any order or removal shall be entered, a full specification of the charges shall be furnished to the magistrate, and he shall be accorded by the judge or judges of the removing court, courts, council, or councils an opportunity to be heard on the charges.

(j) Upon the grant by the appropriate district court or courts of a leave of absence to a magistrate entitled to such relief under chapter 43 of title 38, such court or courts may proceed to appoint, in the manner specified in subsection (a) of this section, another magistrate, qualified for appointment and service under subsections (b), (c), and (d) of this section, who shall serve for the period specified in subsection (e) of this section.

(k) A United States magistrate appointed under this chapter shall be exempt from the provisions of subchapter I of chapter 63 of title 5.

§632. CHARACTER OF SERVICE

(a) Full-time United States magistrates may not engage in the practice of law, and may not engage in any other business, occupation, or employment inconsistent with the expeditious, proper, and impartial performance of their duties as judicial officers.

(b) Part-time United States magistrates shall render such service as judicial officers as is required by law. While so serving they may engage in the practice of law, but may not serve as counsel in any criminal action in any court of the United States, nor act in any capacity that is, under such regulations as the conference may establish, inconsistent with the proper discharge of their office. Within such restrictions, they may engage in any other business, occupation, or employment which is not inconsistent with the expeditious, proper, and impartial performance of their duties as judicial officers.

§636. JURISDICTION, POWERS, AND TEMPORARY ASSIGNMENT

(a) Each United States magistrate serving under this chapter shall have within the territorial jurisdiction prescribed by his appointment —

(1) all powers and duties conferred or imposed upon United States commissioners by law or by the Rules of Criminal Procedure for the United States District Courts;

(2) the power to administer oaths and affirmations, issue orders pursuant to section 3142 of title 18 concerning release or detention of persons pending trial, and take acknowledgements, affidavits, and depositions;

(3) the power to conduct trials under section 3401, title 18, United States Code, in conformity with and subject to the limitations of that section;

(4) the power to enter a sentence for a petty offense; and

(5) the power to enter a sentence for a class A misdemeanor, in a case in which the parties have consented.

(b) (1) Notwithstanding any provision of law to the contrary —

(A) a judge may designate a magistrate to hear and determine any pretrial matter pending before the court, except a motion for injunctive relief, for judgment on the pleadings, for summary judgment, to dismiss or quash an indictment or information made by the defendant, to suppress evidence in a criminal case, to dismiss or to permit maintenance of a class action, to dismiss for failure to state a claim upon which relief can be granted, and to involuntarily dismiss an action. A judge of the court may reconsider any pretrial matter under this subparagraph (A) where it has been shown that the magistrate's order is clearly erroneous or contrary to law.

(B) a judge may also designate a magistrate to conduct hearings, including evidentiary hearings, and to submit to a judge of the court proposed findings of fact and recommendations for the disposition, by a judge of the court, of any motion excepted in subparagraph (A), of applications for post-trial relief made by individuals convicted of criminal offenses and of prisoner petitions challenging conditions of confinement.

(C) the magistrate shall file his proposed findings and recommendations under subparagraph (B) with the court and a copy shall forthwith be mailed to all parties.

Within ten days after being served with a copy, any party may serve and file written objections to such proposed findings and recommendations as provided by rules of court. A judge of the court shall make a de novo determination of those portions of the report or specified proposed findings or recommendations to which objection is made. A judge of the court may accept, reject, or modify, in whole or in part, the findings or recommendations made by the magistrate. The judge may also receive further evidence or recommit the matter to the magistrate with instructions.

(2) A judge may designate a magistrate to serve as a special master pursuant to the applicable provisions of this title and the Federal Rules of Civil Procedure for the United States district courts. A judge may designate a magistrate to serve as a special master in any civil case, upon consent of the parties, without regard to the provisions of rule 53(b) of the Federal Rules of Civil Procedure for the United States district courts.

(3) A magistrate may be assigned such additional duties as are not inconsistent with the Constitution and laws of the United States.

(4) Each district court shall establish rules pursuant to which the magistrates shall discharge their duties.

(c) Notwithstanding any provision of law to the contrary —

(1) Upon the consent of the parties, a full-time United States magistrate or a part-time United States magistrate who serves as a full-time judicial officer may conduct any or all proceedings in a jury or nonjury civil matter and order the entry of judgment in the case, when specially designated to exercise such jurisdiction by the district court or courts he serves. Upon the consent of the parties, pursuant to their specific written request, any other part-time magistrate may exercise such jurisdiction, if such magistrate meets the bar membership requirements set forth in section 631(b)(1) and the chief judge of the district court certifies that a full-time magistrate is not reasonably available in accordance with guidelines established by the judicial council of the circuit. When there is more than one judge of a district court, designation under this paragraph shall be by the concurrence of a majority of all the judges of such district court, and when there is no such concurrence, then by the chief judge.

(2) If a magistrate is designated to exercise civil jurisdiction under paragraph (1) of this subsection, the clerk of court shall, at the time the action is filed, notify the parties of the availability of a magistrate to exercise such jurisdiction. The decision of the parties shall be communicated to the clerk

of court. Thereafter, either the district court judge or the magistrate may again advise the parties of the availability of the magistrate, but in so doing, shall also advise the parties that they are free to withhold consent without adverse substantive consequences. Rules of court for the reference of civil matters to magistrates shall include procedures to protect the voluntariness of the parties' consent.

(3) Upon entry of judgment in any case referred under paragraph (1) of this subsection, an aggrieved party may appeal directly to the appropriate United States court of appeals from the judgment of the magistrate in the same manner as an appeal from any other judgment of a district court. The consent of the parties allows a magistrate designated to exercise civil jurisdiction under paragraph (1) of this subsection to direct the entry of a judgment of the district court in accordance with the Federal Rules of Civil Procedure. Nothing in this paragraph shall be construed as a limitation of any party's right to seek review by the Supreme Court of the United States.

(4) The court may, for good cause shown on its own motion, or under extraordinary circumstances shown by any party, vacate a reference of a civil matter to a magistrate under this subsection.

(5) The magistrate shall, subject to guidelines of the Judicial Conference, determine whether the record taken pursuant to this section shall be taken by electronic sound recording, by a court reporter, or by other means.

(d) The practice and procedure for the trial of cases before officers serving under this chapter shall conform to rules promulgated by the Supreme Court pursuant to section 2072 of this title.

(e) Contempt Authority.

(1) In General. A United States magistrate judge serving under this chapter shall have within the territorial jurisdiction prescribed by the appointment of such magistrate judge the power to exercise contempt authority as set forth in this subsection.

(2) Summary Criminal Contempt Authority. A magistrate judge shall have the power to punish summarily by fine or imprisonment such contempt of the authority of such magistrate judge constituting misbehavior of any person in the magistrate judge's presence so as to obstruct the administration of justice. The order of contempt shall be issued under the Federal Rules of Criminal Procedure.

(3) Additional Criminal Contempt Authority in Civil Consent and Misdemeanor Cases. In any case in which a United States magistrate judge presides with the consent of the parties under subsection (c) of this section, and in any misdemeanor case proceeding before a magistrate judge under section 3401 of title 18, the magistrate judge shall have the power to punish, by fine or imprisonment, criminal contempt constituting disobedience or resistance to the magistrate judge's lawful writ, process, order, rule, decree, or command. Disposition of such contempt shall be conducted upon notice and hearing under the Federal Rules of Criminal Procedure.

(4) Civil Contempt Authority in Civil Consent and Misdemeanor Cases. In any case in which a United States magistrate judge presides with the consent of the parties under subsection (c) of this section, and in any misdemeanor case proceeding before a magistrate judge under section 3401 of title 18, the magistrate judge may exercise the civil contempt authority of the district court. This paragraph shall not be construed to limit the authority of a magistrate judge to order sanctions under any other statute, the Federal Rules of Civil Procedure, or the Federal Rules of Criminal Procedure.

(5) Criminal Contempt Penalties. The sentence imposed by a magistrate judge for any criminal contempt provided for in paragraphs (2) and (3) shall not exceed the penalties for a Class C misdemeanor as set forth in sections 3581(b)(8) and 3571(b)(6) of title 18.

(6) Certification of Other Contempts to the District Court. Upon the commission of any such act

(A) in any case in which a United States magistrate judge presides with the consent of the parties under subsection (c) of this section, or in any misdemeanor case proceeding before a magistrate judge under section 3401 of title 18, that may, in the opinion of the magistrate judge, constitute a serious criminal contempt punishable by penalties exceeding those set forth in paragraph (5) of this subsection, or

(B) in any other case or proceeding under subsection (a) or (b) of this section, or any other statute, where

(i) the act committed in the magistrate judge's presence may, in the opinion of the magistrate judge, constitute a serious criminal contempt punishable by penalties exceeding those set forth in paragraph (5) of this subsection,

(ii) the act that constitutes a criminal contempt occurs outside the presence of the magistrate judge, or

(iii) the act constitutes a civil contempt, the magistrate judge shall forthwith certify the facts to a district judge and may serve or cause to be served, upon any person whose behavior is brought into question under this paragraph, an order requiring such person to appear before a district judge upon a day certain to show cause why that person should not be adjudged in contempt by reason of the facts so certified. The district judge shall thereupon hear the evidence as to the act or conduct complained of and, if it is such as to warrant punishment, punish such person in the same manner and to the same extent as for a contempt committed before a district judge.

(7) Appeals of Magistrate Judge Contempt Orders. The appeal of an order of contempt under this subsection shall be made to the court of appeals in cases proceeding under subsection (c) of this section. The appeal of any other order of contempt issued under this section shall be made to the district court.

(f) In an emergency and upon the concurrence of the chief judges of the districts involved, a United States magistrate may be temporarily assigned to perform any of the duties specified in subsection (a), (b), or (c) of this section in a judicial district other than the judicial district for which he has been appointed. No magistrate shall perform any of such duties in a district to which he has been temporarily assigned until an order has been issued by the chief judge of such district specifying (1) the emergency by reason of which he has been transferred, (2) the duration of his assignment, and (3) the duties which he is authorized to perform. A magistrate so assigned shall not be entitled to additional compensation but shall be reimbursed for actual and necessary expenses incurred in the performance of his duties in accordance with section 635.

(g) A United States magistrate may perform the verification function required by section 4107 of title 18, United States Code. A magistrate may be assigned by a judge of any United States district court to perform the verification required by section 4108 and the appointment of counsel authorized by section 4109 of title 18, United States Code, and may perform such functions beyond the territorial limits of the United States. A magistrate assigned such functions shall have no authority to perform any other function within the territory of a foreign country.

(h) A United States magistrate who has retired may, upon the consent of the chief judge of the district involved, be recalled to serve as a magistrate in any judicial district by the judicial council of the circuit within which such district is located. Upon recall, a magistrate may receive a salary for such service in accordance with regulations promulgated by the Judicial Conference, subject to the restrictions on the payment of an annuity set forth in section 377 of this title or in subchapter III of chapter 83, and chapter 84, of title 5 which are applicable to such magistrate. The requirements set forth in subsections (a), (b)(3), and (d) of section 631, and paragraph (1) of subsection (b) of such section to the extent such paragraph requires membership of the bar of the location in which an individual is to serve as a magistrate, shall not apply to the recall of a retired magistrate under this subsection or section 375 of this title. Any other requirement set forth in section 631(b) shall apply to the recall of a retired magistrate under this subsection or section 375 of this title unless such retired magistrate met such requirement upon appointment or reappointment as a magistrate under section 631.

Chapter 44. Alternative Dispute Resolution

§651. Authorization of Alternative Dispute Resolution

(a) Definition. For purposes of this chapter, an alternative dispute resolution process includes any process or procedure, other than an adjudication by a presiding judge, in which a neutral third party participates to assist in the resolution of issues in controversy, through processes such as early neutral evaluation, mediation, minitrial, and arbitration as provided in sections 654 through 658.

(b) Authority. Each United States district court shall authorize, by local rule adopted under section 2071(a), the use of alternative dispute resolution processes in all civil actions, including adversary proceedings in bankruptcy, in accordance with this chapter, except that the use of arbitration may be authorized only as provided in section 654. Each United States district court shall devise and implement its own alternative dispute resolution program, by local rule adopted under section 2071(a), to encourage and promote the use of alternative dispute resolution in its district.

(c) Existing alternative dispute resolution programs. In those courts where an alternative dispute resolution program is in place on the date of the enactment of the Alternative Dispute Resolution Act of 1998, the court shall examine the effectiveness of that program and adopt such improvements to the program as are consistent with the provisions and purposes of this chapter.

(d) Administration of alternate dispute resolution programs. Each United States district court shall designate an employee, or a judicial officer, who is knowledgeable in alternative dispute resolution practices and processes to implement, administer, oversee, and evaluate the court's alternative dispute resolution program. Such person may also be responsible for recruiting, screening, and training attorneys to serve as neutrals and arbitrators in the court's alternative dispute resolution program. . . .

§652. Jurisdiction

(a) Consideration of alternative dispute resolution in appropriate cases. Notwithstanding any provision of law to the contrary and except as provided in subsections (b) and (c), each district court shall, by local rule adopted under section 2071(a), require that litigants in all civil cases consider the use of an alternative dispute resolution process at an appropriate stage in the litigation. Each district court shall provide litigants in all civil cases with at least one alternative dispute resolution process, including, but not limited to, mediation, early neutral evaluation, minitrial, and arbitration as authorized in sections 654 through 658. Any district court that elects to require the use of alternative dispute resolution in certain cases may do so only with respect to mediation, early neutral evaluation, and, if the parties consent, arbitration.

(b) Actions exempted from consideration of alternative dispute resolution. Each district court may exempt from the requirements of this section specific cases or categories of cases in which use of alternative dispute resolution would not be appropriate. In defining these exemptions, each district court shall consult with members of the bar, including the United States Attorney for that district.

(c) Authority of the Attorney General. Nothing in this section shall alter or conflict with the authority of the Attorney General to conduct litigation on behalf of the United States, with the authority of any Federal agency authorized to conduct litigation in the United States courts, or with any delegation of litigation authority by the Attorney General.

(d) Confidentiality provisions. Until such time as rules are adopted under chapter 131 of this title providing for the confidentiality of alternative dispute resolution processes under this chapter, each district court shall, by local rule adopted under section 2071(a), provide for the confidentiality of the alterna tive dispute resolution processes and to prohibit disclosure of confidential dispute resolution communications.

§653. NEUTRALS

(a) Panel of neutrals. Each district court that authorizes the use of alternative dispute resolution processes shall adopt appropriate processes for making neutrals available for use by the parties for each category of process offered. Each district court shall promulgate its own procedures and criteria for the selection of neutrals on its panels.

(b) Qualifications and training. Each person serving as a neutral in an alternative dispute resolution process should be qualified and trained to serve as a neutral in the appropriate alternative dispute resolution process. For this purpose, the district court may use, among others, magistrate judges who have been trained to serve as neutrals in alternative dispute resolution processes, professional neutrals from the private sector, and persons who have been trained to serve as neutrals in alternative dispute resolution processes. Until such time as rules are adopted under chapter 131 of this title relating to the disqualification of neutrals, each district court shall issue rules under section 2071(a) relating to the disqualification of neutrals (including, where appropriate, disqualification under section 455 of this title, other applicable law, and professional responsibility standards).

§654. ARBITRATION

(a) Referral of actions to arbitration. Notwithstanding any provision of law to the contrary and except as provided in subsections (a), (b), and (c) of section 652 and subsection (d) of this section, a district court may allow the referral to arbitration of any civil action (including any adversary proceeding in bankruptcy) pending before it when the parties consent, except that referral to arbitration may not be made where —

(1) the action is based on an alleged violation of a right secured by the Constitution of the United States;

(2) jurisdiction is based in whole or in part on section 1343 of this title; or

(3) the relief sought consists of money damages in an amount greater than $150,000.

(b) Safeguards in consent cases. Until such time as rules are adopted under chapter 131 of this title relating to procedures described in this subsection, the district court shall, by local rule adopted under section 2071(a), establish procedures to ensure that any civil action in which arbitration by consent is allowed under subsection (a) —

(1) consent to arbitration is freely and knowingly obtained; and

(2) no party or attorney is prejudiced for refusing to participate in arbitration.

(c) Presumptions. For purposes of subsection (a)(3), a district court may presume damages are not in excess of $150,000 unless counsel certifies that damages exceed such amount.

(d) Existing Programs. Nothing in this chapter is deemed to affect any program in which arbitration is conducted pursuant to section title IX of the Judicial Improvements and Access to Justice Act (Public Law 100 — 702), as amended by section 1 of Public Law 105-53.

§655. Arbitrators

(a) Powers of arbitrators. An arbitrator to whom an action is referred under section 654 shall have the power, within the judicial district of the district court which referred the action to arbitration —

(1) to conduct arbitration hearings;

(2) to administer oaths and affirmations; and

(3) to make awards.

(b) Standards for certification. Each district court that authorizes arbitration shall establish standards for the certification of arbitrators and shall certify arbitrators to perform services in accordance with such standards and this chapter. The standards shall include provisions requiring that any arbitrator —

(1) shall take the oath or affirmation described in section 453; and

(2) shall be subject to the disqualification rules under section 455.

(c) Immunity. All individuals serving as arbitrators in an alternative dispute resolution program under this chapter are performing quasi-judicial functions and are entitled to the immunities and protections that the law accords to persons serving in such capacity.

§656. Subpoenas

Rule 45 of the Federal Rules of Civil Procedure (relating to subpoenas) applies to subpoenas for the attendance of witnesses and the production of documentary evidence at an arbitration hearing under this chapter.

§657. Arbitration award and judgment

(a) Filing and effect of arbitration award. An arbitration award made by an arbitrator under this chapter, along with proof of service of such award on the other party by the prevailing party or by the plaintiff, shall be filed promptly after the arbitration hearing is concluded with the clerk of the district court that referred the case to arbitration. Such award shall be entered as the judgment of the court after the time has expired for requesting a trial de novo. The judgment so entered shall be subject to the same provisions of law and shall have the same force and effect as a judgment of the court in a civil action, except that the judgment shall not be subject to review in any other court by appeal or otherwise.

(b) Sealing of arbitration award. The district court shall provide, by local rule adopted under section 2071(a), that the contents of any arbitration award made under this chapter shall not be made known to any judge who might be assigned to the case until the district court has entered final judgment in the action or the action has otherwise terminated.

(c) Trial de novo of arbitration awards.

(1) Time for filing demand. Within 30 days after the filing of an arbitration award with a district court under subsection (a), any party may file a written demand for a trial de novo in the district court.

(2) Action restored to court docket. Upon a demand for a trial de novo, the action shall be restored to the docket of the court and treated for all purposes as if it had not been referred to arbitration.

(3) Exclusion of evidence of arbitration. The court shall not admit at the trial de novo any evidence that there has been an arbitration proceeding, the nature or amount of any award, or any other matter concerning the conduct of the arbitration proceeding, unless —

(A) the evidence would otherwise be admissible in the court under the Federal Rules of Evidence; or

(B) the parties have otherwise stipulated.

Part IV. Jurisdiction and Venue

Chapter 81. Supreme Court

§1251. Original jurisdiction

(a) The Supreme Court shall have original and exclusive jurisdiction of all controversies between two or more States.

(b) The Supreme Court shall have original but not exclusive jurisdiction of:

(1) All actions or proceedings to which ambassadors, other public ministers, consuls, or vice consuls of foreign states are parties;

(2) All controversies between the United States and a State;

(3) All actions or proceedings by a State against the citizens of another State or against aliens.

§1252. [Repealed.]

§1253. Direct appeals from decisions of three-judge courts

Except as otherwise provided by law, any party may appeal to the Supreme Court from an order granting or denying, after notice and hearing, an interlocutory or permanent injunction in any civil action, suit or proceeding required by any Act of Congress to be heard and determined by a district court of three judges.

§1254. Courts of appeals; certiorari; certified questions

Cases in the courts of appeals may be reviewed by the Supreme Court by the following methods:

(1) By writ of certiorari granted upon the petition of any party to any civil or criminal case, before or after rendition of judgment or decree;

(2) By certification at any time by a court of appeals of any question of law in any civil or criminal case as to which instructions are desired, and upon such certification the Supreme Court may give binding instructions or require the entire record to be sent up for decision of the entire matter in controversy.

§1257. State courts; certiorari

(a) Final judgments or decrees rendered by the highest court of a State in which a decision could be had, may be reviewed by the Supreme Court by writ of certiorari where the validity of a treaty or statute of the United States is drawn in question or where the validity of a statute of any State is drawn in question on the ground of its being repugnant to the Constitution, treaties, or laws of the United States, or where any title, right, privilege, or immunity is specially set up or claimed under the Constitution or the treaties or statutes of, or any commission held or authority exercised under, the United States.

(b) For the purposes of this section, the term "highest court of a State" includes the District of Columbia Court of Appeals.

§1258. Supreme court of Puerto Rico; appeal; certiorari

Final judgments or decrees rendered by the Supreme Court of the Commonwealth of Puerto Rico may be reviewed by the Supreme Court by writ of certiorari where the validity of a treaty or statute of the United States is drawn in question or where the validity of a statute of the Commonwealth of Puerto Rico is drawn in question on the ground of its being repugnant to the Constitution, treaties, or laws of the United States, or where any title, right, privilege, or immunity is specially set up or claimed under the Constitution or the treaties or statutes of, or any commission held or authority exercised under, the United States.

Chapter 83. Court of Appeals

§1291. FINAL DECISIONS OF DISTRICT COURTS

The courts of appeals (other than the United States Court of Appeals for the Federal Circuit) shall have jurisdiction of appeals from all final decisions of the district courts of the United States, the United States District Court for the District of the Canal Zone, the District Court of Guam, and the District Court of the Virgin Islands, except where a direct review may be had in the Supreme Court. The jurisdiction of the United States Court of Appeals for the Federal Circuit shall be limited to the jurisdiction described in sections 1292(c) and (d) and 1295 of this title.

§1292. INTERLOCUTORY DECISIONS

(a) Except as provided in subsections (c) and (d) of this section, the courts of appeals shall have jurisdiction of appeals from:

(1) Interlocutory orders of the district courts of the United States, the United States District Court for the District of the Canal Zone, the District Court of Guam, and the District Court of the Virgin Islands, or of the judges thereof, granting, continuing, modifying, refusing or dissolving injunctions, or refusing to dissolve or modify injunctions, except where a direct review may be had in the Supreme Court;

(2) Interlocutory orders appointing receivers, or refusing orders o wind up receiverships or to take steps to accomplish the purposes thereof, such as directing sales or other disposals of property;

(3) Interlocutory decrees of such district courts or the judges thereof determining the rights and liabilities of the parties to admiralty cases in which appeals from final decrees are allowed.

(b) When a district judge, in making in a civil action an order not otherwise appealable under this section, shall be of the opinion that such order involves a controlling question of law as to which there is substantial ground for difference of opinion and that an immediate appeal from the order may materially advance the ultimate termination of the litigation, he shall so state in writing in such order. The Court of Appeals which would have jurisdiction of an appeal of such action may thereupon, in its discretion, permit an appeal to be taken from such order, if application is made to it within ten days after the entry of the order: Provided, however, That application for an appeal hereunder shall not stay proceedings in the district court unless the district judge or the Court of Appeals or a judge thereof shall so order.

(c) The United States Court of Appeals for the Federal Circuit shall have exclusive jurisdiction —

(1) of an appeal from an interlocutory order or decree described in subsection (a) or (b) of this section in any case over which the court would have jurisdiction of an appeal under section 1295 of this title; and

(2) of an appeal from a judgment in a civil action for patent infringement which would otherwise be appealable to the United States Court of Appeals for the Federal Circuit and is final except for an accounting.

(d)(1) When the chief judge of the Court of International Trade issues an order under the provisions of section 256(b) of this title, or when any judge of the Court of International Trade, in issuing any other interlocutory order, includes in the order a statement that a controlling question of law is involved with respect to which there is a substantial ground for difference of opinion and that an immediate appeal from that order may materially advance the ultimate termination of the litigation, the United States Court of Appeals for the Federal Circuit may, in its discretion, permit an appeal to be taken from such order, if application is made to that Court within ten days after the entry of such order.

(2) When the chief judge of the United States Court of Federal Claims issues an order under section 798(b) of this title, or when any judge of the United States Court of Federal Claims, in issuing an interlocutory order, includes in the order a statement that a controlling question of law is involved with respect to which there is a substantial ground for difference of opinion and that an immediate appeal from that order may materially advance the ultimate termination of the litigation, the United States Court of Appeals for the Federal Circuit may, in its discretion, permit an appeal to be taken from such order, if application is made to that Court within ten days after the entry of such order.

(3) Neither the application for nor the granting of an appeal under this subsection shall stay proceedings in the Court of International Trade or in the Claims Court [Court of Federal Claims], as the case may be, unless a stay is ordered by a judge of the Court of International Trade or of the Claims Court [Court of Federal Claims] or by the United States Court of Appeals for the Federal Circuit or a judge of that court.

(4)(A) The United States Court of Appeals for the Federal Circuit shall have exclusive jurisdiction of an appeal from an interlocutory order of a district court of the United States, the District Court of Guam, the District Court of the Virgin Islands, or the District Court for the Northern Mariana Islands, granting or denying, in whole or in part, a motion to transfer an action to the United States Claims Court under section 1631 of this title.

(B) When a motion to transfer an action to the Claims Court [Court of Federal Claims] is filed in a district court, no further proceedings shall be taken in the district court until 60 days after the court has ruled upon the motion. If an appeal is taken from the district court's grant or denial of the motion, proceedings shall be further stayed until the appeal has been decided by the Court of Appeals for the Federal Circuit. The stay of proceedings in the district court shall not bar the granting of preliminary or injunctive relief, where appropriate and where expedition is reasonably necessary. However, during the period in which proceedings are stayed as provided in this subparagraph, no transfer to the Claims Court [Court of Federal Claims] pursuant to the motion shall be carried out.

(e) The Supreme Court may prescribe rules, in accordance with section 2072 of this title, to provide for an appeal of an interlocutory decision to the courts of appeals that is not otherwise provided for under subsection (a), (b), (c), or (d).

§1294. Circuits in which decisions reviewable

Except as provided in sections 1292(c), 1292(d), and 1295 of this title, appeals from reviewable decisions of the district and territorial courts shall be taken to the courts of appeals as follows:

(1) From a district court of the United States to the court of appeals for the circuit embracing the district;

(2) From the United States District Court for the District of the Canal Zone, to the Court of Appeals for the Fifth Circuit;

(3) From the District Court of the Virgin Islands, to the Court of Appeals for the Third Circuit;

(4) From the District Court of Guam, to the Court of Appeals for the Ninth Circuit.

§1295. Jurisdiction of the United States Court of Appeals for the Federal Circuit

(a) The United States Court of Appeals for the Federal Circuit shall have exclusive jurisdiction —

(1) of an appeal from a final decision of a district court of the United States, the United States District Court for the District of the Canal Zone, the District Court of Guam, the District Court of the Virgin Islands, or the District Court for the Northern Mariana Islands, if the jurisdiction of that court was based, in whole or in part, on section 1338 of this title, except that a case involving a claim arising under any Act of Congress relating to copyrights, exclusive rights in mask works, or trademarks and no other claims under section 1338(a) shall be governed by sections 1291, 1292, and 1294 of this title;

(2) of an appeal from a final decision of a district court of the United States, the United States District Court for the District of the Canal Zone, the District Court of Guam, the District Court of the Virgin Islands, or the District Court for the Northern Mariana Islands, if the jurisdiction of that court was based, in whole or in part, on section 1346 of this title, except that jurisdiction of an appeal in a case brought in a district court under section 1346(a)(1), 1346(b), 1346(e), or 1346(f) of this title or under section 1346(a)(2) when the claim is founded upon an Act of Congress or a regulation of an executive department providing for internal revenue shall be governed by sections 1291, 1292, and 1294 of this title;

(3) of an appeal from a final decision of the Claims Court [United States Court of Federal Claims];

(4) of an appeal from a decision of —

(A) the Board of Patent Appeals and Interferences of the United States Patent and Trademark Office with respect to patent applications and interferences, at the instance of an applicant for a patent or any party to a patent interference, and any such appeal shall waive the right of such applicant or party to proceed under section 145 or 146 of title 35;

(B) the Under Secretary of Commerce for Intellectual Property and Director of the United States Patent and Trademark Office or the Trademark Trial and Appeal Board with respect to applications for registration of marks and other proceedings as provided in section 21 of the Trademark Act of 1946 (15 U.S.C. 1071); or

(C) a district court to which a case was directed pursuant to section 145, 146, or 154(b) of title 35;

(5) of an appeal from a final decision of the United States Court of International Trade;

(6) to review the final determinations of the United States International Trade Commission relating to unfair practices in import trade, made under section 337 of the Tariff Act of 1930 (19 U.S.C. 1337);

(7) to review, by appeal on questions of law only, findings of the Secretary of Commerce under general note 2 of the Harmonized Tariff Schedule of the United States (relating to importation of instruments or apparatus);

(8) of an appeal under section 71 of the Plant Variety Protection Act (7 U.S.C. 2461);

(9) of an appeal from a final order or final decision of the Merit Systems Protection Board, pursuant to sections 7703(b)(1) and 7703(d) of title 5;

(10) of an appeal from a final decision of an agency board of contract appeals pursuant to section 8(g)(1) of the Contract Disputes Act of 1978 (41 U.S.C. 607(g)(1));

(11) of an appeal under section 211 of the Economic Stabilization Act of 1970;

(12) of an appeal under section 5 of the Emergency Petroleum Allocation Act of 1973;

(13) of an appeal under section 506(c) of the Natural Gas Policy Act of 1978; and

(14) of an appeal under section 523 of the Energy Policy and Conservation Act.

(b) The head of any executive department or agency may, with the approval of the Attorney General, refer to the Court of Appeals for the Federal Circuit for judicial review any final decision rendered by a board of contract appeals pursuant to the terms of any contract with the United States awarded by that department or agency which the head of such department or agency has concluded is not entitled to finality pursuant to the review standards specified in section 10(b) of the Contract Disputes Act of 1978 (41 U.S.C. 609(b)). The head of each executive department or agency shall make any referral under this section within one hundred and twenty days after the receipt of a copy of the final appeal decision.

(c) The Court of Appeals for the Federal Circuit shall review the matter referred in accordance with the standards specified in section 10(b) of the Contract Disputes Act of 1978. The court shall proceed with judicial review on the administrative record made before the board of contract appeals on matters so referred as in other cases pending in such court, shall determine the issue of finality of the appeal decision, and shall, if appropriate, render judgment thereon, or remand the matter to any administrative or executive body or official with such direction as it may deem proper and just.

§1296. REVIEW OF CERTAIN AGENCY ACTIONS

(a) Jurisdiction. Subject to the provisions of chapter 179, the United States Court of Appeals for the Federal Circuit shall have jurisdiction over a petition for review of a final decision under chapter 5 of title 3 of —

(1) an appropriate agency (as determined under section 454 of title 3);

(2) the Federal Labor Relations Authority made under part D of subchapter II of chapter 5 of title 3, notwithstanding section 7123 of title 5; or

(3) the Secretary of Labor or the Occupational Safety and Health Review Commission, made under part C of subchapter II of chapter 5 of title 3.

(b) Filing of petition. Any petition for review under this section must be filed within 30 days after the date the petitioner receives notice of the final decision.

Chapter 85. District Courts; Jurisdiction

§1331. FEDERAL QUESTION; AMOUNT IN CONTROVERSY; COSTS

The district courts shall have original jurisdiction of all civil actions arising under the Constitution, laws, or treaties of the United States.

§1332. DIVERSITY OF CITIZENSHIP; AMOUNT IN CONTROVERSY; COSTS

(a) The district courts shall have original jurisdiction of all civil actions where the matter in controversy exceeds the sum or value of $75,000, exclusive of interest and costs, and is between —

(1) citizens of different States;

(2) citizens of a State, and citizens and subjects of a foreign state;

(3) citizens of different States and in which foreign states or citizens or subjects thereof are additional parties;

(4) a foreign state, defined in section 1603(a) of this title, as plaintiff and citizens of a State or of different States.

For the purposes of this section, section 1335, and section 1441, an alien admitted to the United States for permanent residence shall be deemed a citizen of the State in which such alien is domiciled.

(b) Except when express provision therefor is otherwise made in a statute of the United States, where the plaintiff who files the case originally in the Federal courts is finally adjudged to be entitled to recover less than the sum or value of $75,000, computed without regard to any setoff or counterclaim to which the defendant may be adjudged to be entitled, and exclusive of interest and costs, the district court may deny costs to the plaintiff and, in addition, may impose costs on the plaintiff.

(c) For the purposes of this section and section 1441 of this title —

(1) a corporation shall be deemed to be a citizen of any State by which it has been incorporated and of the State where it has its principal place of business, except that in any direct action against the insurer of a policy or contract of liability insurance, whether incorporated or unincorporated, to which action the insured is not joined as a party-defendant, such insurer shall be deemed a citizen of the State of which the insured is a citizen, as well as of any State by which the insurer has been incorporated and of the State where it has its principal place of business; and

(2) the legal representative of the estate of a decedent shall be deemed to be a citizen only of the same State as the decedent, and the legal representative of an infant or incompetent shall be a citizen only of the same State as the infant or incompetent.

(d) The word "States," as used in this section, includes the Territories, the District of Columbia, and the Commonwealth of Puerto Rico.

§1333. ADMIRALTY, MARITIME AND PRIZE CASES

The district courts shall have original jurisdiction, exclusive of the courts of the States, of:

(1) Any civil case of admiralty or maritime jurisdiction, saving to suitors in all cases all other remedies to which they are otherwise entitled.

(2) Any prize brought into the United States and all proceedings for the condemnation of property taken as prize.

§1334. BANKRUPTCY CASES AND PROCEEDINGS

(a) Except as provided in subsection (b) of this section, the district court shall have original and exclusive jurisdiction of all cases under title 11.

(b) Notwithstanding any Act of Congress that confers exclusive jurisdiction on a court or courts other than the district courts, the district courts shall have original but not exclusive jurisdiction of all civil proceedings arising under title 11, or arising in or related to cases under title 11.

(c)(1) Nothing in this section prevents a district court in the interest of justice, or in the interest of comity with State courts or respect for State law, from abstaining from hearing a particular proceeding arising under title 11 or arising in or related to a case under title 11.

(2) Upon timely motion of a party in a proceeding based upon a State law claim or State law cause of action, related to a case under title 11 but not arising under title 11 or arising in a case under title 11, with respect to which an action could not have been commenced in a court of the United States absent jurisdiction under this section, the district court shall abstain from hearing such proceeding if an action is commenced, and can be timely adjudicated, in a State forum of appropriate jurisdiction.

(d) Any decision to abstain or not to abstain made under this subsection (other than a decision not to abstain in a proceeding described in subsection (c)(2)) is not reviewable by appeal or otherwise by the court of appeals under section 158(d), 1291, or 1292 of this title or by the Supreme Court of the United States under section 1254 of this title. This subsection shall not be construed to limit the applicability of the stay provided for by section 362 of title 11, United States Code, as such section applies to an action affecting the property of the estate in bankruptcy.

(e) The district court in which a case under title 11 is commenced or is pending shall have exclusive jurisdiction of all of the property, wherever located, of the debtor as of the commencement of such case, and of property of the estate.

§1335. Interpleader

(a) The district courts shall have original jurisdiction of any civil action of interpleader or in the nature of interpleader filed by any person, firm, or corporation, association, or society having in his or its custody or possession money or property of the value of $500 or more, or having issued a note, bond, certificate, policy of insurance, or other instrument of value or amount of $500 or more, or providing for the delivery or payment or the loan of money or property of such amount or value, or being under any obligation written or unwritten to the amount of $500 or more, if

(1) Two or more adverse claimants, of diverse citizenship as defined in section 1332 of this title, are claiming or may claim to be entitled to such money or property, or to any one or more of the benefits arising by virtue of any note, bond, certificate, policy or other instrument, or arising by virtue of any such obligation; and if

(2) the plaintiff has deposited such money or property or has paid the amount of or the loan or other value of such instrument or the amount due under such obligation into the registry of the court, there to abide the judgment of the court, or has given bond payable to the clerk of the court in such amount and with

such surety as the court or judge may deem proper, conditioned upon the compliance by the plaintiff with the future order or judgment of the court with respect to the subject matter of the controversy.

(b) Such an action may be entertained although the titles or claims of the conflicting claimants do not have a common origin, or are not identical, but are adverse to and independent of one another.

[See also §§1397 and 2361.]

§1337. COMMERCE AND ANTITRUST REGULATIONS; AMOUNT IN CONTROVERSY, COSTS

(a) The district courts shall have original jurisdiction of any civil action or proceeding arising under any Act of Congress regulating commerce or protecting trade and commerce against restraints and monopolies: *Provided, however,* That the district courts shall have original jurisdiction of an action brought under section 11706 or 14706 of title 49, only if the matter in controversy for each receipt or bill of lading exceeds $10,000, exclusive of interest and costs.

(b) Except when express provision therefor is otherwise made in a statute of the United States, where a plaintiff who files the case under section 11706 or 14706 of title 49, originally in the Federal courts is finally adjudged to be entitled to recover less than the sum or value of $10,000, computed without regard to any setoff or counterclaim to which the defendant may be adjudged to be entitled, and exclusive of any interest and costs, the district court may deny costs to the plaintiff and, in addition, may impose costs on the plaintiff.

(c) The district courts shall not have jurisdiction under this section of any matter within the exclusive jurisdiction of the Court of International Trade under chapter 95 of this title.

§1338. PATENTS, PLANT VARIETY PROTECTION, COPYRIGHTS, MASK WORKS, DESIGNS, TRADEMARKS AND UNFAIR COMPETITION

(a) The district courts shall have original jurisdiction of any civil action arising under any Act of Congress relating to patents, plant variety protection, copyrights and trademarks. Such jurisdiction shall be exclusive of the courts of the states in patent, plant variety protection and copyright cases.

(b) The district courts shall have original jurisdiction of any civil action asserting a claim of unfair competition when joined with a substantial and related claim under the copyright, patent, plant variety protection, or trademark laws.

(c) Subsections (a) and (b) apply to exclusive rights in mask works under chapter 9 of title 17, and to exclusive rights in designs under chapter 13 of title 17, to the same extent as such subsections apply to copyrights.

§1339. POSTAL MATTERS

The district courts shall have original jurisdiction of any civil action arising under any Act of Congress relating to the postal service.

§1340. Internal revenue; customs duties

The district courts shall have original jurisdiction of any civil action arising under any Act of Congress providing for internal revenue, or revenue from imports or tonnage except matters within the jurisdiction of the Court of International Trade.

§1341. Taxes by States

The district courts shall not enjoin, suspend or restrain the assessment, levy or collection of any tax under State law where a plain, speedy and efficient remedy may be had in the courts of such State.

§1342. Rate orders of State agencies

The district courts shall not enjoin, suspend or restrain the operation of, or compliance with, any order affecting rates chargeable by a public utility and made by a State administrative agency or a rate-making body of a State political subdivision, where:

(1) Jurisdiction is based solely on diversity of citizenship or repugnance of the order to the Federal Constitution; and,

(2) The order does not interfere with interstate commerce; and,

(3) The order has been made after reasonable notice and hearing; and,

(4) A plain, speedy and efficient remedy may be had in the courts of such State.

§1343. Civil rights and elective franchise

(a) The district courts shall have original jurisdiction of any civil action authorized by law to be commenced by any person:

(1) To recover damages for injury to his person or property, or because of the deprivation of any right or privilege of a citizen of the United States, by any act done in furtherance of any conspiracy mentioned in section 1985 of Title 42;

(2) To recover damages from any person who fails to prevent or to aid in preventing any wrongs mentioned in section 1985 of Title 42 which he had knowledge were about to occur and power to prevent;

(3) To redress the deprivation, under color of any State law, statute, ordinance, regulation, custom or usage, of any right, privilege or immunity secured by the Constitution of the United States or by any Act of Congress providing for equal rights of citizens or of all persons within the jurisdiction of the United States;

(4) To recover damages or to secure equitable or other relief under any

Act of Congress providing for the protection of civil rights, including the right to vote.

(b) For purposes of this section —

(1) The District of Columbia shall be considered to be a State; and,

(2) Any Act of Congress applicable exclusively to the District of Columbia shall be considered to be a statute of the District of Columbia.

§1344. Election disputes

The district courts shall have original jurisdiction of any civil action to recover possession of any office, except that of elector of President or Vice President, United States Senator, Representative in or delegate to Congress, or member of a state legislature, authorized by law to be commenced, wherein it appears that the sole question touching the title to office arises out of denial of the right to vote, to any citizen offering to vote, on account of race, color or previous condition of servitude.

The jurisdiction under this section shall extend only so far as to determine the rights of the parties to office by reason of the denial of the right, guaranteed by the Constitution of the United States and secured by any law, to enforce the right of citizens of the United States to vote in all the States.

§1345. United States as plaintiff

Except as otherwise provided by Act of Congress, the district courts shall have original jurisdiction of all civil actions, suits or proceedings commended by the United States, or by any agency or officer thereof expressly authorized to sue by Act of Congress.

§1346. United States as defendant

(a) The district courts shall have original jurisdiction, concurrent with the United States Claims Court, of:

(1) Any civil action against the United States for the recovery of any internal-revenue tax alleged to have been erroneously or illegally assessed or collected, or any penalty claimed to have been collected without authority or any sum alleged to have been excessive or in any manner wrongfully collected under the internal-revenue laws;

(2) Any other civil action or claim against the United States, not exceeding $10,000 in amount, founded either upon the Constitution, or any Act of Congress, or any regulation of an executive department, or upon any express or implied contract with the United States, or for liquidated or unliquidated damages in cases not sounding in tort, except that the district courts shall not have jurisdiction of any civil action or claim against the United States founded upon any express or implied contract with the United States or for liquidated

or unliquidated damages in cases not sounding in tort which are subject to sections 8(g)(1) and 10(a)(1) of the Contract Disputes Act of 1978. For the purpose of this paragraph, and express or implied contract with the Army and Air Force Exchange Service, Navy Exchanges, Marine Corps Exchanges, Coast Guard Exchanges, or Exchange Councils of the National Aeronautics and Space Administration shall be considered an express or implied contract with the United States.

(b)(1) Subject to the provisions of chapter 171 of this title, the district courts, together with the United States District Court for the District of the Canal Zone and the District Court of the Virgin Islands, shall have exclusive jurisdiction of civil actions on claims against the United States, for money damages, accruing on and after January 1, 1945, for injury or loss of property, or personal injury or death caused by the negligent or wrongful act or omission of any employee of the Government while acting within the scope of his office or employment, under circumstances where the United States, if a private person, would be liable to the claimant in accordance with the law of the place where the act or omission occurred.

(2) No person convicted of a felony who is incarcerated while awaiting sentencing or while serving a sentence may bring a civil action against the United States or an agency, officer, or employee of the Government, for mental or emotional injury suffered while in custody without a prior showing of physical injury.

(c) The jurisdiction conferred by this section includes jurisdiction of any set-off, counterclaim, or other claim or demand whatever on the part of the United States against any plaintiff commencing an action under this section.

(d) The district courts shall not have jurisdiction under this section of any civil action or claim for a pension.

(e) The district courts shall have original jurisdiction of any civil action against the United States provided in sections 6226, 6228(a), 7426, or 7428 (in the case of the United States district court for the District of Columbia) or section 7429 of the Internal Revenue Code of 1954.

(f) The district courts shall have exclusive original jurisdiction of civil actions under section 2409a to quiet title to an estate or interest in real property in which an interest is claimed by the United States.

(g) Subject to the provisions of chapter 179, the district courts of the United States shall have exclusive jurisdiction over any civil action commenced under section 453(2) of title 3, by a covered employee under chapter 5 of such title.

§1355. Fine, penalty or forfeiture

(a) The district courts shall have original jurisdiction, exclusive of the courts of the States, of any action or proceeding for the recovery or enforcement of any fine, penalty, or forfeiture, pecuniary or otherwise, incurred under any Act of

Congress, except matters within the jurisdiction of the Court of International Trade under section 1582 of this title.

(b)(1) A forfeiture action or proceeding may be brought in —

(A) the district court for the district in which any of the acts or omissions giving rise to the forfeiture occurred, or

(B) any other district where venue for the forfeiture action or proceeding is specifically provided for in section 1395 of this title or any other statute.

(2) Whenever property subject to forfeiture under the laws of the United States is located in a foreign country, or has been detained or seized pursuant to legal process or competent authority of a foreign government, an action or proceeding for forfeiture may be brought as provided in paragraph (1), or in the United States District court or the District of Columbia.

(c) In any case in which a final order disposing of property in a civil forfeiture action or proceeding is appealed, removal of the property by the prevailing party shall not deprive the court of jurisdiction. Upon motion of the appealing party, the district court or the court of appeals shall issue any order necessary to preserve the right of the appealing party to the full value of the property at issue, including a stay of the judgment of the district court pending appeal or requiring the prevailing party to post an appeal bond.

(d) Any court with jurisdiction over a forfeiture action pursuant to subsection (b) may issue and cause to be served in any other district such process as may be required to bring before the court the property that is the subject of the forfeiture action.

§1359. Parties collusively joined or made

A district court shall not have jurisdiction of a civil action in which any party, by assignment or otherwise, has been improperly or collusively made or joined to invoke the jurisdiction of such court.

§1361. Action to compel an officer of the United States to perform his duty

The district courts shall have original jurisdiction of any action in the nature of mandamus to compel an officer or employee of the United States or any agency thereof to perform a duty owed to the plaintiff.

§1362. Indian tribes

The district courts shall have original jurisdiction of all civil actions, brought by any Indian tribe or band with a governing body duly recognized by the Secretary of the Interior, wherein the matter in controversy arises under the Constitution, laws, or treaties of the United States.

§1364. DIRECT ACTIONS AGAINST INSURERS OF MEMBERS OF DIPLOMATIC MISSIONS AND THEIR FAMILIES

(a) The district courts shall have original and exclusive jurisdiction, without regard to the amount in controversy, of any civil action commenced by any person against an insurer who by contract has insured an individual, who is, or was at the time of the tortious act or omission, a member of a mission (within the meaning of section 2(3) of the Diplomatic Relations Act (22 U.S.C. 254a(3)) or a member of the family of such a member of a mission, or an individual described in section 19 of the Convention on Privileges and Immunities of the United Nations of February 13, 1946, against liability for personal injury, death, or damage to property.

(b) Any direct action brought against an insurer under subsection (a) shall be tried without a jury, but shall not be subject to the defense that the insured is immune from suit, that the insured is an indispensable party, or in the absence of fraud or collusion, that the insured has violated a term of the contract unless the contract was cancelled before the claim arose.

§1367. SUPPLEMENTAL JURISDICTION

(a) Except as provided in subsections (b) and (c) or as expressly provided otherwise by Federal statute, in any civil action of which the district courts have original jurisdiction, the district courts shall have supplemental jurisdiction over all other claims that are so related to claims in the action within such original jurisdiction that they form part of the same case or controversy under Article III of the United States Constitution. Such supplemental jurisdiction shall include claims that involve the joinder or intervention of additional parties.

(b) In any civil action of which the district courts have original jurisdiction founded solely on section 1332 of this title, the district courts shall not have supplemental jurisdiction under subsection (a) over claims by plaintiffs against persons made parties under Rule 14, 19, 20, or 24 of the Federal Rules of Civil Procedure, or over claims by persons proposed to be joined as plaintiffs under Rule 19 of such rules, or seeking to intervene as plaintiffs under Rule 24 of such rules, when exercising supplemental jurisdiction over such claims would be inconsistent with the jurisdictional requirements of section 1332.

(c) The district courts may decline to exercise supplemental jurisdiction over a claim under subsection (a) if —

(1) the claim raises a novel or complex issue of State law,

(2) the claim substantially predominates over the claim or claims over which the district court has original jurisdiction,

(3) the district court has dismissed all claims over which it has original jurisdiction, or

(4) in exceptional circumstances, there are other compelling reasons for declining jurisdiction.

(d) The period of limitations for any claim asserted under subsection (a), and for any other claim in the same action that is voluntarily dismissed at the same time as or after the dismissal of the claim under subsection (a), shall be tolled while the claim is pending and for a period of 30 days after it is dismissed unless State law provides for a longer tolling period.

(e) As used in this section, the term "State" includes the District of Columbia, the Commonwealth of Puerto Rico, and any territory or possession of the United States.

§1369. Multiparty, multiforum jurisdiction

(a) In General.—The district courts shall have original jurisdiction of any civil action involving minimal diversity between adverse parties that arises from a single accident, where at least 75 natural persons have died in the accident at a discrete location, if—

(1) a defendant resides in a State and a substantial part of the accident took place in another State or other location, regardless of whether that defendant is also a resident of the State where a substantial part of the accident took place;

(2) any two defendants reside in different States, regardless of whether such defendants are also residents of the same State or States; or

(3) substantial parts of the accident took place in different States.

(b) Limitation of Jurisdiction of District Courts.—The district court shall abstain from hearing any civil action described in subsection (a) in which—

(1) the substantial majority of all plaintiffs are citizens of a single State of which the primary defendants are also citizens; and

(2) the claims asserted will be governed primarily by the laws of that State.

(c) Special Rules and Definitions.—For purposes of this section—

(1) minimal diversity exists between adverse parties if any party is a citizen of a State and any adverse party is a citizen of another State, a citizen or subject of a foreign state, or a foreign state as defined in section 1603(a) of this title;

(2) a corporation is deemed to be a citizen of any State, and a citizen or subject of any foreign state, in which it is incorporated or has its principal place of business, and is deemed to be a resident of any State in which it is incorporated or licensed to do business or is doing business;

(3)* the term "injury" means—

(A) physical harm to a natural person; and

(B) physical damage to or destruction of tangible property, but only if physical harm described in subparagraph (A) exists;

*[The definitions in subsection 3, carried over from earlier drafts of this statute, do not refer to terms that appear in any enacted legislation. — Ed.]

(4) the term "accident" means a sudden accident, or a natural event culminating in an accident, that results in death incurred at a discrete location by at least 75 natural persons; and

(5) the term "State" includes the District of Columbia, the Commonwealth of Puerto Rico, and any territory or possession of the United States.

(d) Intervening Parties.—In any action in a district court which is or could have been brought, in whole or in part, under this section, any person with a claim arising from the accident described in subsection (a) shall be permitted to intervene as a party plaintiff in the action, even if that person could not have brought an action in a district court as an original matter.

(e) Notification of Judicial Panel on Multidistrict Litigation.—A district court in which an action under this section is pending shall promptly notify the judicial panel on multidistrict litigation of the pendency of the action.

Chapter 87. District Courts; Venue

§1391. Venue generally

(a) A civil action wherein jurisdiction is founded only on diversity of citizenship may, except as otherwise provided by law, be brought only in (1) a judicial district where any defendant resides, if all defendants reside in the same State, (2) a judicial district in which a substantial part of the events or omissions giving rise to the claim occurred, or a substantial part of property that is the subject of the action is situated, or (3) a judicial district in which any defendant is subject to personal jurisdiction at the time the action is commenced, if there is no district in which the action may otherwise be brought.

(b) A civil action wherein jurisdiction is not founded solely on diversity of citizenship may, except as otherwise provided by law, be brought only in (1) a judicial district where any defendant resides, if all defendants reside in the same State, (2) a judicial district in which a substantial part of the events or omissions giving rise to the claim occurred, or a substantial part of property that is the subject of the action is situated, or (3) a judicial district in which any defendant may be found, if there is no district in which the action may otherwise be brought.

(c) For purposes of venue under this chapter, a defendant that is a corporation shall be deemed to reside in any judicial district in which it is subject to personal jurisdiction at the time the action is commenced. In a State which has more than one judicial district and in which a defendant that is a corporation is subject to personal jurisdiction at the time an action is commenced, such corporation shall be deemed to reside in any district in that State within which its contacts would be sufficient to subject it to personal jurisdiction if that district were a separate State, and, if there is no such district, the corporation shall be deemed to reside in the district within which it has the most significant contacts.

(d) An alien may be sued in any district.

(e) A civil action in which a defendant is an officer or employee of the United States or any agency thereof acting in his official capacity or under color of legal authority, or an agency of the United States, or the United States, may, except as otherwise provided by law, be brought in any judicial district in which: (1) a defendant in the action resides, (2) a substantial part of the events or omissions giving rise to the claim occurred, or a substantial part of [the] property that is the subject of the action is situated, or (3) the plaintiff resides if no real property is involved in the action. Additional persons may be joined as parties to any such action in accordance with the Federal Rules of Civil Procedure and with such other venue requirements as would be applicable if the United States or one of its officers, employees, or agencies were not a party.

The summons and complaint in such an action shall be served as provided by the Federal Rules of Civil Procedure except that the delivery of the summons and complaint to the officer or agency as required by the rules may be made by certified mail beyond the territorial limits of the district in which the action is brought.

(f) A civil action against a foreign state as defined in section 1603(a) of this title may be brought —

(1) in any judicial district in which a substantial part of the events or omissions giving rise to the claim occurred, or a substantial part of property that is the subject of the action is situated;

(2) in any judicial district in which the vessel or cargo of a foreign state is situated, if the claim is asserted under section 1605(b) of this title;

(3) in any judicial district in which the agency or instrumentality is licensed to do business or is doing business, if the action is brought against an agency or instrumentality of a foreign state as defined in section 1603(b) of this title; or

(4) in the United States District Court for the District of Columbia if the action is brought against a foreign state or political subdivision thereof.

(g) A civil action in which jurisdiction of the district court is based upon section 1369 of this title may be brought in any district in which any defendant resides or in which a substantial part of the accident giving rise to the action took place.

§1392. Defendants or property in different districts in same State

Any civil action, of a local nature, involving property located in different districts in the same State, may be brought in any of such districts.

§1395. Fine, penalty or forfeiture

(a) A civil proceeding for the recovery of a pecuniary fine, penalty or forfeiture may be prosecuted in the district where it accrues or the defendant is found.

(b) A civil proceeding for the forfeiture of property may be prosecuted in any district where such property is found

§1396. INTERNAL REVENUE TAXES

Any civil action for the collection of internal revenue taxes may be brought in the district where the liability for such tax accrues, in the district of the taxpayer's residence, or in the district where the return was filed.

§1397. INTERPLEADER

Any civil action of interpleader or in the nature of interpleader under section 1335 of this title may be brought in the judicial district in which one or more of the claimants reside.

[See also §§1335 and 2361.]

§1401. STOCKHOLDER'S DERIVATIVE ACTION

Any civil action by a stockholder on behalf of his corporation may be prosecuted in any judicial district where the corporation might have sued the same defendants.

§1402. UNITED STATES AS DEFENDANT

(a) Any civil action in a district court against the United States under subsection (a) of section 1346 of this title may be prosecuted only:

(1) Except as provided in paragraph (2), in the judicial district where the plaintiff resides;

(2) In the case of a civil action by a corporation under paragraph (1) of subsection (a) of section 1346, in the judicial district in which is located the principal place of business or principal office or agency of the corporation; or if it has no principal place of business or principal office or agency in any judicial district (A) in the judicial district in which is located the office to which was made the return of the tax in respect of which the claim is made, or (B) if no return was made, in the judicial district in which lies the District of Columbia. Notwithstanding the foregoing provisions of this paragraph a district court, for the convenience of the parties and witnesses, in the interest of justice, may transfer any such action to any other district or division.

(b) Any civil action on a tort claim against the United States under subsection (b) of section 1346 of this title may be prosecuted only in the judicial district where the plaintiff resides or wherein the act or omission complained of occurred.

(c) Any civil action against the United States under subsection (e) of section 1346 of this title may be prosecuted only in the judicial district where the property is situated at the time of levy, or if no levy is made, in the judicial district in which the event occurred which gave rise to the cause of action.

(d) Any civil action under section 2409a to quiet title to an estate or interest in real property in which an interest is claimed by the United States shall be brought in the district court of the district where the property is located or, if located in different districts, in any of such districts.

§1404. Change of venue

(a) For the convenience of parties and witnesses, in the interest of justice, a district court may transfer any civil action to any other district or division where it might have been brought;

(b) Upon motion, consent or stipulation of all parties, any action, suit or proceeding of a civil nature or any motion or hearing thereof, may be transferred, in the discretion of the court, from the division in which pending to any other division in the same district. Transfer of proceedings in rem brought by or on behalf of the United States may be transferred under this section without the consent of the United States where all other parties request transfer;

(c) A district court may order any civil action to be tried at any place within the division in which it is pending;

(d) As used in this section, the term "district court" includes the District Court of Guam, the District Court for the Northern Mariana Islands, and the District Court of the Virgin Islands, and the term "district" includes the territorial jurisdiction of each such court.

§1406. Cure or waiver of defects

(a) The district court of a district in which is filed a case laying venue in the wrong division or district shall dismiss, or if it be in the interest of justice, transfer such case to any district or division in which it could have been brought.

(b) Nothing in this chapter shall impair the jurisdiction of a district court of any matter involving a party who does not interpose timely and sufficient objection to the venue.

(c) As used in this section, the term "district court" includes the District Court of Guam, the District Court for the Northern Mariana Islands, and the District Court of the Virgin Islands, and the term "district" includes the territorial jurisdiction of each such court.

§1407. Multidistrict litigation

(a) When civil actions involving one or more common questions of fact are pending in different districts, such actions may be transferred to any district for coordinated or consolidated pretrial proceedings. Such transfers shall be made by the judicial panel on multidistrict litigation authorized by this section upon its determination that transfers for such proceedings will be for the convenience of parties and witnesses and will promote the just and efficient conduct of such actions. Each action so transferred shall be remanded by the panel at or before the conclusion of such pretrial proceedings to the district from which it was transferred unless it shall have been previously terminated: *Provided, however,* That the panel may separate any claim, cross-claim, counter-claim, or third-party claim and remand any of such claims before the remainder of the action is remanded.

(b) Such coordinated or consolidated pretrial proceedings shall be conducted by a judge or judges to whom such actions are assigned by the judicial panel on multidistrict litigation. For this purpose, upon request of the panel, a circuit judge or a district judge may be designated and assigned temporarily for service in the transferee district by the Chief Justice of the United States or the chief judge of the circuit, as may be required, in accordance with the provisions of chapter 13 of this title. With the consent of the transferee district court, such actions may be assigned by the panel to a judge or judges of such district. The judge or judges to whom such actions are assigned, the members of the judicial panel on multidistrict litigation, and other circuit and district judges designated when needed by the panel may exercise the powers of a district judge in any district for the purpose of conducting pretrial depositions in such coordinated or consolidated pretrial proceedings.

(c) Proceedings for the transfer of an action under this section may be initiated by —

(1) the judicial panel on multidistrict litigation upon its own initiative, or

(2) motion filed with the panel by a party in any action in which transfer for coordinated or consolidated pretrial proceedings under this section may be appropriate. A copy of such motion shall be filed in the district court in which the moving party's action is pending.

The panel shall give notice to the parties in all actions in which transfers for coordinated or consolidated pretrial proceedings are contemplated, and such notice shall specify the time and place of any hearing to determine whether such transfer shall be made. Orders of the panel to set a hearing and other orders of the panel issued prior to the order either directing or denying transfer shall be filed in the office of the clerk of the district court in which a transfer hearing is to be or has been held. The panel's order of transfer shall be based upon a record of such hearing at which material evidence may be offered by any party to an action pending in any district that would be affected by the proceedings under this section, and shall be supported by findings of fact and conclusions of law based upon such record. Orders of transfer and such other orders as the panel may make thereafter shall be filed in the office of the clerk of the district court of the transferee district and shall be effective when thus filed. The clerk of the transferee district court shall forthwith transmit a certified copy of the panel's order to transfer to the clerk of the district court from which the action is being transferred. An order denying transfer shall be filed in each district wherein there is a case pending in which the motion for transfer has been made.

(d) The judicial panel on multidistrict litigation shall consist of seven circuit and district judges designated from time to time by the Chief Justice of the United States, no two of whom shall be from the same circuit. The concurrence of four members shall be necessary to any action by the panel.

(e) No proceedings for review of any order of the panel may be permitted except by extraordinary writ pursuant to the provisions of title 28, section 1651, United States Code. Petitions for an extraordinary writ to review an order of the panel to set a transfer hearing and other orders of the panel issued prior to the order either directing or denying transfer shall be filed only in the court of appeals having jurisdiction over the district in which a hearing is to be or has been held. Petitions for an extraordinary writ to review an order to transfer or orders subsequent to transfer shall be filed only in the court of appeals having jurisdiction over the transferee district. There shall be no appeal or review or an order of the panel denying a motion to transfer for consolidated or coordinated proceedings.

(f) The panel may prescribe rules for the conduct of its business not inconsistent with Acts of Congress and the Federal Rules of Civil Procedure.

(g) Nothing in this section shall apply to any action in which the United States is a complainant arising under the antitrust laws. "Anti-trust laws" as used herein include those acts referred to in the Act of October 15, 1914, as amended (38 Stat. 730; 15 U.S.C. 12), and also include the Act of June 19, 1936 (49 Stat. 1526; 15 U.S.C. 13, 13a, and 13b) and the Act of September 26, 1914, as added March 21, 1938 (52 Stat. 116, 117; 15 U.S.C. 56); but shall not include section 4A of the Act of October 15, 1914, as added July 7, 1955 (69 Stat. 282; 15 U.S.C. 15a).

(h) Notwithstanding the provisions of section 1404 or subsection (f) of this section, the judicial panel multidistrict litigation may consolidate and transfer with or without the consent of the parties, for both pretrial purposes and for trial, any action brought under section 4C of the Clayton Act.

Chapter 89. District Courts; Removal of Cases from State Courts

§1441. Actions removable generally

(a) Except as otherwise expressly provided by Act of Congress, any civil action brought in a State court of which the district courts of the United States have original jurisdiction, may be removed by the defendant or the defendants, to the district court of the United States for the district and division embracing the place where such action is pending. For purposes of removal under this chapter, the citizenship of defendants sued under fictitious names shall be disregarded.

(b) Any civil action of which the district courts have original jurisdiction founded on a claim or right arising under the Constitution, treaties or laws of the United States shall be removable without regard to the citizenship or residence of the parties. Any other such action shall be removable only if none of the parties in interest properly joined and served as defendants is a citizen of the State in which such action is brought.

(c) Whenever a separate and independent claim or cause of action within the jurisdiction conferred by section 1331 of this title is joined with one or more otherwise non-removable claims or causes of action, the entire case may be removed and the district court may determine all issues therein, or, in its discretion, may remand all matters in which State law predominates.

(d) Any civil action brought in a State court against a foreign state as defined in section 1603(a) of this title may be removed by the foreign state to the district court of the United States for the district and division embracing the place where such action is pending. Upon removal the action shall be tried by the court without jury. Where removal is based upon this subsection, the time limitations of section 1446(b) of this chapter may be enlarged at any time for cause shown.

(e)(1) Notwithstanding the provisions of subsection (b) of this section, a defendant in a civil action in a State court may remove the action to the district court of the United States for the district and division embracing the place where the action is pending if—

(A) the action could have been brought in a United States district court under section 1369 of this title; or

(B) the defendant is a party to an action which is or could have been brought, in whole or in part, under section 1369 in a United States district court and arises from the same accident as the action in State court, even if the action to be removed could not have been brought in a district court as an original matter.

The removal of an action under this subsection shall be made in accordance with section 1446 of this title, except that a notice of removal may also be filed before trial of the action in State court within 30 days after the date on which the defendant first becomes a party to an action under section 1369 in a United States district court that arises from the same accident as the action in State court, or at a later time with leave of the district court.

(2) Whenever an action is removed under this subsection and the district court to which it is removed or transferred under section 1407(j)* has made a liability determination requiring further proceedings as to damages, the district court shall remand the action to the State court from which it had been removed for the determination of damages, unless the court finds that, for the convenience of parties and witnesses and in the interest of justice, the action should be retained for the determination of damages.

(3) Any remand under paragraph (2) shall not be effective until 60 days after the district court has issued an order determining liability and has certified its intention to remand the removed action for the determination of damages.

*[28 U.S.C. §1407(j), which appeared in earlier drafts of a legislative proposal, was never enacted — ED.]

An appeal with respect to the liability determination of the district court may be taken during that 60-day period to the court of appeals with appellate jurisdiction over the district court. In the event a party files such an appeal, the remand shall not be effective until the appeal has been finally disposed of. Once the remand has become effective, the liability determination shall not be subject to further review by appeal or otherwise.

(4) Any decision under this subsection concerning remand for the determination of damages shall not be reviewable by appeal or otherwise.

(5) An action removed under this subsection shall be deemed to be an action under section 1369 and an action in which jurisdiction is based on section 1369 of this title for purposes of this section and sections 1407, 1697, and 1785 of this title.

(6) Nothing in this subsection shall restrict the authority of the district court to transfer or dismiss an action on the ground of inconvenient forum.

(f) The court to which a civil action is removed under this section is not precluded from hearing and determining any claim in such civil action because the State court from which civil action is removed did not have jurisdiction over that claim.

§1442. FEDERAL OFFICERS OR AGENCIES SUED OR PROSECUTED

(a) A civil action or criminal prosecution commenced in a State court against any of the following may be removed by them to the district court of the United States for the district and division embracing the place wherein it is pending:

(1) The United States or any agency thereof or any officer (or any person acting under that officer) of the United States or of any agency thereof, sued in an official or individual capacity for any act under color of such office or on account of any right, title or authority claimed under any Act of Congress for the apprehension or punishment of criminals or the collection of the revenue.

(2) A property holder whose title is derived from any such officer, where such action of prosecution affects the validity of any law of the United States.

(3) Any officer of the courts of the United States, for any Act under color of office or in the performance of his duties;

(4) Any officer of either House of Congress, for any act in the discharge of his official duty under an order of such House.

(b) A personal action commenced in any State court by an alien against any citizen of a State who is, or at the time the alleged action accrued was, a civil officer of the United States and is a nonresident of such State, wherein jurisdiction is obtained by the State court by personal service of process, may be removed by the defendant to the district court of the United States for the district and division in which the defendant was served with process.

§1442a. MEMBERS OF ARMED FORCES SUED OR PROSECUTED

A civil or criminal prosecution in a court of a State of the United States against a member of the armed forces of the United States on account of an act done under color of his office or status, or in respect to which he claims any right, title, or authority under a law of the United States respecting the armed forces thereof, or under the law of war, may at any time before the trial or final hearing thereof be removed for trial into the district court of the United States for the district where it is pending in the manner prescribed by law, and it shall thereupon be entered on the docket of the district court, which shall proceed as if the cause had been originally commenced therein and shall have full power to hear and determine the cause.

§1443. CIVIL RIGHTS CASES

Any of the following civil actions or criminal prosecutions, commenced in a State court may be removed by the defendant to the district court of the United States for the district and division embracing the place wherein it is pending:

(1) Against any person who is denied or cannot enforce in the courts of such State a right under any law providing for the equal civil rights of citizens of the United States, or of all persons within the jurisdiction thereof;

(2) For any act under color of authority derived from any law providing for equal rights, or for refusing to do any act on the ground that it would be inconsistent with such law.

§1445. NONREMOVABLE ACTIONS

(a) A civil action in any State court against a railroad or its receivers or trustees, arising under sections 1-4 and 5-10 of the Act of April 22, 1908 (45 U.S.C. 51-54, 55-60), may not be removed to any district court of the United States.

(b) A civil action in any State court against a carrier or its receivers or trustees to recover damages for delay, loss, or injury of shipments, arising under section 11706 or 14706 of Title 49, may not be removed to any district court of the United States unless the matter in controversy exceeds $10,000, exclusive of interest and costs.

(c) A civil action in any State court arising under the workmen's compensation laws of such State may not be removed to any district court of the United States.

(d) A civil action in any State court arising under section 40302 of the Violence Against Women Act of 1994 may not be removed to any district court of the United States.

§1446. Procedure for removal

(a) A defendant or defendants desiring to remove any civil action or criminal prosecution from a State court shall file in the district court of the United States for the district and division within which such action is pending a notice of removal signed pursuant to Rule 11 of the Federal Rules of Civil Procedure and containing a short and plain statement of the grounds for removal, together with a copy of all process, pleadings, and orders served upon such defendant or defendants in such action.

(b) The notice of removal of a civil action or proceeding shall be filed within thirty days after the receipt by the defendant, through service or otherwise, of a copy of the initial pleading setting forth the claim for relief upon which such action or proceeding is based, or within thirty days after the service of summons upon the defendant if such initial pleading has then been filed in court and is not required to be served on the defendant, whichever period is shorter.

If the case stated by the initial pleading is not removable, a notice of removal may be filed within thirty days after receipt by the defendant, through service or otherwise, of a copy of an amended pleading, motion, order or other paper from which it may first be ascertained that the case is one which is or has become removable, except that a case may not be removed on the basis of jurisdiction conferred by section 1332 of this title more than 1 year after commencement of the action. . . .

(d) Promptly after the filing of such notice the defendant or defendants shall give written notice thereof to all adverse parties and shall file a copy of the notice with the clerk of such State court, which shall effect removal and the State court shall proceed no further unless and until the case is remanded. . . .

§1447. Procedure after removal generally

(a) In any case removed from a State court, the district court may issue all necessary orders and process to bring before it all proper parties whether served by process issued by the State court or otherwise.

(b) It may require the removing party to file with its clerk copies of all records and proceedings in such State court or may cause the same to be brought before it by writ of certiorari issued to such State court.

(c) A motion to remand the case on the basis of any defect other than lack of subject matter jurisdiction must be made within 30 days after the filing of the notice of removal under section 1446(a). If at any time before final judgment it appears that the district court lacks subject matter jurisdiction, the case shall be remanded. An order remanding the case may require payment of just costs and any actual expenses, including attorney fees, incurred as a result of the removal. A certified copy of the order of remand shall be mailed by the clerk to the clerk of the State court. The State court may thereupon proceed with such case.

(d) An order remanding a case to the State court from which it was removed is not reviewable on appeal or otherwise, except that an order remanding a case to the State court from which it was removed pursuant to section 1443 of this title shall be reviewable by appeal or otherwise.

(e) If after removal the plaintiff seeks to join additional defendants whose joinder would destroy subject matter jurisdiction, the court may deny joinder, or permit joinder and remand the action to the State court.

§1448. Process after removal

In all cases removed from any State court to any district court of the United States in which any one or more of the defendants has not been served with process or in which the service has not been perfected prior to removal, or in which process served proves to be defective, such process or service may be completed or new process issued in the same manner as in cases originally filed in such district court.

This section shall not deprive any defendant upon whom process is served after removal of his right to move to remand the case.

§1451. Definitions

For purposes of this chapter —

(1) The term "State court" includes the Superior Court of the District of Columbia.

(2) The term "State" includes the District of Columbia.

§1452. Removal of claims related to bankruptcy cases

(a) A party may remove any claim or cause of action in a civil action other than a proceeding before the United States Tax Court or a civil action by a governmental unit to enforce such governmental unit's police or regulatory power, to the district court for the district where such civil action is pending, if such district court has jurisdiction of such claim or cause of action under section 1334 of this title.

(b) The court to which such claim or cause of action is removed may remand such claim or cause of action on any equitable ground. An order entered under this subsection remanding a claim or cause of action, or a decision to not remand, is not reviewable by appeal or otherwise by the court of appeals under section 158(d), 1291, or 1292 of this title or by the Supreme Court of the United States under section 1254 of this title.

Chapter 99. General Provisions

§1631. TRANSFER TO CURE WANT OF JURISDICTION

Whenever a civil action is filed in a court as defined in section 610 of this title or an appeal, including a petition for review of administrative action, is noticed for or filed with such a court and that court finds that there is a want of jurisdiction, the court shall, if it is in the interest of justice, transfer such action or appeal to any other such court in which the action or appeal could have been brought at the time it was filed or noticed, and the action or appeal shall proceed as if it had been filed in or noticed for the court to which it is transferred on the date upon which it was actually filed in or noticed for the court from which it is transferred.

Part V. Procedure

Chapter 111. General Provisions

§1651. WRITS

(a) The Supreme Court and all courts established by Act of Congress may issue all writs necessary or appropriate in aid of their respective jurisdictions and agreeable to the usages and principles of law.

(b) An alternative writ or rule nisi may be issued by a justice or judge of a court which has jurisdiction.

§1652. STATE LAWS AS RULES OF DECISION

The laws of the several states, except where the Constitution or treaties of the United States or Acts of Congress otherwise require or provide, shall be regarded as rules of decision in civil actions in the courts of the United States, in cases where they apply.

§1654. APPEARANCE PERSONALLY OR BY COUNSEL

(a) In all courts of the United States the parties may plead and conduct their own cases personally or by counsel, as, by the rules of such courts, respectively, are permitted to manage and conduct causes therein.

§1658. TIME LIMITATIONS ON THE COMMENCEMENT OF CIVIL ACTIONS ARISING UNDER ACTS OF CONGRESS

(a) Except as otherwise provided by law, a civil action arising under an Act of Congress enacted after the date of the enactment of this section may not be commenced later than 4 years after the cause of action accrues.

(b) Notwithstanding subsection (a), a private right of action that involves a claim of fraud, deceit, manipulation, or contrivance in contravention of a regulatory requirement concerning the securities laws, as defined in section 3(a)(47) of the Securities Exchange Act of 1934 (15 U.S.C. 78c(a)(47)), may be brought not later than the earlier of—

(1) 2 years after the discovery of the facts constituting the violation; or

(2) 5 years after such violation.

Chapter 113. Process

§1693. Place of arrest in civil action

Except as otherwise provided by Act of Congress, no person shall be arrested in one district for trial in another in any civil action in a district court.

§1694. Patent infringement action

In a patent infringement action commenced in a district where the defendant is not a resident but has a regular and established place of business, service of process, summons or subpoena upon such defendant may be made upon his agent or agents conducting such business.

§1695. Stockholder's derivative action

Process in a stockholder's action in behalf of his corporation may be served upon such corporation in any district where it is organized or licensed to do business or is doing business.

§1696. Service in foreign and international litigation

(a) The district court of the district in which a person resides or is found may order service upon him of any document issued in connection with a proceeding in a foreign or international tribunal. The order may be made pursuant to a letter rogatory issued, or request made, by a foreign or international tribunal or upon application of any interested person and shall direct the manner of service. Service pursuant to this subsection does not, of itself, require the recognition or enforcement in the United States of a judgment, decree, or order rendered by a foreign or international tribunal.

(b) This section does not preclude service of such a document without an order of court.

§1697. SERVICE IN MULTIPARTY, MULTIFORUM ACTIONS

When the jurisdiction of the district court is based in whole or in part upon section 1369 of this title, process, other than subpoenas, may be served at any place within the United States, or anywhere outside the United States if otherwise permitted by law.

Chapter 115. Evidence; Documentary

§1738. STATE AND TERRITORIAL STATUTES AND JUDICIAL PROCEEDINGS; FULL FAITH AND CREDIT

The Acts of the legislature of any State, Territory, or Possession of the United States, or copies thereof, shall be authenticated by affixing the seal of such State, Territory or Possession thereto.

The records and judicial proceedings of any court of any such State, Territory or Possession, or copies thereof, shall be proved or admitted in other courts within the United States and its Territories and Possessions by the attestation of the clerk and seal of the court annexed, if a seal exists, together with a certificate of a judge of the court that the said attestation is in proper form.

Such Acts, records and judicial proceedings or copies thereof, so authenticated, shall have the same full faith and credit in every court within the United States and its Territories and Possessions as they have by law or usage in the courts of such State, Territory or Possession from which they are taken.

§1738A. FULL FAITH AND CREDIT GIVEN TO CHILD CUSTODY DETERMINATIONS

(a) The appropriate authorities of every State shall enforce according to its terms, and shall not modify except as provided in subsections (f), (g), and (h) of this section, any custody determination or visitation determination made consistently with the provisions of this section by a court of another State.

(b) As used in this section, the term —

(1) "child" means a person under the age of eighteen;

(2) "contestant" means a person, including a parent or grandparent, who claims a right to custody or visitation of a child;

(3) "custody determination" means a judgment, decree, or other order of a court providing for the custody of a child, and includes permanent and temporary orders, and initial orders and modifications;

(4) "home State" means the State in which, immediately preceding the time involved, the child lived with his parents, a parent, or a person acting as parent, for at least six consecutive months, and in the case of a child less than six months old, the State in which the child lived from birth with any of such

persons. Periods of temporary absence of any of such persons are counted as part of the six-month or other period;

(5) "modification" and "modify" refer to a custody or visitation determination which modifies, replaces, supersedes, or otherwise is made subsequent to, a prior custody or visitation determination concerning the same child, whether made by the same court or not;

(6) "person acting as a parent" means a person, other than a parent, who has physical custody of a child and who has either been awarded custody by a court or claims a right to custody;

(7) "physical custody" means actual possession and control of a child;

(8) "State" means a State of the United States, the District of Columbia, the Commonwealth of Puerto Rico, or a territory or possession of the United States; and

(9) "visitation determination" means a judgment, decree, or other order of a court providing for the visitation of a child and includes permanent and temporary orders and initial orders and modifications.

(c) A child custody or visitation determination made by a court of a State is consistent with the provisions of this section only if —

(1) such court has jurisdiction under the law of such State; and

(2) one of the following conditions is met:

(A) such State (i) is the home State of the child on the date of the commencement of the proceeding, or (ii) had been the child's home State within six months before the date of the commencement of the proceeding and the child is absent from such State because of his removal or retention by a contestant or for other reasons, and a contestant continues to live in such State;

(B) (i) it appears that no other State would have jurisdiction under subparagraph (A), and

(ii) it is in the best interest of the child that a court of such State assume jurisdiction because

(I) the child and his parents, or the child and at least one contestant, have a significant connection with such State other than mere physical presence in such State, and

(II) there is available in such State substantial evidence concerning the child's present or future care, protection, training, and personal relationships;

(C) the child is physically present in such State and

(i) the child has been abandoned, or

(ii) it is necessary in an emergency to protect the child because the child, a sibling, or parent of the child has been subjected to or threatened with mistreatment or abuse;

(D)(i) it appears that no other State would have jurisdiction under subparagraph (A), (B), (C), or (E), or another State has declined to exercise jurisdication on the ground that the State whose jurisdiction is in issue is the more appropriate forum to determine the custody or visitation of the child, and

(ii) it is in the best interest of the child that such court assume jurisdiction; or

(E) the court has continuing jurisdiction pursuant to subsection (d) of this section.

(d) The jurisdiction of a court of a State which has made a child custody or visitation determination consistently with the provisions of this section continues as long as the requirement of subsection (c)(1) of this section continues to be met and such State remains the residence of the child or of any contestant.

(e) Before a child custody or visitation determination is made, reasonable notice and opportunity to be heard shall be given to the contestants, any parent whose parental rights have not been previously terminated and any person who has physical custody of a child.

(f) A court of a State may modify a determination of the custody of the same child made by a court of another State, if —

(1) it has jurisdiction to make such a child custody determination; and

(2) the court of the other State no longer has jurisdiction, or it has declined to exercise such jurisdiction to modify such determination.

(g) A court of a State shall not exercise jurisdiction in any proceeding for a custody or visitation determination commenced during the pendency of a proceeding in a court of another State where such court of that other State is exercising jurisdiction consistently with the provisions of this section to make a custody or visitation determination.

(h) A court of a State may not modify a visitation determination made by a court of another State unless the court of the other State no longer has jurisdiction to modify such determination or has declined to exercise jurisdiction to modify such determination.

§1738B. FULL FAITH AND CREDIT FOR CHILD SUPPORT ORDERS

(a) General Rule. The appropriate authorities of each State —

(1) shall enforce according to its terms a child support order made consistently with this section by a court of another State; and

(2) shall not seek or make a modification of such an order except in accordance with subsections (e), (f), and (i).

(b) Definitions. In this section:

"child" means —

(A) a person under 18 years of age; and

(B) a person 18 or more years of age with respect to whom a child support order has been issued pursuant to the laws of a State.

"child's State" means the State in which a child resides.

A "child's home State" means the State in which a child lived with a parent or a person acting as parent for at least six consecutive months immediately preceding the time of filing of a petition or comparable pleading for support and, if a child is less than six months old, the State in which the child lived from birth with any of them. A period of temporary absence of any of them is counted as part of the six-month period.

"child support" means a payment of money, continuing support, or arrearages or the provision of a benefit (including payment of health insurance, child care, and educational expenses) for the support of a child.

"child support order" —

(A) means a judgment, decree, or order of a court requiring the payment of child support in periodic amounts or in a lump sum; and

(B) includes —

(i) a permanent or temporary order; and

(ii) an initial order or a modification of an order.

"contestant" means —

(A) a person (including a parent) who —

(i) claims a right to receive child support;

(ii) is a party to a proceeding that may result in the issuance of a child support order; or

(iii) is under a child support order; and

(B) a State or political subdivision of a State to which the right to obtain child support has been assigned.

"court" means a court or administrative agency of a State that is authorized by State law to establish the amount of child support payable by a contestant or make a modification of a child support order.

"modification" means a change in a child support order that affects the amount, scope, or duration of the order and modifies, replaces, supersedes, or otherwise is made subsequent to the child support order.

"State" means a State of the United States, the District of Columbia, the Commonwealth of Puerto Rico, the territories and possessions of the United States, and Indian country (as defined in section 1151 of title 18).

(c) Requirements of Child Support Orders. A child support order made by a court of a State is made consistently with this section if —

(1) a court that makes the order, pursuant to the laws of the State in which the court is located —

(A) has subject matter jurisdiction to hear the matter and enter such an order; and

(B) has personal jurisdiction over the contestants; and

(2) reasonable notice and opportunity to be heard is given to the contestants.

(d) Continuing Jurisdiction. A court of a State that has made a child support order consistently with this section has continuing, exclusive jurisdiction over the order if the State is the child's State or the residence of any individual contestant unless the court of another State, acting in accordance with subsections (e) and (f), has made a modification of the order.

(e) Authority to Modify Orders. A court of a State may modify a child support order issued by a court of another State if —

(1) the court has jurisdiction to make such a child support order pursuant to subsection (i); and

(2)(A) the court of the other State no longer has continuing, exclusive jurisdiction of the child support order because that State no longer is the child's State or the residence of any individual contestant; or

(B) each individual contestant has filed written consent with the State of continuing exclusive jurisdiction for a court of another State to modify the order and assume continuing, exclusive jurisdiction over the order.

(f) Recognition of child support orders. — If one or more child support orders have been issued with regard to an obligor and a child, a court shall apply the following rules in determining which order to recognize for purposes of continuing, exclusive jurisdiction and enforcement:

(1) If only one court has issued a child support order, the order of that court must be recognized.

(2) If two or more courts have issued child support orders for the same obligor and child, and only one of the courts would have continuing, exclusive jurisdiction under this section, the order of that court must be recognized.

(3) If two or more courts have issued child support orders for the same obligor and child, and more than one of the courts would have continuing, exclusive jurisdiction under this section, an order issued by a court in the current home State of the child must be recognized, but if an order has not been issued in the current home State of the child, the order most recently issued must be recognized.

(4) If two or more courts have issued child support orders for the same obligor and child, and none of the courts would have continuing, exclusive jurisdiction under this section, a court having jurisdiction over the parties shall issue a child support order, which must be recognized.

(5) The court that has issued an order recognized under this subsection is the court having continuing, exclusive jurisdiction under subsection (d).

(g) Enforcement of Modified Orders. — A court of a State that no longer has continuing, exclusive jurisdiction of a child support order may enforce the order with respect to nonmodifiable obligations and unsatisfied obligations that accrued before the date on which a modification of the order is made under subsections (e) and (f).

(h) Choice of law. —

(1) In General. — In a proceeding to establish, modify, or enforce a child support order, the forum State's law shall apply except as provided in paragraphs (2) and (3).

(2) Law of State of Issuance of Order. — In interpreting a child support order including the duration of current payments and other obligations of support, a court shall apply the law of the State of the court that issued the order.

(3) Period of Limitation. — In an action to enforce a child support order, a court shall apply the statute of limitation of the forum State or the State of the court that issued the order, whichever statute provides the longer period of limitation.

(i) Registration for Modification. — If there is no individual contestant or child residing in the issuing State, the party or support enforcement agency seeking to modify, or to modify and enforce, a child support order issued in another State shall register that order in a State with jurisdiction over the nonmovant for the purpose of modification.

§1739. State and Territorial nonjudicial records; full faith and credit

All nonjudicial records or books kept in any public office of any State, Territory, or Possession of the United States, or copies thereof, shall be proved or admitted in any court or office in any other State, Territory, or Possession by the attestation of the custodian of such records or books, and the seal of his office annexed, if there be a seal, together with a certificate of a judge of a court of record of the county, parish, or district in which such office may be kept, or of the Governor, or secretary of state, the chancellor or keeper of the great seal, off the State, Territory, or Possession that the said attestation is in due form and by the proper officers.

If the certificate is given by a judge, it shall be further authenticated by the clerk or prothonotary of the court, who shall certify, under his hand and the seal of his office, that such judge is duly commissioned and qualified; or, if given by such Governor, secretary, chancellor, or keeper of the great seal, it shall be under the great seal of the State, Territory, or Possession in which it is made.

Such records or books, or copies thereof, so authenticated, shall have the same full faith and credit in every court and office within the United States and its Territories and Possessions as they have by law or usage in the courts or offices of the State, Territory, or Possession from which they are taken.

Chapter 117. Evidence; Depositions

§1785. Subpoenas in multiparty, multiforum actions

When the jurisdiction of the district court is based in whole or in part upon section 1369 of this title, a subpoena for attendance at a hearing or trial may, if authorized by the court upon motion for good cause shown, and upon such terms and conditions as the court may impose, be served at any place within the United States, or anywhere outside the United States if otherwise permitted by law.

Chapter 119. Evidence; Witnesses

§1821. PER DIEM AND MILEAGE GENERALLY; SUBSISTENCE

(a)(1) Except as otherwise provided by law, a witness in attendance at any court of the United States, or before a United States Magistrate, or before any person authorized to take his deposition pursuant to any rule or order of a court of the United States, shall be paid the fees and allowances provided by this section.

(2) As used in this section, the term "court of the United States" includes, in addition to the courts listed in section 451 of this title, any court created by Act of Congress in a territory which is invested with any jurisdiction of a district court of the United States.

(b) A witness shall be paid an attendance fee of $40 per day for each day's attendance. A witness shall also be paid the attendance fee for the time necessarily occupied in going to and returning from the place of attendance at the beginning and end of such attendance or at any time during such attendance.

(c)(1) A witness who travels by common carrier shall be paid for the actual expenses of travel on the basis of the means of transportation reasonably utilized and the distance necessarily traveled to and from such witness's residence by the shortest practical route in going to and returning from the place of attendance. Such a witness shall utilize a common carrier at the most economical rate reasonably available. A receipt or other evidence of actual cost shall be furnished.

(2) A travel allowance equal to the mileage allowance which the Administrator of General Services has prescribed, pursuant to section 5704 of title 5, for official travel of employees of the Federal Government shall be paid to each witness who travels by privately owned vehicle. Computation of mileage under this paragraph shall be made on the basis of a uniformed table of distances adopted by the Administrator of General Services.

(3) Toll charges for toll roads, bridges, tunnels, and ferries, taxicab fares between places of lodging and carrier terminals, and parking fees (upon presentation of a valid parking receipt), shall be paid in full to a witness incurring such expenses.

(4) All normal travel expenses within and outside the judicial district shall be taxable as costs pursuant to section 1920 of this title.

(d)(1) A subsistence allowance shall be paid to a witness when an overnight stay is required at the place of attendance because such place is so far removed from the residence of such witness as to prohibit return thereto from day to day.

(2) A subsistence allowance for a witness shall be paid in an amount not to exceed the maximum per diem allowance prescribed by the Administrator of General Services, pursuant to section 5702(a) of title 5, for official travel in the area of attendance by employees of the Federal Government.

(3) A subsistence allowance for a witness attending in an area designated by the Administrator of General Services as a high-cost area shall be paid in

an amount not to exceed the maximum actual subsistence allowance prescribed by the Administrator, pursuant to section 5702(c)(B) of title 5, for official travel in such area by employees of the Federal Government.

(4) When a witness is detained pursuant to section 3144 of title 18 for want of security for his appearance, he shall be entitled for each day of detention when not in attendance at court, in addition to his subsistence, to the daily attendance fee provided by subsection (b) of this section.

(e) An alien who has been paroled into the United States for prosecution, pursuant to section 212(d)(5) of the Immigration and Nationality Act (8 U.S.C. 1182(d)(5)), or an alien who either has admitted belonging to a class of aliens who are deportable or has been determined pursuant to section 240 of such Act (8 U.S.C. 1252(b)) to be deportable, shall be ineligible to receive the fees or allowances provided by this section.

(f) Any witness who is incarcerated at the time that his or her testimony is given (except for a witness to whom the provisions of section 3144 of title 18 apply) may not receive fees or allowances under this section, regardless of whether such witness is incarcerated at the time he or she makes a claim for fees or allowances under this section.

§1824. Mileage fees under summons as both witness and juror

No constructive or double mileage fees shall be allowed by reason of any person being summoned both as a witness and a juror.

§1825. Payment of fees

(a) In any case in which the United States or an officer or agency of the United States is a party, the United States marshal for the district shall pay all fees of witnesses on the certificate of the United States attorney or assistant United States attorney, and in the proceedings before a United States magistrate, on the certificate of such magistrate, except that any fees of defense witnesses, other than experts, appearing pursuant to subpoenas issued upon approval of the court, shall be paid by the United States marshal for the district —

(1) on the certificate of a Federal public defender or assistant Federal public defender, in a criminal case in which the defendant is represented by such Federal public defender or assistant Federal public defender, and

(2) on the certificate of the clerk of the court upon the affidavit of such witnesses' attendance given by other counsel appointed pursuant to section 3006A of title 18, in a criminal case in which a defendant is represented by such other counsel.

(b) In proceedings in forma pauperis for a writ of habeas corpus, and in proceedings in forma pauperis under section 2255 of this title, the United States marshal for the district shall pay, on the certificate of the district judge, all fees of witnesses for the party authorized to proceed in forma pauperis, except that any fees of witnesses for such party, other than experts, appearing pursuant to subpoenas issued upon approval of the court, shall be paid by the United States marshal for the district —

(1) on the certificate of a Federal public defender or assistant Federal public defender, in any such proceedings in which a party is represented by such Federal public defender or assistant Federal public defender, and

(2) on the certificate of the clerk of the court upon the affidavit of such witnesses' attendance given by other counsel appointed pursuant to section 3006A of title 18, in any such proceedings in which a party is represented by such other counsel.

(c) Fees and mileage need not by tendered to a witness upon service of a subpoena issued on behalf of the United States or an officer or agency of the United States, upon service of a subpoena issued on behalf of a defendant represented by a Federal public defender, assistant Federal public defender, or other attorney appointed pursuant to section 3006A of title 18, or upon service of a subpoena issued on behalf of a party authorized to proceed in forma pauperis, if the payment of such fees and mileage is to be made by the United States marshal under this section.

§1826. Recalcitrant witnesses

(a) Whenever a witness in any proceeding before or ancillary to any court or grand jury of the United States refuses without just cause shown to comply with an order of the court to testify or provide other information, including any book, paper, document, record, recording or other material, the court, upon such refusal, or when such refusal is duly brought to its attention, may summarily order his confinement at a suitable place until such time as the witness is willing to give such testimony or provide such information. No period of such confinement shall exceed the life of —

(1) the court proceeding, or

(2) the term of the grand jury, including extensions, before which such refusal to comply with the court order occurred, but in no event shall such confinement exceed eighteen months.

(b) No person confined pursuant to subsection (a) of this section shall be admitted to bail pending the determination of an appeal taken by him from the order for his confinement if it appears that the appeal is frivolous or taken for delay. Any appeal from an order of confinement under this section shall be disposed of as soon as practicable, but not later than thirty days from the filing of such appeal.

(c) Whoever escapes or attempts to escape from the custody of any facility or from any place in which or to which he is confined pursuant to this section or section 4243 of title 18, or whoever rescues or attempts to rescue or instigates, aids, or assists the escape or attempt to escape of such a person, shall be subject to imprisonment for not more than three years, or a fine of not more than $10,000, or both.

Chapter 121. Juries; Trial by Jury

§1861. Declaration of policy

It is the policy of the United States that all litigants in Federal courts entitled to trial by jury shall have the right to grand and petit juries selected at random from a fair cross section of the community in the district or division wherein the court convenes. It is further the policy of the United States that all citizens shall have the opportunity to be considered for service on grand and petit juries in the district courts of the United States, and shall have an obligation to serve as jurors when summoned for that purpose.

§1862. Discrimination prohibited

No citizen shall be excluded from service as a grand or petit juror in the district courts of the United States or in the Court of International Trade on account of race, color, religion, sex, national origin, or economic status.

§1863. Plan for random jury selection

(a) Each United States district court shall devise and place into operation a written plan for random selection of grand and petit jurors that shall be designed to achieve the objectives of sections 1861 and 1862 of this title, and that shall otherwise comply with the provisions of this title. The plan shall be placed into operation after approval by a reviewing panel consisting of the members of the judicial council of the circuit and either the chief judge of the district whose plan is being reviewed or such other active district judge of that district as the chief judge of the district may designate. The panel shall examine the plan to ascertain that it complies with the provisions of this title. If the reviewing panel finds that the plan does not comply, the panel shall state the particulars in which the plan fails to comply and direct the district court to present within a reasonable time an alternative plan remedying the defect or defects. Separate plans may be adopted for each division or combination of divisions within a judicial district. The district court may modify a plan at any time and it shall modify the plan when so directed by the reviewing panel. The district court shall promptly notify the panel, the Administrative Office of the United States Courts, and the Attorney General of the United States, of the initial adoption and future modifications of the plan by filing copies therewith. Modifications of the plan made at the instance of the district court shall become effective after approval by the panel. Each district court shall submit a report on the jury selection process within its jurisdiction to the Administrative Office of the United States Courts in such form and at such times as the Judicial Conference of the United States may specify. The Judicial Conference of the United States may, from time to time, adopt rules and regulations governing the provisions and the operation of the plans formulated under this title.

(b) Among other things, such plan shall —

(1) either establish a jury commission, or authorize the clerk of the court, to manage the jury selection process. If the plan establishes a jury commission, the district court shall appoint one citizen to serve with the clerk of the court as the jury commission: *Provided, however,* That the plan for the District of Columbia may establish a jury commission consisting of three citizens. The citizen jury commissioner shall not belong to the same political party as the clerk serving with him. The clerk or the jury commission, as the case may be, shall act under the supervision and control of the chief judge of the district court or such other judge of the district court as the plan may provide. Each jury commissioner shall, during his tenure in office, reside in the judicial district or division for which he is appointed. Each citizen jury commissioner shall receive compensation to be fixed by the district court plan at a rate not to exceed $50 per day for each day necessarily employed in the performance of his duties, plus reimbursement for travel, subsistence, and other necessary expenses incurred by him in the performance of such duties. The Judicial Conference of the United States may establish standards for allowance of travel, subsistence, and other necessary expenses incurred by jury commissioners.

(2) specify whether the names of prospective jurors shall be selected from the voter registration lists or the lists of actual voters of the political subdivisions within the district or division. The plan shall prescribe some other source or sources of names in addition to voter lists where necessary to foster the policy and protect the rights secured by sections 1861 and 1862 of this title. The plan for the District of Columbia may require the names of prospective jurors to be selected from the city directory rather than from voter lists. The plans for the districts of Puerto Rico and the Canal Zone may prescribe some other source or sources of names of prospective jurors in lieu of voter lists, the use of which shall be consistent with the policies declared and rights secured by sections 1861 and 1862 of this title. The plan for the district of Massachusetts may require the names of prospective jurors to be selected from the resident list provided for in chapter 234A, Massachusetts General Laws, or comparable authority, rather than from voter lists.

(3) specify detailed procedures to be followed by the jury commission or clerk in selecting names from the sources specified in paragraph (2) of this subsection. These procedures shall be designed to ensure the random selection of a fair cross section of the persons residing in the community in the district or division wherein the court convenes. They shall ensure that names of persons residing in each of the counties, parishes, or similar political subdivisions within the judicial district or division are placed in a master jury wheel; and shall

ensure that each county, parish, or similar political subdivision within the district or division is substantially proportionally represented in the master jury wheel for that judicial district, division, or combination of divisions. For the purposes of determining proportional representation in the master jury wheel, either the number of actual voters at the last general election in each county, party, or similar political subdivision, or the number of registered voters if registration of voters is uniformly required throughout the district or division, may be used.

(4) provide for a master jury wheel (or a device similar in purpose and function) into which the names of those randomly selected shall be placed. The plan shall fix a minimum number of names to be placed initially in the master jury wheel, which shall be at least one-half of 1 per centum of the total number of persons on the lists used as a source of names for the district or division; but if this number of names is believed to be cumbersome and unnecessary, the plan may fix a smaller number of names to be placed in the master wheel, but in no event less than one thousand. The chief judge of the district court, or such other district court judge as the plan may provide, may order additional names to be placed in the master jury wheel from time to time as necessary. The plan shall provide for periodic emptying and refilling of the master jury wheel at specified times, the interval for which shall not exceed four years.

(5)(A) except as provided in subparagraph (B), specify those groups of persons or occupational classes whose members shall, on individual request therefor, be excused from jury service. Such groups or classes shall be excused only if the district court finds, and the plan states, that jury service by such class or group would entail undue hardship or extreme inconvenience to the members thereof, and excuse of members thereof would not be inconsistent with sections 1861 and 1862 of this title.

(B) specify that volunteer safety personnel, upon individual request, shall be excused from jury service. For purposes of this subparagraph, the term "volunteer safety personnel" means individuals serving a public agency (as defined in section 1203(6) of title I of the Omnibus Crime Control and Safe Streets Act of 1968) in an official capacity, without compensation, as firefighters or members of a rescue squad or ambulance crew.

(6) specify that the following persons are barred from jury service on the ground that they are exempt: (A) members in active service in the Armed Forces of the United States; (B) members of the fire or police departments of any State, the District of Columbia, any territory or possession of the United States, or any subdivision of a State, the District of Columbia, or such territory or possession; (C) public officers in the executive, legislative, or judicial branches of the Government of the United States, or of any State, the District of Columbia, any territory or possession of the United States, or any subdivision of a State, the District of Columbia, or such territory or possession, who are actively engaged in the performance of official duties.

(7) fix the time when the names drawn from the qualified jury wheel shall be disclosed to parties and to the public. If the plan permits these names to be made public, it may nevertheless permit the chief judge of the district court, or such other district court judge as the plan may provide, to keep these names confidential in any case where the interests of justice so require.

(8) specify the procedures to be followed by the clerk or jury commission in assigning persons whose names have been drawn from the qualified jury wheel to grand and petit jury panels.

(c) The initial plan shall be devised by each district court and transmitted to the reviewing panel specified in subsection (a) of this section within one hundred and twenty days of the date of enactment of the Jury Selection and Service Act of 1968. The panel shall approve or direct the modification of each plan so submitted within sixty days thereafter. Each plan or modification made at the direction of the panel shall become effective after approval at such time thereafter as the panel directs, in no event to exceed ninety days from the date of approval. Modifications made at the instance of the district court under subsection (a) of this section shall be effective at such time thereafter as the panel directs, in no event to exceed ninety days from the date of modification.

(d) State, local, and Federal officials having custody, possession, or control of voter registration lists, lists of actual voters, or other appropriate records shall make such lists and records available to the jury commission or clerks for inspection, reproduction, and copying at all reasonable times as the commission or clerk may deem necessary and proper for the performance of duties under this title. The district courts shall have jurisdiction upon application by the Attorney General of the United States to compel compliance with this subsection by appropriate process.

§1864. DRAWING OF NAMES FROM THE MASTER JURY WHEEL; COMPLETION OF JUROR QUALIFICATION FORM

(a) From time to time as directed by the district court, the clerk or a district judge shall publicly draw at random from the master jury wheel the names of as many persons as may be required for jury service. The clerk or jury commission may, upon order of the court, prepare an alphabetical list of the names drawn from the master jury wheel. Any list so prepared shall not be disclosed to any person except pursuant to the district court plan or pursuant to section 1867 or 1868 of this title. The clerk or jury commission shall mail to every person whose name is drawn from the master wheel a juror qualification form accompanied by instructions to fill out and return the form, duly signed and sworn, to the clerk or jury commission by mail within ten days. If the person is unable to fill out the form, another shall do it for him, and shall indicate that he has done so and the reason therefor. In any case in which it appears that there is an omission, ambiguity, or error in a form, the clerk or jury commission shall return the form with instructions to the person to make such additions or corrections as may be necessary and to return the form to the clerk or jury commission within ten days. Any person who fails to return a completed juror qualification form as instructed may be summoned by the clerk or jury commission forthwith to appear before the clerk or jury commission to fill out a juror qualification form. A person summoned to appear because of failure to return a juror qualification form as instructed who personally appears and executes a juror qualification form before the clerk or jury commission may, at the discretion of the district court, except where his prior failure to execute and mail such form was willful, be entitled to receive for such appearance the same fees and travel allowances paid to jurors under section 1871 of this title. At the time of his appearance for jury service, any person may be required to fill out another juror qualification form in the presence of the jury commission or the clerk or the court, at which time, in such cases as it appears warranted, the person may be questioned, but only with regard to his responses to questions contained on the form. Any information thus acquired by the clerk or jury commission may be noted on the juror qualification form and transmitted to the chief judge or such district court judge as the plan may provide.

(b) Any person summoned pursuant to subsection (a) of this section who fails to appear as directed shall be ordered by the district court forthwith to appear and show cause for his failure to comply with the summons. Any person who fails to appear pursuant to such order or who fails to show good cause for noncompliance with the summons may be fined not more than $100 or imprisoned not more than three days, or both. Any person who willfully misrepresents a material fact on a juror qualification form for the purpose of avoiding or securing service as a juror may be fined not more than $100 or imprisoned not more than three days, or both.

§1865. QUALIFICATIONS FOR JURY SERVICE

(a) The chief judge of the district court, or such other district court judge as the plan may provide, on his initiative or upon recommendation of the clerk or jury commission, or the clerk under supervision of the court if the court's jury selection plan so authorizes, shall determine solely on the basis of information provided on the juror qualification form and other competent evidence whether a person is unqualified for, or exempt, or to be excused from jury service. The clerk shall enter such determination in the space provided on the juror qualification form and in any alphabetical list of names drawn from the master jury wheel. If a person did not appear in response to a summons, such fact shall be noted on said list.

(b) In making such determination the chief judge of the district court, or such other district court judge as the plan may provide, or the clerk if the court's jury selection plan so provides, shall deem any person qualified to serve on grand and petit juries in the district court unless he —

(1) is not a citizen of the United States eighteen years old who has resided for a period of one year within the judicial district;

(2) is unable to read, write, and understand the English language with a degree of proficiency sufficient to fill out satisfactorily the juror qualification form;

(3) is unable to speak the English language;

(4) is incapable, by reason of mental or physical infirmity, to render satisfactory jury service; or

(5) has a charge pending against him for the commission of, or has been convicted in a State or Federal court of record of, a crime punishable by imprisonment for more than one year and his civil rights have not been restored.

§1866. Selection and summoning of jury panels

(a) The jury commission, or in the absence thereof the clerk, shall maintain a qualified jury wheel and shall place in such wheel names of all persons drawn from the master jury wheel who are determined to be qualified as jurors and not exempt or excused pursuant to the district court plan. From time to time, the jury commission or the clerk shall publicly draw at random from the qualified jury wheel such number of names of persons as may be required for assignment to grand and petit jury panels. The jury commission or the clerk shall prepare a separate list of names of persons assigned to each grand and petit jury panel.

(b) When the court orders a grand or petit jury to be drawn, the clerk or jury commission or their duly designated deputies shall issue summonses for the required number of jurors.

Each person drawn for jury service may be served personally, or by registered, certified or first-class mail addressed to such person at his usual residence or business address.

If such service is made personally, the summons shall be delivered by the clerk or the jury commission or their duly designated deputies to the marshal who shall make such service.

If such service is made by mail, the summons may be served by the marshal or by the clerk, the jury commission or their duly designated deputies, who shall make affidavit of service and shall attach thereto any receipt from the addressee for a registered or certified summons.

(c) Except as provided in section 1865 of this title or in any jury selection plan provision adopted pursuant to paragraph (5) or (6) of section 1863(b) of this title, no person or class of persons shall be disqualified, excluded, excused, or exempt from service as jurors: *Provided,* That any person summoned for jury service may be (1) excused by the court, or by the clerk under supervision of the court if the court's jury selection plan so authorizes, upon a showing of undue hardship or extreme inconvenience, for such period as the court deems necessary, at the conclusion of which such person either shall be summoned again for jury service under subsections (b) and (c) of this section or, if the court's jury selection plan so provides, the name of such person shall be reinserted into the qualified jury wheel for selection pursuant to subsection (a) of this section, or (2) excluded by the court on the ground that such person may be unable to render impartial jury service or that his service as a juror would be likely to disrupt the proceedings, or (3) excluded upon peremptory challenge as provided by law, or (4) excluded pursuant to the procedure specified by law upon a challenge by any party for good cause shown, or (5) excluded upon determination by the court that his service as a juror would be likely to threaten the secrecy of the proceedings, or otherwise adversely affect the integrity of jury deliberations. No person shall be excluded under clause (5) of this subsection unless the judge, in open court, determines that such is warranted and that exclusion of the person will not be inconsistent with sections 1861 and 1862 of this title. The number of persons excluded under clause (5) of this subsection shall not exceed one per centum of the number of persons who return executed jury qualification forms during the period, specified in the plan, between two consecutive fillings of the master jury wheel. The names of persons excluded under clause (5) of this subsection, together with detailed explanations for the exclusions, shall be forwarded immediately to the judicial council of the circuit, which shall have the power to make any appropriate order, prospective or retroactive, to redress any misapplication of clause (5) of this subsection, but otherwise exclusions effectuated under such clause shall not be subject to challenge under the provisions of this title. Any person excluded from a particular jury under clause (2), (3), or (4) of this subsection shall be eligible to sit on another jury if the basis for his initial exclusion would not be relevant to his ability to serve on such other jury.

(d) Whenever a person is disqualified, excused, exempt, or excluded from jury service, the jury commission or clerk shall note in the space provided on his juror qualification form or on the juror's card drawn from the qualified jury wheel the specific reason therefor.

(e) In any two-year period, no person shall be required to (1) serve or attend court for prospective service as a petit juror for a total of more than thirty days, except when necessary to complete service in a particular case, or (2) serve on more than one grand jury, or (3) serve as both a grand and petit juror.

(f) When there is an unanticipated shortage of available petit jurors drawn from the qualified jury wheel, the court may require the marshal to summon a sufficient number of petit jurors selected at random from the voter registration lists, lists of actual voters, or other lists specified in the plan, in a manner ordered by the court consistent with sections 1861 and 1862 of this title.

(g) Any person summoned for jury service who fails to appear as directed shall be ordered by the district court to appear forthwith and show cause for his failure to comply with the summons. Any person who fails to show good cause for noncompliance with a summons may be fined not more than $100 or imprisoned not more than three days, or both.

§1867. CHALLENGING COMPLIANCE WITH SELECTION PROCEDURES

(a) In criminal cases, before the voir dire examination begins, or within seven days after the defendant discovered or could have discovered, by the exercise of diligence, the grounds therefor, whichever is earlier, the defendant may move to dismiss the indictment or stay the proceedings against him on the ground of substantial failure to comply with the provisions of this title in selecting the grand or petit jury.

(b) In criminal cases, before the voir dire examination begins, or within seven days after the Attorney General of the United States discovered or could have discovered, by the exercise of diligence, the grounds therefor, whichever is earlier, the Attorney General may move to dismiss the indictment or stay the proceedings on the ground of substantial failure to comply with the provisions of this title in selecting the grand or petit jury.

(c) In civil cases, before the voir dire examination begins, or within seven days after the party discovered or could have discovered, by the exercise of diligence, the grounds therefor, whichever is earlier, any party may move to stay the proceedings on the ground of substantial failure to comply with the provisions of this title in selecting the petit jury.

(d) Upon motion filed under subsection (a), (b), or (c) of this section, containing a sworn statement of facts which, if true, would constitute a substantial failure to comply with the provisions of this title, the moving party shall be entitled to present in support of such motion the testimony of the jury commission or clerk, if available, any relevant records and papers not public or otherwise available used by the jury commissioner or clerk, and any other relevant evidence. If the court determines that there has been a substantial failure to comply with the provisions of this title in selecting the grand jury, the court shall stay the proceedings pending the selection of a grand jury in conformity with this title or dismiss the indictment, whichever is appropriate. If the court determines that there has been a substantial failure to comply with the provisions of this title in selecting the petit jury, the court shall stay the proceedings pending the selection of a petit jury in comformity with this title.

(e) The procedures prescribed by this section shall be the exclusive means by which a person accused of a Federal crime, the Attorney General of the United States or a party in a civil case may challenge any jury on the ground that such jury was not selected in conformity with the provisions of this title. Nothing in this section shall preclude any person or the United States from pursuing any other remedy, civil or criminal, which may be available for the vindication or enforcement of any law prohibiting discrimination on account of race, color, religion, sex, national origin or economic status in the selection of persons for service on grand or petit juries.

(f) The contents of records or papers used by the jury commission or clerk in connection with the jury selection process shall not be disclosed, except pursuant to the district court plan or as may be necessary in the preparation or presentation of a motion under subsection (a), (b), or (c) or this section, until after the master jury wheel has been emptied and refilled pursuant to section 1863(b)(4) of this title and all persons selected to serve as jurors before the master wheel was emptied have completed such service. The parties in a case shall be allowed to inspect, reproduce, and copy such records or papers at all reasonable times during the preparation and pendency of such a motion. Any person who discloses the contents of any record or paper in violation of this subsection may be fined not more than $1,000 or imprisoned not more than one year, or both.

§1868. Maintenance and inspection of records

After the master jury wheel is emptied and refilled pursuant to section 1863(b)(4) of this title, and after all persons selected to serve as jurors before the master wheel was emptied have completed such service, all records and papers compiled and maintained by the jury commission or clerk before the master wheel was emptied shall be preserved in the custody of the clerk for four years or for such longer period as may be ordered by a court, and shall be available for public inspection for the purpose of determining the validity of the selection of any jury.

§1869. Definitions

For purposes of this chapter —

(a) "clerk" and "clerk of the court" shall mean the clerk of the district court of the United States, any authorized deputy clerk, and any other person authorized by the court to assist the clerk in the performance of functions under this chapter;

(b) "chief judge" shall mean the chief judge of any district court of the United States;

(c) Voter Registration lists shall mean the official records maintained by State or local election officials of persons registered to vote in either the most recent State or the most recent Federal general election, or, in the case of a State or political subdivision thereof that does not require registration as a prerequisite to voting, other official lists of persons qualified to vote in such election. The term shall also include the list of eligible voters maintained by any Federal examiner pursuant to the Voting Rights Act of 1965 where the names on such list have not been included on the official registration lists or other official lists maintained by the appropriate State or local officials. With respect to the districts of Guam and the Virgin Islands, "voter registration lists" shall mean the official records maintained by territorial election officials of persons registered to vote in the most recent territorial general election;

(d) "lists of actual voters" shall mean the official lists of persons actually voting in either the most recent State or the most recent Federal general election;

(e) "division" shall mean: (1) one or more statutory divisions of a judicial district; or (2) in statutory divisions that contain more than one place of holding court, or in judicial districts where there are no statutory divisions, such counties, parishes, or similar political subdivisions surrounding the places where court is held as the district court plan shall determine: *Provided,* That each county, parish, or similar political subdivision shall be included in some such division;

(f) "district court of the United States," "district court," and "court" shall mean any district court established by chapter 5 of this title, and any court which is created by an Act of Congress in a territory and is invested with any jurisdiction of a district court established by chapter 5 of this title.

(g) "jury wheel" shall include any device or system similar in purpose or function, such as a properly programmed electronic data processing system or device;

(h) "juror qualification form" shall mean a form prescribed by the Administrative Office of the United States Courts and approved by the Judicial Conference of the United States, which shall elicit the name, address, age, race, occupation, education, length of residence within the judicial district, distance from residence to place of holding court, prior jury service, and citizenship of a potential juror, and whether he should be excused or exempted from jury service, has any physicial or mental infirmity impairing his capacity to serve as juror, is able to read, write, speak, and understand the English language, has pending against him any charge for the commission of a State or Federal criminal offense punishable by imprisonment for more than one year, or has been convicted in any State or Federal court of record of a crime punishable by imprisonment for more than one year and has not had his civil rights restored. The form shall request, but not require, any other information not inconsistent with the provisions of this title and required by the district court plan in the interests of the sound administration of justice. The form shall also elicit the sworn statement that his responses are true to the best of his knowledge. Notarization shall not be required. The form shall contain words clearly informing the person that the furnishing of any information with respect to his religion, national origin, or economic status is not a prerequisite to his qualification for jury service, that such information need not be furnished if the person finds it objectionable to do so, and that information concerning race is required solely to enforce nondiscrimination in jury selection and has no bearing on an individual's qualification for jury service.

(i) "public officer" shall mean a person who is either elected to public office or who is directly appointed by a person elected to public office.

§1870. Challenge

In civil cases, each party shall be entitled to three peremptory challenges. Several defendants or several plaintiffs may be considered as a single party for the purposes of making challenges, or the court may allow additional peremptory challenges and permit them to be exercised separately or jointly.

All challenges for cause or favor, whether to the array or panel or to individual jurors, shall be determined by the court.

§1871. FEES

(a) Grand and petit jurors in district courts appearing pursuant to this chapter shall be paid the fees and allowances provided by this section. The requisite fees and allowances shall be disbursed on the certificate of the clerk of court in accordance with the procedure established by the Director of the Administrative Office of the United States Courts. Attendance fees for extended service under subsection (b) of this section shall be certified by the clerk only upon the order of a district judge.

(b)(1) A juror shall be paid an attendance fee of $40 per day for actual attendance at the place of trial or hearing. A juror shall also be paid the attendance fee for the time necessarily occupied in going to and returning from such place at the beginning and end of such service or at any time during such service.

(2) A petit juror required to attend more than thirty days in hearing one case may be paid, in the discretion of the trial judge, an additional fee, not exceeding $10 more than the attendance fee, for each day in excess of thirty days on which he is required to hear such case.

(3) A grand juror required to attend more than forty-five days of actual service may be paid, in the discretion of the district judge in charge of the particular grand jury, an additional fee, not exceeding $10 more than the attendance fee, for each day in excess of forty-five days of actual service.

(4) A grand or petit juror required to attend more than ten days of actual service may be paid, in the discretion of the judge, the appropriate fees at the end of the first ten days and at the end of every ten days of service thereafter.

(5) Certification of additional attendance fees may be ordered by the judge to be made effective commencing on the first day of extended service, without reference to the date of such certification.

(c)(1) A travel allowance not to exceed the maximum rate per mile that the Director of the Administrative Office of the United States Courts has prescribed pursuant to section 604(a)(7) of this title for payment to supporting court personnel in travel status using privately owned automobiles shall be paid to each juror, regardless of the mode of transportation actually employed. The prescribed rate shall be paid for the distance necessarily traveled to and from a juror's residence by the shortest practical route in going to and returning from the place of service. Actual mileage in full at the prescribed rate is payable at the beginning and at the end of a juror's term of service.

(2) The Director shall promulgate rules regulating interim travel allowances to jurors. Distances traveled to and from court should coincide with the shortest practical route.

(3) Toll charges for toll roads, bridges, tunnels, and ferries shall be paid in full to the juror incurring such charges. In the discretion of the court, reasonable parking fees may be paid to the juror incurring such fees upon presentation of a valid parking receipt. Parking fees shall not be included in any tabulation of mileage cost allowances.

(4) Any juror who travels to district court pursuant to summons in an area outside of the contiguous forty-eight States of the United States shall be paid the travel expenses provided under this section, or actual reasonable transportation expenses subject to the discretion of the district judge or clerk of court as circumstances indicate, exercising due regard for the mode of transportation, the availability of alternative modes, and the shortest practical route between residence and court.

(5) A grand juror who travels to district court pursuant to a summons may be paid the travel expenses provided under this section or, under guidelines established by the Judicial Conference, the actual reasonable costs of travel by aircraft when travel by other means is not feasible and when certified by the chief judge of the district court in which the grand juror serves.

(d)(1) A subsistence allowance covering meals and lodging of jurors shall be established from time to time by the Director of the Administrative Office of the United States Courts pursuant to section 604(a)(7) of this title, except that such allowance shall not exceed the allowance for supporting court personnel in travel status in the same geographical area. Claims for such allowance shall not require itemization.

(2) A subsistence allowance shall be paid to a juror when an overnight stay is required at the place of holding court, and for the time necessarily spent in traveling to and from the place of attendance if an overnight stay is required.

(3) A subsistence allowance for jurors serving in district courts outside of the contiguous forty-eight States of the United States shall be allowed at a rate not to exceed that per diem allowance which is paid to supporting court personnel in travel status in those areas where the Director of the Administrative Office of the United States Courts has prescribed an increased per diem fee pursuant to section 604(a)(7) of this title.

(e) During any period in which a jury is ordered to be kept together and not to separate, the actual cost of subsistence shall be paid upon the order of the court in lieu of the subsistence allowances payable under subsection (d) of this section. Such allowance for the jurors ordered to be kept separate or sequestered shall include the cost of meals, lodging, and other expenditures ordered in the discretion of the court for their convenience and comfort.

(f) A juror who must necessarily use public transportation in travelling to and from court, the full cost of which is not met by the transportation expenses allowable under subsection (c) of this section on account of the short distance traveled in miles, may be paid, in the discretion of the court, the actual reasonable expense of such public transportation, pursuant to the methods of payment provided by this section. Jurors who are required to remain at the court beyond the normal business closing hour for deliberation or for any other reason may be transported to their homes, or to temporary lodgings where such lodgings are ordered by the court, in a manner directed by the clerk and paid from funds authorized under this section.

(g) The Director of the Administrative Office of the United States Courts shall promulgate such regulations as may be necessary to carry out his authority under this section.

§1872. Issues of fact in Supreme Court

In all original actions at law in the Supreme Court against citizens of the United States, issues of fact shall be tried by a jury.

§1873. Admiralty and maritime cases

In any case of admiralty and maritime jurisdiction relating to any matter of contract or tort arising upon or concerning any vessel of twenty tons or upward, enrolled and licensed for the coasting trade, and employed in the business of commerce and navigation between places in different states upon the lakes and navigable waters connecting said lakes, the trial of all issues of fact shall be by jury if either party demands it.

§1875. Protection of jurors' employment

(a) No employer shall discharge, threaten to discharge, intimidate, or coerce any permanent employee by reason of such employee's jury service, or the attendance or scheduled attendance in connection with such service, in any court of the United States.

(b) Any employer who violates the provisions of this section —

(1) shall be liable for damages for any loss of wages or other benefits suffered by an employee by reason of such violation;

(2) may be enjoined from further violations of this section and ordered to provide other appropriate relief, including but not limited to the reinstatement of any employee discharged by reason of his jury service; and

(3) shall be subject to a civil penalty of not more than $1,000 for each violation as to each employee.

(c) Any individual who is reinstated to a position of employment in accordance with the provisions of this section shall be considered as having been on furlough or leave of absence during his period of jury service, shall be reinstated to his position of employment without loss of seniority, and shall be entitled to participate in insurance or other benefits offered by the employer pursuant to established rules and practices relating to employees on furlough or leave of absence in effect with the employer at the time such individual entered upon jury service.

(d)(1) An individual claiming that his employer has violated the provisions of this section may make application to the district court for the district in which such employer maintains a place of business and the court shall, upon finding probable merit in such claim, appoint counsel to represent such individual in any action in the district court necessary to the resolution of such claim. Such counsel shall be compensated and necessary expenses repaid to the extent provided by section 3006A of title 18, United States Code.

(2) In any action or proceeding under this section, the court may award a prevailing employee who brings such action by retained counsel a reasonable attorney's fee as part of the costs. The court may tax a defendant employer, as costs payable to the court, the attorney fees and expenses incurred on behalf of a prevailing employee, where such costs were expended by the court pursuant to paragraph (1) of this subsection. The court may award a prevailing employer a reasonable attorney's fee as part of the costs only if the court finds that the action is frivolous, vexatious, or brought in bad faith.

Chapter 123. Fees and Costs

§1914. DISTRICT COURT; FILING AND MISCELLANEOUS FEES; RULES OF COURT

(a) The clerk of each district court shall require the parties instituting any civil action, suit or proceeding in such court, whether by original process, removal or otherwise, to pay a filing fee of $150, except that on application for a writ of habeas corpus the filing fee shall be $5.

(b) The clerk shall collect from the parties such additional fees only as are prescribed by the Judicial Conference of the United States.

(c) Each district court by rule or standing order may require advance payment of fees.

§1915. PROCEEDINGS IN FORMA PAUPERIS

(a)(1) Subject to subsection (b), any court of the United States may authorize the commencement, prosecution or defense of any suit, action or proceeding, civil or criminal, or appeal therein, without prepayment of fees or security therefor, by a person who submits an affidavit that includes a statement of all assets such prisoner possesses that the person is unable to pay such fees or give security therefor. Such affidavit shall state the nature of the action, defense or appeal and affiant's belief that the person is entitled to redress.

(2) A prisoner seeking to bring a civil action or appeal a judgment in a civil action or proceeding without prepayment of fees or security therefor, in addition to filing the affidavit filed under paragraph (1), shall submit a certified copy of the trust fund account statement (or institutional equivalent) for the prisoner for the six-month period immediately preceding the filing of the complaint or notice of appeal, obtained from the appropriate official of each prison at which the prisoner is or was confined.

(3) An appeal may not be taken in forma pauperis if the trial court certifies in writing that it is not taken in good faith.

(b)(1) Notwithstanding subsection (a), if a prisoner brings a civil action or files an appeal in forma pauperis, the prisoner shall be required to pay the full amount of a filing fee. The court shall assess and, when funds exist, collect, as a partial payment of any court fees required by law, an initial partial filing fee of 20 percent of the greater of —

(A) the average monthly deposits to the prisoner's account; or

(B) the average monthly balance in the prisoner's account for the 6-month period immediately preceding the filing of the complaint or notice of appeal.

(2) After payment of the initial partial filing fee, the prisoner shall be required to make monthly payments of 20 percent of the preceding month's income credited to the prisoner's account. The agency having custody of the prisoner shall forward payments from the prisoner's account to the clerk of the court each time the amount in the account exceeds $10 until the filing fees are paid.

(3) In no event shall the filing fee collected exceed the amount of fees permitted by statute for the commencement of a civil action or an appeal of a civil action or criminal judgment.

(4) In no event shall a prisoner be prohibited from bringing a civil action or appealing a civil or criminal judgment for the reason that the prisoner has no assets and no means by which to pay the initial partial filing fee.

(c) Upon the filing of an affidavit in accordance with subsections (a) and (b) and the prepayment of any partial filing fee as may be required under subsection (b), the court may direct payment by the United States of the expenses of (1) printing the record on appeal in any civil or criminal case, if such printing is required by the appellate court; (2) preparing a transcript of proceedings before a United States magistrate in any civil or criminal case, if such transcript is required by the district court, in the case of proceedings conducted under section 636(b) of this title or under section 3401(b) of title 18, United States Code; and (3) printing the record on appeal if such printing is required by the appellate court, in the case of proceedings conducted pursuant to section 636(c) of this title. Such expenses shall be paid when authorized by the Director of the Administrative Office of the United States Courts.

(d) The officers of the court shall issue and serve all process, and perform all duties in such cases. Witnesses shall attend as in other cases, and the same remedies shall be available as are provided for by law in other cases.

(e)(1) The court may request an attorney to represent any person unable to afford counsel.

(2) Notwithstanding any filing fee, or any portion thereof, that may have been paid, the court shall dismiss the case at any time if the court determines that —

(A) the allegation of poverty is untrue; or

(B) the action or appeal —

(i) is frivolous or malicious;

(ii) fails to state a claim on which relief may be granted; or

(iii) seeks monetary relief against a defendant who is immune from such relief.

(f)(1) Judgment may be rendered for costs at the conclusion of the suit or action as in other proceedings, but the United States shall not be liable for any of the costs thus incurred. If the United States has paid the cost of a stenographic transcript or printed record for the prevailing party, the same shall be taxed in favor of the United States.

(2)(A) If the judgment against a prisoner includes the payment of costs under this subsection, the prisoner shall be required to pay the full amount of the costs ordered.

(B) The prisoner shall be required to make payments for costs under this subsection in the same manner as is provided for filing fees under subsection (a)(2).

(C) In no event shall the costs collected exceed the amount of the costs ordered by the court.

(g) In no event shall a prisoner bring a civil action or appeal a judgment in a civil action or proceeding under this section if the prisoner has, on three or more prior occasions, while incarcerated or detained in any facility, brought an action or appeal in a court of the United States that was dismissed on the grounds that it is frivolous, malicious, or fails to state a claim upon which relief may be granted, unless the prisoner is under imminent danger of serious physical injury.

(h) As used in this section, the term 'prisoner' means any person incarcerated or detained in any facility who is accused of, convicted of, sentenced for, or adjudicated delinquent for, violations of criminal law or the terms and conditions of parole, probation, pretrial release, or diversionary program.

§1919. Dismissal for lack of jurisdiction

Whenever any action or suit is filed in any district court, the Court of International Trade, or the Court of Federal Claims for want of jurisdiction, such court may order the payment of just costs.

§1920. Taxation of costs

A judge or clerk of any court of the United States may tax as costs the following:

(1) Fees of the clerk and marshal;

(2) Fees of the court reporter for all or any part of the stenographic transcript necessarily obtained for use in the case;

(3) Fees and disbursements for printing and witnesses;

(4) Fees for exemplification and copies of papers necessarily obtained for use in the case;

(5) Docket fees under section 1923 of this title.

(6) Compensation of court appointed experts, compensation of interpreters, and salaries, fees, expenses, and costs of special interpretation services under section 1828 of this title.

A bill of costs shall be filed in the case and, upon allowance, included in the judgment or decree.

§1923. Docket fees and costs of briefs

(a) Attorney's and proctor's docket fees in courts of the United States may be taxed as costs as follows:

$20 on trial or final hearing (including a default judgment whether entered by the court or by the clerk) in civil, criminal, or admiralty cases, except that in cases of admiralty and maritime jurisdiction where the libellant recovers less than $50 the proctor's docket fee shall be $10;

$20 in admiralty appeals involving not over $1,000;

$50 in admiralty appeals involving not over $5,000;

$100 in admiralty appeals involving more than $5,000;

$5 on discontinuance of a civil action;

$5 on motion for judgment and other proceedings on recognizances;

$2.50 for each deposition admitted in evidence.

(b) The docket fees of the United States attorneys and United States trustees shall be paid to the clerk of court and by him paid into the Treasury.

(c) In admiralty appeals the court may allow as costs for printing the briefs of the successful party not more than:

$25 where the amount involved is not over $1,000;

$50 where the amount involved is not over $5,000;

$75 where the amount involved is over $5,000.

§1927. Counsel's liability for excessive costs

Any attorney or other person admitted to conduct cases in any court of the United States or any Territory thereof who so multiplies the proceedings in any case as to increase costs unreasonably and vexatiously may be required by the court to satisfy personally the excess costs, expenses, and attorneys' fees reasonably incurred because of such conduct.

§1929. Extraordinary expenses not expressly authorized

Where the ministerial officers of the United States incur extraordinary expense in executing Acts of Congress, the payment of which is not specifically provided for, the Attorney General may allow the payment thereof.

Chapter 125. Pending Actions and Judgments

§1961. Interest

(a) Interest shall be allowed on any money judgment in a civil case recovered in a district court. Execution therefor may be levied by the marshal, in any case where, by the law of the State in which such court is held, execution may be levied for interest on judgments recovered in the courts of the State. Such interest shall be calculated from the date of the entry of the judgment, at a rate equal to the coupon issue yield equivalent (as determined by the Secretary of the Treasury) of the average accepted auction price for the last auction of fifty-two-week United States Treasury bills settled immediately prior to the date of the judgment. The Director of the Administrative Office of the United States Courts shall distribute notice of that rate and any changes in it to all Federal judges; and

(b) Interest shall be computed daily to the date of payment except as provided in section 2516(b) of title 28, and section 1304(b) of title 31, and shall be compounded annually.

(c)(1) This section shall not apply in any judgment of any court with respect to any internal revenue tax case. Interest shall be allowed in such cases at the underpayment rate or overpayment rate (whichever is appropriate) established under section 6621 of the Internal Revenue Code of 1954 [26 U.S.C.A. §6621].

(2) Except as otherwise provided in paragraph (1) of this subsection, interest shall be allowed on all final judgments against the United States in the United States Court of Appeals for the Federal Circuit, at the rate provided in subsection (a) and as provided in subsection (b).

(3) Interest shall be allowed, computed, and paid on judgments of the United States Claims Court only as provided in paragraph (1) of this subsection or in any other provision of law.

(4) This section shall not be construed to affect the interest on any judgment of any court not specified in this section.

§1963. Registration of judgments for enforcement in other districts

A judgment in an action for the recovery of money or property entered in any court of appeals, district court, bankruptcy court or in the Court of International Trade may be registered by filing a certified copy of the judgment in any other district or, with respect to the Court of International Trade, in any judicial district, when the judgment has become final by appeal or expiration of the time for appeal or when ordered by the court that entered the judgment for good cause shown. Such a judgment entered in favor of the United States may be so registered any time after judgment is entered. A judgment so registered shall have the same effect as a judgment of the district court of the district where registered and may be enforced in like manner.

A certified copy of the satisfaction of any judgment in whole or in part may be registered in like manner in any district in which the judgment is a lien.

The procedure prescribed under this section is in addition to other procedures provided by law for the enforcement of judgments.

§1964. Constructive notice of pending actions

Where the law of a State requires a notice of an action concerning real property pending in a court of the State to be registered, recorded, docketed, or indexed in a particular manner, or in a certain office or county or parish in order to give constructive notice of the action as it relates to the real property, and such law authorizes a notice of an action concerning real property pending in a United States district court to be registered, recorded, docketed, or indexed in the same manner, or in the same place, those requirements of the State law must be complied with in order to give constructive notice of such an action pending in a United States district court as it relates to real property in such State.

Chapter 131. Rules of Courts

§2071. Rule-making power generally

(a) The Supreme Court and all courts established by Act of Congress may from time to time prescribe rules for the conduct of their business. Such rules shall be consistent with Acts of Congress and rules of practice and procedure prescribed under section 2072 of this title.

(b) Any rule prescribed by a court, other than the Supreme Court, under subsection (a) shall be prescribed only after giving appropriate public notice and an opportunity for comment. Such rule shall take effect upon the date specified by the prescribing court and shall have such effect on pending proceedings as the prescribing court may order.

(c)(1) A rule of a district court prescribed under subsection (a) shall remain in effect unless modified or abrogated by the judicial council of the relevant circuit.

(2) Any other rule prescribed by a court other than the Supreme Court under subsection (a) shall remain in effect unless modified or abrogated by the Judicial Conference.

(d) Copies of rules prescribed under subsection (a) by a district court shall be furnished to the judicial council, and copies of all rules prescribed by a court other than the Supreme Court under subsection (a) shall be furnished to the Director of the Administrative Office of the United States Courts and made available to the public.

(e) If the prescribing court determines that there is an immediate need for a rule, such court may proceed under this section without public notice and opportunity for comment, but such court shall promptly thereafter afford such notice and opportunity for comment.

(f) No rule may be prescribed by a district court other than under this section.

§2072. Rules of procedure and evidence; power to prescribe

(a) The Supreme Court shall have the power to prescribe general rules of practice and procedure and rules of evidence for cases in the United States district courts (including proceedings before magistrates thereof) and courts of appeals.

(b) Such rules shall not abridge, enlarge, or modify any substantive right. All laws in conflict with such rules shall be of no further force or effect after such rules have taken effect.

(c) Such rules may define when a ruling of a district court is final for the purposes of appeal under section 1291 of this title.

§2073. Rules of procedure and evidence; method of prescribing

(a)(1) The Judicial Conference shall prescribe and publish the procedures for the consideration of proposed rules under this section.

(2) The Judicial Conference may authorize the appointment of committees to assist the Conference by recommending rules to be prescribed under sections 2072 and 2075 of this title. Each such committee shall consist of members of the bench and the professional bar, and trial and appellate judges.

(b) The Judical Conference shall authorize the appointment of a standing committee on rules of practice, procedure, and evidence under subsection (a) of this section. Such standing committee shall review each recommendation of any other committees so appointed and recommend to the Judicial Conference rules of practice, procedure, and evidence and such changes in rules proposed by a committee appointed under subsection (a)(2) of this section as may be necessary to maintain consistency and otherwise promote the interest of justice.

(c)(1) Each meeting for the transaction of business under this chapter by any committee appointed under this section shall be open to the public, except when the committee so meeting, in open session and with a majority present, determines that it is in the public interest that all or part of the remainder of the meeting on that day shall be closed to the public, and states the reason for so closing the meeting. Minutes of each meeting for the transaction of business under this chapter shall be maintained by the committee and made available to the public, except that any portion of such minutes, relating to a closed meeting and made available to the public, may contain such deletions as may be necessary to avoid frustrating the purposes of closing the meeting.

(2) Any meeting for the transaction of business under this chapter, by a

committee appointed under this section, shall be preceded by sufficient notice to enable all interested persons to attend.

(d) In making a recommendation under this section or under section 2072 or 2075, the body making that recommendation shall provide a proposed rule, an explanatory note on the rule, and a written report explaining the body's action, including any minority or other separate views.

(e) Failure to comply with this section does not invalidate a rule prescribed under section 2072 or 2075 of this title.

§2074. Rules of procedure and evidence; submission to Congress; effective date

(a) The Supreme Court shall transmit to the Congress not later than May 1 of the year in which a rule prescribed under section 2072 is to become effective a copy of the proposed rule. Such rule shall take effect no earlier than December 1 of the year in which such rule is so transmitted unless otherwise provided by law. The Supreme Court may fix the extent such rule shall apply to proceedings then pending, except that the Supreme Court shall not require the application of such rule to further proceedings then pending to the extent that, in the opinion of the court in which such proceedings are pending, the application of such rule in such proceedings would not be feasible or would work injustice, in which event the former rule applies.

(b) Any such rule creating, abolishing, or modifying an evidentiary privilege shall have no force or effect unless approved by Act of Congress.

§2075. Bankruptcy rules

The Supreme Court shall have the power to prescribe by general rules, the forms of process, writs, pleadings, and motions, and the practice and procedure in cases under title 11.

Such rules shall not abridge, enlarge, or modify any substantive right.

The Supreme Court shall transmit to Congress not later than May 1 of the year in which a rule prescribed under this section is to become effective a copy of the proposed rule. The rule shall take effect no earlier than December 1 of the year in which it is transmitted to Congress unless otherwise provided by law.

§2077. Publication of rules; advisory committees

(a) The rules for the conduct of the business of each court except the Supreme Court, that is authorized to prescribe rules of the conduct of such court's business under section 2071 of this title, including the operating procedures of such court, shall be published. Each such court shall print or cause to be printed necessary copies of the rules. The Judicial Conference shall prescribe the fees for sales of copies under section 1913 of this title, but the Judicial

Conference may provide for free distribution of copies to members of the bar of each court and to other interested persons.

(b) Each court, except the Supreme Court, that is authorized to prescribe rules of conduct of such court's business under section 2071 of this title shall appoint an advisory committee for the study of the rules of practice and internal operating procedures of the court of appeals and, in the case of an advisory committee appointed by a court of appeals, of the rules of the judicial council of the circuit. The advisory committee shall make recommendations to the court concerning such rules and procedures. Members of the committee shall serve without compensation, but the Director may pay travel and transportation expenses in accordance with section 5703 of title 5.

Chapter 133. Review — Miscellaneous Provisions

§2101. Supreme Court; time for appeal or certiorari; docketing; stay

(a) A direct appeal to the Supreme Court from any decision under section 1253 of this title, holding unconstitutional in whole or in part, any Act of Congress, shall be taken within thirty days after the entry of the interlocutory or final order, judgment or decree. The record shall be made up and the case docketed within sixty days from the time such appeal is taken under rules prescribed by the Supreme Court.

(b) Any other direct appeal to the Supreme Court which is authorized by law, from a decision of a district court in any civil action, suit or proceeding, shall be taken within thirty days from the judgment, order or decree, appealed from, if interlocutory, and within sixty days if final.

(c) Any other appeal or any writ of certiorari intended to bring any judgment of decree in a civil action, suit or proceeding before the Supreme Court for review shall be taken or applied for within ninety days after the entry of such judgment or decree. A justice of the Supreme Court, for good cause shown, may extend the time for applying for a writ of certiorari for a period not exceeding sixty days.

(d) The time for appeal or application for a writ of certiorari to review the judgment of a State court in a criminal case shall be as prescribed by rules of the Supreme Court;

(e) An application to the Supreme Court for a writ of certiorari to review a case before judgment has been rendered in the court of appeals may be made at any time before judgment;

(f) In any case in which the final judgment or decree of any court is subject to review by the Supreme Court on writ of certiorari, the execution and enforcement of such judgment or decree may be stayed for a reasonable time to enable the party aggrieved to obtain a writ of certiorari from the Supreme

Court. The stay may be granted by a judge of the court rendering the judgment or decree or by a justice of the Supreme Court, and may be conditioned on the giving of security, approved by such judge or justice, that if the aggrieved party fails to make application for such writ within the period allotted therefor, or fails to obtain an order granting his application, or fails to make his plea good in the Supreme Court, he shall answer for all damages and costs which the other party may sustain by reason of the stay.

(g) The time for application for a writ of certiorari to review a decision of the United States Court of Appeals for the Armed Forces shall be as prescribed by rules of the Supreme Court.

§2102. Priority of criminal case on appeal from state court

Criminal cases on review from State courts shall have priority, on the docket of the Supreme Court, over all cases except cases to which the United States is a party and such other cases as the court may decide to be of public importance.

§2103. [Repealed.]

§2104. Reviews of State court deicsions

A review by the Supreme Court of a judgment or decree of a State court shall be conducted in the same manner and under the same regulations, and shall have the same effect, as if the judgment or decree reviewed had been rendered in a court of the United States.

§2105. Scope of review; abatement

There shall be no reversal in the Supreme Court or a court of appeals for error in ruling upon matters in abatement which do not involve jurisdiction.

§2106. Determination

The Supreme Court or any other court of appellate jurisdiction may affirm, modify, vacate, set aside or reverse any judgment, decree, or order of a court lawfully brought before it for review, and may remand the cause and direct the entry of such appropriate judgment, decree, or order, or require such further proceedings to be had as may be just under the circumstances.

§2107. Time for appeal to court of appeals

(a) Except as otherwise provided in this section, no appeal shall bring any judgment, order or decree in an action, suit or proceeding of a civil nature before a court of appeals for review unless notice of appeal is filed, within thirty days after the entry of such judgment, order or decree.

(b) In any such action, suit or proceeding in which the United States or an officer or agency thereof is a party, the time as to all parties shall be sixty days from such entry.

(c) The district court may, upon motion filed not later than 30 days after the expiration of the time otherwise set for bringing appeal, extend the time for appeal upon a showing of excusable neglect or good cause. In addition, if the district court finds —

(1) that a party entitled to notice of the entry of a judgment or order did not receive such notice from the clerk or any party within 21 days of its entry, and

(2) that no party would be prejudiced, the district court may, upon motion filed within 180 days after entry of the judgment or order or within 7 days after receipt of such notice, whichever is earlier, reopen the time for appeal for a period of 14 days from the date of entry of the order reopening the time for appeal.

(d) This section shall not apply to bankruptcy matters or other proceedings under Title 11.

§2108. Proof of amount in controversy

Where the power of any court of appeals to review a case depends upon the amount or value in controversy, such amount or value, if not otherwise satisfactorily disclosed upon the record, may be shown and ascertained by the oath of a party to the case or by other competent evidence.

§2109. Quorum of supreme Court justices absent

If a case brought to the Supreme Court by direct appeal from a district court cannot be heard and determined because of the absence of a quorum of qualified justices, the Chief Justice of the United States may order it remitted to the court of appeals for the circuit including the district in which the case arose, to be heard and determined by that court either sitting in banc or specially constituted and composed of the three circuit judges senior in commission who are able to sit, as such order may direct. The decision of such court shall be final and conclusive. In the event of the disqualification or disability of one or more of such circuit judges, such court shall be filled as provided in chapter 15 of this title.

In any other case brought to the Supreme Court for review, which cannot be heard and determined because of the absence of a quorum of qualified justices, if a majority of the qualified justices shall be of opinion that the case cannot be heard and determined at the next ensuing term, the court shall enter its order affirming the judgment of the court from which the case was brought for review with the same effect as upon affirmance by an equally divided court.

§2111. HARMLESS ERROR

On the hearing of any appeal or writ of certiorari in any case, the court shall give judgment after an examination of the record without regard to errors or defects which do not affect the substantial rights of the parties.

§2113. DEFINITION

For purposes of this chapter, the terms "State court," "State courts," and "highest court of a State" include the District of Columbia Court of Appeals.

Part VI. Particular Proceedings

Chapter 151. Declaratory Judgments

§2201. CREATION OF REMEDY

(a) In a case of actual controversy within its jurisdiction, except with respect to Federal taxes other than actions brought under section 7428 of the Internal Revenue Code of 1986 or a proceeding under section 505 or 1146 of title 11, or in any civil action involving an antidumping or countervailing duty proceeding regarding a class or kind of merchandise of a free trade area country (as defined in section 510A(f)(10) of the Tariff Act of 1930), as determined by the administering authority, any court of the United States, upon the filing of an appropriate pleading, may declare the rights and other legal relations of any interested party seeking such declaration, whether or not further relief is or could be sought. Any such declaration shall have the force and effect of a final judgment or decree and shall be reviewable as such.

(b) For limitations on actions brought with respect to drug patents see section 505 of the Federal Food, Drug, and Cosmetic Act.

§2202. FURTHER RELIEF

Further necessary or proper relief based on a declaratory judgment or decree may be granted, after reasonable notice and hearing, against any adverse party whose rights have been determined by such judgment.

Chapter 155. Injunctions; Three-Judge Courts

§2281. [REPEALED.]

§2282. [REPEALED.]

§2283. STAY OF STATE COURT PROCEEDINGS

A court of the United States may not grant an injunction to stay proceedings in a State court except as expressly authorized by Act of Congress, or where necessary in aid of its jurisdiction, or to protect or effectuate its judgments.

§2284. THREE-JUDGE COURT; WHEN REQUIRED; COMPOSITION; PROCEDURE

(a) A district court of three judges shall be convened when otherwise required by Act of Congress, or when an action is filed challenging the constitutionality of the apportionment of congressional districts or the apportionment of any statewide legislative body.

(b) In any action required to be heard and determined by a district court of three judges under subsection (a) of this section, the composition and procedure of the court shall be as follows:

(1) Upon the filing of a request for three judges, the judge to whom the request is presented shall, unless he determines that three judges are not required, immediately notify the chief judge of the circuit, who shall designate two other judges, at least one of whom shall be a circuit judge. The judges so designated, and the judge to whom the request was presented, shall serve as members of the court to hear and determine the action or proceeding.

(2) If the action is against a State, or officer or agency thereof, at least five days' notice of hearing of the action shall be given by registered or certified mail to the Governor and attorney general of the State.

(3) A single judge may conduct all proceedings except the trial, and enter all orders permitted by the rules of civil procedure except as provided in this subsection. He may grant a temporary restraining order on a specific finding, based on evidence submitted, that specified irreparable damage will result if the order is not granted, which order, unless previously revoked by the district judge, shall remain in force only until the hearing and determination by the district court of three judges of an application for a preliminary injunction. A single judge shall not appoint a master, or order a reference, or hear and determine any application for a preliminary or permanent injunction or motion to vacate such an injunction, or enter judgment on the merits. Any action of a single judge may be reviewed by the full court at any time before final judgment.

Chapter 159. Interpleader

§2361. PROCESS AND PROCEDURE

In any civil action of interpleader or in the nature of interpleader under section 1335 of this title, a district court may issue its process for all claimants and enter its order restraining them from instituting or prosecuting any proceeding in any State or United States court affecting the property, instrument or obligation involved in the interpleader action until further order of the court. Such process and order shall be returnable at such time as the court or judge thereof directs, and shall be addressed to and served by the United States marshals for the respective districts where the claimants reside or may be found.

Such district court shall hear and determine the case, and may discharge the plaintiff from further liability, make the injunction permanent, and make all appropriate orders to enforce its judgment.

[See also §§1335 and 1397.]

Chapter 161. United States as Party Generally

§2401. Time for commencing action against United States

(a) Except as provided by the Contract Disputes Act of 1978, every civil action commenced against the United States shall be barred unless the complaint is filed within six years after the right of action first accrues. The action of any person under legal disability or beyond the seas at the time the claim accrues may be commenced within three years after the disability ceases.

(b) A tort claim against the United States shall be forever barred unless it is presented in writing to the appropriate Federal agency within two years after such claim accrues or unless action is begun within six months after the date of mailing, by certified or registered mail, of notice of final denial of the claim by the agency to which it was presented.

§2402. Jury trial in actions against United States

Subject to chapter 179 of this title, any action against the United States under section 1346 shall be tried by the court without a jury, except that any action against the United States under section 1346(a)(1) shall, at the request of either party to such action, be tried by the court with a jury.

§2403. Intervention by United States or a State; constitutional question

(a) In any action, suit or proceeding in a court of the United States to which the United States or any agency, office or employee thereof is not a party, wherein the constitutionality of any Act of Congress affecting the public interest is drawn in question, the court shall certify such fact to the Attorney General, and shall permit the United States to intervene for presentation of evidence, if evidence is otherwise admissible in the case, and for argument on the question of constitutionality. The United States shall, subject to the applicable provisions of law, have all the rights of a party and be subject to all liabilities of a party as to court costs to the extent necessary for a proper presentation of the facts and law relating to the question of constitutionality.

(b) In any action, suit, or proceeding in a court of the United States to which a State or any agency, officer, or employee thereof is not a party wherein the constitutionality of any statute of that State affecting the public interest is drawn in question, the court shall certify such fact to the attorney general of the State, and shall permit the State to intervene for presentation of evidence, if evidence is otherwise admissible in the case, and for argument on the question of constitutionality. The State shall, subject to the applicable provisions of law, have all the rights of a party and be subject to all liabilities of a party as to court costs to the extent necessary for a proper presentation of the facts and law relating to the question of constitutionality.

§2412. Costs and fees

(a)(1) Except as otherwise specifically provided by statute, a judgment for costs, as enumerated in section 1920 of this title, but not including the fees and expenses of attorneys, may be awarded to the prevailing party in any civil action brought by or against the United States or any agency or any official of the United States acting in his or her official capacity in any court having jurisdiction of such action. A judgment for costs when taxed against the United States shall, in an amount established by statute, court rule, or order, be limited to reimbursing in whole or in part the prevailing party for the costs incurred by such party in the litigation.

(2) A judgment for costs, when awarded in favor of the United States in an action brought by the United States, may include an amount equal to the filing fee prescribed under section 1914(a) of this title. The preceding sentence shall not be construed as requiring the United States to pay any filing fee.

(b) Unless expressly prohibited by statute, a court may award reasonable fees and expenses of attorneys, in addition to the costs which may be awarded pursuant to subsection (a), to the prevailing party in any civil action brought by or against the United States or any agency or any official of the United States acting in his or her official capacity in any court having jurisdiction of such action. The United States shall be liable for such fees and expenses to the same extent that any other party would be liable under the common law or under the terms of any statute which specifically provides for such an award.

(c)(1) Any judgment against the United States or any agency and any official of the United States acting in his or her official capacity for costs pursuant to subsection (a) shall be paid as provided in sections 2414 and 2517 of this title and shall be in addition to any relief provided in the judgment.

(2) Any judgment against the United States or any agency and any official of the United States acting in his or her official capacity for fees and expenses of attorneys pursuant to subsection (b) shall be paid as provided in sections 2414 and 2517 of this title, except that if the basis for the award is a finding

that the United States acted in bad faith, then the award shall be paid by any agency found to have acted in bad faith and shall be in addition to any relief provided in the judgment.

(d)(1)(A) Except as otherwise specifically provided by statute, a court shall award to a prevailing party other than the United States fees and other expenses, in addition to any costs awarded pursuant to subsection (a), incurred by that party in any civil action (other than cases sounding in tort), including proceedings for judicial review of agency action, brought by or against the United States in any court having jurisdiction of that action, unless the court finds that the position of the United States was substantially justified or that special circumstances make an award unjust.

(B) A party seeking an award of fees and other expenses shall, within thirty days of final judgment in the action, submit to the court an application for fees and other expenses which shows that the party is a prevailing party and is eligible to receive an award under this subsection, and the amount sought, including an itemized statement from any attorney or expert witness representing or appearing in behalf of the party stating the actual time expended and the rate at which fees and other expenses are computed. The party shall also allege that the position of the United States was not substantially justified. Whether or not the position of the United States was substantially justified shall be determined on the basis of the record (including the record with respect to the action or failure to act by the agency upon which the civil action is based) which is made in the civil action for which fees and other expenses are sought.

(C) The court, in its discretion, may reduce the amount to be awarded pursuant to this subsection, or deny an award, to the extent that the prevailing party during the course of the proceedings engaged in conduct which unduly and unreasonably protracted the final resolution of the matter in controversy.

(D) If, in a civil action brought by the United States or a proceeding for judicial review of an adversary adjudication described in section 504(a)(4) of title 5, the demand by the United States is substantially in excess of the judgment finally obtained by the United States and is unreasonable when compared with such judgment, under the facts and circumstances of the case, the court shall award to the party the fees and other expenses related to defending against the excessive demand, unless the party has committed a willful violation of law or otherwise acted in bad faith, or special circumstances make an award unjust. Fees and expenses awarded under this subparagraph shall be paid only as a consequence of appropriations provided in advance.

(2) For the purposes of this subsection —

(A) "fees and other expenses" includes the reasonable expenses of expert witnesses, the reasonable cost of any study, analysis, engineering report, test, or project which is found by the court to be necessary for the preparation of the party's case, and reasonable attorney fees (The amount of fees awarded under this subsection shall be based upon prevailing market rates for the kind and quality of the services furnished, except that

(i) no expert witness shall be compensated at a rate in excess of the highest rate of compensation for expert witnesses paid by the United States; and

(ii) attorney fees shall not be awarded in excess of $125 per hour unless the court determines that an increase in the cost of living or a special factor, such as the limited availability of qualified attorneys for the proceedings involved, justifies a higher fee.);

(B) "party" means

(i) an individual whose net worth did not exceed $2,000,000 at the time the civil action was filed, or

(ii) any owner of an unincorporated business, or any partnership, corporation, association, unit of local government, or organization, the net worth of which did not exceed $7,000,000 at the time the civil action was filed, and which had not more than 500 employees at the time the civil action was filed; except that an organization described in section 501(c)(3) of the Internal Revenue Code of 1986 (26 U.S.C. 501(c)(3)) exempt from taxation under section 501(a) of such Code, or a cooperative association as defined in section 15(a) of the Agricultural Marketing Act (12 U.S.C. 1141j(a)), may be a party regardless of the net worth of such organization or cooperative association or for purposes of subsection (d)(1)(D), a small entity as defined in section 601 of Title 5;

(C) "United States" includes any agency and any official of the United States acting in his or her official capacity;

(D) "position of the United States" means, in addition to the position taken by the United States in the civil action, the action or failure to act by the agency upon which the civil action is based; except that fees and expenses may not be awarded to a party for any portion of the litigation in which the party has unreasonably protracted the proceedings;

(E) "civil action brought by or against the Unites States" includes an appeal by a party, other than the United States, from a decision of a contracting officer rendered pursuant to a disputes clause in a contract with the Government or pursuant to the Contract Disputes Act of 1978;

(F) "court" includes the United States Claims Court and the United States Court of Appeals for Veterans Claims;

(G) "final judgment" means a judgment that is final and not appealable, and includes an order of settlement;

(H) "prevailing party", in the case of eminent domain proceedings, means a party who obtains a final judgment (other than by settlement), exclusive of interest, the amount of which is at least as close to the highest valuation of the property involved that is attested to at trial on behalf of the property owner as it is to the highest valuation of the property involved that is attested to at trial on behalf of the Government; and

(I) "demand" means the express demand of the United States which led to the adversary adjudication, but shall not include a recitation of the maximum statutory penalty (i) in the complaint, or (ii) elsewhere when accompanied by an express demand for a lesser amount.

(3) In awarding fees and other expenses under this subsection to a prevailing party in any action for judicial review of an adversary adjudication, as defined in subsection (b)(1)(C) of section 504 of title 5, United States Code, or an adversary adjudication subject to the contract Disputes Act of 1978, the court shall include in that award fees and other expenses to the same extent authorized in subsection (a) of such section, unless the court finds that during such adversary adjudication the position of the United States was substantially justified, or that special circumstances make an award unjust.

(4) Fees and other expenses awarded under this subsection to a party shall be paid by any agency over which the party prevails from any funds made available to the agency, by appropriation or otherwise.

(e) The provisions of this section shall not apply to any costs, fees, and other expenses in connection with any proceeding to which section 7430 of the Internal Revenue Code of 1954 applies (determined without regard to subsections (b) and (f) of such section). Nothing in the preceding sentence shall prevent the awarding under subsection (a) of section 2412 of title 28, United States Code, of costs enumerated in section 1920 of such title (as in effect on October 1, 1981).

(f) If the United States appeals an award of costs or fees and other expenses made against the United States under this section and the award is affirmed in whole or in part, interest shall be paid on the amount of the award as affirmed. Such interest shall be computed at the rate determined under section 1961(a) of this title, and shall run from the date of the award through the day before the date of the mandate of affirmance.

PART II

SUPPLEMENTARY CASES, NOTES, AND OTHER MATERIALS

PERSONAL JURISDICTION

II

B. The Modern Constitutional Formulation of Power

2. Absorbing in rem jurisdiction

Page 114. After Note 6 add:

In rem jurisdiction, an old idea, and the Internet, a newer one, have come together in an interesting way. Like other trademarks, Internet domain names are valuable pieces of intellectual property, and legislation protects them from various sorts of abuse and poaching. Because of the ease of establishing a web site and the ubiquity of the Internet, plaintiffs seeking to protect domain names sometimes have difficulty in locating the defendant. Even if the defendant's whereabouts are known, the defendant may not be subject to personal jurisdiction in the United States. Congress has responded with the Anti-Cybersquatting Consumer Protection Act (15 U.S.C. §1125(d)(2) (2000)), whose procedural portions exploit the architecture of the Internet and the concept of in rem jurisdiction.

Understanding the statutory scheme requires understanding how the network routes traffic in cyberspace. Individual computers in the Internet have numerical "addresses." But long strings of numbers are more difficult to remember than ibm.com, so the Internet uses a domain name system, which is a table of names associated with computer addresses. Whenever an Internet user requests a domain name site, its numerical address has to be matched with a number by searching a list acquired from "directory computers" that maintain lists matching site names with numerical addresses. The domain name registrar keeps the most current tables matching names and numbers. The registrar thus functions both as a keeper of title records and as a continually updated directory that facilitates the matching process that allows the Internet to function.

In addition to establishing liability for various forms of "cybersquatting," the statute exploits this system. It allows a plaintiff to bring an in rem action in the location of the registrar of domain names:

> The owner of a mark may file an in rem civil action against a domain name in the judicial district in which the domain name registrar, domain name registry, or other domain name authority that registered or assigned the domain name is located if . . .
>
> (ii) the court finds that the owner —

(I) is not able to obtain in personam jurisdiction over a person who would have been a defendant in a civil action under paragraph (1); or

(II) through due diligence was not able to find a person who would have been a defendant in a civil action under paragraph (1) by —

(aa) sending a notice of the alleged violation and intent to proceed under this paragraph to the registrant of the domain name at the postal and e-mail address provided by the registrant to the registrar; and

(bb) publishing notice of the action as the court may direct promptly after filing the action.

(B) The actions under subparagraph (A)(ii) shall constitute service of process.

Upon receiving such a notice, the domain name registrar is to "deposit" the disputed domain with the court during the suit's pendency. Consider some issues raised by these provisions:

a. Are they fair to defendants, many of whom believe they have either legitimate property rights or free speech rights to their domain names? Consider López, an Arizona defendant who establishes a "SmithBad.com" site, criticizing the actions of Smith, Inc. The domain registry of SmithBad is in Virginia, the location of Network Solutions, Inc., the world's largest domain name registrar (with more than a million registrations). Smith, Inc. brings an action in Virginia invoking the statute just quoted. What objections might López have to the invocation of the in rem procedure? What additional facts would you want to know?

b. Are these provisions consistent with your understanding of *Shaffer*? Suppose a defendant located in California allegedly infringes a domain name of a New York plaintiff, who brings suit in the Eastern District of Virginia. What will the domain name registrar do when it receives notice of the action? Is the in rem solution as applied to these facts constitutional?

c. Could one also think of the Act as a sort of interpleader (see Chapter XIII), in which an "asset" (the domain name file or the computer holding that file) of a stakeholder (the domain name registrar) is sought by two competing claimants (the holder and the alleged "squatter")? In such a setting, even in the absence of an in rem proceeding, one could imagine the domain name holder "depositing" the name (or the database entry for that name) in court and asking the tribunal to adjudicate the contest between the holder and the challenger. If that framing of the issue is right, does it help to rescue the constitutionality of the in rem proceeding?

3. Specific Jurisdiction: The Modern Cases

Page 120. At the end of the first full paragraph insert:

. . . Petitioners then sought a writ of prohibition in the Supreme Court of Oklahoma to restrain the District Judge, respondent Charles S. Woodson, from exercising in personam jurisdiction over them. . . .

Page 139. At the end of the first paragraph, following the citation to International Shoe, *insert:*

Thus courts in "appropriate case[s]" may evaluate "the burden on the defendant," "the forum State's interest in adjudicating the dispute," "the interstate judicial system's interest in obtaining the most efficient resolution of controversies," and the "shared interest of the several States in furthering fundamental substantive social policies." World-Wide Volkswagen v. Woodson.

Page 145. Before Note 5 insert:

Compare *Burger King* with Diamond HealthCare of Ohio, Inc. v. Humility of Mary Health Partners, 229 Fed. 3d 448 (4th Cir. 2000). Diamond, based in Virginia, contracted with HMH, in Ohio, to provide various health services, including hospitalization for the elderly. Diamond had approached HMH in Ohio, where the contract was negotiated, where most of the services were to be performed and whose law governed the contract. But all the paperwork passed through Virginia, and some parts of the agreement were also performed there. Diamond sued HMH for breach of contract in federal district court in Virginia. The two-person majority rejected Virginia's jurisdiction; the dissent, citing *Burger King*, said that case was indistinguishable and governed. Who's right?

Page 146. Before "4. General Jurisdiction" insert:

7. Recent Internet cases involving personal jurisdiction have reinforced the analytical framework suggested in note 6. A recent California case reviews the case law while considering the fate of a talented college student whose freelance programming landed him in hot water.

Pavlovich v. Superior Court (DVD Copy Control Association, Real Party in Interest)

29 Cal. 4th 262, 58 P.3d 2 (2002)

BROWN, J.

"The Internet is an international network of interconnected computers" which "enables tens of millions of people to communicate with one another and to access vast amounts of information from around the world." (Reno v. ACLU (1997) 521 U.S. 844, 849-850). . . .

Not surprisingly, the so-called Internet revolution has spawned a host of new legal issues as courts have struggled to apply traditional legal frameworks to this new communication medium. Today, we join this struggle and consider the impact of the Internet on the determination of personal jurisdiction. In this case, a California court exercised personal jurisdiction over a defendant based on a posting on an Internet Web site. Under the particular facts of this case, we conclude the court's exercise of jurisdiction was improper.

Digital versatile discs (DVDs) "provide high quality images, such as motion pictures, digitally formatted on a convenient 5-inch disc . . . ." Before the commercial release of DVDs containing motion pictures, the Content Scrambling System (CSS), a system used to encrypt and protect copyrighted motion pictures on DVDs, was developed. The CSS technology prevents the playing or copying of copyrighted motion pictures on DVDs without the algorithms and keys necessary to decrypt the data stored on the disc.

Real party in interest DVD Copy Control Association, Inc. (DVD CCA) . . . [,] a nonprofit trade association organized under the laws of the State of Delaware with its principal place of business in California, . . . acquired the licensing rights to the CSS technology and became the sole licensing entity for this technology in the DVD video format.

Petitioner Matthew Pavlovich is currently a resident of Texas and the president of Media Driver, LLC, a technology consulting company in Texas. During the four years before he moved to Texas, he studied computer engineering at Purdue University in Indiana, where he worked as a systems and network administrator. Pavlovich does not reside or work in California. He has never had a place of business, telephone listing, or bank account in California and has never owned property in California. Neither Pavlovich nor his company has solicited any business in California or has any business contacts in California.

At Purdue, Pavlovich was the founder and project leader of the LiVid video project (LiVid), which operated a Web site located at "livid.on.openprojects.net." The site consisted of a single page with text and links to other Web sites. The site only provided information; it did not solicit or transact any business and permitted no interactive exchange of information between its operators and visitors.

According to Pavlovich, the goal of LiVid was "to improve video and DVD support for Linux and to . . . combine the resources and the efforts of the various individuals that were working on related things . . . ." To reach this goal, the project sought to defeat the CSS technology and enable the decryption and copying of DVDs containing motion pictures. Consistent with these efforts, LiVid posted the source code of a program named DeCSS on its Web site. . . . DeCSS allows users to circumvent the CSS technology by decrypting data contained on DVDs and enabling the placement of this decrypted data onto computer hard drives or other storage media.

At the time LiVid posted DeCSS, Pavlovich knew that DeCSS "was derived from CSS algorithms" and that reverse engineering these algorithms was probably illegal. He had also "heard" that "there was an organization which you had to file for or apply for a license" to the CSS technology. He did not, however, learn that the organization was DVD CCA or that DVD CCA had its principal place of business in California until after DVD CCA filed this action.

In its complaint, DVD CCA alleged that Pavlovich misappropriated its trade secrets by posting the DeCSS program on the LiVid Web site. . . . The complaint sought injunctive relief but did not seek monetary damages. In response, Pavlovich filed a motion to quash service of process, contending that California lacked jurisdiction over his person. . . .

II

California courts may exercise personal jurisdiction on any basis consistent with the Constitutions of California and the United States. (Code Civ. Proc., §410.10.) . . .

When determining whether specific jurisdiction exists, courts consider the " 'relationship among the defendant, the forum, and the litigation.' " (Helicopteros Nacionales de Colombia v. Hall (1984) 466 U.S. 408, 414, quoting Shaffer v. Heitner.) A court may exercise specific jurisdiction over a nonresident defendant only if: (1) "the defendant has purposefully availed himself or herself of forum benefits"; (2) "the 'controversy is related to or "arises out of" [the] defendant's contacts with the forum' "; and (3) " 'the assertion of personal jurisdiction would comport with "fair play and substantial justice[.]" ' "

[The opinion reviewed cases applying the purposeful availment test, focusing on the analogy of this case with defamation.]

In the defamation context, the United States Supreme Court has described an "effects test" for determining purposeful availment. In [Jones v.] Calder, a reporter in Florida wrote an article for the National Enquirer about Shirley Jones, a well-known actress who lived and worked in California. The president and editor of the National Enquirer reviewed and approved the article, and the National Enquirer published the article. Jones sued, among others, the reporter and editor (individual defendants) for libel in California. The individual defendants moved to quash service of process, contending they lacked minimum contacts with California.

The United States Supreme Court disagreed and held that California could exercise jurisdiction over the individual defendants "based on the 'effects' of their Florida conduct in California." . . . The court . . . noted that the individual defendants wrote or edited "an article that they knew would have a potentially devastating impact upon [Jones]. And they knew that the brunt of that injury would be felt by [Jones] in the State in which she lives and works and in which the National Enquirer has its largest circulation." . . .

[C]ourts have "struggled somewhat with *Calder*'s import, recognizing that the case cannot stand for the broad proposition that a foreign act with foreseeable effects in the forum state always gives rise to specific jurisdiction." . . .

. . . In this case, Pavlovich's sole contact with California is LiVid's posting of the DeCSS source code containing DVD CCA's proprietary information on an Internet Web site accessible to any person with Internet access. . . .

Although we have never considered the scope of personal jurisdiction based solely on Internet use, other courts have considered this issue, and most have adopted a sliding scale analysis. "At one end of the spectrum are situations where a defendant clearly does business over the Internet. If the defendant enters into contracts with residents of a foreign jurisdiction that involve the knowing and repeated transmission of computer files over the Internet, personal jurisdiction is proper. At the opposite end are situations where a defendant has simply posted information on an Internet Web site which is accessible to users in foreign jurisdictions. A passive Web site that does little more than make information available to those who are interested in it is not grounds for the exercise of personal jurisdiction. The middle ground is occupied by interactive Web sites where a user can exchange information with the host computer. In these cases, the exercise of jurisdiction is determined by examining the level of interactivity and commercial nature of the exchange of information that occurs on the Web site." Zippo Manufacturing Co. v. Zippo Dot Com, Inc. (W.D. Pa. 1997) 952 F. Supp. 1119, 1124.

Here, LiVid's Web site merely posts information and has no interactive features. There is no evidence in the record suggesting that the site targeted California. Indeed, there is no evidence that any California resident ever visited, much less downloaded the DeCSS source code from, the LiVid Web site. Thus, Pavlovich's alleged "conduct in . . . posting [a] passive Web site[] on the Internet is not," by itself, "sufficient to subject" him "to jurisdiction in California." " 'Creating a site, like placing a product into the stream of commerce, may be felt nationwide—or even worldwide—but, without more, it is not an act purposefully directed toward the forum state.' " (*Cybersell*, quoting Bensusan Restaurant Corp. v. King (S.D.N.Y. 1996) 937 F. Supp. 295, 301, affd. (2d Cir. 1997).) Otherwise, "personal jurisdiction in Internet-related cases would almost always be found in any forum in the country." (GTE New Media Services Inc. v. BellSouth Corp. (D.C. Cir. 2000) 199 F.3d 1343, 1350.) Such a result would "vitiate long-held and inviolate principles of" personal jurisdiction.

Nonetheless, DVD CCA contends posting the misappropriated source code on an Internet Web site is sufficient to establish purposeful availment in this case because Pavlovich knew the posting would harm not only a licensing entity but also the motion picture, computer and consumer electronics industries centered in California. According to DVD CCA, this knowledge establishes that Pavlovich intentionally targeted California and is sufficient to confer jurisdiction under the *Calder* effects test. Although the question is close, we disagree. As an initial matter, DVD CCA's reliance on Pavlovich's awareness that an entity owned the licensing rights to the CSS technology is misplaced. Although Pavlovich knew about this entity, he did not know that DVD CCA was that entity or that DVD CCA's primary place of business was California until *after* the filing of this lawsuit. . . .

Thus, the only question in this case is whether Pavlovich's knowledge that his tortious conduct may harm certain industries centered in California—i.e., the motion picture, computer, and consumer electronics industries—is sufficient to establish express aiming at California. As explained below, we conclude that this knowledge, by itself, cannot establish purposeful availment under the effects test. . . .

First . . . the foreseeability that third parties may use DeCSS to harm the motion picture industry cannot, by itself, satisfy the express aiming requirement. Because nothing in the record suggests that Pavlovich encouraged Web site visitors to use DeCSS to illegally pirate copyrighted motion pictures, his mere "awareness" they might do so does not show purposeful availment. (See *Asahi Metal Industry*.)

Second, Pavlovich's knowledge of the effects of his tortious conduct on the consumer electronics and computer industries centered in California is an even more attenuated basis for jurisdiction. . . . Otherwise, the commission of any intentional tort affecting industries in California would subject a defendant to jurisdiction in California. . . .

[C]onsider the ramifications of a contrary holding. According to DVD CCA, California should exercise jurisdiction over Pavlovich because he *should have known* that third parties *may* use the misappropriated code to illegally copy movies on DVDs and that licensees of the misappropriated technology resided in California. In other words, DVD CCA is asking this court to exercise jurisdiction over a defendant because he *should have known* that his conduct *may* harm—not a California plaintiff—but industries associated with that plaintiff. . . .

Indeed, such a broad interpretation of the effects test would effectively eliminate the purposeful availment requirement in the intentional tort context for select plaintiffs. In most, if not all, intentional tort cases, the defendant is or should be aware of the industries that may be affected by his tortious conduct. Consequently, any plaintiff connected to industries centered in California—i.e., the motion picture, computer, and consumer electronics industries—could sue an out-of-state defendant in California for intentional torts that *may* harm those industries. For example, any creator or purveyor of technology that enables copying of movies or computer software—including a student in Australia who develops a program for creating backup copies of software and distributes it to some of his classmates or a store owner in Africa who sells a device that makes digital copies of movies on videotape—would be subject to suit in California because they should have known their conduct may harm the motion picture or computer industries in California. Indeed, DVD CCA's interpretation would subject any defendant who commits an intentional tort affecting the motion picture, computer, or consumer electronics industries to jurisdiction in California even if the plaintiff was not a California resident. Under this logic, plaintiffs connected to the auto industry could sue any defendant in Michigan, plaintiffs connected to the financial industry could sue any defendant in New York, and plaintiffs connected to the potato industry could sue any defendant in Idaho. Because finding jurisdiction under the facts in this case would effectively subject all intentional tortfeasors whose conduct may harm industries in California to jurisdiction in California, we decline to do so.

We, however, emphasize the narrowness of our decision. A defendant's knowledge that his tortious conduct may harm industries centered in California is undoubtedly relevant to any determination of personal jurisdiction and may support a finding of jurisdiction. We merely hold that this knowledge *alone* is insufficient to establish express aiming at the forum state as required by the effects test. Because the only evidence in the record even suggesting express aiming is Pavlovich's knowledge that his conduct may harm industries centered in California, due process requires us to decline jurisdiction over his person.

In addition, we are not confronted with a situation where the plaintiff has no other forum to pursue its claims and therefore do not address that situation. DVD CCA has the ability and resources to pursue Pavlovich in another forum such as Indiana or Texas. Our decision today does not foreclose it from doing so. Pavlovich may still face the music—just not in California.

III

Accordingly, we reverse the judgment of the Court of Appeal and remand for further proceedings consistent with this opinion.

KENNARD, WERDEGAR and MORENO, JJ., concur.

BAXTER, J., joined by GEORGE, C.J., and CHIN, J., dissenting:

I respectfully dissent. That this case involves a powerful new medium of electronic communication, usable for good or ill, should not blind us to the essential facts and principles. The record indicates that, by intentionally posting an unlicensed decryption code for the Content Scrambling System (CSS) on their Internet Web sites, defendant and his network of "open source" associates sought to undermine and defeat the very purposes of the licensed CSS encryption technology, i.e., *copyright protection* for movies recorded on digital versatile discs (DVDs) and *limitation of playback* to operating systems licensed to unscramble the encryption code. The intended targets of this effort were not individual persons or businesses, but entire industries. Defendant knew at least two of the intended targets—the movie industry and the computer industry involved in producing the licensed playback systems—either were centered in California or maintained a particularly substantial presence here. Thus, the record amply supports the trial court's conclusion, for purposes of specific personal jurisdiction, that defendant's intentional act, even if committed outside California, was "expressly aimed" at California. (See Calder v. Jones.)

In the particular circumstances, it cannot matter that defendant may not have known or cared about the *exact identities* or *precise locations* of each individual target, or that he happened to employ a so-called passive Internet Web site, or whether any California resident visited the site. By acting with the broad intent to harm *industries he knew were centered or substantially present in this state*, defendant forged sufficient "minimum contacts" with *California* "that he should reasonably anticipate being haled into court [*here*]" (*World-Wide Volkswagen Corp.*) for litigation " 'arising out of' " his forum-related conduct. . . .

NOTES AND PROBLEMS

1. The caption of the case is potentially confusing. The California Supreme Court heard the case before final judgment by granting an interlocutory writ of mandate. In that writ the nominal defendant is the trial court—hence the caption of the case. Ordinarily, as here, the party who stands to gain from the trial court's ruling (the "real party in interest," here the plaintiff in the underlying lawsuit) assumes responsibility for defending the ruling in question.

2. The court split 4-3 in this case. Did it reach the right result?

3. The majority opinion seems to turn on Pavlovich's knowledge that his action would cause damage in California.

a. The premise is that a state has jurisdiction over a defendant who acts in a way that he knows will cause harm in another state. Firing a bullet over a state line supplies a classic example. A less violent example occurred in *Calder* (discussed above), in which the defendant newspaper knew that the plaintiff lived in California and that, if its article caused her harm, it would occur there.

b. Suppose that the lawyers for DVD Copy Control located a former classmate of Pavlovich who will under oath swear that he heard defendant say of his decryption program, "This ought to show those creeps in Silicon Valley that they aren't as smart as they think they are." Would such a statement, if properly in evidence, be enough to lead to a different outcome in this case? Or is there something else that leads the court to deny jurisdiction?

c. In *Calder* the defendant newspaper profited from the scandalous (and allegedly defamatory statements) about the plaintiff. In *Pavlovich* the defendant, although reducing the value of others' intellectual property, did not himself profit. Suppose he had; should the case have come out differently if Pavlovich had sold copies of his decrypting programs?

4. The plaintiff's lawyers were hired by the holders of the intellectual property at stake in this case. Pavlovich was represented pro bono by a lawyer located in Silicon Valley. Pavlovich is not the average pro bono client; why do you suppose his lawyer took on this uncompensated representation?

4. General Jurisdiction

Page 158. Replace the second sentence in Note 2 with:

Having personally guaranteed the payment for his company's machines, the owner of Concrete Placing travels to Washington to attend a sporting event.

D. The Constitutional Requirement of Notice

Page 174. Before Note 4 insert:

c. The Anti-Cybersquatting Consumer Protection Act (15 U.S.C. §1125(d)(2)(A) (2000)) provides for an "in rem" action against domain names on the Internet. The statute allows a plaintiff to commence the action by notifying the domain name registrar, who will then "deposit" the domain name with the court (presumably by allowing the court to order the blocking of Internet access to that name while the suit is pending), and provides for notice to the owner of the name as follows:

> The owner of a mark may file an in rem civil action against a domain name in the judicial district in which the domain name registrar . . . if
>
> (ii) the court finds that the owner —
>
> (I) is not able to obtain in personam jurisdiction over a person who would have been a defendant in a civil action under [the substantive provisions of the statute]; or
>
> (II) through due diligence was not able to find a person who would have been a defendant [under the substantive provisions of the statute] by —
>
> (aa) sending a notice of the alleged violation and intent to proceed under this paragraph to the registrant of the domain name at the postal and e-mail address provided by the registrant to the registrar; and
>
> (bb) publishing notice of the action as the court may direct promptly after filing the action.

A trademark owner seeking to invoke this provision sent notice to the domain name owners, then eight days later filed an in rem action. The defendant challenged the short time between notice and suit. What result? Lucent Technologies Inc. v. Lucentsucks.com, 95 F. Supp. 2d 528 (E.D. Va. 2000) (eight days insufficient time to satisfy "due diligence" provision of subsections II(i) and (II)(ii) when interpreted in light of due process clause).

Page 190. Before Note 6a insert:

For example, consider a Michigan case in which a process server, having had someone point the defendant out to him, asked the defendant to confirm his identity. After defendant twice denied his identity, he entered a door which he locked behind him. The server "served" process by leaving a copy of the complaint at the door, and shouting through it that the defendant had been served. Adequate process to satisfy a state statute requiring "delivering a summons and a copy of the complaint to the defendant personally"? Barclay v. Crown Building & Developing, 241 Mich. App. 639 (2000) (yes).

E. Self-Imposed Restraints

1. Long-Arm Statutes as a Restraint on Jurisdiction

Page 196. Before Note 4b insert:

One court has limited this power by interpreting "service of process" to be distinct from personal jurisdiction. In Peay v. BellSouth Medical Assistance Plan, 205 Fed. 3d 1206 (10th Cir. 2000), the court held that the nationwide service of process in federal pension legislation did not confer personal jurisdiction, whose requirements had to be separately satisfied.

3. Declining Jurisdiction: Transfer and Forum Non Conveniens

a. Forum Non Conveniens

Page 209. Before Notes and Problems insert:

With *Piper* compare Guidi v. Inter-Continental Hotels Corp., 224 F.3d 142 (2d. Cir. 2000). Plaintiffs were a survivor and heirs of the victims of shootings in an Egyptian hotel operated by defendant, where a gunman had shot six. Plaintiffs brought a federal diversity action in New York against the New York-based corporate hotel operator. The district court dismissed on forum non conveniens grounds, finding that an Egyptian court would be more familiar with Egyptian law, which governed the action, that Egypt's commitment to tourism assured that the suit would be handled properly, and that there was already related litigation pending in Egypt-suits brought by the families of French and Italian victims. The Second Circuit reversed, holding that the district court had abused its discretion in dismissing. The inconvenience and "emotional burden" on plaintiffs outweighed the "slight[ly]" greater convenience of litigation in Egypt, said the court. Can you distinguish *Piper*?

SUBJECT MATTER JURISDICTION OF THE FEDERAL COURTS

III

B. Federal Question Jurisdiction

Page 226. Replace the first sentence in the first full paragraph with:

But suppose that the defendant does not move to dismiss under either Rule 12(b)(1) or 12(b)(6)?

Page 226. Replace the last paragraph with:

In one respect *Capron* and *Caterpillar* agree: Both treat challenges to subject matter jurisdiction in a way that differs sharply from personal jurisdiction. On one hand, personal jurisdiction may be waived by failing to raise it at the threshold of litigation: if in *Capron* an objection to *personal* jurisdiction had been raised for the first time on appeal, the objection would be treated as having been waived. On the other hand, challenges to personal jurisdiction, if properly raised at the threshold of the case, are treated seriously on appeal: For example, suppose one of the defendants in *Caterpillar* had raised a well-grounded challenge to personal jurisdiction; such a challenge to personal jurisdiction would presumably have prevailed on appeal. Does the difference in treatment make sense? Consider the differences in the values protected by personal and subject matter jurisdiction.

C. Diversity Jurisdiction

Page 233. Before Note 5 insert:

c. Beyond interpleader, in one somewhat confusingly defined situation, Congress has specifically authorized minimal diversity as a basis for federal jurisdiction. The Multiparty Multiforum Trial Jurisdiction Act of 2002, 28 U.S.C. §1369, applies to mass disasters such as airplane crashes. It gives the federal courts jurisdiction "where at least 75 natural persons have died in the accident at a discrete location" and one of three additional conditions is met: (1) defendants reside in a state different from that where the accident occurred, (2) two or more defendants "reside in different States," or (3) substantial parts of the accident occurred in two or more states. If the two triggering conditions are met, the federal court has jurisdiction if "minimal" diversity exits, a condition defined by the statute in these terms: "any party is a citizen of a State and any adverse party is a citizen of another State, a citizen or subject of a foreign state." There is no amount-in-controversy requirement, though common sense suggests that 75 deaths will create substantial amounts in controversy. Legislative history suggests that the statute was intended to create federal jurisdiction over lawsuits involving crashes of airplanes flying interstate routes; can you imagine other circumstances when it might apply? Such an extension of diversity is clearly constitutional; as a matter of legislative policy, should it be cast in more general terms?

Page 243. Before Note 3 insert:

The issue remains, however, undecided by the Supreme Court, which in Free v. Abbot Laboratories affirmed the lower court by an evenly divided vote when Justice O'Connor recused herself from participation in the case. 529 U.S. 333 (2000).

D. Supplemental Jurisdiction

Page 251. Before "E. Removal" insert:

6. Supplemental jurisdiction can create difficult problems for plaintiffs who guess wrong in invoking federal question jurisdiction. Suppose plaintiff has employment discrimination claims. Believing the claims involve both state and federal law and preferring a federal forum, plaintiff files in federal court, invoking supplemental jurisdiction for the state claims. It turns out that plaintiff was wrong about the federal claims: after the state statute of limitations has run, the federal court dismisses the federal claims and declines to exercise jurisdiction over the remaining state law claims. What can plaintiff do?

a. Some states have "savings" statutes that toll the state statute of limitations under such circumstances, so plaintiff could refile in state court.

b. But not all states have such statutes. In such cases §1367(d) seeks to address the problem by opening a 30-day "window." Suppose our hypothetical plaintiff is in a state which has no "savings" statute; how does §1367(d) help her? What should she do?

c. Courts have wrestled with interpreting §1367(d). The Minnesota Supreme Court has held the 30-day extension unconstitutional as applied to a claim against a state agency that had not consented to such a provision. Univ. of Minn. v. Ragor, 620 N.W.2d 680 (Minn. 2001). By contrast, a Florida appellate court has held that §1367(d) tolls state statutes not only as to claims dismissed by a federal court but to those the plaintiff voluntarily dismisses in order to pursue state litigation instead. Blinn v. Fla. Dept. of Transp., 781 So. 2d 1103 (Fl. App. 2000).

E. Removal

Page 257. Before Note 3b insert:

Apparently post-removal manipulation of the amount in controversy will not work. In Rogers v. Wal-Mart Stores, Inc., 230 F.3d 868 (6th Cir. 2000), plaintiff filed a state law negligence action seeking $950,000 in damages. Defendant removed, invoking diversity. After the case was removed, plaintiff sought remand to state court, offering to stipulate that she would seek less than $75,000 in damages and the case therefore fell below the amount in controversy requirement. The Sixth Circuit affirmed a denial of the remand petition, saying that the removal petition should be judged by the apparent amount in controversy at the time removal is sought. Suppose plaintiff, like Lewis in *Caterpillar*, strongly prefers state court. With the advantage of hindsight, how could he have manipulated the amount in controversy to prevent removal?

THE *ERIE* PROBLEM

IV

B. The Limits of State Power in Federal Courts

3. Determining the Scope of Federal Law: Avoiding and Accommodating *Erie*

Page 298. Insert before Notes and Problems:

Semtek International Inc. v. Lockheed Martin Corp.

531 U.S. 497 (2001)

Justice SCALIA delivered the opinion of the Court.

This case presents the question whether the claim-preclusive effect of a federal judgment dismissing a diversity action on statute-of-limitations grounds is determined by the law of the State in which the federal court sits.

I

Petitioner filed a complaint against respondent in California state court, alleging breach of contract and various business torts. Respondent removed the case to the United States District Court for the Central District of California on the basis of diversity of citizenship, and successfully moved to dismiss petitioner's claims as barred by California's 2-year statute of limitations. In its order of dismissal, the District Court, adopting language suggested by respondent, dismissed petitioner's claims "in [their] entirety on the merits and with prejudice." Without contesting the District Court's designation of its dismissal as "on the merits," petitioner appealed to the Court of Appeals for the Ninth Circuit, which affirmed the District Court's order. Petitioner also brought suit against respondent in the State Circuit Court for Baltimore City, Maryland, alleging the same causes of action, which were not time barred under Maryland's 3-year statute of limitations . . . . Following a hearing, the Maryland state court granted respondent's motion to dismiss on the ground of res judicata. . . . The [Maryland] Court of Special Appeals affirmed, holding that, regardless of whether California would have accorded claim-preclusive effect to a statute-of-limitations dismissal by one of its own courts, the dismissal by the California federal court barred the complaint filed in Maryland, since the res judicata effect of federal diversity judgments is prescribed by federal law, under which the earlier dismissal was on the merits and claim preclusive . . . .

II

Petitioner contends that the outcome of this case is controlled by Dupasseur v. Rochereau, 21 Wall. 130, 135 (1875), which held that the res judicata effect of a federal diversity judgment "is such as would belong to judgments of the State courts rendered under similar circumstances," and may not be accorded any "higher sanctity or effect." Since, petitioner argues, the dismissal of an action on statute-of-limitations grounds by a California state court would not be claim preclusive, it follows that the similar dismissal of this diversity action by the California federal court cannot be claim preclusive. While we agree that this would be the result demanded by *Dupasseur*, the case is not dispositive because it was decided under the Conformity Act of 1872 [the pre-Rules legislation] which required federal courts to apply the procedural law of the forum State in nonequity cases. That arguably affected the outcome of the case . . . .

Respondent, for its part, contends that the outcome of this case is controlled by Federal Rule of Civil Procedure 41(b), which provides as follows:

> Involuntary Dismissal: Effect Thereof. For failure of the plaintiff to prosecute or to comply with these rules or any order of court, a defendant may move for dismissal of an action or of any claim against the defendant. Unless the court in its order for dismissal otherwise specifies, a dismissal under this subdivision and any dismissal not provided for in this rule, other than a dismissal for lack of jurisdiction, for improper venue, or for failure to join a party under Rule 19, operates as an adjudication upon the merits.

Since the dismissal here did not "otherwise specify" (indeed, it specifically stated that it *was* "on the merits"), and did not pertain to the excepted subjects of jurisdiction, venue, or joinder, it follows, respondent contends, that the dismissal "is entitled to claim preclusive effect."

Implicit in this reasoning is the unstated minor premise that all judgments denominated "on the merits" are entitled to claim-preclusive effect. That premise is not necessarily valid. The original connotation of an "on the merits" adjudication is one that actually "passes directly on the substance of [a particular] claim" before the court. Restatement §19, Comment *a*, at 161. That connotation remains common to every jurisdiction of which we are aware . . . . And it is, we think, the meaning intended in those many statements to the effect that a judgment "on the merits" triggers the doctrine of res judicata or claim preclusion. See, e.g., Parklane Hosiery Co. v. Shore, 439 U.S. 322, 326, n.5 (1979).

But over the years the meaning of the term "judgment on the merits" "has gradually undergone change," R. Marcus, M. Redish, & E. Sherman, Civil Procedure: A Modern Approach 1140-1141 (3d ed. 2000), and it has come to be applied to some judgments (such as the one involved here) that do *not* pass

Petitioner not claim preclusive

Respondent is claim preclusive FRCP

upon the substantive merits of a claim and hence do *not* (in many jurisdictions) entail claim-preclusive effect.

In short, it is no longer true that a judgment "on the merits" is necessarily a judgment entitled to claim-preclusive effect; and there are a number of reasons for believing that the phrase "adjudication upon the merits" does not bear that meaning in Rule 41(b). To begin with, Rule 41(b) sets forth nothing more than a default rule for determining the import of a dismissal (a dismissal is "upon the merits," with the three stated exceptions, unless the court "otherwise specifies"). This would be a highly peculiar context in which to announce a federally prescribed rule on the complex question of claim preclusion, saying in effect, "All federal dismissals (with three specified exceptions) preclude suit elsewhere, unless the court otherwise specifies."

And even apart from the purely default character of Rule 41(b), it would be peculiar to find a rule governing the effect that must be accorded federal judgments by other courts ensconced in rules governing the internal procedures of the rendering court itself. Indeed, such a rule would arguably violate the jurisdictional limitation of the Rules Enabling Act: that the Rules "shall not abridge, enlarge or modify any substantive right," 28 U.S.C. §2072(b) . . . . In the present case, for example, if California law left petitioner free to sue on this claim in Maryland even after the California statute of limitations had expired, the federal court's extinguishment of that right (through Rule 41(b)'s mandated claim-preclusive effect of its judgment) would seem to violate this limitation.

Moreover, as so interpreted, the Rule would in many cases violate the federalism principle of Erie R. Co. v. Tompkins, 304 U.S. 64, 78-80 (1938), by engendering " 'substantial' variations [in outcomes] between state and federal litigation" which would "likely . . . influence the choice of a forum," Hanna v. Plumer, 380 U.S. 460, 467-468 (1965). See also Guaranty Trust Co. v. York, 326 U.S. 99, 108-110 (1945). With regard to the claim-preclusion issue involved in the present case, for example, the traditional rule is that expiration of the applicable statute of limitations merely bars the remedy and does not extinguish the substantive right, so that dismissal on that ground does not have claim-preclusive effect in other jurisdictions with longer, unexpired limitation periods. Out-of-state defendants sued on stale claims in California and in other States adhering to this traditional rule would systematically remove state-law suits brought against them to federal court — where, unless otherwise specified, a statute-of-limitations dismissal would bar suit everywhere.[1]

We think the key to a more reasonable interpretation of the meaning of "operates as an adjudication upon the merits" in Rule 41(b) is to be found in

1. Rule 41(b), interpreted as a preclusion-establishing rule, would not have the two effects described in the preceding paragraphs — arguable violation of the Rules Enabling Act and incompatibility with Erie R. Co. v. Tompkins — if the court's failure to specify an other-than-on-the-merits dismissal were subject to reversal on appeal whenever it would alter the rule of claim preclusion applied by the State in which the federal court sits. No one suggests that this is the rule, and we are aware of no case that applies it.

Rule 41(a), which, in discussing the effect of voluntary dismissal by the plaintiff, makes clear that an "adjudication upon the merits" is the opposite of a "dismissal without prejudice":

> Unless otherwise stated in the notice of dismissal or stipulation, the dismissal is without prejudice, except that a notice of dismissal operates as an adjudication upon the merits when filed by a plaintiff who has once dismissed in any court of the United States or of any state an action based on or including the same claim.

The primary meaning of "dismissal without prejudice," we think, is dismissal without barring the defendant from returning later, to the same court, with the same underlying claim. That will also ordinarily (though not always) have the consequence of not barring the claim from *other* courts, but its primary meaning relates to the dismissing court itself. . . .

We think, then, that the effect of the "adjudication upon the merits" default provision of Rule 41(b) — and, presumably, of the explicit order in the present case that used the language of that default provision — is simply that, unlike a dismissal "without prejudice," the dismissal in the present case barred refiling of the same claim in the United States District Court for the Central District of California. That is undoubtedly a necessary condition, but it is not a sufficient one, for claim-preclusive effect in other courts.[2]

III

Having concluded that the claim-preclusive effect, in Maryland, of this California federal diversity judgment is dictated neither by Dupasseur v. Rochereau, as petitioner contends, nor by Rule 41(b), as respondent contends, we turn to consideration of what determines the issue. Neither the Full Faith and Credit Clause, U.S. Const., Art. IV, §1,[3] nor the full faith and credit statute, 28 U.S.C. §1738,[4] addresses the question. By their terms they govern the effects to be given only to state-court judgments (and, in the case of the statute, to judgments by

2. We do not decide whether, in a diversity case, a federal court's "dismissal upon the merits" (in the sense we have described), under circumstances where a state court would decree only a "dismissal without prejudice," abridges a "substantive right" and thus exceeds the authorization of the Rules Enabling Act. We think the situation will present itself more rarely than would the arguable violation of the Act that would ensue from interpreting Rule 41(b) as a rule of claim preclusion; and if it is a violation, can be more easily dealt with on direct appeal.

3. Article IV, §1 provides as follows:

> Full Faith and Credit shall be given in each State to the public Acts, Records, and judicial Proceedings of every other State. And the Congress may by general Laws prescribe the Manner in which such Acts, Records and Proceedings shall be proved, and the Effect thereof.

4. Title 28 U.S.C. §1738 provides in relevant part as follows:

> The records and judicial proceedings of any court of any . . . State, Territory or Possession . . . shall have the same full faith and credit in every court within the United States and its Territories and Possessions as they have by law or usage in the courts of such State, Territory or Possession from which they are taken.

courts of territories and possessions). And no other federal textual provision, neither of the Constitution nor of any statute, addresses the claim-preclusive effect of a judgment in a federal diversity action.

It is also true, however, that no federal textual provision addresses the claim-preclusive effect of a federal-court judgment in a federal-question case, yet we have long held that States cannot give those judgments merely whatever effect they would give their own judgments, but must accord them the effect that this Court prescribes. The reasoning of [the cases so holding] suggests, moreover, that even when States are allowed to give federal judgments (notably, judgments in diversity cases) no more than the effect accorded to state judgments, that disposition is by direction of *this* Court, which has the last word on the claim-preclusive effect of *all* federal judgments:

> It is true that for some purposes and within certain limits it is only required that the judgments of the courts of the United States shall be given the same force and effect as are given the judgments of the courts of the States wherein they are rendered; but it is equally true that whether a Federal judgment has been given due force and effect in the state court is a Federal question reviewable by this court, which will determine for itself whether such judgment has been given due weight or otherwise. . . .
>
> When is the state court obliged to give to Federal judgments only the force and effect it gives to state court judgments within its own jurisdiction? Such cases are distinctly pointed out in the opinion of Mr. Justice Bradley in *Dupasseur* v. *Rochereau* [which stated that the case was a diversity case, applying state law under state procedure].

[Deposit Bank v. Frankfort, 191 U.S. 514-515 (1903)].

In other words, in *Dupasseur* the State was allowed (indeed, required) to give a federal diversity judgment no more effect than it would accord one of its own judgments only because reference to state law was *the federal rule that this Court deemed appropriate*. In short, federal common law governs the claim-preclusive effect of a dismissal by a federal court sitting in diversity.

It is left to us, then, to determine the appropriate federal rule. And despite the sea change that has occurred in the background law since *Dupasseur* was decided — not only repeal of the Conformity Act but also the watershed decision of this Court in *Erie* — we think the result decreed by *Dupasseur* continues to be correct for diversity cases. Since state, rather than federal, substantive law is at issue there is no need for a uniform federal rule. And indeed, nationwide uniformity in the substance of the matter is better served by having the same claim-preclusive rule (the state rule) apply whether the dismissal has been ordered by a state or a federal court. This is, it seems to us, a classic case for adopting, as the federally prescribed rule of decision, the law that would be applied by state courts in the State in which the federal diversity court sits. See Gasperini v. Ctr. for Humanities, Inc. As we have alluded to above, any other rule would produce the sort of "forum-shopping . . . and . . . inequitable administration of the laws" that *Erie* seeks to avoid, *Hanna*, since filing in, or removing to, federal court would be encouraged by the divergent effects that the litigants would anticipate from likely grounds of dismissal. See Guaranty Trust Co. v. York.

This federal reference to state law will not obtain, of course, in situations in which the state law is incompatible with federal interests. If, for example, state law did not accord claim-preclusive effect to dismissals for willful violation of discovery orders, federal courts' interest in the integrity of their own processes might justify a contrary federal rule. No such conflict with potential federal interests exists in the present case. Dismissal of this state cause of action was decreed by the California federal court only because the California statute of limitations so required; and there is no conceivable federal interest in giving that time bar more effect in other courts than the California courts themselves would impose.

Because the claim-preclusive effect of the California federal court's dismissal "upon the merits" of petitioner's action on statute-of-limitations grounds is governed by a federal rule that in turn incorporates California's law of claim preclusion (the content of which we do not pass upon today), the Maryland Court of Special Appeals erred in holding that the dismissal necessarily precluded the bringing of this action in the Maryland courts. The judgment is reversed, and the case remanded for further proceedings not inconsistent with this opinion.

It is so ordered.

NOTES AND PROBLEMS

1. Notice the common analytic problems presented by these four cases. In each there is a state practice.

a. Begin by identifying the state practice in each case. What did the state courts do differently than a federal court would do?

b. Consider which of these state policies one might call substantive. Two — in *Ricoh* and *Gasperini* — seem to meet this criteria pretty clearly, the former seeking not to disadvantage home-state litigants, the latter trying to hold down tort damage judgments. *Burlington Northern*'s appeals penalty is more difficult to characterize, but it has a clear pro-plaintiff effect. California's law of claim preclusion does not seem to fit well into this group: it neither favors a class of litigants nor seems to express any policy governing what Justice Harlan might call "primary human behavior."

2. Now consider the Supreme Court's treatment of these cases. In each one it locates a provision of federal law in arguable variance with the state practice. That step involves at least two moves. First, one has to find that there is pertinent federal law. Second, one has to find whether the federal law conflicts with the state practice and, if so, whether the federal law controls. Neither step is obvious.

a. In *Burlington Northern* the Court read a Federal Rule of Appellate Procedure dealing with frivolous appeals as if it also addressed nonfrivolous but unsuccessful appeals, the subject of the state statute. According to the Court, the *silence* of Fed. R. App. P. 38 about nonfrivolous appeals dictated a practice at odds with the state statute, which therefore yielded to the federal Rule.

b. In *Ricoh* the Court read 28 U.S.C. §1404, usually thought to address questions of forum non conveniens, as if it covered — and therefore displaced — state law on forum selection clauses. Again, there was an obvious argument that §1404 applied only in the usual cases, in which there was neither a forum selection clause nor a state law forbidding the enforcement of such clauses.

c. In *Gasperini* the federal law was more obviously applicable: both the Reexamination Clause and case law suggested that there was a serious question of whether federal appellate courts could exercise verdict reduction power.

d. In *Semtek* the search for governing federal law is more subtle. The Court first *rejects* some bodies of federal law (including Rule 41) that might be thought to apply, then locates the governing federal common law, which it can then cast in suitably flexible terms — permitting deference to the state law of claim preclusion in federal diversity cases except when "state law is incompatible with federal interests."

3. Notice the outcome: in each case federal law provides the criterion by which the case will be decided, but whether the federal law will displace or accommodate the state practice varies.

a. In *Gasperini* the Constitution appears to be the source of federal supremacy. In *Burlington Northern* and *Ricoh* federal Rules or statutes provide the basis for federal dominance. And in *Semtek* the federal judge-made law of judgments provides the basis.

b. But in three of the four cases the content of the governing law turns out to be quite deferential to state practice, shaping either the content or the application of federal law. Only in *Burlington Northern* does the federal statute categorically displace state law.

c. And the federal courts get the last say about how much and when the federal courts will defer to state law.

4. One can view this pattern in several ways. Cynically, one could note that at the end of the day federal judges will be able to decide whether and how to accommodate state procedural practices. This is a result technically consistent with *Erie* but one that might induce discomfort in Justices Brandeis and Frankfurter and might to some even look like a tiptoed step back towards the world of Swift v. Tyson. More charitably, one might view this pattern as an inching away from the over-mechanical world imagined in York v. Guaranty Trust, a retreat perhaps encouraged by the difficulty encountered by a federal judge who conscientiously decides that state law *does* govern — except that no one knows what the state law is. The next section describes that problem.

INCENTIVES TO LITIGATE

V

B. Substitutionary Remedies

2. Liquidated, Statutory, and Punitive Damages

Page 326. For the third sentence in the bracketed summary at the bottom of the page, substitute:

Upon discovering that his vehicle had been repainted, Gore sued. He introduced evidence both of the reduction in value of his own vehicle and, in support of his claim for punitive damages, that BMW had sold as new in the U.S. 983 other vehicles which had been similarly repainted.

Page 330. In place of Note 5 insert:

5. *Oberg* made it clear that due process requires some judicial review, but did not have occasion to be explicit about whether that review could be by a trial judge or whether it must be by an appellate court. The question was answered in Cooper Indus. Inc. v. Leatherman Tool Group, Inc., 532 U.S. 424 (2001). *Cooper Industries*, implicitly assuming that appellate review of punitive damages awards was necessary, went on to hold that the Constitution required *de novo* appellate review of the three *Gore* factors: (1) degree of reprehensibility of defendant's conduct; (2) disparity between harm suffered by the plainitiff and the punitive damage award; and (3) the difference between the jury's punitive award and the civil penalties authorized in comparable cases. The opinion justified this standard by pointing out that a punitive damage award differed from the usual "fact" found by a jury, as to which great appellate deference is required. If such review is constitutionally required, state as well as federal courts must make it part of their procedure for reviewing punitive damage awards.

6. The Supreme Court has apparently concluded that state courts have not heard the message transmitted by this string of cases; the most recent case suggests the majority's impatience, as well as a willingness to lay down clearer guidelines.

State Farm Mutual Automobile Insurance Co. v. Campbell

__ U.S. __, 2003 U.S. LEXIS 2713 (2003)

JUSTICE KENNEDY delivered the opinion of the Court.

We address once again the measure of punishment, by means of punitive damages, a State may impose upon a defendant in a civil case. The question is whether, in the circumstances we shall recount, an award of $145 million in punitive damages, where full compensatory damages are $1 million, is excessive and in violation of the Due Process Clause of the Fourteenth Amendment to the Constitution of the United States.

I

In 1981, Curtis Campbell (Campbell) was driving with his wife, Inez Preece Campbell, in Cache County, Utah. He decided to pass six vans traveling ahead of them on a two-lane highway. Todd Ospital was driving a small car approaching from the opposite direction. To avoid a head-on collision with Campbell, who by then was driving on the wrong side of the highway and toward oncoming traffic, Ospital swerved onto the shoulder, lost control of his automobile, and collided with a vehicle driven by Robert G. Slusher. Ospital was killed, and Slusher was rendered permanently disabled. The Campbells escaped unscathed.

In the ensuing wrongful death and tort action, Campbell insisted he was not at fault. Early investigations did support differing conclusions as to who caused the accident, but "a consensus was reached early on by the investigators and witnesses that Mr. Campbell's unsafe pass had indeed caused the crash." Campbell's insurance company, petitioner State Farm Mutual Automobile Insurance Company (State Farm), nonetheless decided to contest liability and declined offers by Slusher and Ospital's estate (Ospital) to settle the claims for the policy limit of $50,000 ($25,000 per claimant). State Farm also ignored the advice of one of its own investigators and took the case to trial, assuring the Campbells that "their assets were safe, that they had no liability for the accident, that [State Farm] would represent their interests and that they did not need to procure separate counsel." To the contrary, a jury determined that Campbell was 100 percent at fault, and a judgment was returned for $185,849, far more than the amount offered in settlement.

At first State Farm refused to cover the $135,849 in excess liability. Its counsel made this clear to the Campbells: " 'You may want to put for sale signs on your property to get things moving.' " Nor was State Farm willing to post a supersedeas bond to allow Campbell to appeal the judgment against him. Campbell obtained his own counsel to appeal the verdict. During the pendency of the appeal, in late 1984, Slusher, Ospital, and the Campbells reached an agreement whereby Slusher and Ospital agreed not to seek satisfaction of their claims against the Campbells. In exchange the Campbells agreed to pursue a bad faith action against State Farm and to be represented by Slusher's and Ospital's attorneys. The Campbells also agreed that Slusher and Ospital would have a right to play a part in all major decisions concerning the bad faith action. No settlement could be concluded without Slusher's and Ospital's approval, and Slusher and Ospital would receive 90 percent of any verdict against State Farm.

In 1989, the Utah Supreme Court denied Campbell's appeal in the wrongful death and tort actions. State Farm then paid the entire judgment, including the amounts in excess of the policy limits. The Campbells nonetheless filed a complaint against State Farm alleging bad faith, fraud, and intentional infliction of emotional distress. . . .

[The Utah Supreme Court described State Farm's stance in the bad faith case:]

> State Farm argued . . . that its decision to take the case to trial was an 'honest mistake' that did not warrant punitive damages. In contrast, the Campbells introduced evidence that State Farm's decision to take the case to trial was a result of a national scheme to meet corporate fiscal goals by capping payouts on claims company-wide. This scheme was referred to as State Farm's "Performance, Planning and Review," or PP & R, policy. To prove the existence of this scheme, the trial court allowed the Campbells to introduce extensive expert testimony regarding fraudulent practices by State Farm in its nation-wide operations. . . .

Evidence pertaining to the PP&R policy concerned State Farm's business practices for over 20 years in numerous States. Most of these practices bore no relation to third-party automobile insurance claims, the type of claim underlying the Campbells' complaint against the company. The jury awarded the Campbells $2.6 million [later reduced to $1 million] in compensatory damages and $145 million in punitive damages . . . .

II

[The Court reviewed its punitive damages cases, stressing the importance of careful judicial oversight:]

Although these awards serve the same purposes as criminal penalties, defendants subjected to punitive damages in civil cases have not been accorded the protections applicable in a criminal proceeding. This increases our concerns over the imprecise manner in which punitive damages systems are administered. . . .

In light of these concerns, in [BMW of North America v.] *Gore*, we instructed courts reviewing punitive damages to consider three guideposts: (1) the degree of reprehensibility of the defendant's misconduct; (2) the disparity between the actual or potential harm suffered by the plaintiff and the punitive damages award; and (3) the difference between the punitive damages awarded by the jury and the civil penalties authorized or imposed in comparable cases. We reiterated the importance of these three guideposts in *Cooper Industries* and mandated appellate courts to conduct de novo review of a trial court's application of them to the jury's award. . . .

III

Under the principles outlined in BMW of North America, Inc. v. Gore, this case is neither close nor difficult. It was error to reinstate the jury's $145 million punitive damages award. We address each guidepost of *Gore* in some detail.

A

"[T]he most important indicium of the reasonableness of a punitive damages award is the degree of reprehensibility of the defendant's conduct." *Gore*. We have instructed courts to determine the reprehensibility of a defendant by considering whether: the harm caused was physical as opposed to economic; the tortious conduct evinced an indifference to or a reckless disregard of the health or safety of others; the target of the conduct had financial vulnerability; the conduct involved repeated actions or was an isolated incident; and the harm was the result of intentional malice, trickery, or deceit, or mere accident. The existence of any one of these factors weighing in favor of a plaintiff may not be sufficient to sustain a punitive damages award; and the absence of all of them renders any award suspect. It should be presumed a plaintiff has been made whole for his injuries by compensatory damages, so punitive damages should only be awarded if the defendant's culpability, after having paid compensatory damages, is so reprehensible as to warrant the imposition of further sanctions to achieve punishment or deterrence.

Applying these factors in the instant case, we must acknowledge that State Farm's handling of the claims against the Campbells merits no praise. The trial court found that State Farm's employees altered the company's records to make Campbell appear less culpable. State Farm disregarded the overwhelming likelihood of liability and the near-certain probability that, by taking the case to trial, a judgment in excess of the policy limits would be awarded. State Farm amplified the harm by at first assuring the Campbells their assets would be safe from any verdict and by later telling them, postjudgment, to put a for-sale sign on their house. While we do not suggest there was error in awarding punitive damages based upon State Farm's conduct toward the Campbells, a more modest punishment for this reprehensible conduct could have satisfied the State's legitimate objectives, and the Utah courts should have gone no further.

This case, instead, was used as a platform to expose, and punish, the perceived deficiencies of State Farm's operations throughout the country. The Utah Supreme Court's opinion makes explicit that State Farm was being condemned for its nationwide policies rather than for the conduct direct[ed] toward the Campbells. . . .

A State cannot punish a defendant for conduct that may have been lawful where it occurred. *Gore*. . . . Nor, as a general rule, does a State have a legitimate concern in imposing punitive damages to punish a defendant for unlawful acts committed outside of the State's jurisdiction. Any proper adjudication of conduct that occurred outside Utah to other persons would require their inclusion, and, to those parties, the Utah courts, in the usual case, would need to apply the laws of their relevant jurisdiction. Phillips Petroleum Co. v. Shutts, [casebook page 990] (1985). . . .

For a more fundamental reason, however, the Utah courts erred in relying upon this and other evidence: The courts awarded punitive damages to punish and deter conduct that bore no relation to the Campbells' harm. A defendant's dissimilar acts, independent from the acts upon which liability was premised, may not serve as the basis for punitive damages. A defendant should be punished for the conduct that harmed the plaintiff, not for being an unsavory individual or business. Due process does not permit courts, in the calculation of punitive damages, to adjudicate the merits of other parties' hypothetical claims against a defendant under the guise of the reprehensibility analysis, but we have no doubt the Utah Supreme Court did that here. . . .

The Campbells have identified scant evidence of repeated misconduct of the sort that injured them. Nor does our review of the Utah courts' decisions convince us that State Farm was only punished for its actions toward the Campbells. Although evidence of other acts need not be identical to have relevance in the calculation of punitive damages, the Utah court erred here because evidence pertaining to claims that had nothing to do with a third-party lawsuit was introduced at length. Other evidence concerning reprehensibility was even more tangential. For example, the Utah Supreme Court criticized State Farm's investigation into the personal life of one of its employees and, in a broader approach, the manner in which State Farm's policies corrupted its employees. . . .

B

Turning to the second *Gore* guidepost, we have been reluctant to identify concrete constitutional limits on the ratio between harm, or potential harm, to the plaintiff and the punitive damages award. . . . We decline again to impose a bright-line ratio which a punitive damages award cannot exceed. Our jurisprudence and the principles it has now established demonstrate, however, that, in practice, few awards exceeding a single-digit ratio between punitive and compensatory damages, to a significant degree, will satisfy due process. [The Court reviewed its cases, summing up as follows:] They demonstrate what should be obvious: Single-digit multipliers are more likely to comport with due process, while still achieving the State's goals of deterrence and retribution, than awards with ratios in range of 500 to 1 or, in this case, of 145 to 1.

Nonetheless, because there are no rigid benchmarks that a punitive damages award may not surpass, ratios greater than those we have previously upheld may comport with due process where "a particularly egregious act has resulted in only a small amount of economic damages." The converse is also true, however. When compensatory damages are substantial, then a lesser ratio, perhaps only equal to compensatory damages, can reach the outermost limit of the due process guarantee. . . .

In the context of this case, we have no doubt that there is a presumption against an award that has a 145-to-1 ratio. The compensatory award in this case was substantial; the Campbells were awarded $1 million for a year and a half of emotional distress. This was complete compensation. The harm arose from a transaction in the economic realm, not from some physical assault or trauma; there were no physical injuries; and State Farm paid the excess verdict before the complaint was filed, so the Campbells suffered only minor economic injuries for the 18-month period in which State Farm refused to resolve the claim against them. The compensatory damages for the injury suffered here, moreover, likely were based on a component which was duplicated in the punitive award. Much of the distress was caused by the outrage and humiliation the Campbells suffered at the actions of their insurer; and it is a major role of punitive damages to condemn such conduct. . . .

The remaining premises for the Utah Supreme Court's decision bear no relation to the award's reasonableness or proportionality to the harm. . . . The wealth of a defendant cannot justify an otherwise unconstitutional punitive damages award. *Gore* ("The fact that BMW is a large corporation rather than an impecunious individual does not diminish its entitlement to fair notice of the demands that the several States impose on the conduct of its business"); ("[Wealth] provides an open-ended basis for inflating awards when the defendant is wealthy . . . . That does not make its use unlawful or inappropriate; it simply means that this factor cannot make up for the failure of other factors, such as 'reprehensibility,' to constrain significantly an award that purports to punish a defendant's conduct"). The principles set forth in *Gore* must be implemented with care, to ensure both reasonableness and proportionality.

C

The third guidepost in *Gore* is the disparity between the punitive damages award and the "civil penalties authorized or imposed in comparable cases." . . . Here, we need not dwell long on this guidepost. The most relevant civil sanction under Utah state law for the wrong done to the Campbells appears to be a $10,000 fine for an act of fraud, an amount dwarfed by the $145 million punitive damages award. . . .

IV

An application of the *Gore* guideposts to the facts of this case, especially in light of the substantial compensatory damages awarded (a portion of which contained a punitive element), likely would justify a punitive damages award at or near the amount of compensatory damages. The punitive award of $145 million, therefore, was neither reasonable nor proportionate to the wrong committed, and it was an irrational and arbitrary deprivation of the property of the defendant. The proper calculation of punitive damages under the principles we have discussed should be resolved, in the first instance, by the Utah courts.

The judgment of the Utah Supreme Court is reversed, and the case is remanded for proceedings not inconsistent with this opinion.

It is so ordered.

[Justices Scalia and Thomas dissented separately on the grounds that neither the due process clause nor the rest of the Constitution provided a basis for controlling states' awards of punitive damages.]

[Justice Ginsburg dissented on two grounds: that it was unwise for the Court to use the Constitution to lay down the kind of rules that were essentially legislative; and that in this case the behavior of State Farm (which included the apparent destruction of materials that had been requested in discovery) warranted the award in question:]

I remain of the view that this Court has no warrant to reform state law governing awards of punitive damages. Even if I were prepared to accept the flexible guides prescribed in *Gore*, I would not join the Court's swift conversion of those guides into instructions that begin to resemble marching orders. For the reasons stated, I would leave the judgment of the Utah Supreme Court undisturbed.

NOTES AND PROBLEMS

1. The case is both a significant punitive damages opinion and an illustration of some of the maneuverings characteristic of modern tort litigation, with insurers and plaintiffs' lawyers engaging in high-stakes moves. To get this aspect of the case clear, reread Part I of Justice Kennedy's opinion.

a. How many lawsuits are involved here? Who were the parties to each?

b. What behavior in which lawsuit provided the basis for a possible punitive damage award?

c. What happened after the first lawsuit? Who will share in what proportions any damage award after the Court's remand?

2. What should the Utah courts—and the plaintiffs—do on remand? They know that $145 million is too much, maybe a lot too much. What else?

a. Is an award of any punitives justified? Does the opinion speak clearly to this point?

b. If so, how much? The opinion suggests that "single-digit" multipliers will usually mark the outer bounds of due process. Does this mean that a $9 million award should be upheld (nine times the amount of the already-reduced compensatory damages)? Or, as the majority suggests, is the fact that this is a case in which substantial compensatory damages were awarded justify only a lower multiplier? How much lower?

3. What does *Campbell* say about future punitive damages claims? Take some easy-to-imagine hypotheticals:

a. The opinion stresses that the Campbells suffered no physical injuries. Suppose they had, and that State Farm had also declined to pay their medical expenses (on the grounds that they were exaggerating their condition or seeking medically unnecessary treatment). All other things being equal, the opinion suggests a higher multiplier than with solely economic damages. How much higher? Higher than the single-digit presumption?

b. Suppose the same compensatory damages (economic loss only) but evidence that defendant had used the same tactic multiple times in Utah (thus eliminating the problem of applying Utah punitives to out-of-state conduct). What multiplier?

4. To what extent does the opinion require state and federal courts to alter existing procedures in punitive damage cases?

a. Does the opinion suggest that trial courts may (or should) instruct juries in multipliers, telling them to choose among single-digits, except in egregious cases? Or is this instruction directed primarily to judges? If the courts should not instruct juries as to multipliers, can lawyers use them in arguments directed to juries? Suppose on remand plaintiffs' lawyer says to the jury: "I suggest to you that an award of $1 million would adequately compensate the Campbells for the ordeal to which the defendants have subjected them; and I suggest that another $9 million would send defendant the right kind of message about the evil of its conduct." Error?

b. Many states now allow plaintiffs to introduce evidence of defendants' wealth in punitive damage cases, on the grounds that such evidence allows juries to fit the punishment not just to the "crime" but to the defendant. Reread the last paragraph in section III B of the opinion. Does it hold such evidentiary practices unconstitutional? Or does it say that the wealth of the defendant cannot be used as a substitute for a careful consideration of the amount of harm and the "badness" of the defendant's conduct? The answer matters, because the ability to introduce defendant's wealth in evidence is a powerful tool, many lawyers would say.

5. When the opinion came down, the legal press suggested it was a big victory for insurers and "repeat defendants." That assessment might be wrong on several levels.

a. Good empirical studies of actual punitive damage awards suggest that in the 5-7 percent of trials where punitive damages are awarded, the amounts typically exhibit a ratio of about 1:1 with compensatory damages—whether consciously or not judges and jurors were essentially matching the amount of compensatory damages. Theodore Eisenberg et al., *The Predictability of Punitive Damages*, 26

J. Legal Stud. 623, 634 (1997) (reporting a mean compensatory damage award of $49,000 and a mean punitive damage award of $50,000). If this data is representative, the decision will not reduce many punitive awards.

b. In fact, were the *Campbell* multiplier range to reach the ears of jurors, either through instructions or lawyers' argument, it might, by encouraging juries not just to "match" compensatory damages but to multiply them, actually increase the median punitive damage award.

E. Financing Litigation

4. From Fee Spreading to Fee Shifting

d. By Statute

Page 355. Before "5. Fee Shifting and Settlement" insert:

3. What sort of victory should justify a fee award under a fee-shifting statute? A prevailing plaintiff who has won a jury verdict or summary judgment is obviously entitled to attorneys' fees. Presumably many out-of-court settlements reflect the parties' awareness that if plaintiffs prevail on some substantial part of the lawsuit they will be entitled to fees under such a statute; Evans v. Jeff D., casebook page 358, reveals a defendant's lawyer all too aware of attorneys' fee statutes.

a. What of the plaintiff who wins just by filing a lawsuit? In Buckhannon v. West Virginia, 532 U.S. 598 (2001), plaintiff operator of an assisted living residence challenged a state statute under whose terms plaintiff would have to close its facilities. After suit was filed the state agreed to suspend the orders requiring the homes' closure. Then, while suit was pending, the state legislature amended the relevant statutes, eliminating the challenged provision. The defendant state then moved to dismiss the lawsuit as moot. Plaintiff moved for its attorneys' fees as a "prevailing party," citing cases in which Courts of Appeals had awarded fees to analogously situated parties who were "catalysts" for legal change. No, said the U.S. Supreme Court. Plaintiff may have "won" in the ordinary sense of that word, but it had not prevailed in litigation, and was therefore not entitled to fees under the relevant statute (an analogue to §1988(b)). Judicial relief is required to qualify for fees under such a statute.

b. Should Congress (or a state legislature) amend the fee statutes to permit such "catalyst" parties to earn fees? Suppose the statute was so amended. Would the reasonable fees be measured by the litigation expenses or by the same attorneys' time spent in lobbying the legislature to make the change in the challenged statutory scheme?

5. Fee Shifting and Settlement

a. Rule 68

Page 356. Replace second sentence in Note 2b with:

No: Plaintiff, who recovered less than the offer amount, will have to pay post-offer costs, but these costs do not include attorneys' fees.

PLEADING

VI

B. Pleading in a Modern Regime

3. Ethical Limitations and Disfavored Claims

a. Ethical Principles as a Limitation

Page 435. Substitute the following for Note 12:

12. Consider the incentives created by the current Rule. Party files a groundless paper. Opponent challenges it, giving Party the required notice and 21-day period before filing the Rule 11 motion. Party fails to withdraw the groundless paper. Opponent makes the necessary substantive motion to defeat the groundless paper (e.g., a 12(b)(6) motion, a Rule 56 motion, etc.). Ideally, Opponent would then like to be able to collect its legal fees for opposing the groundless paper. But the court may not impose any sanction at all, and if it does, that sanction may not require any payment to Opponent. Moreover, Opponent cannot combine its Rule 11 motion with the substantive motion because of the separate motion requirement. Under these circumstances, if Opponent has already won the underlying lawsuit, is it worth the effort to bring a separate Rule 11 motion? Will Rule 11 motions be confined to "grudge matches" between lawyers or parties who have developed strong personal animosity in the course of litigation?

Page 436. Before "b. Disfavored Claims?" insert:

14. Finally, consider what effect a sanction imposed under Rule 11 should have in subsequent litigation.

a. Baker serves as Adam's financial adviser. Dissatisfied with the results, Adam sues Baker. Baker wins both a dismissal and Rule 11 sanctions because Adam failed to comply with discovery requests and produced no evidentiary basis for alleging Baker's involvement in the challenged transactions. Adam then publishes an article disparaging Baker's skill as a financial adviser. Baker sues Adam for libel. Baker seeks partial summary judgment in the libel action, arguing that prior litigation — and specifically the Rule 11 motion — established that she had nothing to do with the transactions in question and that the publication was therefore knowingly false. Is Baker entitled to summary judgment because of the Rule 11 ruling? Faigin v. Kelly, 184 F.3d 67 (1st Cir. 1999) (Rule 11 motion decided whether party had "abused judicial process" by failing to produce evidence, not whether the underlying claims were true or false; no issue preclusion because a different "issue" in two proceedings).

b. Carla faces disbarment proceedings, based in part on four Rule 11 sanctions awarded against her in various lawsuits in which she has appeared. She seeks to defend her conduct, but the bar prosecutor contends that the sanctions in the four cases preclude Carla from relitigating her behavior. Is she precluded? In re Gwen G. Caranchini, 956 S.W.2d 910 (Mo. 1997) (factual findings of disciplinary sanctions precluded from relitigation).

b. Disfavored Claims?

(2) Civil Rights

Page 445. Before "4. Allocating the Elements" insert:

3. The Supreme Court has reinforced the holding of *Leatherman*, extending it to other civil rights claims. In Swierkiewicz v. Sorema, N.A., 534 U.S. 506 (2002), the Court held that Rule 8(a) also governs in employment discrimination cases, where case law has established that to prevail on such a claim, a plaintiff lacking proof of intentional discrimination has to prove a "prima facie" case by showing (1) membership in a protected group, (2) qualification for the job in question, (3) an adverse employment action, and (4) circumstances that support an inference of discrimination. The Court distinguished between proof and pleading; though the plaintiff might have to produce evidence of each of these elements to survive summary judgment, he need not include them in the complaint:

> Other provisions of the Federal Rules of Civil Procedure are inextricably linked to Rule 8(a)'s simplified notice pleading standard. Rule 8(e)(1) states that "no technical forms of pleading or motions are required," and Rule 8(f) provides that "all pleadings shall be so construed as to do substantial justice." Given the Federal Rules' simplified standard for pleading, "[a] court may dismiss a complaint only if it is clear that no relief could be granted under any set of facts that could be proved consistent with the allegations." Hishon v. King & Spalding , 467 U.S. 69, 73 (1984). If a pleading fails to specify the allegations in a manner that provides sufficient notice, a defendant can move for a more definite statement under Rule 12(e) before responding. Moreover, claims lacking merit may be dealt with through summary judgment under Rule 56. The liberal notice pleading of Rule 8(a) is the starting point of a simplified pleading system, which was adopted to focus litigation on the merits of a claim. ("The Federal Rules reject the approach that pleading is a game of skill in which one misstep by counsel may be decisive to the outcome and accept the principle that the purpose of pleading is to facilitate a proper decision on the merits").

Id. at 513-514.

DISCOVERY

VII

A. Modern Discovery

Page 486. Before "B. The Possibility and Limits of Discovery: Relevance and Privilege" insert:

Recent years have seen this debate intensify, with focus directed less to discovery in general than to more specific questions: Should parties be required to disclose, without a request from the opposition, materials supporting their case? Should the scope of discovery be limited in some way? Could abusive deposition practice be controlled? How broadly should information discovered in one lawsuit be available to parties in related litigation? Each of these issues was addressed in a substantial — and controversial — revision of the Rules that took effect in December 2000. Both the changes and their possible effects are addressed in the materials below.

As an introduction to these changes a short history of the debates surrounding the discovery portion of the Rules is instructive. The desirability of amendments to the discovery rules has been under debate for more than twenty years. Roughly speaking, one could see the two sides as disagreeing about whether it was possible to throw out the bath water without harming the baby and, if so, how. The "baby" in this debate was the general acknowledgement that the U.S. discovery system (every state has adopted something like the broad discovery regime of the Rules) makes it possible to ferret out much information and thus to allow parties with good counsel and adequate resources to litigate in full possession of the relevant information. The "bathwater" is composed of several elements, depending on who was doing the analysis. One group focused on the extent of expensive "over-discovery," another on "under-discovery" and stonewalling, a third on the asserted decline of professional civility and cooperation, a fourth on the failure of judicial supervision. These different definitions of the problem led to differing remedies. The 2000 amendments, promulgated after an elaborate process of hearings and comment, had four central features: changes in required disclosures by the parties; a narrowing of the definition of material discoverable without judicial order; imposition of national restrictions on the number of interrogatories and depositions and the length of depositions in the absence of judicial order; and a set of changes designed to encourage judicial monitoring and possible cost-sharing of discovery.

Page 486. For "B. The Possibilities and Limits of Discovery: Relevance and Privilege, 1. Relevance" substitute:

B. The Possibility and Limits of Discovery: Relevance and Privilege

Both the power and the destructive potential of discovery hinge on the principles governing its use. From 1938 until 2000 Rule 26(b)(1) gave the parties a right to discover "any matter, not privileged, which is *relevant* to the *subject matter* involved in the pending action" (emphasis added). The new version of this section authorizes discovery of "any matter, not privileged, that is *relevant to the claim or defense* of any party" (emphasis added). In either version the concept of relevance both grants power and limits it; privilege operates solely as a limitation.

1. Relevance

To be discoverable information must be "relevant to a claim or defense." That short phrase links the concept of relevance to the law of pleading, to the law of evidence, and to common sense. Start with common sense. Relevance defines a relationship between pieces of information: how I tie my shoelaces is irrelevant to whether it will rain today; how the sky looks is highly relevant to that question. But legal relevance demands more than this. For a piece of information to be relevant to a legal proposition means, according to the governing substantive law — enforced by the rules of evidence — that the information tends to prove or disprove something the law says matters. For example, if in a contract dispute the defendant contends that he failed to pay for goods because the goods were defective, the condition of the goods will be relevant. If the defendant instead contends that he failed to pay for the goods because he used the money to support a sick relative, the state of the relative's health would be irrelevant. Its irrelevance flows from the law of contract, which says that one's motives for breaching a contract don't matter. Finally, consider the new role of pleading in defining relevance for the purposes of discovery. In the contract case imagined above, suppose the defendant pleaded, as its sole defense, the running of the statute of limitations. On the basis of that pleading, would information about whether the plaintiff had fulfilled his part of the agreement be "relevant to a claim or defense"? The next two cases illustrate the relation among substantive law, relevance, and discoverability.

Blank v. Sullivan & Cromwell

16 Fair Empl. Prac. Cas. (BNA) 87 (S.D.N.Y. 1976)

MOTLEY, J.

[Plaintiffs were female lawyers who had unsuccessfully applied for positions as associates around 1970; they sued, alleging sexual discrimination in hiring.]

Plaintiffs have moved for a rehearing and modification of so much of this court's order of May 24, 1976 as denied plaintiffs the discovery sought in Interrogatories 60(f) and (g), 61, 62, and 63 of their First Interrogatories[1] (filed in court on April 18, 1976). That order adopted the report of Magistrate Harold J. Raby, to whom plaintiffs' Rule 37 motion had previously been referred, but modified the report insofar as it had recommended compliance with the Interrogatories here in question. Specifically, with respect to these Interrogatories (and certain others not in issue on the motion for rehearing), the court held that "the defendant need not respond in any form to such interrogatories since the information sought therein relates to defendant's partners and employees who became partners, and is not relevant to the subject matter of the suit before this court." However, upon reconsideration and upon careful examination of the arguments submitted by plaintiffs, defendant, and amicus Equal Employment Opportunity Commission, the court has decided to order defendants to respond to the interrogatories here in issue. . . .

In reversing its prior ruling, this court also is mindful of the fact that a plaintiff may not sue for injuries that he or she has not suffered, and he or she may not sue on behalf of a class of which he or she is not a member. Plaintiff, therefore, cannot represent in this action those who may be aggrieved by defendant's partner selection criteria. However, defendant is incorrect in suggesting that because the individual plaintiff here has not alleged that she was denied partnership due to her sex, she is not entitled to the requested discovery.

Under Rule 26, Fed. R. Civ. P., a party is entitled to discovery, not only of material which is relevant and admissible at trial, but also of information which "appears reasonably calculated to lead to the discovery of admissible evidence."

1. "60. Identify each and every female permanent associate at Sullivan & Cromwell prior to August 30, 1970 and indicate as to each . . .

(f) whether each was offered an opportunity to become a partner; and

(g) whether each became a partner.

"61. State the average length of service at the firm as an associate, of all associates who were offered partnerships in the firm between 1961 and the present date.

"62. If any person listed in answer to Question 60 was not offered an opportunity to become a partner within the average length of service period noted in answer to Question 61, state the reason why she was not extended such an offer.

"63. State the name of each male attorney hired by the firm after the earliest date listed in answer to Question 60(b) who was offered an opportunity to become a partner at the firm, and indicate:

(a) the date when each person started work at the firm;

(b) the date on which each person was offered the opportunity to become a partner; and

(c) the area of specialization of each person."

More specifically, in Title VII cases, in which a plaintiff alleges discriminatory employment practices, both the Supreme Court, in McDonnell Douglas Corp. v. Green, 411 U.S. 792, 804-805 (1973), and the Second Circuit in Kohn v. Royall, Koegel & Wells, 496 F.2d 1094, 1101 (1974) have ruled that general information on defendant's labor hierarchy may be reflective of restrictive or exclusionary hiring practices within the contemplation of the statute.

Thus, the narrow inquiry is whether the information requested is so unrelated to plaintiffs' claim that women are discriminated against by defendant on account of sex that it cannot be said to be "relevant" within the expansive meaning of that term in Rule 26. In the court's view, this connection is not nearly so tenuous as defendant suggests.

By order dated June 13, 1975, this court ruled that "the class represented by plaintiff is defined to include all women qualified to hold legal positions at the law firm of Sullivan and Cromwell who have been or would be denied employment because of their sex." Judge Lasker of this Court dealt with a plaintiff class similarly constituted in a suit against the law firm of Royall, Koegel & Wells. By order dated January 7, 1975, he granted plaintiffs in that suit similar discovery with respect to advancement to partnership, endorsing the recommendation of Magistrate, now Judge Goettel, who had commented as follows: "It is difficult to conceive of anything more telling with respect to whether or not these [female] associates are being subject to employment discrimination than whether they proceed on to partnerships in the firm in the same manner as male attorneys with similar capabilities."

The court is, of course, aware that the numerous factors which bear upon the admission to partnership make it impossible to equate that decision with the decision to hire an associate. However, it does not follow from that recognition that a firm's practices in advancing, or failing to advance, associates to partnership have no probative bearing upon allegations of improper discrimination in hiring associates. Even assuming arguendo, that Title VII does not proscribe the use of sex as a criterion for admission to partnership, that legal conclusion does not necessarily indicate that evidence of sexually oriented discrimination at that level might not be probative of a similar pattern in the selection of associates, where it would be illegal.

Accordingly, defendant is directed to answer the Interrogatories referred to above.

Steffan v. Cheney

920 F.2d 74 (D.C. Cir. 1990)

Per Curiam

Joseph C. Steffan resigned from the United States Naval Academy in 1987, after an administrative board recommended that he be discharged. The board's recommendation was based solely upon Steffan's statements proclaiming himself a homosexual; he was not charged with any homosexual conduct. In 1988 he filed this action, claiming that he was constructively discharged and challenging the constitutionality of the regulations that provided for the discharge of admitted homosexuals. The factual and procedural background of the case is set out in the opinion of the district court, and will not be repeated in detail here.

The matter is before this court now because Steffan, claiming his Fifth Amendment privilege against self-incrimination, refused to answer deposition questions directed to whether he had engaged in homosexual conduct during or after his tenure as a midshipman. He also objected that the questions were not relevant to the legality of his separation. The district court, having issued a prior warning, dismissed Steffan's action for failure to comply with its discovery order, see Fed. R. Civ. P. 37(b)(2), and Steffan appeals. Although the district court has broad discretion in choosing a sanction under Rule 37, no sanction may be upheld if its imposition was based upon an error of law. Because this is such a case, we reverse.

The district court acknowledged that "the record is clear that [Steffan] was separated from the Naval Academy based on his admission that he is a homosexual rather than on any evidence of misconduct." Nevertheless, the court thought that the questions about homosexual conduct were "highly relevant" because, it believed, the Navy could "refuse reinstatement on the grounds that an individual has engaged in homosexual acts." The court held that "in seeking reinstatement and award of his diploma, [Steffan] through his claims has placed in issue whether he is qualified for such relief."

Judicial review of an administrative action is confined to "the grounds . . . upon which the record discloses that [the] action was based." SEC v. Chenery Corp., 318 U.S. 80, 87 (1943). This rule applies with equal force to judicial review of administrative actions by the military.

Here Steffan is challenging the Navy's administrative determination that he is unfit for continued service because he stated that he is a homosexual. That he seeks reinstatement as relief for an allegedly invalid separation does not put into issue the question whether he engaged in potentially disqualifying conduct unless such conduct was a basis for his separation. See White v. Secretary of the Army, 878 F.2d 501, 505 (D.C. Cir. 1989).* If Steffan was discharged wrongfully, he "has never been discharged[;] . . . in the eyes of the law, [he] remains in service." Dilley v. Alexander, 627 F.2d 407, 411 (D.C. Cir. 1980).

The district court therefore erred in finding the inquiry into homosexual conduct vel non to be relevant on the ground asserted in its opinion. Should the district court find that the questions are relevant on any other ground, it must of course balance anew the interests of the parties before deciding upon a sanction.

*The Government now argues that Steffan's admission of homosexuality raised a "rebuttable regulatory presumption that he had a predilection [sic] to commit, and had committed, homosexual acts." This argument, not raised in the district court, finds no support in the record. Cf. Ben-Shalom v. Marsh, 881 F.2d 454, 457 (7th Cir. 1989) (soldier given written notice of presumption).

We reverse the judgment of the district court and remand for further proceedings consistent with this opinion.

So ordered.

NOTES AND PROBLEMS

1. How does one explain the different results in the two cases? In both cases one party (plaintiffs in *Blank*, the defendant in *Steffan*) asked a broad question; in one case the court orders an answer, in the other it refuses to order Steffan to answer. Why?

2. Focus on the procedural moves that led these two courts to issue their discovery rulings.

a. Which actions by which parties led the district court to issue its ruling?

b. How did *Steffan* reach an appellate court?

c. Suppose the defendant in *Blank* wanted to challenge the district court ruling. Could it have appealed?

d. What do your answers tell you about the power of district courts in discovery matters?

3. Develop your understanding of the concept of relevance by working through the following problems:

a. Albert and Barbara are involved in an automobile collision. Albert sues Barbara, alleging negligence. Barbara denies liability. Albert seeks to discover the size of Barbara's bank account. (He wants to know whether she will be capable of satisfying a damage judgment.) Is this information "relevant to a claim or defense" and thus discoverable?

b. Same facts as in Problem 3a, except that in addition to asserting negligence, Albert alleges that Barbara intentionally collided with him. Intentional torts carry with them punitive damages, and under some conditions a jury asked to award punitive damages may consider the wealth of the defendant, the idea being that the punishment should be tailored to the defendant's circumstances. Albert again seeks to discover the size of Barbara's bank account. Is it now "relevant to a claim or defense" and thus discoverable?

c. Same lawsuit as in Problem 3a — that is, a negligence action, with no allegations of intentional harm. Albert, fearing that Barbara may lack assets to pay damages, seeks to discover whether Barbara has a liability insurance policy that would be available to satisfy a damage judgment if he wins the suit. If one considers only relevance to a claim or defense, is the policy discoverable? Now consider how Rule 26(a)(1)(D) changes this result. What might justify this exception to the ordinary rules of relevance?

4. Now consider a variation on this problem, one in which you begin to confront some of the techniques of discovery. The current version of Rule 26 provides for a three-stage discovery process. In the first, set forth in Rule 26(a), the parties come forward with certain basic information "that the disclosing party may use to *support* its claims or defenses" (emphasis added). In the second stage,

they may, without seeking judicial permission, ask each other for additional information under the guidelines described in Rule 26(b)(1). In the third stage, the parties may, with judicial permission and a showing of good cause, seek either deeper or broader discovery, extending their discovery beyond claims or defenses to the "subject matter" of the suit, or increasing the number or duration of interrogatories and depositions beyond those specified in the rules. Read Rule 26(a) and (b) and answer the following questions:

a. Albert alleges that Barbara "negligently collided" with his car; Barbara's answer has denied negligence. (For an example of such an exchange of general pleadings, see casebook pages 20 and 23.) Albert's lawyer has interviewed him, obtained copies of his medical and wage records, and has spoken with various other potential witnesses. Albert's lawyer intends to present a straightforward version of the case: Barbara ran a red light, collided with Albert, who as a result lost wages and incurred medical expenses. A witness at the intersection will testify that Barbara ran the light. There are, however, some soft spots in the case: Albert has a poor driving record and has himself been cited for running red lights; his job situation has been precarious and Albert thinks that his boss might testify that he was about to be fired (thus reducing potential damages for lost wages). What disclosures must Albert make under 26(a)(1)?

b. Now consider Barbara's disclosures. Her lawyer has interviewed her and knows the name and address of a mechanic who can testify about the maintenance of her car (he will say it was well maintained), her boss (with whom she had a major argument just before the accident), and a bystander who saw the accident. The bystander, let us suppose, is not the same one located by Albert. This witness is not an attractive one — a vagrant with a long history of minor drug arrests — but he says he thinks the light was green for Barbara when she entered the intersection. Explain how each of these witnesses might have information relevant to the lawsuit. Which of their names should Barbara's lawyer supply at the time appropriate for the disclosure required in Rule 26(a)(1)(A)?

5. Notice that the 2000 revisions of the disclosure provisions require parties to disclose information that they "may use" "to support" their claims or defenses. By contrast, the general discovery provisions of 26(b)(1) require discovery of any unprivileged matter "relevant to the claim or defense of any party." Consider how those provisions would bear on the following problems:

a. Barbara has told her lawyer that she had a violent argument with her boss just before the accident and was still fuming as she drove. Her lawyer is also debating whether to use the testimony of the vagrant who will testify that the traffic light was in her favor. Must she disclose her boss as a witness pursuant to 26(a)(1)? The vagrant?

b. Suppose, after the initial disclosures, Barbara is served with an interrogatory asking her to supply the name of any witness with information relevant to plaintiff's claim. Must she now list her boss as such a witness?

6. How specific must a pleading be to trigger the "claim or defense" requirement of Rule 26(a)(1) and 26(b)(1)? Consider whether the following case gives any definition to this phrase.

Johnson Matthey, Inc. v. Research Corp.

2002 WL 31235717 (S.D.N.Y. 2002)

MAAS, Magistrate J.

I. Introduction . . .

Following a referral from Judge Mukasey, I resolved a series of discovery disputes in this action [involving a dispute arising from an agreement to develop and market certain chemicals used in treating cancer]. The motion filed by plaintiff Johnson Matthey, Inc. ("JM") asks me to reconsider my determination that information concerning a 1995 lawsuit between defendant Research Corp. ("Research") and Michigan State University ("MSU") (the "MSU litigation") need not be produced by Research. . . .

II. Discussion. . . .

B. JM Motion

In its April 19, 2002 letter, JM originally sought the materials related to the MSU litigation because the limited available public record indicated that it concerned [the same chemicals involved in the present suit] and sought recovery for unjust enrichment, one of the legal theories that JM seeks to assert against Research here. The complaint in the MSU litigation alleged that Research had breached its contract with MSU in various ways, including Research's failure to use enough of its income for scientific investigation and other contractually-specified goals. The complaint further alleged that the failure to expend its money for these purposes had unjustly enriched Research.

During the May 10 discovery conference, I indicated that I would likely deny JM's request for documents related to the MSU litigation because neither of the specific claims raised there was at issue in this action. As I observed at the time, the mere fact that an unjust enrichment theory was advanced in both lawsuits was insufficient to establish the relevance of the MSU litigation. Nevertheless, I agreed to review the complaint in the MSU litigation in further detail before making a final determination. My subsequent review of the complaint confirmed my initial conclusion.

JM seeks reconsideration of my decision concerning the MSU litigation on . . . grounds . . . that I overlooked a controlling decision which "make[s] clear" that materials from the MSU litigation are discoverable. In Burda Media, Inc. v. Blumenberg, Judge Sweet held that " 'any possibility' that the sought-after information may be relevant to the *subject matter* of the action will satisfy Rule 26(b)(1)'s requirements" (quoting Daval Steel Prods. v. M/V Fakerdine, 951 F.2d 1357, 1367 (2d Cir. 1991) (emphasis added)). This expansive language accurately summarizes the law as it stood at the time. Thereafter, however, Rule 26(b)(1) of the Federal Rules of Civil Procedure was amended to narrow the scope of relevancy from "subject matter" of the action to "claim or defense of any party." See Fed. R. Civ. P. 26(b)(1), adv. comm. note to 2000 amendment. In order to compel the production of information which is relevant only to the subject matter of an action, the Rule requires that the party seeking discovery demonstrate "good cause." See id.

Although the relationship between JM and Research began at MSU, the complaint in the MSU litigation establishes that it concerned matters which are in no way relevant to a claim or defense at issue here. JM also has failed to demonstrate good cause for expanding the scope of discovery to incorporate the materials generated in that lawsuit. JM's motion for reconsideration is therefore denied. . . .

SO ORDERED.

NOTES AND PROBLEMS

1. The quotation from *Burda Media*, applying the now-superseded standard, suggests the breadth with which some courts had applied the earlier version of Rule 26.

2. How does "claim or defense" change the nature of the discoverable material? Suppose the plaintiff in *Johnson Matthey* had alleged that the defendant was continuing a course of wrongful behavior that it had begun in relation to other parties; would that render the earlier suit discoverable?

3. The phrase "relevant to the subject matter involved in the action" no longer defines the initial scope of disclosure and discovery, but it continues to exist in Rule 26(b). It now defines a broader stage of discovery that is available only if the judge so orders "for good cause," a finding that Magistrate Judge Maas declined to make in *Johnson Matthey*. What should count as good cause? What if the *Johnson Matthey* plaintiff had frankly admitted that information in the prior suit was not relevant to a present claim or defense, but told the judge that it believed defendant had engaged in a pattern of repeated conduct (and might therefore be liable for punitive damages) and that it needed judicial permission to explore that belief?

C. Surveying Discovery: Procedures and Methods

Page 496. For "1. Required Disclosures" substitute:

1. Required Disclosures

Rule 26(a)(1) describes the first stage, which it calls "required disclosures." For types of cases in which disclosure is required, the parties must meet early in the suit; within 14 days after that meeting, each party must offer the other side the names of witnesses and descriptions of documents "that the disclosing party may use to support its claims or defenses," as well as calculations of damages, and copies of insurance agreements. The parties must exchange such information without its having been requested by their opponent. Once these initial disclosures have occurred, the parties may then request additional information using interrogatories, depositions, requests for inspection of documents and physical objects, requests for physical and mental examinations, and for admissions. All this requires cooperation by the lawyers, a timetable, and mechanisms for enforcing discovery and disclosure obligations. Disclosure, though an important part of discovery, will not occur in all cases. The provisions of Rule 26 (a)(1)(E) exempt many kinds of smaller or simpler cases; one estimate by the Federal Judicial Center suggested that as many as a third of federal filings fall into the eight exempt categories.

NOTES AND PROBLEMS

1. Your client, Baker, gives you a state court complaint from a state employing the current version of the discovery rules. The plaintiff, Alice, alleges that Baker agreed to sell her his car, and then refused to go through with the transaction; Alice seeks damages. Baker tells you that he and Alice discussed such a possibility, but that they never agreed. In response to your questions, Baker tells you no one witnessed their discussion. You file an answer denying that there was a contract. You know that Rule 26(a)(1) requires some disclosures.

a. On this state of the pleadings, what information would you have to prepare for disclosure?

b. On this state of the pleadings, what would be the only information you would be confident Alice would have to disclose to you?

c. What does "unless solely for impeachment," a phrase used in Rules 26(a)(1)(A) and (B) mean? Suppose that Baker's lawyer has learned that Alice has a reputation for lying, and that a prior lawsuit of a similar sort was dismissed when the judge found that she was not a credible witness. If we imagine that Baker will use this information solely to attack Alice's credibility if she testifies, then Baker need not disclose it as part of the initial disclosures. What if the central element of Baker's defense is that Alice is lying when she says she and Baker agreed to the sale? Is her credibility now "solely for impeachment"?

2. Assuming a party must make some disclosure, when must that disclosure occur? Answering this question requires a close reading of Rules 4, 16(b), 26(a)(1), and 26(f). Together these provisions establish a time line that starts when the defendant has been served or has "appeared" in the lawsuit. Service occurs when the defendant has been served or when the defendant, pursuant to Rule 4(d), has waived formal service. Appearance refers to the defendant's filing some paper or motion that evinces its participation in the lawsuit; it would include an answer as well as various Rule 12(b) motions.

At this point a series of time sequences that govern pretrial procedure begins to run. One appears in Rule 16(b), which requires that within 90 days after a defendant's appearance or 120 days after service, the judge shall hold a "scheduling conference," to discuss the way discovery and other pretrial matters should proceed. Rule 26(f) requires the parties meet themselves, without the judge, to discuss the case "as soon as practicable and in any event at least 21 days before a scheduling conference is held." Finally, to complete the link to disclosure, Rule 26(a)(1) requires the parties, at this meeting or within 14 days after it, to exchange disclosure lists.

The result of these interlocking provisions is to require the parties to exchange the required disclosures at least seven days before the scheduling conference and, at the latest, four months after the complaint is served on defendant. More commonly, where defendant has appeared, the disclosure will occur no later than 85 days after that appearance.

3. Disclosure will not occur in all cases. The 2000 revisions made disclosure mandatory in all federal court cases but at the same time suggested that very small and very large cases will be exempted from disclosure. Rule 26(a)(1)(E) lists a number of exempt categories — smaller claims and those in which either a well-developed record or the absence of counsel make disclosure unnecessary or potentially unfair. The advisory committee notes suggest that very large cases, in which one imagines that close judicial supervision will displace the Rules, may also be exempted.

4. Rule 26(d) says that the parties may not use other forms of discovery — depositions, interrogatories, etc. — until after the meeting required by Rule 26(f). The exchange of disclosures must closely follow the Rule 26(f) meeting. The other forms of discovery will thus come into play only after the initial disclosures.

5. Suppose a party has fully complied with its disclosure requirements, but then learns of an additional witness or document. Read Rule 26(e) and Rule 37(c)(1).

a. Albert, suing Barbara for negligently inflicted injuries in an auto accident, supplies her with all of his medical bills pursuant to Rule 26(a)(1)(B) and (C). Thereafter, he receives a substantial new bill from the treating surgeon. What must Albert do?

b. Albert does not inform Barbara of the new surgeon's bill, but its existence comes to light in a deposition of the surgeon. Thereafter, Barbara seeks to block admission of the bill as part of the evidence on damages. How should the judge rule?

Page 498. The text for "2. Asking Questions: Interrogatories and Depositions (Rules 28, 30, 31, 32, 33, and 37)" should read:

One may send one's opponent a list of questions to answer (interrogatories) or one may take a witness's deposition ("depose" him or her). What is the difference between the two? The answer usually involves balancing utility and cost; in discovery one often gets what one pays for.

Interrogatories (Rule 33) are typically much cheaper for the interrogator (the "propounder" of the interrogatories) because one can inexpensively frame a set of appropriate questions, send it to an adverse party, and sit back and wait for the answers; the recipient (and his lawyer) must either answer the questions or object to them. A drawback to interrogatories is that, because the questioner cannot follow up evasive answers with a question designed to pin things down, interrogatories that go beyond fairly routine specific information — such as the names and addresses of witnesses — may yield little valuable information. And because much routine information will ordinarily emerge as part of the disclosure required by Rule 26(a)(1), there may be only a few situations in which interrogatories serve a useful role. Moreover, parties must seek permission of the court — or a stipulation from their opponents — before propounding more than 25 questions. Note also that interrogatories may be sent only to a party; nonparty witnesses may be deposed but need not answer written interrogatories.

Depositions (Rules 28, 30, 31, 32) present the opposite balance of cost and usefulness. A deposition is like questioning a witness at trial without the judge: Depositions usually occur in lawyers' offices, and the lawyers are present, as is the witness and a court reporter or recording device. The lawyers ask questions that the witness must answer under oath. The advantage is that the lawyer can ask a series of questions that force the witness to take a position as to the matters at issue, and the lawyer can follow up with further questions if the witness is evasive, or if the witness' testimony opens up new avenues of inquiry. The disadvantage is expense to all concerned. In a full-blown deposition both sides have their lawyers there; if the witness is not one of the parties he or she may also be represented by a lawyer. In addition, the deposing party must arrange for some form of recording or transcription of the deposition. In a case with multiple parties, each hour of deposition time may amount to thousands of dollars in legal fees and costs. As with interrogatories, the Rules place limits on depositions. Without seeking permission, the total number of depositions taken by one side (plaintiff(s), defendant(s), third-party defendant(s)) may not exceed ten, no deposition may exceed a day of seven hours, and no person may be deposed a second time without the permission of the court or the other side.

Halfway between interrogatories and a deposition is a deposition on written questions (Rule 31); in this rarely-used procedure the lawyer writes down the questions and sends them to the court reporter presiding at the deposition who asks the questions and records the witness's answers. This is a good deal cheaper than a deposition on oral examination but usually yields less information than a "live" deposition. To understand the reason for this low yield, think how difficult it would be to compose such a set of questions: The first one or two inquiries are straightforward, but how does one frame follow-up questions without knowing what the witness will say to the initial inquiry? A related question is what happens if there is a disagreement about whether a question in a deposition or an interrogatory is justified? The procedure differs according to the device being used.

Read Rules 30(d) and 33(b), together with Rule 37(a)(2) and (4), and apply them to the questions below.

PROBLEMS

1. Having sustained injuries from a household appliance, Cora sues Manufacturer. The required discovery conference and the ensuing disclosures occur. Cora then serves 55 interrogatories on Manufacturer and 20 interrogatories on Department Store, which sold her the product. Both Store and Manufacturer refuse to answer.

a. Explain why Store needn't answer even if the questions are relevant and not privileged. By what procedural step might Cora induce Store to answer?

b. Can Cora get a court to compel Manufacturer's answers? How?

2. Pursuant to Rule 30(b)(6), Cora serves on Manufacturer a request to depose an employee or officer responsible for the "design and safety engineering" of the appliance in question. Manufacturer designates Geraldine Chen, a vice president for product design. At the deposition, Cora's lawyer asks Chen a series of questions about her qualifications and responsibilities. She then asks Chen a question about the financial structure of the company. Manufacturer's lawyer believes that question is outside the subject matter specified in the Rule 30(b)(6) notice (and Chen is therefore less well prepared to answer).

a. May Manufacturer's lawyer instruct Chen not to answer the line of questions to which he objects? See Rule 30(d)(1).

b. What should Manufacturer's lawyer do? See Rule 30(d)(4).

c. In part because Manufacturer's lawyer has lodged numerous objections to the questions asked by Cora's lawyer, the deposition, which started at 9 a.m., ends at 5 (having been interrupted only for a lunch hour) without Cora's lawyer having reached her most important questions. When Cora's lawyer asks that the deposition be continued, Manufacturer's lawyer refuses, citing Rule 30(d)(2). What can Cora's lawyer do? What is Cora's lawyer's strongest argument for a continuation of the deposition?

d. After Chen's deposition, Cora's lawyer schedules another deposition, of another witness — Cora's eleventh deposition. What objection can Manufacturer make? See Rule 30(a)(2)(A).

3. In the same deposition, Cora's lawyer asks Chen a series of questions that Manufacturer's lawyer believes constitute violations of the attorney-client privilege ("Have you consulted with counsel about potential liability for a product with this design characteristic?"). Many lawyers would respond to such a question by instructing their client not to answer the question, a course of action explicitly permitted by Rule 30(d)(1). Having elicited this response to a series of similar questions, Cora's lawyer moves to another subject and thereafter ends the deposition. If Cora's lawyer believes that some of the unanswered questions were not subject to any privilege, how should she proceed to require answers?

4. One should not overlook the deposition as a source of unintentional

humor. Consider the following excerpts, collected by Mary Louise Gilman, the editor of *National Shorthand Reporter* and published in Richard Lederer, Anguished English (1987):

Q. Doctor, did you say he was shot in the woods?
A. No, I said he was shot in the lumbar region.

Q. What is your name?
A. Ernestine McDowell.

Q. And what is your marital status?
A. Fair.

Q. Mrs. Smith, do you believe that you are emotionally unstable?
A. I should be.
Q. How many times have you committed suicide?
A. Four times.

Q. When he went, had you gone and had she, if she wanted to and were able, for the time being excluding all the restraints on her not to go, gone also, would he have brought you, meaning you and she, with him to the station?
Mr. Brooks: Objection. That question should be taken out and shot.

Finally, consider what Professor Richard Friedman reports as "an actual trial transcript," whose accuracy he has confirmed with one of the lawyers:

The Court: Next witness.
Ms. Olschner: Your Honor, at this time I would like to swat Mr. Buck in the head with his client's deposition.
The Court: You mean read it?
Ms. Olschner: No, sir. I mean to swat him [in] the head with it. Pursuant to Rule 32, I may use the deposition "for any purpose" and that is the purpose for which I want to use it.
The Court: Well, it does say that.
(Pause.)
The Court: There being no objection, you may proceed.
Ms. Olschner: Thank you, Judge Hanes.
(Whereupon Ms. Olschner swatted Mr. Buck in the head with a deposition.)
Mr. Buck: But Judge . . .
The Court: Next witness.
Mr. Buck: We object.
The Court: Sustained. Next witness.

3. Examining Things and People: Production and Inspection of Documents and Things; Physical and Mental Examinations (Rules 34 and 35)

Page 503. In place of Problem 1, insert:

1. Alice brings suit against Centerville Village, claiming that its police officers assaulted her during an afternoon political demonstration. Her complaint alleges

that the assault "severely injured her." The city attorney assigned to the case uncovers a photograph of Alice, taken the night after the incident, showing her participating enthusiastically in a local dance contest. At the Rule 26(f) conference with Alice's lawyer, Centerville's lawyer learns that she will contend that the police assault injured her leg.

a. Must the defendant produce the photograph as part of the disclosures required within ten days of the lawyers' conference? Read Rule 26(a)(1)(B). What risk does defendant run if it does not disclose the photograph? Read Rule 37(c)(1).

b. Assume that the defendant does not disclose the existence of the photograph in the initial round of disclosures. Thereafter Alice makes a Rule 34 demand that Centerville produce "all documents, memoranda, and reports relating to the incident." As attorney for Centerville, must you now produce the photograph?

c. Suppose Centerville produces the photograph in response to the Rule 34 demand. Can Alice seek sanctions? Of what sort? Read Rule 37(c)(1). Can Centerville argue that any failure to disclose initially is harmless because the evidence eventually came to light?

5. Ensuring Compliance

Page 506. Substitute the following new Problems:

PROBLEMS

1. Producer Corp. sues Supplier, Inc., alleging failure to fulfill the conditions of a contract; Supplier denies the allegations of the complaint and counterclaims for Producer's alleged failure to pay for goods delivered. As soon as pleadings have closed, and before the disclosures have occurred, Producer *notices* (that is, notifies of the intention to take) the depositions of several of Supplier's officers and employees.

a. Explain why Supplier can object to this course of action. See Rule 26(d).

b. After the initial round of disclosures, Producer again seeks to depose the officers and employees. Supplier objects to this course of action, believing that without more groundwork these depositions will prove a waste of time and expense — and will have to be repeated later in the action once Producer has developed more information. Can Supplier refuse to attend the depositions and avoid sanctions on the grounds that Producer should first have built a stronger foundation for an efficient use of deposition time? If not, what can Supplier do? See Rule 26(b)(2) and Rule 26(c).

2. In the lawsuit described in Problem 1, Producer's disclosures fail to list a former officer who was present at the negotiations of the agreement and who could testify as to the parties' intent. At trial Producer seeks to have this person testify. What objection can Supplier make? See Rule 37(c)(1).

3. Suppose the same situation as in the preceding problem. After initial

disclosures Supplier sends Producer an interrogatory asking for the name of any witness with information about the contract negotiation. Producer fails to supply witness's name; Supplier nonetheless learns of the witness at a subsequent deposition. What sanction can the court can impose on Producer for its failure to disclose the identity of this witness in the original interrogatory?

4. As the lawsuit described in Problem 1 proceeds, Supplier serves Producer with a request to produce documents relevant to the suit.

a. First suppose that Producer simply fails to respond to the requests for documents. What steps must Supplier follow to force Producer either to comply or suffer sanctions. Read carefully Rule 37(a)(1)-(2). See Shuffle Master Inc. v. Progressive Games, Inc., 170 F.R.D. 166 (D. Nev. 1996) (refusing to order sanctions in the absence of a certificate demonstrating good faith effort to confer with adversary).

b. Now suppose two of the documents sought are letters from Producer's lawyer to Producer, answering questions about the interpretation of the contract in question; Producer believes that both documents are protected by the attorney-client privilege. How should Producer raise such a contention? See Rules 26(c) and 37(a). What tactical advantages might accrue from using Rule 26(c) rather than 37(a) as the setting in which to raise the privilege?

c. Producer's response to Supplier's request states simply, "The requested documents have not been produced because they are protected by the attorney-client privilege." What should Supplier do? See Rules 26(b)(5) and 37(a)(2)(B).

E. Discovery in an Adversary System

2. Expert Information

Page 539. In place of Note 3 insert:

3. Assume that John's lawyer decides early on—before initial disclosures are due—that he will not use Dr. Welby to testify at trial.

a. Under these circumstances John's lawyer need not list Welby as a potential expert witness as required in Rule 26(a)(2).

b. Suppose that, after the required disclosures have been made, Mary, through interrogatories, seeks the name of any person who may have information concerning John's medical condition. Welby, having examined John, has such information. Rule 26(a)(4) states that "facts known or opinions held" by a nontestifying expert retained in anticipation of litigation may be discovered only under special circumstances. But what about the identity of such experts?

c. If John does disclose Welby's name, can he get a protective order forbidding Mary to depose Welby? Explain why such an order is probably required by Rule 26(a)(4).

F. Ensuring Compliance and Controlling Abuse of Discovery

Pages 544-548. Replace the material preceding "2. Sanctions as a Remedy" with:

Even with the preceding doctrinal framework in mind, one of the hardest concepts for the student to grasp is the "culture" of discovery. *Hickman*'s fears that the advent of discovery would mean the demise of the adversary system appear to have been greatly exaggerated. Instead, discovery has become the field on which some of unrestrained advocacy's least attractive features sometimes display themselves. Delay, evasiveness, use of discovery to buy time or to force a hard-pressed opponent to settle for less, abusive use of various discovery devices, and the like appear on lawyers' lists of such tactics. One study, reprinted in part below, catalogues some common abuses.

> **Interrogatories and Document Productions**
> Attorneys drafting interrogatories do not view them primarily as means of openly exploring the data . . . [but] as weapons to be used in the manner that best advances the competitive interests of their client. . . . Many litigators feel compelled to use written interrogatories as weapons for purely tactical purposes. . . . Some attorneys serve lengthy sets of "canned" interrogatories if they perceive some advantage to be gained by psychologically or economically harassing an opposing party or counsel. Litigators may also use interrogatories to pressure or manipulate opposing counsel into doing such initial case preparation as factual investigation and legal research and analysis that properly should be undertaken by the propounding counsel and paid for by that counsel's client. . . .
>
> The responding adversary's first impulse is to construe all inquiries and requests as narrowly as possible, thereby limiting the amount of useful information that must be divulged. . . . Nor will litigators necessarily answer a request even if they have construed it as narrowly as possible and have objected to every arguable technical deficiency. Responding counsel's next line of defense is built on the use of privileges and the work product doctrine. . . .
>
> When responding to document production demands, litigators sometimes resort to the obstructive device of burying significant documents in mounds of irrelevant or innocuous materials. . . . If the tactics discussed above fail to conceal damaging information, counsel may feel constrained to refuse to respond to interrogatories or document production requests until compelled to do so. The first ploy is to ignore the original discovery probe and its deadlines. At least among seasoned litigators the fear of sanctions for missing one deadline is not great.
>
> **Depositions**
> An aggressive litigator bent on straining the resources and testing the will of an adversary can notice numerous depositions and can prolong each examination for extended periods of time . . . [with the effect of] harassing and embarrassing adverse parties or witnesses and . . . disrupting their lives and businesses. . . .*

*Brazil, The Adversary Character of Civil Discovery: A Critique and Proposals for Change, 31 Vand. L. Rev. 1295, 1320-1324, 1329 (1978).

Such depressing observations have several sources, some of which lie in the design of the discovery system itself. The original Federal Rules envisioned discovery's operating largely without judicial supervision, and the Rules therefore speak of lawyers' exchanging various discovery requests without intervention by the court. In that scheme judges became involved only when the system breaks down — for example, in the event of a motion for a protective order, a request to compel discovery, or a motion for sanctions. But when such judicial intervention comes, the judge steps into a dispute about which she might know little, and may therefore be inclined to tread rather warily. Moreover, many judges routinely assign discovery matters to federal magistrate judges and hear only appeals from their orders. Thus judges faced with discovery battles often have very little feel for the dispute before them. Recent revisions to the Rules have sought to address these issues in several ways, and a debate revolves around whether these efforts will succeed and, if so, whether they will have done more harm than good.

1. An Anatomy of Discovery Abuses

Before assessing the effectiveness of these efforts, it may help to construct an anatomy of discovery abuses. There are three basic patterns: too little discovery, too much discovery, and mismatched discovery. The first, sometimes called "stonewalling," occurs when one party refuses or resists appropriate requests for discovery. The second occurs when one party seeks more discovery than the case justifies so as to discourage or hamper the opponent. The last pattern, "mismatched" discovery, occurs when the two parties have significantly unequal wealth; the richer party, even if it does not abuse discovery, may seem to have an unfair advantage. The Rules offer partial solutions to the first two problems but deal less well with the third. The Rules employ three tools: limits on discovery, sanctions for bad behavior, and judicial supervision.

Start with stonewalling. Refusal to cooperate with justifiable discovery requests can subject a party to sanctions. Read Rules 26(g) and 37, noting the range of propositions to which the signature of the lawyer certifies under 26(g). Some report that early judicial supervision is effective in reducing stonewalling; if so, the mandatory scheduling conference required by the 2000 revisions, combined with the mandatory disclosures, may have the desired effect.

Over-discovery has a similar set of control mechanisms. If the information requested is irrelevant or privileged, one may simply decline to answer; the 2000 revisions further limited the scope of material discoverable without a judicial order to "matter relevant to [a] claim or defense," requiring a judicial order to broaden the scope. Discovery can also be excessive because cumulative or burdensome; note the provision in Rule 26(g) in which the signing lawyer certifies that discovery is not "unreasonable or unduly burdensome or expensive, given the needs of the case." The Rules also impose some mechanical limits — 25 interrogatories and ten depositions, none of which can last more than seven hours.

For cases in which these provisions fail to solve the problem, Rule 26(c) permits any party to seek a protective order. That Rule permits a court to limit discovery, even though the information sought might otherwise be discoverable, if it would produce "annoyance, embarrassment, oppression, or undue burden or expense." For problems that do not fit neatly into any of these categories, one might consider a discovery conference (under Rule 16), which involves the judge in the framing of a discovery plan. Such a conference may be convened by the court on its own motion; judges who wish to manage discovery may use such conferences as a tool. Indeed, the 2000 revisions, without explicitly saying so, have divided discovery into two sorts — that which can occur without judicial supervision or permission, and a second phase in which judicial permission and, probably, supervision will be required.

PROBLEMS

1. Having filed a complaint against Baxter Corp. for breach of contract and received the required disclosures, Arthur Corp. sends Baxter a set of additional interrogatories seeking some routine information about the details of company organization, such as which officers and employees are responsible for which aspects of the company's affairs. Baxter refuses to answer any of the questions, noting in its response that these matters are not relevant to the claims and defenses of the action. Arthur's lawyer believes that such questions are entirely proper because they enable her to decide which officers to depose — and that they are thus included within Rule 26(b)(1) as "reasonably calculated to lead to the discovery of admissible evidence."

a. How should Arthur's lawyer proceed to get answers to his interrogatories?

b. Can Arthur seek sanctions? Under what Rule(s)?

2. Baxter serves a notice to take the deposition of Alice Arthur, the President of Arthur Corp. On the appointed day, Alice Arthur doesn't show up. As attorney for Baxter, what remedies would you seek? See Rule 37(d).

3. When Baxter seeks sanctions, Arthur claims that Baxter purposefully scheduled the deposition at an extremely inconvenient place and requests that the location be changed. Should that argument, if true, block or mitigate sanctions?

4. When Baxter deposes Alice Arthur, her lawyer interposes numerous objections, with the result that at the end of seven hours, the deposition is just getting into the core inquiries Baxter has planned. Alice and her lawyer stand, call for the end of the deposition, and draw Baxter's attention to the seven-hour provision of Rule 30(d)(2). What should Baxter do?

5. Arthur and Baxter serve a series of requests for discovery on each other, including interrogatories, notices of depositions, and various requests for the production of documents. Arthur believes that it has responded in good faith to

Baxter's requests but that Baxter has been systematically uncooperative, raising many barely tenable objections, declining to produce documents until threatened with a court order, producing incomplete sets of documents, then producing overwhelming quantities of documents in which the relevant material is buried, and similar tactics. What should Arthur do?

6. The amount at stake in Arthur v. Baxter is $80,000 — all but $5,000 of that amount representing Arthur's claim against Baxter. In connection with its counterclaim, Baxter serves on Arthur notices for a series of depositions of Arthur's officers. When Arthur's lawyer calls Baxter's lawyer to discuss the scheduling of these depositions, she learns that the series of depositions will take 30 hours to complete. Given the billing rates of the two attorneys and the cost of a stenographer, the cost of such a series of depositions could exceed $10,000. Is that troubling? Is there anything Arthur's lawyer can do about it?

We have not yet addressed one of the more difficult discovery problems — how the legal system should cope with substantial imbalance in the parties' wealth. Because discovery is conducted by the parties' lawyers, the litigants must bear the costs. Some of the more elaborate forms, particularly depositions, can cost a lot. Can the wealthier party prevail simply by dint of greater resources? The problem has two versions. First, what happens if one party lacks resources to do adequate discovery? The most troubling case would arise if most of the likely evidence was in defendant's hands, and the case suggested that assembly of evidence would be complex — perhaps in a product liability or environmental hazard claim. Without access to discovery, such a claim has no chance of succeeding. Although the Rules nowhere address this problem specifically, several possibilities present themselves. The party with fewer resources may be able to conduct "discovery" from various public sources — government or public documents, press sources, and the like. Digital media and the Internet have made such searches much faster and cheaper than they were fifty years ago. Moreover, a disciplined discovery scheme making maximum use of "cheap" discovery (such as document requests and interrogatories) may yield a good deal. With large public and private institutions, well-planned document requests can produce rich veins of information. Finally, it may be possible to ride free on the discovery efforts of other parties if they are involved: a deposition conducted by one party will likely yield useful information. One change in the 2000 amendments to the Rules made this avenue more difficult to pursue. Rule 5(d) now forbids parties from filing any discovery materials with the court until they are used in a "proceeding" (including a pretrial motion). The motivation behind this amendment was simple: courts were running out of space to store such documents. But the consequences may be to curtail the availability of discovery materials in separate but factually related cases, making it harder for an ill-funded party to "piggy-back" on another's previous efforts.

2. Sanctions as a Remedy

Page 560. Before Note 2 insert:

d. The 2000 amendments to the discovery rules were designed as a response to what some thought were widespread discovery problems. Consider whether any of the amended Rules would have affected the present case, litigated and decided before the amendments. The amended Rule 26(b) limits discovery to matters relevant to the parties "claims or defenses." Would that have had any effect, given the continued existence of the plaintiffs' broad fraud allegation? Presumably the limitation of interrogatories to 25 might have caused the plaintiffs to seek court permission for a larger number of interrogatories, but it is hard to imagine the court's failing to grant such a request, given the number of counts in the complaint. The amended rules place no numerical limit on document requests. And the dispute, rancorous as it was, did not involve depositions, so the number and time limits in Rule 30 would have no effect.

RESOLUTION WITHOUT TRIAL

VIII

A. The Pressure to Choose Adjudication or an Alternative

3. Voluntary Dismissal

Page 576. Before "B. Avoiding Adjudication" insert:

d. With *Grover* and *Manshack* contrast Doe v. Urohealth Sys., Inc., 216 F.3d 157 (1st Cir. 2000). Plaintiff alleged a defective medical product, conducted a year of discovery (including several discovery disputes drawing reprimands from the judge), and on the eve of defendant's summary judgment motion, sought to dismiss the federal action without prejudice so that he could consolidate it with recently filed parallel state litigation. The First Circuit held it was an abuse of discretion for the district court to allow such a dismissal:

> Although the courts talk about "legal prejudice," the governing Federal Rule of Civil Procedure lays down no specific test, see Fed. R. Civ. P. 41(a)(2), and the precedents could be read as saying that everything depends on the particular circumstances and that a range of factors could be taken into account. . . .
>
> At the same time, it is very difficult to imagine in the circumstances of this case a no-prejudice dismissal at plaintiff's behest that would not involve payment by the plaintiff of the defendant's attorney's fees and other expenses of litigation in federal court to date.

Id. at 163.

B. Avoiding Adjudication

1. Negotiation and Settlement

b. Contracting for Confidentiality

Page 594. Before "c. Contracting for a Judgment" insert:

4. A revision made as part of the 2000 amendments to the Federal Rules of Civil Procedure may have the effect of substantially restricting non-party access

to discovery materials even if these materials are not part of a confidentiality agreement or court order. As amended, Rule 5(d), which governs service of papers, provides that "discovery requests and responses *must not be filed* until they are used in the proceeding or the court orders filing" (emphasis added). Unless documents are filed with the court they will remain in lawyers' files and not become part of a publicly available record. The reason for the amended rule is straightforward: courthouses were running out of space to file the sometimes voluminous products of discovery, and many local rules already barred routine filing of discovery requests.

a. Consider a deposition of an expert in a product liability suit. During that deposition, the parties show the witness numerous documents produced in earlier rounds of discovery. Are these documents now "used in the proceeding" and thus required to be filed? The Advisory Committee Notes say no.

b. The same documents are now made part of a motion for summary judgment; they are presumably now "used in the proceeding" and must be filed (subject to any protective order the judge issues). But, if the parties acting pursuant to local rule, attach to their motions only those parts of the documents and depositions that are the subject of argument, only those portions will be filed and part of the public record.

TRIAL

X

B. Procedural Control of Rational Proof

5. Controlling Juries After the Verdict

b. New Trial

Page 742. After Note 5 insert:

6. Consider the procedural dilemmas of a plaintiff, who, having won a trial court verdict, finds it attacked on appeal. Chad Weisgram's mother died in an apartment fire; he sued the manufacturer of an allegedly defective electric baseboard heater. To prove the defect in the heater, Weisgram offered at trial three expert witnesses, whose testimony the defendant challenged. The jury returned a verdict for plaintiff and defendant moved for new trial and for judgment as a matter of law (renewing a similar pre-verdict motion), which the trial court denied, instead entering judgment on the verdict for the plaintiff. Defendant appealed, contending that the experts' testimony should not have been admitted.

a. Consider the strategic choice confronting Weisgram. He has the right to cross-appeal, arguing that *if* the trial court ruling is reversed, there were other errors that entitled him to a new trial. But as a matter of strategy it is awkward to argue that the trial court judgment was correct and at the same time to contend that there were sufficient errors in various rulings to entitle him to a new trial if the judgment is reversed. Weisgram chose not to make such an argument.

b. That may have been a bad choice, because the appellate court reversed on the ground that that the experts' testimony should not have been admitted (because their testimony was scientifically unsound and speculative) and that without that testimony there was no evidence that defendant was responsible for the death. The appellate court then faced the question of whether it should simply grant judgment for the defendant or remand for the trial court to allow Weisgram to move for a new trial; circuits had split on the issue. Resolving a split in the circuits, the Supreme Court unanimously affirmed the appellate court's power to enter judgment for defendant without remanding. Weisgram v. Marley Co., 528 U.S. 440 (2000).

APPEAL

XI

A. Who Can Appeal?

1. A Losing Party: Adversity

NOTES AND PROBLEMS

Page 757. Before "2. Who Raised the Issue Below: Waiver" add:

5. Class actions present special problems of appealability. Formally, only the named class representatives are parties. Does that mean that only they can appeal? Does a represented absentee class member have to intervene, thus becoming a formal party, before he can appeal? Suppose a class action comes to a proposed settlement, of which the class members receive notice. One such member objects to the settlement, but does not intervene. Can he nevertheless appeal? Yes; in Devlin v. Scardelletti, 536 U.S. 1 (2002), over a dissent arguing that the ruling upset long-standing rules of appealability, the Court held that such a class member could bring an appeal:

> What is most important to this case is that unnamed class members are parties to the proceedings in the sense of being bound by the settlement. It is this feature of class action litigation that requires that class members be allowed to appeal the approval of a settlement when they have objected at the fairness hearing. To hold otherwise would deprive unnamed class members of the power to preserve their own interests in a settlement that will ultimately bind them, despite their expressed objections before the trial court.

Id. at 17.

RESPECT FOR JUDGMENTS

XII

A. Claim Preclusion

4. After a Judgment "on the Merits"

Page 830. In place of Note 4 insert:

4. This chapter has thus far implicitly assumed that the preclusive effect of a judgment would be that attached to it by the court rendering the judgment. For example, in Frier v. City of Vandalia, the federal court was seeking to discern the claim preclusion law of Illinois, the state whose courts rendered the initial judgment on Frier's replevin claims. The United States Supreme Court has said the matter is more complicated than that — at least in federal diversity cases.

a. In Semtek International Inc. v. Lockheed Martin Corp., 531 U.S. 497 (2001), supra supplement page 395, the Court held that the preclusive effect of a judgment rendered in a federal diversity action should be the same that would be attached to that judgment if a *state* court in the forum state had rendered it. Thus a Maryland court should give to a federal court judgment rendered in California (in a diversity action), the same effect as would be accorded to a California state court rendering the same judgment. According to the unanimous opinion of the Court, that result flows neither from statute nor the Constitution but from the federal common law of former adjudication. That common law, however, said *Semtek*, has some flexibility: "This federal reference to state law will not obtain, of course, in situations in which the state law is incompatible with federal interests. If, for example, state law did not accord preclusive effect to dismissals for willful violations of discover orders, federal courts' interest in the integrity of their own processes might justify a contrary federal rule."

b. Notice the result of *Semtek*, as applied to some of the hypothetical cases above. For federal claims the preclusive effect of a Rule 12(b)(6) dismissal bars not only the claim pleaded but all claims arising from the same transaction or occurrence. Some states, including California, apparently have different rules (see Note 3c). In a federal court lawsuit based on federal claims, a 12(b)(6) dismissal will bar a new complaint based on the same occurrence. In a federal court lawsuit brought in California, in which federal jurisdiction was based exclusively in diversity, would a 12(b)(6) dismissal bar a new claim, based on the same transaction, but now properly pleaded?

c. The answer may not be clear. On one hand, if California would permit such a repleading of the case, *Semtek* suggests that the federal court should do likewise in a diversity action. What, though, should we make of the caution, noted in Note 4a, that state preclusion law should not apply if it is "incompatible with federal interests"? The federal courts almost invariably allow plaintiffs an opportunity to amend their complaints, and they have less technical pleading requirements than some states. Is the federal "interest" in getting all the pleading out of the way in a single suit enough of a federal interest to justify disregarding state law? Or would such an approach be insufficiently deferential to state law?

d. *Semtek* raises still another set of questions when a federal judgment is entered in a case in which the court's jurisdiction rests both on federal questions and diversity. Does the preclusive effect of the judgment differ by claim? Or is less deference to state preclusion law required when the federal courts' jurisdiction rests on a basis other than diversity?

5. *Semtek* used as an example a dismissal for failure to comply with discovery orders. The excerpt quoted in Note 4a suggested that, whatever a state's own claim preclusion rules, a federal dismissal for failure to comply with discovery rules would require precluding the same claim refiled in a state court.

a. Why? Explain why the *Semtek* court would think that permitting a plaintiff who had suffered such a dismissal should not be permitted to refile.

b. The next case tries to extract itself from the quicksand of the opposite situation: a *state-court* dismissal of a claim for non-compliance with discovery, with the added attraction that the claim dismissed ought not to have been in state court in the first place.

B. Issue Preclusion

2. The Same Issue

Page 836. Before "2. An Issue 'Actually Litigated and Determined' " insert:

4. Courts regularly award sanctions and discipline lawyers under procedural rules like Rule 11. Awarding a sanction under that Rule will sometimes involve a finding that a claim or defense is not "warranted by existing law" or that "the allegations and other factual contentions" lack "evidentiary support." What should be the effect of such findings in subsequent litigation?

a. Suppose Plaintiff brings a claim against Defendant, who successfully challenges the complaint under Rule 11(b)(3) (lacks evidentiary support). The court finds that Plaintiff had no evidence when he filed the suit and awards sanctions, following which action plaintiff voluntarily dismisses the case. Plaintiff now files a second suit making similar allegations. Defendant moves for summary judgment, contending that the court's findings in the first suit establish the lack of evidence for the claim and are entitled to issue preclusive effect. How should the court rule? Faigin v. Kelly, 184 F.3d 67 (1st Cir. 1999) (Rule 11 motion decided whether party had "abused judicial process" by failing to produce evidence, not whether the underlying claims were true or false; no issue preclusion because a different "issue" in two proceedings).

b. Suppose that Plaintiff does not file a second suit, but Defendant files an action for malicious prosecution, contending that Plaintiff lacked probable cause to bring the first suit. Can Defendant (now plaintiff in the second action) assert the sanctions findings as preclusive of whether Plaintiff had probable cause to bring the first action? Cf. Xantech Corp. v. Ramco Indus. Inc., 159 F.3d 1098, 1094 (7th Cir. 1998) (no *claim* preclusion on similar facts).

c. Finally, suppose that after a series of sanctions under Rule 11, Lawyer faces disciplinary action from the bar. Should the findings in the Rule 11 motions be determinative of whether Lawyer has breached ethical duties in those instances? In re Gwen G. Caranchini, 956 S.W.2d 910, (Mo. 1997) (factual findings of disciplinary sanctions precluded from relitigation in bar proceedings).

JOINDER

XIII

B. Joinder of Parties

2. By Defendants: Third Party Claims

Page 911. For the bracketed summary of the facts of Watergate Landmark Condominium Unit Owners' Association v. Wiss, Janey, Elstner Associates *substitute:*

[A condominium association hired Legum & Norman, a real estate management firm, to oversee maintenance of the units. When owners reported that their balconies were crumbling, the condo association asked the real estate managers for a recommendation. The management firm recommended that the condo association hire Wiss, Janey — an engineering firm. The condo association did hire Wiss, Janey, who prepared specifications for balcony repairs. The condo association then hired Brisk Waterproofing to perform the repairs in accord with the Wiss, Janey specifications. When those repairs failed to remedy the problem, the condo association sued both the engineering firm and the real estate management firm, but not the waterproofers.]

E. The Class Action

2. Statutory Requirements

Page 977. The citation for Heaven v. Trust Bank *is* 118 F.3d 735 (11th Cir. 1997).